Fundamentals of Christian Education

Ellen G. White

Original Copyright © 1923 by the
Southern Publishing Association
Nashville, Tennessee

Copyright © 2020 by
A Thinking Generation Ministries
ISBN 978-0-9977124-6-9

1. Proper Education 7
2. Christ an Educator 27
3. An Appeal for Our Students 29
4. Thoughts on Education 35
5. A Visit to College City 39
6. The Home and the School 41
7. The Importance of Physical Training 47
8. Daniel's Integrity Under Test 51
9. The Importance of Education 55
10. Danger of Reading Fictitious or Infidel Books 61
11. The Schools of the Ancient Hebrews 63
12. Courtship and Marriage 67
13. Importance of Training in the Work of God 73
14. Proper Education of the Young 77
15. The Value of Bible Study 83
16. The Book of Books 87
17. Parental Responsibility 93
18. Education and Health 97
19. Home Education 99
20. Mental Inebriates 109
21. Books in Our Schools 113
22. The Teacher of Truth the Only Safe Educator 117
23. The Treasures With Which to Store the Mind 123
24. The Science of Salvation the First of Sciences 127
25. Christian Character Exemplified in Teachers and Students ... 131
26. The World By Wisdom Knew Not God 135
27. The Relation of Education to the Work of God 139
28. The Need of Trained Workers 147
29. To Teachers and Students 153
30. The Best Education and Its Purpose 161
31. Christ as Teacher 165
32. The Education Most Essential for Gospel Workers 169
33. Students Deciding Their Eternal Destiny 171
34. Formality, Not Organization, an Evil 177
35. To Teachers 183
36. Suspension of Students 195
37. To the Students at Battle Creek College 201
38. Students Required to be Workers with God 205

39. Words to Students 209
40. Study the Bible for Yourselves 215
41. Work and Education 217
42. The Basis of True Education 229
43. Beware of Imitations 231
44. Speedy Preparation For the Work 233
45. The Essential Education 255
46. Diligent and Thorough Education 259
47. Books and Authors in Our Schools 265
48. The Great Lesson Book 271
49. Higher Education 273
50. The Divine Teacher 277
51. True Education 283
52. Manual Training 291
53. Educational Influence of Surroundings 295
54. Importance of Physical Culture 299
55. The True Higher Education 303
56. Christ's Example in Contrast with Formalism 309
57. A Divine Example 313
58. The Bible the Most Important Book for Education in Our Schools   315
59. Correct School Discipline 321
60. The Bible in Our Schools 329
61. Special Testimony Relating to Politics 335
62. Sowing Beside All Waters 343
63. The Work of Our Training Schools 345
64. Shall We Colonize Around Our Institutions 349
65. Lessons from the Life of Solomon 353
66. Teachers as Examples of Christian Integrity 357
67. The Essential in Education 363
68. A Message to Teachers 365
69. Provision Made for Our Schools 369
70. Teacher, Know Thyself 373
71. The Work Before Us 375
72. Counsel to Teachers 379
73. The True Ideal for Our Youth 385
74. A Message for Our Young People 389

Proper Education

It is the nicest work ever assumed by men and women to deal with youthful minds. The greatest care should be taken in the education of youth to so vary the manner of instruction as to call forth the high and noble powers of the mind. Parents and school-teachers are certainly disqualified to properly educate children, if they have not first learned the lesson of self-control, patience, forbearance, gentleness, and love. What an important position for parents, guardians, and teachers! There are very few who realize the most essential wants of the mind, and how to direct the developing intellect, the growing thoughts and feelings of youth.

There is a time for training children and a time for educating youth; and it is essential that in school both of these be combined in a great degree. Children may be trained for the service of sin or for the service of righteousness. The early education of youth shapes their characters both in their secular and in their religious life. Solomon says, "Train up a child in the way he should go: and when he is old, he will not depart from it." This language is positive. The training which Solomon enjoins is to direct, educate, and develop. In order for parents and teachers to do this work, they must themselves understand "the way" the child should go. This embraces more than merely having a knowledge of books. It takes in everything that is good, virtuous, righteous, and holy. It comprehends the practice of temperance, godliness, brotherly kindness, and love to God and to one another. In order to attain this object, the physical, mental, moral, and religious education of children must have attention.

The education of children, at home or at school, should not be like the training of dumb animals; for children have an intelligent will, which should be directed to control all their powers. Dumb animals need to be trained; for they have not reason and intellect. But the human mind must be taught self-control. It must be educated to rule the human being, while animals are controlled by a master, and are trained to be submissive to him. The master is mind, judgment, and will for his beast. A child may be so trained as to have, like the beast, no will of his own. Even his individuality may be merged in the one who superintends his training; his will, to all intents and purposes, is subject to the will of the teacher.

Children who are thus educated will ever be deficient in moral energy and individual responsibility. They have not been taught to move from reason and principle; their wills have been controlled by another, and the mind has not been called out, that it might expand and strengthen by exercise. They have not been directed and disciplined with respect to their peculiar constitutions and capabilities of mind, to put forth their strongest powers when required. Teachers should not stop here, but should give special attention to the cultivation of the weaker faculties, that all the powers may be brought into exercise, and carried forward from one degree of strength to another, that the mind may attain due proportions.

There are many families of children who appear to be well trained, while under the training discipline; but when the system which has held them to set rules is broken up, they seem to be incapable of thinking, acting, or deciding for themselves. These children have been so long under iron rule, not allowed to think and act for themselves in those things in which it was highly proper that they should, that they have no confidence in themselves to move out upon their own judgment, having an opinion of their own. And when they go out from their parents to act for themselves, they are easily led by others' judgment in the wrong direction. They have not stability of character. They have not been thrown upon their own judgment as fast and as far as practicable, and therefore their minds have not been properly developed and strengthened. They have so long been absolutely controlled by their parents that they rely wholly upon them; their parents are mind and judgment for them.

On the other hand, the young should not be left to think and act independently of the judgment of their parents and teachers. Children should be taught to respect experienced judgment, and to be guided by their parents and teachers. They should be so educated that their minds will be united with the minds of their parents and teachers, and so instructed that they can see the propriety of heeding their counsel. Then when they go forth from the guiding hand of their parents and teachers, their characters will not be like the reed trembling in the wind.

The severe training of youth, without properly directing them to think and act for themselves as their own capacity and turn of mind will allow, that by this means they may have growth of thought, feelings of self-respect, and confidence in their own ability to perform, will ever produce a class who are weak in mental and moral power. And when they stand in the world to act for themselves, they will reveal the fact that they are trained, like the animals, and not educated. Their wills, instead of being guided, were forced into subjection by the harsh discipline of parents and teachers.

Those parents and teachers who boast of having complete control of the minds and wills of the children under their care, would cease their boastings, could they trace out the future lives of the children who are thus brought into subjection by force or through fear. These are almost wholly unprepared to share in the stern responsibilities of life. When these youth are no longer under their parents and teachers, and are compelled to think and act for themselves, they are almost sure to take a wrong course, and yield to the power of temptation. They do not make this life a success, and the same deficiencies are seen in their religious life. Could the instructors of children and youth have the future result of their mistaken discipline mapped out before them, they would change their plan of education. That class of teachers who are gratified that they have almost complete control of the wills of their scholars, are not the most successful teachers, although the appearance for the time being may be flattering.

God never designed that one human mind should be under the complete control of another. And those who make efforts to have the individuality of their pupils merged in themselves, and to be mind, will, and conscience for them, assume fearful responsibilities. These scholars may, upon certain occasions, appear like well-drilled soldiers. But when the restraint is removed, there will be seen a want of independent action from firm principle existing in them. Those who make it their object to so educate their pupils that they may see and feel that the power lies in themselves to make men and women of firm principle, qualified for any position in life, are the most useful and permanently successful teachers. Their work may not show to the very best advantage to careless observers, and their labors may not be valued as highly as are those of the teacher who holds the minds and wills of his scholars by absolute authority; but the future lives of the pupils will show the fruits of the better plan of education.

There is danger of both parents and teachers commanding and dictating too much, while they fail to come sufficiently into social relation with their children or scholars. They often hold themselves too much reserved, and exercise their authority in a cold, unsympathizing manner which cannot win the hearts of their children and pupils. If they would gather the children close to them, and show that they love them, and would manifest an interest in all their efforts, and even in their sports, sometimes even being a child among children, they would make the children very happy, and would gain their love and win their confidence. And the children would sooner respect and love the authority of their parents and teachers.

The habits and principles of a teacher should be considered of even greater importance than his literary qualifications. If he is a sincere Christian, he will feel the necessity of having an equal interest in the physical, mental, moral, and spiritual education of his scholars. In order to exert the right influence, he should have perfect control over himself, and his own heart should be richly imbued with love for his pupils, which will be seen in his looks, words, and acts. He should have firmness of character, and then he can mold the minds of his pupils, as well as instruct them in the sciences. The early education of youth generally shapes their characters for life. Those who deal with the young should be very careful to call out the qualities of the mind, that they may better know how to direct its power so that they may be exercised to the very best account.

Close Confinement at School

The system of education carried out for generations back has been destructive to health and even life itself. Many young children have passed five hours each day in schoolrooms not properly ventilated, nor sufficiently large for the healthful accommodation of the scholars. The air of such rooms soon becomes poison to the lungs that inhale it. Little children, whose limbs and muscles are not strong, and whose brains are undeveloped, have been kept confined indoors to their injury. Many have but a slight hold on life to begin with. Confinement in school from day to day makes them nervous and diseased. Their bodies are dwarfed because of the exhausted condition of the nervous system. And if the lamp of life goes out, the parents and teachers do not consider that they had any direct influence in quenching the vital spark. When standing by the graves of their children, the afflicted parents look upon their bereavement as a special dispensation of Providence, when, by inexcusable ignorance, their own course has destroyed the lives of their children. To then charge their death to Providence, is blasphemy. God wanted the little ones to live and be disciplined, that they might have beautiful characters, and glorify Him in this world, and praise Him in the better world.

Parents and teachers, in taking the responsibility of training these children, do not feel their accountability before God to become acquainted with the physical organism, that they may treat the bodies of their children and pupils in a manner to preserve life and health. Thousands of children die because of the ignorance of parents and teachers. Mothers will spend hours over needless work upon their own dresses and those of their children, to fit them for display, and will then plead that they cannot find time to read up, and obtain the information necessary to take care of the health of their children. They think it less trouble to trust their bodies to the doctors. In order to be in accordance with fashion and custom, many parents have sacrificed the health and lives of their children.

To become acquainted with the wonderful human organism, the bones, muscles, stomach, liver, bowels, heart, and pores of the skin, and to understand the dependence of one organ upon another for the healthful action of all, is a study in which most mothers take no interest. They know nothing of the influence of the body upon mind, and of the mind upon the body. The mind, which allies finite to the infinite, they do not seem to understand. Every organ of the body was made to be servant to the mind. The mind is the capital of the body. Children are allowed to eat flesh-meats, spices, butter, cheese, pork, rich pastry, and condiments generally. They are also allowed to eat irregularly and between meals of unhealthful food. These things do their work of deranging the stomach, exciting the nerves of unnatural action, and enfeebling the intellect. Parents do not realize that they are sowing the seed which will bring forth disease and death.

Many children have been ruined for life by urging the intellect, and neglecting to strengthen the physical powers. Many have died in childhood because of the course pursued by injudicious parents and school-teachers in forcing their young intellects, by flattery or fear, when they were too young to see the inside of a school room. Their minds have been taxed with lessons, when they should not have been called out, but kept back until the physical constitution was strong enough to endure mental effort. Small children should be left as free as lambs to run out-of-doors, to be free and happy, and should be allowed the most favorable opportunities to lay the foundation for sound constitutions.

Parents should be the only teachers of their children until they have reached eight or ten years of age. As fast as their minds can comprehend it, the parents should open before them God's great book of nature. The mother should have less love for the artificial in her house, and in the preparation of her dress for display, and should find time to cultivate, in herself and in her children, a love for the beautiful buds and opening flowers. By calling the attention of her children to their different colors and variety of forms, she can make them acquainted with God, who made all the beautiful things which attract and delight them. She can lead their minds up to their Creator, and awaken in their young hearts a love for their heavenly Father, who has manifested so great love for them. Parents can associate God with all His created works. The only schoolroom for children from eight to ten years of age should be in the open air, amid the opening flowers and nature's beautiful scenery. And their only textbook should be the treasures of nature. These lessons, imprinted upon the minds of young children amid the pleasant, attractive scenes of nature, will not soon be forgotten.

In order for children and youth to have health, cheerfulness, vivacity, and well-developed muscles and brains, they should be much in the open air, and have well-regulated employment and amusement. Children and youth who are kept at school and confined to books, cannot have sound physical constitutions. The exercise of the brain in study, without corresponding physical exercise, has a tendency to attract the blood to the brain, and the circulation of the blood through the system becomes unbalanced. The brain has too much blood, and the extremities too little. There should be rules regulating their studies to certain hours, and then a portion of their time should be spent in physical labor. And if their habits of eating, dressing, and sleeping are in accordance with physical law, they can obtain an education without sacrificing physical and mental health.

Physical Decline of the Race

The book of Genesis gives quite a definite account of social and individual life, and yet we have no record of an infant being born blind, deaf, crippled, deformed, or imbecile. There is not an instance upon record of a natural death in infancy, childhood, or early manhood. There is no account of men and women dying of disease. Obituary notices in the book of Genesis run thus: "And all the days that Adam lived were nine hundred and thirty years; and he died." "And all the days of Seth were nine hundred and twelve years; and he died." Concerning others, the record states: He lived to a good old age; and he died. It was so rare for a son to die before the father that such an occurrence was considered worthy of record: "And Haran died before his father Terah." Haran was a father of children before his death.

God endowed man with so great vital force that he has withstood the accumulation of disease brought upon the race in consequence of perverted habits, and has continued for six thousand years. This fact of itself is enough to evidence to us the strength and electrical energy that God gave to man at his creation. It took more than two thousand years of crime and indulgence of base passions to bring bodily disease upon the race to any great extent. If Adam, at his creation, had not been endowed with twenty times as much vital force as men now have, the race, with their present habits of living in violation of natural law, would have become extinct. At the time of Christ's first advent, the race had degenerated so rapidly that an accumulation of disease pressed upon that generation, bringing in a tide of woe, and a weight of misery inexpressible.

The wretched condition of the world at the present time has been presented before me. Since Adam's fall, the race has been degenerating. Some of the reasons for the present deplorable condition of men and women, formed in the image of God, were shown me. And a sense of how much must be done to arrest, even in a degree, the physical, mental, and moral decay, caused my heart to be sick and faint. God did not create the race in its present feeble condition. This state of things is not the work of Providence, but the work of man; it has been brought about by wrong habits and abuses, by violating the laws that God has made to govern man's existence. Through the temptation to indulge appetite, Adam and Eve first fell from their high, holy, and happy estate. And it is through the same temptation that the race have become enfeebled. They have permitted appetite and passion to take the throne, and to bring into subjection reason and intellect.

The violation of physical law, and the consequence, human suffering, have so long prevailed that men and women look upon the present state of sickness, suffering, debility, and premature death as the appointed lot of humanity. Man came from the hand of his Creator, perfect and beautiful in form, and so filled with vital force that it was more than a thousand years before his corrupt appetites and passions, and general violations of physical law, were sensibly felt upon the race. More recent generations have felt the pressure of infirmity and disease still more rapidly and heavily with every generation. The vital forces have been greatly weakened by the indulgence of appetite and lustful passion.

The patriarchs from Adam to Noah, with but few exceptions, lived nearly a thousand years. Since the days of Noah, the length of life has been tapering. Those suffering with disease were brought to Christ from every city, town, and village for Him to heal; for they were afflicted with all manner of diseases. And disease has been steadily on the increase through successive generations since that period. Because of the continued violation of the laws of life, mortality has increased to a fearful extent. The years of man have been shortened, so that the present generation pass to the grave, even before the age at which the generations that lived the first few thousand years after the creation came upon the stage of action.

Disease has been transmitted from parents to children, from generation to generation. Infants in the cradle are miserably afflicted because of the sins of their parents, which have lessened their vital force. Their wrong habits of eating and dressing, and their general dissipation, are transmitted as an inheritance to their children. Many are born insane, deformed, blind, deaf, and a very large class are deficient in intellect. The strange absence of principle which characterizes this generation, and which is shown in their disregard of the laws of life and health, is astonishing. Ignorance prevails upon this subject, while light is shining all around them. With the majority, their principal anxiety is, What shall I eat? what shall I drink? and wherewithal shall I be clothed? Notwithstanding all that is said and written in regard to how we should treat our bodies, appetite is the great law which governs men and women generally.

The moral powers are weakened, because men and women will not live in obedience to the laws of health, and make this great subject a personal duty. Parents bequeath to their offspring their own perverted habits, and loathsome diseases corrupt the blood and enervate the brain. The majority of men and women remain in ignorance of the laws of their being, and indulge appetite and passion at the expense of intellect and morals, and seem willing to remain in ignorance of the result of their violation of nature's laws. They indulge the depraved appetite in the use of slow poisons, which corrupt the blood, and undermine the nervous forces, and in consequence bring upon themselves sickness and death. Their friends call the result of this course the dispensation of Providence. In this they insult Heaven. They rebelled against the laws of nature, and suffered the punishment for thus abusing her laws. Suffering and mortality now prevail everywhere, especially among children. How great is the contrast between this generation, and those who lived during the first two thousand years!

Importance of Home Training

I inquired if this tide of woe could not be prevented, and something be done to save the youth of this generation from the ruin which threatens them. I was shown that one great cause of the existing deplorable state of things is that parents do not feel under obligation to bring up their children to conform to physical law. Mothers love their children with an idolatrous love, and indulge their appetite when they know that it will injure their health, and thereby bring upon them disease and unhappiness. This cruel kindness is manifested to a great extent in the present generation. The desires of children are gratified at the expense of health and happy tempers, because it is easier for the mother, for the time being, to gratify them than to withhold that for which they clamor.

Thus mothers are sowing the seed that will spring up and bear fruit. The children are not educated to deny their appetites and restrict their desires. And they become selfish, exacting, disobedient, unthankful, and unholy. Mothers who are doing this work will reap with bitterness the fruit of the seed they have sown. They have sinned against Heaven and against their children, and God will hold them accountable.

Had education for generations back been conducted upon altogether a different plan, the youth of this generation would not now be so depraved and worthless. The managers and teachers of schools should have been those who understood physiology, and who had an interest, not only to educate the youth in the sciences, but to teach them how to preserve health, so that they might use their knowledge to the best account after they had obtained it. There should have been connected with the schools, establishments for carrying on various branches of labor, that the students might have employment, and the necessary exercise out of school hours.

The students' employment and amusements should have been regulated with reference to physical law, and should have been adapted to preserve to them the healthy tone of all the powers of body and mind. Then a practical knowledge of business could have been obtained while their literary education was being gained. Students at school should have had their moral sensibilities aroused to see and feel that society has claims upon them, and that they should live in obedience to natural law, so that they can, by their existence and influence, by precept and example, be an advantage and blessing to society. It should be impressed upon the youth that all have an influence that is constantly telling upon society, to improve and elevate, or to lower and debase. The first study of the young should be to know themselves and how to keep their bodies in health.

Many parents keep their children at school nearly the year round. These children go through the routine of study mechanically, but do not retain that which they learn. Many of these constant students seem almost destitute of intellectual life. The monotony of continual study wearies the mind, and they take but little interest in their lessons; and to many the application to books becomes painful. They have not an inward love of thought, and an ambition to acquire knowledge. They do not encourage in themselves habits of reflection and investigation.

Children are in great need of proper education, in order that they may be of use in the world. But any effort that exalts intellectual culture above moral training is misdirected. Instructing, cultivating, polishing, and refining youth and children should be the main burden with both parents and teachers. Close reasoners and logical thinkers are few, for the reason that false influences have checked the development of the intellect. The supposition of parents and teachers that continual study would strengthen the intellect, has proved erroneous; for in many cases it has had the opposite effect.

In the early education of children, many parents and teachers fail to understand that the greatest attention needs to be given to the physical constitution, that a healthy condition of body and brain may be secured. It has been the custom to encourage children to attend school when they are mere babies, needing a mother's care. When of a delicate age, they are frequently crowded into ill-ventilated schoolrooms, where they sit in wrong positions upon poorly constructed benches, and as the result the young and tender frames of some have become deformed.

The disposition and habits of youth will be very likely to be manifested in mature manhood. You may bend a young tree into almost any shape that you choose, and if it remains and grows as you have bent it, it will be a deformed tree, and will ever tell of the injury and abuse received at your hand. You may, after years of growth, try to straighten the tree, but all your efforts will prove unavailing. It will ever be a crooked tree. This is the case with the minds of youth. They should be carefully and tenderly trained in childhood. They may be trained in the right direction or in the wrong, and in their future lives they will pursue the course in which they were directed in youth. The habits formed in youth will grow with the growth and strengthen with the strength, and will generally be the same in after life, only continually growing stronger.

We are living in an age when almost everything is superficial. There is but little stability and firmness of character, because the training and education of children from their cradle is superficial. Their characters are built upon sliding sand. Self-denial and self-control have not been molded into their characters. They have been petted and indulged until they are spoiled for practical life. The love of pleasure controls minds, and children are flattered and indulged to their ruin. Children should be so trained and educated that they will expect temptations, and calculate to meet difficulties and dangers. They should be taught to have control over themselves, and to nobly overcome difficulties; and if they do not willfully rush into danger, and needlessly place themselves in the way of temptation; if they shun evil influences and vicious society, and then are unavoidably compelled to be in dangerous company, they will have strength of character to stand for the right and preserve principle, and will come forth in the strength of God with their morals untainted. If youth who have been properly educated, make God their trust, their moral powers will stand the most powerful test.

But few parents realize that their children are what their example and discipline have made them, and that they are responsible for the characters their children develop. If the hearts of Christian parents were in obedience to the will of Christ, they would obey the injunction of the heavenly Teacher: "But seek ye first the kingdom of God and His righteousness; and all these things shall be added unto you." If those who profess to be followers of Christ would only do this, they would give, not only to their children, but to the unbelieving world, examples that would rightly represent the religion of the Bible.

If Christian parents lived in obedience to the requirements of the divine Teacher, they would preserve simplicity in eating and in dressing, and would live more in accordance with natural law. They would not then devote so much time to artificial life, in making for themselves cares and

Fundamentals of Christian Education

burdens that Christ has not laid upon them, but that He has positively bid them shun. If the kingdom of God and His righteousness were the first and all-important consideration with parents, but little precious time would be lost in useless outward ornamentation, while the minds of their children are almost entirely neglected. The precious time devoted by many parents to dressing their children for display in their scenes of amusement would better, far better, be spent in cultivating their own minds, in order that they may be competent to properly instruct their children. It is not essential to the salvation or happiness of these parents that they use the precious probationary time that God has lent them, in dressing, visiting, and gossiping.

Many parents plead that they have so much to do that they have no time to improve their minds, to educate their children for practical life, or to teach them how they may become lambs of Christ's fold. Not until the final settlement, when the cases of all will be decided, and the acts of our entire lives will be laid open to our view in the presence of God and the Lamb and all the holy angels, will parents realize the almost infinite value of their misspent time. Very many will then see that their wrong course has determined the destiny of their children. Not only have they failed to secure for themselves the words of commendation from the King of glory, "Well done, thou good and faithful servant, enter thou into the joy of thy Lord," but they hear pronounced upon their children the terrible denunciation, "Depart!" This separates their children forever from the joys and glories of Heaven, and from the presence of Christ. And they themselves also receive the denunciation, Depart, "thou wicked and slothful servant." Jesus will never say, "Well done," to those who have not earned the "well done" by their faithful lives of self-denial and self-sacrifice to do others good and to promote His glory. Those who live principally to please themselves instead of to do others good, will meet with infinite loss.

If parents could be aroused to a sense of the fearful responsibility which rests upon them in the work of educating their children, more of their time would be devoted to prayer, and less to needless display. They would reflect, and study, and pray earnestly to God for wisdom and divine aid, to so train their children that they may develop characters that God will approve. Their anxiety would not be to know how they can educate their children so that they will be praised and honored of the world, but how they can educate them to form beautiful characters that God can approve.

Much study and earnest prayer for heavenly wisdom are needed to know how to deal with youthful minds; for very much depends upon the direction parents give to the minds and wills of their children. To balance their minds in the right direction and at the right time, is a most important work; for their eternal destiny may depend on the decisions made at some critical moment. How important, then, that the minds of parents be as free as possible from perplexing, wearing care in temporal things, that they may think and act with calm consideration, wisdom, and love, and make the salvation of the souls of their children the first and highest consideration! The great object which parents should seek to attain for their dear children should be the inward adorning. Parents cannot afford to allow visitors and strangers to claim their attention, and by robbing them of time, which is life's great capital, make it impossible for them to give their children each day that patient instruction which they must have to give right direction to their developing minds.

This lifetime is too short to be squandered in vain and trifling diversion, in unprofitable visiting, in needless dressing for display, or in exciting amusements. We cannot afford to squander the time given us of God in which to bless others, and in which to lay up for ourselves a treasure in heaven. We have none too much time for the discharge of necessary duties. We should give time to the culture of our own hearts and minds, in order that we may be qualified for our life work. By neglecting these essential duties, and conforming to the habits and customs of fashionable, worldly society, we do ourselves and our children a great wrong.

Mothers who have youthful minds to train, and the characters of children to form, should not seek the excitement of the world in order to be cheerful and happy. They have an important life work, and they and theirs cannot afford to spend time in an unprofitable manner. Time is one of the important talents which God has entrusted to us, and for which He will call us to account. A waste of time is a waste of intellect. The powers of the mind are susceptible of high cultivation. It is the duty of mothers to cultivate their minds, and keep their hearts pure. They should improve every means within their reach for their intellectual and moral improvement, that they may be qualified to improve the minds of their children. Those who indulge their disposition to be in company, will soon feel restless unless visiting or entertaining visitors. Such have not the power of adaptation to circumstances. The necessary, sacred home duties seem commonplace and uninteresting to them. They have no love for self-examination or self-discipline. The mind hungers for the varying, exciting scenes of worldly life; children are neglected for the indulgence of inclination; and the recording angel writes, "Unprofitable servants." God designs that our minds should not be purposeless, but should accomplish good in this life.

If parents would feel that it is a solemn duty enjoined upon them of God to educate their children for usefulness in this life; if they would adorn the inner temple of the souls of their sons and daughters for the immortal life, we should see a great change in society for the better. There would not then be manifest so great indifference to practical godliness, and it would not be so difficult to arouse the moral sensibilities of children to understand the claims that God has upon them. But parents become more and more careless in the education of their children in the useful branches. Many parents allow their children to form wrong habits and to follow their own inclination, and fail to impress upon their minds the danger of their doing this, and the necessity of their being controlled by principle.

Children frequently begin a piece of work with enthusiasm, but, becoming perplexed or wearied with it, they wish to change and take hold of something new. Thus they may take hold of several things, meet with a little discouragement, and give them up; and so they pass from one thing to another, perfecting nothing. Parents should not allow the love of change to control their children. They should not be so much engaged with other things that they will have no time to patiently discipline the developing minds. A few words of encouragement, or a little help at the right time, may carry them over their trouble and discouragement, and the satisfaction they will derive from seeing the task completed that they undertook, will stimulate them to greater exertion.

Many children, for want of words of encouragement, and a little assistance in their efforts, become disheartened, and change from one thing to another. And they carry this sad defect with them in mature life. They fail to make a success of anything they engage in, for they have not been taught to persevere under discouraging circumstances. Thus the entire lifetime of many proves a failure, because they did not have correct discipline when young. The education received in childhood and youth, affects their entire business career in mature life, and their religious experience bears a corresponding stamp.

Physical Labor for Students

With the present plan of education, a door of temptation is opened to the youth. Although they generally have too many hours of study, they have many hours without anything to do. These leisure hours are frequently spent in a reckless manner. The knowledge of bad habits is communicated from one to another, and vice is greatly increased. Very many young men who have been religiously instructed at home, and who go out to the schools comparatively innocent and virtuous, become corrupt by associating with vicious companions. They lose self-respect, and sacrifice noble principles. Then they are prepared to pursue the downward path; for they have so abused their consciences that sin does not appear so exceeding sinful. These evils, which exist in the schools that are conducted according to the present plan, might be remedied in a great degree if study and labor could be combined. The same evils exist in the higher schools, only in a greater degree; for many of the youth have educated themselves in vice, and their consciences are seared.

Many parents overrate the stability and good qualities of their children. They do not seem to consider that they will be exposed to the deceptive influences of vicious youth. Parents have their fears as they send them some distance away to school, but flatter themselves that as they have had good examples and religious instruction, they will be true to principle in their high school life. Many parents have but a faint idea to what extent licentiousness exists in these institutions of learning. In many cases the parents have labored hard and suffered many privations for the cherished object of having their children obtain a finished education. And after all their efforts, many have the bitter experience of receiving their children from their course of studies with dissolute habits and ruined constitutions. And frequently they are disrespectful to their parents, unthankful, and unholy. These abused parents, who are thus rewarded by ungrateful children, lament that they sent their children from them, to be exposed to temptations, and come back to them physical, mental, and moral wrecks. With disappointed hopes and almost broken hearts, they see their children, of whom they had high hopes, follow in a course of vice and drag out a miserable existence.

But there are those of firm principles, who answer the expectation of parents and teachers. They go through the course of schooling with clear consciences, and come forth with good constitutions, and morals unstained by corrupting influences. But the number is few.

Some students put their whole being into their studies, and concentrate their mind upon the object of obtaining an education. They work the brain, but allow the physical powers to remain inactive. The brain is overworked, and the muscles become weak because they are not exercised. When these students graduate, it is evident that they have obtained their education at the expense of life. They have studied day and night, year after year, keeping their minds continually upon the stretch, while they have failed to sufficiently exercise their muscles. They sacrifice all for a knowledge of the sciences, and pass to their graves.

Young ladies frequently give themselves up to study, to the neglect of other branches of education even more essential for practical life than the study of books. And after having obtained their education, they are often invalids for life. They neglected their health by remaining too much indoors, deprived of the pure air of heaven, and of the God-given sunlight. These young ladies might have come from their schools in health, had they combined with their studies household labor and exercise in the open air.

Health is a great treasure. It is the richest possession mortals can have. Wealth, honor, or learning is dearly purchased, if it be at the loss of the vigor of health. None of these attainments can secure happiness, if health is wanting. It is a terrible sin to abuse the health that God has given us; for every abuse of health enfeebles us for life, and makes us losers, even if we gain any amount of education.

In many cases parents who are wealthy do not feel the importance of giving their children an education in the practical duties of life as well as in the sciences. They do not see the necessity, for the good of their children's minds and morals, and for their future usefulness, of giving them a thorough understanding of useful labor. This is due their children, that, should misfortune come, they could stand forth in noble independence, knowing how to use their hands. If they have a capital of strength, they cannot be poor, even if they have not a dollar. Many who in youth were in affluent circumstances, may be robbed of all their riches, and be left with parents and brothers and sisters dependent upon them for sustenance. Then how important that every youth be educated to labor, that they may be prepared for any emergency! Riches are indeed a curse when their possessors let them stand in the way of their sons and daughters obtaining a knowledge of useful labor, that they may be qualified for practical life.

Those who are not compelled to labor, frequently do not have sufficient active exercise for physical health. Young men, for want of having their minds and hands employed in active labor, acquire habits of indolence, and frequently obtain what is most to be dreaded, a street education, lounging about stores, smoking, drinking, and playing cards.

Young ladies will read novels, excusing themselves from active labor because they are in delicate health. Their feebleness is the result of their lack of exercising the muscles God has given them. They may think they are too feeble to do housework, but will work at crochet and tatting, and preserve the delicate paleness of their hands and faces, while their care-burdened mothers toil hard to wash and iron their garments. These ladies are not Christians, for they transgress the fifth commandment. They do not honor their parents. But the mother is the one who is most to blame. She has indulged her daughters and excused them from bearing their share of household duties, until work has become distasteful to them, and they love and enjoy delicate idleness. They eat, and sleep, and read novels, and talk of the fashions, while their lives are useless.

Poverty, in many cases, is a blessing; for it prevents youth and children from being ruined by inaction. The physical as well as the mental powers should be cultivated and properly developed. The first and constant care of parents should be to see that their children have firm constitutions, that they may be sound men and women. It is impossible to attain this object without physical exercise. For their own physical health and moral good, children should be taught to work, even if there is no necessity so far as want is concerned. If they would have pure and virtuous characters, they must have the discipline of well-regulated labor, which will bring into exercise all the muscles. The satisfaction that children will have in being useful, and in denying themselves to help others, will be the most healthful pleasure they ever enjoyed. Why should the wealthy rob themselves and their dear children of this great blessing?

Parents, inaction is the greatest curse that ever came upon youth. Your daughters should not be allowed to lie in bed late in the morning sleeping away the precious hours lent them of God to be used for the best purpose, and for which they will have to give an account to Him. The mother does her daughters great injury by bearing the burdens that they should share with her for their own present and future good. The course that many parents pursue in allowing their children to be indolent, and to gratify their desire for reading romance, is unfitting them for real life. Novel and story-book reading are the greatest evils in which youth can indulge. Novel and love-story readers always fail to make good, practical mothers. They are air-castle builders, living in an unreal, an imaginary world. They become sentimental, and have sick fancies. Their artificial life spoils them for anything useful. They are dwarfed in intellect, although they may flatter themselves that they are superior in mind and manners. Exercise in household labor is of the greatest advantage to young girls.

Physical labor will not prevent the cultivation of the intellect. Far from it. The advantages gained by physical labor will balance a person and prevent the mind from being overworked. The toil will come upon the muscles, and relieve the wearied brain. There are many listless, useless girls who consider it unladylike to engage in active labor. But their characters are too transparent to deceive sensible persons in regard to their real worthlessness. They simper and giggle, and are all affectation. They appear as though they could not speak their words fairly and squarely, but torture all they say with lisping and simpering. Are these ladies? They were not born fools, but were educated such. It does not require a frail, helpless, overdressed, simpering thing to make a lady. A sound body is required for a sound intellect. Physical soundness, and a practical knowledge of all the necessary household duties, will never be hindrances to a well-developed intellect; both are highly important for a lady.

All the powers of the mind should be called into use and developed, in order for men and women to have well-balanced minds. The world is full of one-sided men and women, who have become such because one set of their faculties was cultivated, while others were dwarfed from inaction. The education of most youth is a failure. They over-study, while they neglect that which pertains to practical business life. Men and women become parents without considering their responsibilities, and their offspring sink lower in the scale of human deficiency than they themselves. Thus the race is fast degenerating. The constant application to study, as the schools are now conducted, is unfitting youth for practical life. The human mind will have action. If it is not active in the right direction, it will be active in the wrong. In order to preserve the balance of the mind, labor and study should be united in the schools.

Provision should have been made in past generations for education upon a larger scale. In connection with the schools should have been agricultural and manufacturing establishments. There should also have been teachers of household labor. And a portion of the time each day should have been devoted to labor, that the physical and mental powers might be equally exercised. If schools had been established upon the plan we have mentioned, there would not now be so many unbalanced minds.

God prepared for Adam and Eve a beautiful garden. He provided for them everything that their wants required. He planted for them fruit-bearing trees of every variety. With a liberal hand He surrounded them with His bounties. The trees for usefulness and beauty, and the lovely flowers, which sprung up spontaneously, and flourished in rich profusion around them, were to know nothing of decay. Adam and Eve were rich indeed. They possessed Eden. Adam was lord in his beautiful domain. None can question the fact that he was rich. But God knew that Adam could not be happy unless he had employment. Therefore He gave him something to do; he was to dress the garden.

If men and women of this degenerate age have a large amount of earthly treasure, which, in comparison with that paradise of beauty and wealth given the lordly Adam, is very insignificant, they feel themselves above labor, and educate their children to look upon it as degrading. Such rich parents, by precept and example, instruct their children that money makes the gentleman and the lady. But our idea of the gentleman and the lady is measured by the intellect and the moral worth. God estimates not by dress. The exhortation of the inspired apostle Peter is, "Whose adorning let it not be that outward adorning of plaiting the hair, and of wearing of gold, or of putting on of apparel; but let it be the hidden man of the heart, in that which is not corruptible, even the ornament of a meek and quiet spirit, which is in the sight of God of great price." A meek and quiet spirit is exalted above worldly honor or riches.

The Lord illustrates how He estimates the worldly wealthy, who lift up their souls unto vanity because of their earthly possessions, by the rich man who tore down his barns and built greater, that he might have room to bestow his goods. Forgetful of God, he failed to acknowledge whence all his possessions came. No grateful thanks ascended to his gracious Benefactor. He congratulated himself thus: "Soul, thou hast much goods laid up for many years; take thine ease, eat, drink, and be merry." The Master, who had entrusted to him earthly riches with which to bless his fellow men and glorify his Maker, was justly angry at his ingratitude, and said, "Thou fool, this night thy soul shall be required of thee: then whose shall those things be, which thou hast provided? So is he that layeth up treasure for himself, and is not rich toward God." Here we have an illustration of how the infinite God estimates man. An extensive fortune, or any degree of wealth, will not secure the favor of God. All these bounties and blessings come from Him, to prove, test, and develop the character of man.

Men may have boundless wealth; yet if they are not rich toward God, if they have no interest to secure to themselves the heavenly treasure and divine wisdom, they are counted fools by their Creator, and we leave them just where God leaves them. Labor is a blessing. It is impossible for us to enjoy health without labor. All the faculties should be called into use that they may be properly developed, and that men and women may have well-balanced minds. If the young had been given a thorough education in the different branches of labor, if they had been taught labor as well as the sciences, their education would have been of greater advantage to them.

A constant strain upon the brain while the muscles are inactive, enfeebles the nerves, and students have an almost uncontrollable desire for change and exciting amusements. And when they are released, after being confined to study several hours each day, they are nearly wild. Many have never been controlled at home. They have been left to follow inclination, and they think that the restraint of the hours of study is a severe tax upon them; and not having anything to do after study hours, Satan suggests sport and mischief for a change. Their influence over other students is demoralizing. Those students who have had the benefits of religious teaching at home, and who are ignorant of the vices of society, frequently become the best acquainted with those whose minds have been cast in an inferior mold, and whose advantages for mental culture and religious training have been very limited. And they are in danger, by mingling in the society of this class, and by breathing an atmosphere that is not elevating, but that tends to lower and degrade the morals, of sinking to the same low level as their companions. It is the delight of a large class of students, in their unemployed hours, to have a high time. And very many of those who leave their homes innocent and pure, become corrupted by their associations at school.

I have been led to inquire, Must all that is valuable in our youth be sacrificed in order that they may obtain a school education? Had there been agricultural and manufacturing establishments connected with our schools, and had competent teachers been employed to educate the youth in the different branches of study and labor, devoting a portion of each day to mental improvement, and a portion to physical labor, there would now be a more elevated class of youth to come upon the stage of action to have influence in molding society. Many of the youth who would graduate at such institutions would come forth with stability of character. They would have perseverance, fortitude, and courage to surmount obstacles, and such principles that they would not be swayed by a wrong influence, however popular. There should have been experienced teachers to give lessons to young ladies in the cooking department. Young girls should have been instructed to manufacture wearing apparel, to cut, make, and mend garments, and thus become educated for the practical duties of life.

For young men, there should be establishments where they could learn different trades, which would bring into exercise their muscles as well as their mental powers. If the youth can have but a one-sided education, which is of the greater consequence, a knowledge of the sciences, with all the disadvantages to health and life, or a knowledge of labor for practical life? We unhesitatingly answer, The latter. If one must be neglected, let it be the study of books.

There are very many girls who have married and have families, who have but little practical knowledge of the duties devolving upon a wife and mother. They can read, and play upon an instrument of music; but they cannot cook. They cannot make good bread, which is very essential to the health of the family. They cannot cut and make garments, for they never learned how. They considered these things unessential, and in their married life they are as dependent upon someone to do these things for them as are their own little children. It is this inexcusable ignorance in regard to the most needful duties of life which makes very many unhappy families.

The impression that work is degrading to fashionable life has laid thousands in the grave who might have lived. Those who perform only manual labor, frequently work to excess without giving themselves periods of rest; while the intellectual class overwork the brain, and suffer for want of the healthful vigor that physical labor gives. If the intellectual would to some extent share the burden of the laboring class, and thus strengthen the muscles, the laboring class might do less, and devote a portion of their time to mental and moral culture. Those of sedentary and literary habits should take physical exercise, even if they have no need to labor so far as means are concerned. Health should be a sufficient inducement to lead them to unite physical with mental labor.

Moral, intellectual, and physical culture should be combined in order to have well-developed, well-balanced men and women. Some are qualified to exercise greater intellectual strength than others, while others are inclined to love and enjoy physical labor. Both of these classes should seek to improve where they are deficient, that they may present to God their entire being, a living sacrifice, holy and acceptable to Him, which is their reasonable service. The habits and customs of fashionable society should not gauge their course of action. The inspired apostle Paul adds, "And be not conformed to this world; but be ye transformed by the renewing of your mind, that ye may prove what is that good, and acceptable, and perfect will of God."

The minds of thinking men labor too hard. They frequently use their mental powers prodigally; while there is another class whose highest aim in life is physical labor. The latter class do not exercise the mind. Their muscles are exercised, while their brains are robbed of intellectual strength; just as the minds of thinking men are worked, while their bodies are robbed of strength and vigor by their neglect to exercise the muscles. Those who are content to devote their lives to physical labor, and leave others to do the thinking for them, while they simply carry out what other brains have planned, will have strength of muscle, but feeble intellects. Their influence for good is small in comparison to what it might be if they would use their brains as well as their muscles. This class fall more readily if attacked by disease, because the system is vitalized by the electrical force of the brain to resist disease.

Men who have good physical powers should educate themselves to think as well as to act, and not depend upon others to be brains for them. It is a popular error with a large class to regard work as degrading. Therefore young men are very anxious to educate themselves to become teachers, clerks, merchants, lawyers, and to occupy almost any position that does not require physical labor. Young women regard housework as demeaning. And although the physical exercise required to perform household labor, if not too severe, is calculated to promote health, yet they will seek for an education that will fit them to become teachers or clerks, or will learn some trade which will confine them indoors to sedentary employment. The bloom of health fades from their cheeks, and disease fastens upon them, because they are robbed of physical exercise, and their habits are perverted generally. All this because it is fashionable! They enjoy delicate life, which is feebleness and decay.

True, there is some excuse for young women not choosing housework for employment, because those who hire kitchen girls generally treat them as servants. Frequently their employers do not respect them, and treat them as though they were unworthy to be members of their families. They do not give them the privileges they do the seamstress, the copyist, and the teacher of music. But there can be no employment more important than that of housework. To cook well, to present healthful food upon the table in an inviting manner, requires intelligence and experience. The one who prepares the food that is to be placed in our stomachs, to be converted into blood to nourish the system, occupies a most important and elevated position. The position of copyist, dressmaker, or music teacher cannot equal in importance that of the cook.

44

The foregoing is a statement of what might have been done by a proper system of education. Time is too short now to accomplish that which might have been done in past generations; but we can do much, even in these last days, to correct the existing evils in the education of youth. And because time is short, we should be in earnest, and work zealously to give the young that education which is consistent with our faith. We are reformers. We desire that our children should study to the best advantage. In order to do this, employment should be given them which will call the muscles into exercise. Daily, systematic labor should constitute a part of the education of the youth, even at this late period. Much can now be gained by connecting labor with schools. In following this plan, the students will realize elasticity of spirit and vigor of thought, and will be able to accomplish more mental labor in a given time than they could by study alone. And they can leave school with their constitutions unimpaired, and with strength and courage to persevere in any position in which the providence of God may place them.

Because time is short, we should work with diligence and double energy. Our children may never enter college, but they can obtain an education in those essential branches which they can turn to a practical use, and which will give culture to the mind, and bring its powers into use. Very many youth who have gone through a college course have not obtained that true education that they can put to practical use. They may have the name of having a collegiate education, but in reality they are only educated dunces.

There are many young men whose services God would accept, if they would consecrate themselves to Him unreservedly. If they would exercise those powers of the mind in the service of God which they use in serving themselves and in acquiring property, they would make earnest, persevering, successful laborers in the vineyard of the Lord. Many of our young men should turn their attention to the study of the Scriptures, that God may use them in His cause. But they do not become as intelligent in spiritual knowledge as in temporal things; therefore they fail to do the work of God which they could do with acceptance. There are but few to warn sinners and win souls to Christ, when there should be many. Our young men generally are wise in worldly matters, but not intelligent in regard to the things of the kingdom of God. They might turn their minds in a heavenly, divine channel, and walk in the light, going on from one degree of light and strength to another, until they could turn sinners to Christ, and point the unbelieving and desponding to a bright track heavenward. And when the warfare is ended, they might be welcomed to the joy of their Lord.

Young men should not enter upon the work of explaining the Scriptures and lecturing upon the prophecies, when they do not have a knowledge of the important Bible truths they try to explain to others. They may be deficient in the common branches of education, and therefore fail to do the amount of good they could do if they had had the advantages of a good school. Ignorance will not increase the humility or spirituality of any professed follower of Christ. The truths of the divine word can be best appreciated by an intellectual Christian. Christ can be best glorified by those who serve Him intelligently. The great object of education is to enable us to use the powers which God has given us in such a manner as will best represent the religion of the Bible and promote the glory of God.

We are indebted to Him who gave us existence, for all the talents which have been entrusted to us; and it is a duty we owe to our Creator to cultivate and improve upon the talents He has committed to our trust. Education will discipline the mind, develop its powers, and understandingly direct them, that we may be useful in advancing the glory of God. We need a school where those who are just entering the ministry may be taught at least the common branches of education, and where they may also learn more perfectly the truths of God's word for this time. In connection with these schools, lectures should be given upon the prophecies. Those who really have good abilities such as God will accept to labor in His vineyard, would be very much benefited by only a few months' instruction at such a school.--Test., Vol. III, pages 131-160, 1872.

FOR ADDITIONAL READING

Life of Christ (12 Articles), The Youth's Instructor, March 1, 1872 to March 3, 1874

Dangers and Duties of Youth, Testimonies for the Church 3:221-227 (1872)

Appeal to the Youth, Idem., 362-380 (1875)

Christ an Educator

The human mind is susceptible of the highest cultivation. A life devoted to God should not be a life of ignorance. Many speak against education because Jesus chose uneducated fishermen to preach His gospel. They assert that He showed preference for the uneducated. Many learned and honorable men believed His teaching. Had these fearlessly obeyed the convictions of their consciences, they would have followed Him. Their abilities would have been accepted, and employed in the service of Christ, had they offered them. But they had not moral power, in face of the frowning priests and jealous rulers, to confess Christ, and venture their reputation in connection with the humble Galilean.

He who knew the hearts of all, understood this. If the educated and noble would not do the work they were qualified to do, Christ would select men who would be obedient and faithful in doing His will. He chose humble men and connected them with Himself, that He might educate them to carry forward the great work on earth when He should leave it.

Christ was the light of the world. He was the fountain of all knowledge. He was able to qualify the unlearned fishermen to receive the high commission He would give them. The lessons of truth given these lowly men were of mighty significance. They were to move the world. It seemed but a simple thing for Jesus to connect these humble persons with Himself; but it was an event productive of tremendous results. Their words and their works were to revolutionize the world.

Jesus did not despise education. The highest culture of the mind, if sanctified through the love and the fear of God, receives His fullest approval. The humble men chosen by Christ were with Him three years, subject to the refining influence of the Majesty of Heaven. Christ was the greatest educator the world ever knew.

God will accept the youth with their talent, and their wealth of affection, if they will consecrate themselves to Him. They may reach to the highest point of intellectual greatness; and if balanced by religious principle they can carry forward the work which Christ came from Heaven to accomplish, and in thus doing be co-workers with the Master.

The students at our College have valuable privileges, not only of obtaining a knowledge of the sciences, but also of learning how to cultivate and practice virtues which will give them symmetrical characters. They are God's responsible moral agents. The talents of wealth, station, and intellect are given of God in trust to man for his wise improvement. These varied trusts He has distributed proportionately to the known powers and capacities of His servants, to everyone his work.

The Giver expects returns corresponding to the gifts. The humblest gift is not to be despised or left inactive. The little rivulet does not say,

I will not flow along my narrow channel because I am not a mighty river. The spires of grass do not refuse to grow because they are not forest trees. The lamp does not refuse to give its little light because it is not a star. The moon and stars do not refuse to shine because they have not the brilliant light of the sun. Every person has his own peculiar sphere and vocation. Those who make the most of their God-given opportunities will return to the Giver, in their improvement, an interest proportionate to the entrusted capital.

The Lord does not reward the great amount of labor. He does not regard the greatness of the work so much as the fidelity with which it is done. The good and faithful servants are rewarded. As we cultivate the powers God has given us here, we shall increase in knowledge and perception, and be enabled to comprehend and value the immortal life. Those who have abused their God-given privileges in this life, and have been content with their ignorance, having their minds completely occupied with subjects of trivial value to themselves or others, will not comprehend personal responsibility, subdue evil tendencies, and strengthen high resolves for a purer, higher, holier life.

The youth should be learners for the next world. Perseverance in the acquisition of knowledge, controlled by the fear and love of God, will give them an increased power for good in this life, and those who have made the most of their privileges to reach the highest attainments here, will take these valuable acquisitions with them into the future life. They have sought and obtained that which is imperishable. The capability to appreciate the glories that "eye hath not seen, nor ear heard," will be proportionate to the attainments reached in the cultivation of the faculties in this life.

Those who will empty their hearts of vanity and rubbish, through the grace of God may purify the chambers of the mind, and make it a storehouse of knowledge, purity, and truth. And it will be continually reaching beyond the narrow boundaries of worldly thought, into the vastness of the Infinite. The justice and mercy of God will be unfolded to the moral perceptions. The grievous character of sin, with its results, will be discerned. The character of God, His love manifested in giving His Son to die for the world, and the beauty of holiness, are exalted themes for contemplation. These will strengthen the intellect, and bring man into close communion with the Infinite One.--Review and Herald, June 21, 1877.

FOR ADDITIONAL READING

Battle Creek College, Signs of the Times, February 7, 14, 1878

An Appeal for Our Students

We have had many fears that students who attend Battle Creek College will fail to receive all the benefit they might, in the way of religious culture, from the families that furnish them rooms. Some families do not enjoy the sweet influences of the religion of Christ, although they are professed Christians. The influence which this class of persons exert over the students is more objectionable than that of those who make no pretensions to godliness. These irreligious, irresponsible formalists may stand forth before the world in pretentious leaves, while, like the barren fig-tree they are wholly destitute of that which alone our Saviour values,--fruit to His glory. The work wrought on the heart by the grace of God, they know nothing about. These persons exert an influence which is detrimental to all with whom they associate. There should be committees, to see that the homes provided for the students are not with mere formalists, who have no burden for the souls of the dear youth.

Very much may be done for those who are deprived of the softening, subduing influences of the home circle. The spirit manifested by many shows that the language of the heart is, "'Am I my brother's keeper?' I have no burden or responsibility aside from my own family. I have no special burden or interest for the students who occupy rooms in my house." I would ask these persons if they have burdens and feel responsibilities for their own children. I am sorry to see so little anxiety on the part of some parents that all the influences surrounding their children should be favorable to the formation of Christian character; but those who do have soul-burdens for their own loved ones should not selfishly confine their interest to their own family. Jesus is our example in all things; but He has given us no example of such selfishness as we see manifested by many who profess to be His followers. If we abide in Christ, and His love abides in us, we shall love those for whom Christ died; for He has commanded His followers to love one another as He has loved them. Do we who profess His name obey this injunction? If we fail in this point we shall in others also. Had Christ studied His own profit, convenience, and pleasure, the world would have been left to perish in its sin and corruption.

A strange indifference in reference to the salvation of souls seems to have taken possession of many professed Christians. Sinners may be perishing all around them, and they have no particular burden in the matter. Will Christ say to these indifferent ones, "Well done, good and faithful servant, enter thou into the joy of thy Lord"? The joy of Christ consists in seeing souls redeemed through the sacrifice He has made for them.

Young men and women who are not under home influences need someone to look after them, and to manifest some interest for them; and those who do this are supplying a great lack, and are as verily doing a work for God and the salvation of souls as the minister in the pulpit. This work of disinterested benevolence in laboring for the good of the youth is no more than God requires of everyone of us. How earnestly should the experienced Christian work to prevent the formation of those habits that indelibly mar the character. Let the followers of Christ make the word of God attractive to the youth. Let your own characters, softened and subdued by the beauties of holiness, be a daily, hourly sermon to the youth. Manifest no spirit of grumbling; but win them to holiness of life and obedience to God. Some professors, by their sourness, repel the young. The hearts of youth are now like impressible wax, and you may lead them to admire the Christian character; but in a few years the wax may become granite.

I call upon the professed Christians of Battle Creek as a church and as individuals, take up your God-given responsibilities. Walk with God yourselves; and exert an influence over the young which shall preserve them from falling under the manifold temptations made attractive to seduce the young of this generation. Satan is getting the start of God's professed people. They seem to be asleep to the dangers of the young, and the ruin that threatens them. Satan exultingly displays his victories gained over the youth; and those who profess to be soldiers of the cross allow him to take his victims from under the very rooftree, and appear wonderfully reconciled.

The cases of many are looked upon as hopeless by those who did not reach out a helping hand to save them. Some of these might have been saved; and even now, if proper interest was manifested in them, they could be reached. What have any of us that we did not receive? We are debtors to Christ for every ability, every grace, every good thought, and every proper action. Of ourselves we have nothing of which to boast. In lowliness and humility, let us bow at the foot of the cross; and let all our words and acts be such as shall win others to Christ, and not drive them farther from Him.

I address you who reside at the great center of the work. You cannot be careless, irreverent formalists all to yourselves. Many witnesses are looking upon you, and many pattern after your course. An irreligious life not only seals your own condemnation, but ruins others also. You who live where such weighty interests are to be maintained, should be minute men, faithful sentinels, never off guard. One incautious moment spent in selfish ease or in self-gratification may give the enemy an advantage which years of hard labor may not recover. Those who choose Battle Creek for their home should be men and women of faith and prayer, true to the interests of those around them. There is no safety only as they walk with God.

There will be diversity of character among the youth who attend the College at Battle Creek. They have been differently educated and trained. Many have been left to follow the bent of their own inexperienced minds. The parents have thought they loved their children, but have proved themselves their worst enemies. They have let evil go unrestrained. They have allowed their children to cherish sin, which is like cherishing and petting a viper, that will not only sting the victim who cherishes it, but all with whom he is connected.

Some of these petted children are among the students who attend our College. Teachers, and all who are interested in the students and would help them, have an unenviable task in seeking to benefit this class of untamed youth. They have not been in subjection to their parents at home, and have no idea of having a head at school or in the homes where they board. What faith, and patience, and grace, and wisdom are required to deal with these neglected, much-to-be-pitied youth. The deceived parents may even take sides with the children against school and home discipline. They would restrain others from doing the duty God requires of them, and which they have grossly neglected. What wisdom from God is needed to deal justly and love mercy under these trying circumstances. How difficult to balance in the right direction minds that have been warped by this mismanagement. While some have been unrestrained, others have been governed too much; and when away from the vigilant hands that held the reins of control harshly, leaving love and mercy out of the question, they have felt that they would not be dictated to by anyone. They despise the very thought of restraint.

Should not those who have the difficult task of educating these young people and molding their characters have the faithful prayers of the children of God? Care, burdens, and weighty responsibilities must fall to the lot of the conscientious, God-fearing teacher, as well as that of the burden-bearing fathers and mothers in Israel who reside in Battle Creek. All sincere Christians, who value souls for whom Christ died, will make earnest efforts to do all in their power to correct even the wrongs and neglects of the natural parents. The teachers will feel that they have a duty devolving upon them to present their pupils before the world and before God with symmetrical characters and well-balanced minds. But the teachers cannot bear all this burden, and should not be expected to be alone responsible for the good manners and elevated morals of their pupils. Every family that provides rooms for them should have rules to which they must conform. It will not be doing them or their parents a kindness to allow them to form lawless habits and break or deface furniture. If they have exuberant spirits and pent-up energy, let them do vigorous manual labor, until weariness prepares them to appreciate rest in their rooms.

The rooms of some of the students last year bore an unfavorable record of the roomers. If students are coarse and rude, their rooms frequently make this fact apparent. Reckless sport, boisterous laughter, and late hours should not be tolerated by those who rent rooms. If they allow this conduct in the students, they do them a serious wrong, and make themselves, in a great degree, responsible for the misconduct. The rooms of students should be frequently visited, to see if they are favorable to health and comfort, and to ascertain if all are living in accordance with the rules of the school. Any remissness should be pointed out, and the students should be faithfully labored with. If they are insubordinate and will not be controlled, they are better off at home, and the school is better off without them. Our College should not become depraved for the sake of a few lawless students. The colleges in our land are many of them places where the youth are in danger of becoming immoral and depraved through these evil associations.

The associations of our students is an important matter, and should not be neglected. Many who come to our College are professed Christians. Especial interest should be manifested in these, and they should be encouraged in their endeavors to live a Christian life. They should be guarded, as far as possible, from the temptations that meet the youth whichever way they may turn. To those who have had years of experience, the temptations which overcome these young people may seem so light and trivial that they will withdraw their sympathies from the tempted and tried ones. This is wrong. Their own life and early experience may have been even more varying than those of the youth they would censure for their weakness.

Many who profess to be followers of Christ are weak in moral power. They have never been heroes of the cross, and are easily attracted from their allegiance to God by selfish pleasures or amusements. These persons should be helped. They should not be left to chance in choosing their companions and roommates. Those who love and fear God should bear the burden of these cases upon their souls, and should move discreetly in changing unfavorable associations. Christian youth who are inclined to be influenced by irreligious associates should have for companions those who will strengthen good resolutions and religious inclinations. A well-disposed, religiously inclined youth, and even a professor of religion, may lose his religious impressions by association with one who speaks lightly of sacred and religious things, and perhaps ridicules them, and who lacks reverence and conscientiousness. A little leaven may leaven the lump. Some are weak in faith; but if placed with proper roommates, whose influence is strong for the right, they may be balanced in the right direction, obtain a valuable religious experience, and be successful in the formation of Christian character.

I would that our brethren and sisters would watch for souls as they that must give an account. My mind has been deeply exercised upon this subject. I would urge upon those who profess Christ the necessity of putting on the whole armor; then work for our youth who attend Battle Creek College. They may not need sermons and long censorious lectures as much as they need genuine interest. Let them know by your works that you love them and have a care for their souls. If you would manifest for the tender youth now coming to Battle Creek, who are thrown into the very arms of the church, one half the care you have for your temporal interests, you might bind them to you by the strongest bonds of sympathy; and your influence over them would be a power for good.--Review and Herald, February 21, 1878.

FOR ADDITIONAL READING

Joseph in Egypt, Signs of the Times, January 8, 1880-February 5, 1880

Cultivation of the Voice, The Review and Herald, February 5, 1880

Early Life and Call of Moses, Signs of the Times, February 4, 1880-March 4, 1880

Our College Test, Testimonies for the Church, 4: 418-429

College Students, Idem, 4: 430-437

Improvement of Talents, Idem, 4: 519-522

Warning and Admonition, Idem, 4: 537-544

Moral and Intellectual Culture, Idem, 4: 545-549

Influence of Associates, Idem, 4: 587-591

Simplicity in Dress, Idem, 4: 628-648

Proper Education, Idem, 4: 648-653

Literary Societies, The Review and Herald, January 4, 1881

Bible Study, The Review and Herald, January 11, 1881

The Life of Daniel, The Review and Herald, January 25, 1881-February 15, 1881

Thoughts on Education

No work every undertaken by man requires greater care and skill than the proper training and education of youth and children. There are no influences so potent as those which surround us in our early years. Says the wise man, "Train up a child in the way he should go: and when he is old, he will not depart from it." The nature of man is threefold, and the training enjoined by Solomon comprehends the right development of the physical, intellectual, and moral powers. To perform this work aright, parents and teachers must themselves understand "the way the child should go." This embraces more than a knowledge of books or the learning of the schools. It comprehends the practice of temperance, brotherly kindness, and godliness; the discharge of our duty to ourselves, to our neighbors, and to God.

The training of children must be conducted on a different principle from that which governs the training of irrational animals. The brute has only to be accustomed to submit to its master; but the child must be taught to control himself. The will must be trained to obey the dictates of reason and conscience. A child may be so disciplined as to have, like the beast, no will of its own, his individuality being lost in that of his teacher. Such training is unwise, and its effect disastrous. Children thus educated will be deficient in firmness and decision. They are not taught to act from principle; the reasoning powers are not strengthened by exercise. So far as possible, every child should be trained to self-reliance. By calling into exercise the various faculties, he will learn where he is strongest, and in what he is deficient. A wise instructor will give special attention to the development of the weaker traits, that the child may form a well-balanced, harmonious character.

In some schools and families, children appear to be well-trained, while under the immediate discipline, but when the system which has held them to set rules is broken up, they seem to be incapable of thinking, acting, or deciding for themselves. Had they been taught to exercise their own judgment as fast and as far as practicable, the evil would have been obviated. But they have so long been controlled by parents or teachers as to wholly rely upon them. He who seeks to have the individuality of his scholars merged in his own, so that reason, judgment, and conscience shall be subject to his control, assumes an unwarranted and fearful responsibility. Those who train their pupils to feel that the power lies in themselves to become men and women of honor and usefulness, will be the most permanently successful. Their work may not appear to the best advantage to careless observers, and their labor may not be valued so highly as that of the instructor who holds absolute control, but the after-life of the pupils will show the results of the better plan of education.

Both parents and teachers are in danger of commanding and dictating too much, while they fail to come sufficiently into social relation with their children or their scholars. They maintain too great a reserve, and exercise their authority in a cold, unsympathizing manner, which tends to repel instead of winning confidence and affection. If they would oftener gather the children about them, and manifest an interest in their work, and even in their sports, they would gain the love and confidence of the little ones, and the lesson of respect and obedience would be far more readily learned; for love is the best teacher. A similar interest manifested for the youth will secure like results. The young heart is quick to respond to the touch of sympathy.

Let it never be forgotten that the teacher must be what he desires his pupils to become. Hence, his principles and habits should be considered as of greater importance than even his literary qualifications. He should be a man who fears God, and feels the responsibility of His work. He should understand the importance of physical, mental, and moral training, and should give due attention to each. He who would control his pupils must first control himself. To gain their love, he must show by look and word and act that his heart is filled with love for them. At the same time, firmness and decision are indispensable in the work of forming right habits, and developing noble characters.

Physical training should occupy an important place in every system of education. It is the duty of parents and teachers to become acquainted with the human organism and the laws by which it is governed, and so far as possible, to secure to their children and pupils that greatest of all earthly blessings, "a sound mind in a sound body." Myriads of children die annually, and many more are left to drag out a life of wretchedness, perhaps of sin, because of the ignorance or neglect of parents and teachers.

Many a mother spends hours and even days in needless work merely for display, and yet has no time to obtain the information necessary that she may preserve the health of her children. She trusts their bodies to the doctor, and their souls to the minister, that she may go on undisturbed in her worship of fashion. To become acquainted with the wonderful mechanism of the human frame, to understand the dependence of one organ upon another, for the healthful action of all, is a work in which she has no interest. Of the mutual influence of mind and body, she knows little. The mind itself, that wonderful endowment which allies the finite with the infinite, she does not understand.

For generations, the system of popular education, for children especially, has been destructive to health, and even to life itself. Five and even six hours a day young children have passed in schoolrooms not properly ventilated nor sufficiently large for the healthful accommodation of the scholars. The air of such rooms soon becomes poisonous to the lungs that inhale it. And here the little ones, with their active, restless bodies, and no less active and restless minds, have been kept unoccupied during the long summer days, when the fair world without called them to gather health and happiness with the birds and flowers. Many children have at best but a slight hold on life. Confinement in school makes them nervous and diseased. Their bodies become dwarfed from want of exercise and the exhausted condition of the nervous system. If the lamp of life goes out, parents and teachers are far from suspecting that they themselves had aught to do with quenching the vital spark. The sad bereavement is looked upon as a special dispensation of Providence, when the truth is, inexcusable ignorance and neglect of nature's laws had destroyed the life of these children. God designed them to live in the enjoyment of health and vigor, to develop pure, noble, and lovely characters, to glorify Him in this life and to praise Him forever in the future life.

Who can estimate the lives that have been wrecked by cultivating the intellectual to the neglect of the physical powers? The course of injudicious parents and teachers in stimulating the young mind by flattery or fear, has proved fatal to many a promising pupil. Instead of urging them on with every possible incentive, a judicious instructor will rather restrain the too active mind until the physical constitution has become strong enough to sustain mental effort.

That the youth may have health and cheerfulness, which are dependent upon normal physical and mental development, care must be given to the proper regulation of study, labor, and amusement. Those who are closely confined to study to the neglect of physical exercise, are injuring the health by so doing. The circulation is unbalanced, the brain having too much blood and the extremities too little. Their studies should be restricted to a proper number of hours, and then time should be given to active labor in the open air.

Little children should be permitted to run and play out of doors, enjoying the fresh, pure air, and the life-giving sunshine. Let the foundation of a strong constitution be laid in early life. Parents should be the only teachers of their children, until they are eight or ten years of age. Let the mother have less care for the artificial, let her refuse to devote her powers to the slavery of fashionable display, and find time to cultivate in herself and her children a love for the beautiful things of nature. Let her point them to the glories spread out in the heavens, to the thousand forms of beauty that adorn the earth, and then tell them of Him who made them all. Thus she can lead their young minds up to the Creator, and awaken in their hearts reverence and love for the Giver of every blessing. The fields and hills--nature's audience chamber--should be the schoolroom for little children. Her treasures should be their textbook. The lessons thus imprinted upon their minds will not be soon forgotten. [61]

God's works in nature have lessons of wisdom and gifts of healing for all. The ever-varying scenes of the recurring seasons constantly present fresh tokens of His glory, His power, and His love. Well were it for older students, while they labor to acquire the arts and learning of men, to also seek more of the wisdom of God,--to learn more of the divine laws, both natural and moral. In obedience to these are life and happiness, in this world and in the world to come.--Review and Herald, Jan. 10, 1882.

FOR ADDITIONAL READING

Should Christians Dance? The Review and Herald, February 28, 1882

Parental Responsibility, Testimonies for the Church, 5: 319-323

Training of Children, Idem, 5: 323-331

Business and Religion, Idem, 5: 422-429

A Visit to College City

A few weeks since, I visited College City (California), to speak, by invitation, upon the subject of temperance. The church was tendered for the occasion, and there was a good attendance. The people of this place have already taken a praiseworthy stand upon temperance principles. In fact, it was upon this condition that a college was established here. The land upon which the college building stands, with a large tract surrounding it, was donated to the Christian Church for educational purposes, with the stipulation that no saloon should ever be opened within three miles of the college. This agreement seems to have been faithfully kept. We would feel that the youth were much safer in attending school in such a town than where there are saloons open day and night on every street corner.

The rules of this college strictly guard the association of young men and young women during the school term. It is only when these rules are temporarily suspended, as is sometimes the case, that gentlemen are permitted to accompany ladies to and from public gatherings. Our own College at Battle Creek has similar regulations, though not so stringent. Such rules are indispensable to guard the youth from the danger of premature courtship and unwise marriage. Young people are sent to school by their parents to obtain an education, not to flirt with the opposite sex. The good of society, as well as the highest interest of the students, demands that they shall not attempt to select a life partner while their own character is yet undeveloped, their judgment immature, and while they are at the same time deprived of parental care and guidance.

It is because the home training is defective that the youth are so unwilling to submit to proper authority. I am a mother; I know whereof I speak, when I say that youth and children are not only safer but happier under wholesome restraint than when following their own inclination. Parents, your sons and daughters are not properly guarded. They should never be permitted to go and come when they please, without your knowledge and consent. The unbounded freedom granted to children at this age has proved the ruin of thousands. How many are allowed to be in the streets at night, and parents are content to be ignorant of the associates of their children. Too often, companions are chosen whose influence tends only to demoralize.

Under the cover of darkness, boys collect in groups to learn their first lessons in card-playing, gambling, smoking, and wine or beer sipping. The sons of religious parents venture into the saloons for an oyster supper, or some similar indulgence, and thus place themselves in the way of temptation. The very atmosphere of these resorts is redolent with blasphemy and pollution. No one can long remain in it without becoming corrupted. It is by such associations that promising youth are becoming inebriates and criminals. The very beginnings of the evil should be guarded against. Parents, unless you know that their surroundings are unexceptionable, do not permit your children to go into the streets after nightfall to engage in out-door sports, or to meet other boys for amusement. If this rule be rigidly enforced, obedience to it will become habitual, and the desire to transgress will soon cease.

Those who are seeking to shield the youth from temptation and to prepare them for a life of usefulness, are engaged in a good work. We are glad to see in any institution of learning a recognition of the importance of proper restraint and discipline for the young. May the efforts of all such instructors be crowned with success.--Signs of the Times, March 2, 1882

The Home and the School

It is the boast of the present age that never before did men possess so great facilities for the acquirement of knowledge, or manifest so general an interest in education. Yet despite this vaunted progress, there exists an unparalleled spirit of insubordination and recklessness in the rising generation; mental and moral degeneracy are well-nigh universal. Popular education does not remedy the evil. The lax discipline in many institutions of learning has nearly destroyed their usefulness, and in some cases rendered them a curse rather than a blessing. This fact has been seen and deplored, and earnest efforts have been made to remedy the defects in our educational system. There is urgent need of schools in which the youth may be trained to habits of self-control, application, and self-reliance, of respect for superiors and reverence for God. With such training, we might hope to see the young prepared to honor their Creator and to bless their fellow men.

It was to secure these objects that our own College at Battle Creek was founded. But those who endeavor to accomplish such a work, find that their undertaking is fraught with many and grave difficulties. The evil which underlies all others, and which often counteracts the efforts of the best instructors, is to be found in the home discipline. Parents do not see the importance of shielding their children from the gilded temptations of this age. They do not exercise proper control themselves, and hence do not rightly appreciate its value.

Many fathers and mothers err in failing to second the efforts of the faithful teacher. Youth and children, with their imperfect comprehension and undeveloped judgment, are not always able to understand all the teacher's plans and methods. Yet when they bring home reports of what is said and done at school, these are discussed by the parents in the family circle, and the course of the teacher is criticised without restraint. Here the children learn lessons that are not easily unlearned. Whenever they are subjected to unaccustomed restraint, or required to apply themselves to hard study, they appeal to their injudicious parents for sympathy and indulgence. Thus a spirit of unrest and discontent is encouraged, the school as a whole suffers from the demoralizing influence, and the teacher's burden is rendered much heavier. But the greatest loss is sustained by the victims of parental mismanagement. Defects of character which a right training would have corrected, are left to strengthen with years, to mar and perhaps destroy the usefulness of their possessor.

As a rule it will be found that the students most ready to complain of school discipline are those who have received a superficial education. Having never been taught the necessity of thoroughness, they regard it with dislike. Parents have neglected to train their sons and daughters to the faithful performance of domestic duties. Children are permitted to spend their hours in play, while father and mother toil on unceasingly. Few young persons feel that it is their duty to bear a part of the family burden. They are not taught that the indulgence of appetite, or the pursuit of ease or pleasure, is not the great aim of life.

The family circle is the school in which the child receives its first and most enduring lessons. Hence parents should be much at home. By precept and example, they should teach their children the love and the fear of God; teach them to be intelligent, social, affectionate, to cultivate habits of industry, economy, and self-denial. By giving their children love, sympathy, and encouragement at home, parents may provide for them a safe and welcome retreat from many of the world's temptations.

"No time," says the father, "I have no time to give to the training of my children, no time for social and domestic enjoyments." Then you should not have taken upon yourself the responsibility of a family. By withholding from them the time which is justly theirs, you rob them of the education which they should have at your hands. If you have children, you have a work to do, in union with the mother, in the formation of their characters. Those who feel that they have an imperative call to labor for the improvement of society, while their own children grow up undisciplined, should inquire if they have not mistaken their duty. Their own household is the first missionary field in which parents are required to labor. Those who leave the home garden to grow up to thorns and briers, while they manifest great interest in the cultivation of their neighbor's plot of ground, are disregarding the word of God.

I repeat, it is the lack of love and piety, and the neglect of proper discipline at home, that creates so much difficulty in schools and colleges. There is a fearful state of coldness and apathy among professed Christians. They are unfeeling, uncharitable, unforgiving. These evil traits, first indulged at home, exert their baleful influence in all the associations of daily life. If the spirit of kindness and courtesy were cherished by parents and children, it would be seen also in the intercourse between teacher and pupil. Christ should be an honored guest in the family circle, and His presence is no less needed in the class room. Would that the converting power of God might soften and subdue the hearts of parents and children, teachers and students, and transform them into the likeness of Christ.

Fathers and mothers should carefully and prayerfully study the characters of their children. They should seek to repress and restrain those traits that are too prominent, and to encourage others which may be deficient, thus securing harmonious development. This is no light matter. The father may not consider it a great sin to neglect the training of his children; but thus does God regard it. Christian parents need a thorough conversion upon this subject. Guilt is accumulating upon them, and the consequences of their actions reach down from their own children to children's children. The ill-balanced mind, the hasty temper, the fretfulness, envy, or jealousy,

The Home and the School

bear witness to parental neglect. These evil traits of character bring great unhappiness to their possessors. How many fail to receive from companions and friends the love which they might have, if they were more amiable. How many create trouble wherever they go, and in whatever they are engaged!

Children have claims which their parents should acknowledge and respect. They have a right to such an education and training as will make them useful, respected, and beloved members of society here, and give them a moral fitness for the society of the pure and holy hereafter. The young should be taught that both their present and their future well-being depend to a great degree on the habits they form in childhood and youth. They should be early accustomed to submission, self-denial, and a regard for others' happiness. They should be taught to subdue the hasty temper, to withhold the passionate word, to manifest unvarying kindness, courtesy, and self-control. Fathers and mothers should make it their life-study that their children may become as nearly perfect in character as human effort, combined with divine aid, can make them. This work, with all its importance and responsibility, they have accepted, in that they have brought children into the world.

Parents must see that their own hearts and lives are controlled by the divine precepts, if they would bring up their children in the nurture and admonition of the Lord. They are not authorized to fret and scold and ridicule. They should never taunt their children with perverse traits of character, which they themselves have transmitted to them. This mode of discipline will never cure the evil. Parents, bring the precepts of God's word to admonish and reprove your wayward children. Show them a "thus saith the Lord" for your requirements. A reproof which comes as the word of God is far more effective than one falling in harsh, angry tones from the lips of parents.

Wherever it seems necessary to deny the wishes or oppose the will of a child, he should be seriously impressed with the thought that this is not done for the gratification of the parents, or to indulge arbitrary authority, but for his own good. He should be taught that every fault uncorrected will bring unhappiness to himself, and will displease God. Under such discipline, children will find their greatest happiness in submitting their own will to the will of their Heavenly Father.

Some parents--and some teachers, as well--seem to forget that they themselves were once children. They are dignified, cold, and unsympathetic. Wherever they are brought in contact with the young,--at home, in the day school, the Sabbath school, or the church,--they maintain the same air of authority, and their faces habitually wear a solemn, reproving expression. Childish mirth or waywardness, the restless activity of the young life, finds no excuse in their eyes. Trifling misdemeanors are treated as grave sins. Such discipline is not Christlike. Children thus trained fear their parents or teachers, but do not love them; they do not confide to them their childish experiences. Some of the most valuable qualities of mind and heart are chilled to death, as a tender plant before the wintry blast.

Smile, parents; smile, teachers. If your heart is sad, let not your face reveal the fact. Let the sunshine from a loving, grateful heart light up the countenance. Unbend from your iron dignity, adapt yourselves to the children's needs, and make them love you. You must win their affection, if you would impress religious truth upon their heart.

Jesus loved the children. He remembered that He was once a child, and His benevolent countenance won the affections of the little ones. They loved to play around Him, and to stroke that loving face with their innocent hands. When the Hebrew mothers brought their babes to be blessed by the dear Saviour the disciples deemed the errand of too little importance to interrupt His teachings. But Jesus read the earnest longing of those mothers' hearts, and checking His disciples, He said, "Suffer little children, and forbid them not, to come unto Me: for of such is the kingdom of heaven."

Parents, you have a work to do for your children which no other can do. You cannot shift your responsibilities upon another. The father's duty to his children cannot be transferred to the mother. If she performs her own duty, she has burden enough to bear. Only by working in unison, can the father and mother accomplish the work which God has committed to their hands.

That time is worse than lost to parents and children which is devoted to the acquirement of wealth, while mental improvement and moral culture are neglected. Earthly treasures must pass away; but nobility of character, moral worth, will endure forever. If the work of parents be well done, it will through eternity testify of their wisdom and faithfulness. Those who tax their purses and their ingenuity to the utmost to provide for their households costly apparel and dainty food, or to maintain them in ignorance of useful labor, will be repaid only by the pride, envy, willfulness, and disrespect of their spoiled children.

The young need to have a firm barrier built up from their infancy between them and the world, that its corrupting influence may not affect them. Parents must exercise increasing watchfulness, that their children be not lost to God. If it were considered as important that the young possess a beautiful character and amiable disposition as it is that they imitate the fashions of the world in dress and deportment, we would see hundreds where there is one today coming upon the stage of active life prepared to exert an ennobling influence upon society.

The parents' work of education, instruction, and discipline underlies every other. The efforts of the best teachers must often bear little fruit, if fathers and mothers fail to act their part with faithfulness. God's word must ever be their guide. We do not endeavor to present a new line of duty. We set before all the teachings of that word by which our work must be judged, and we inquire, Is this the standard which we as Christian parents are endeavoring to reach?--Review and Herald, March 21, 1882.

FOR ADDITIONAL READING

The Teacher and His Work, Signs of the Times, April 27, 1882

Labor as a Blessing, Signs of the Times, May 4, 1882

Our School at Healdsburg, Signs of the Times, May 4, 1882

Home Training — Its Importance and Results, Signs of the Times, May 25, 1882

Home Discipline, The Review and Herald, June 13, 1882

The Importance of Physical Training

The present age is one of unparalleled interest in education. The wide diffusion of knowledge through the agency of the press, placing the means for self-culture within the reach of all, has awakened a general desire for mental improvement.

While we acknowledge with gratitude our increased facilities, we should not close our eyes to the defects in the present system of education. In the eager effort to secure intellectual culture, physical as well as moral training has been neglected. Many youth come forth from institutions of learning with morals debased, and physical powers enfeebled; with no knowledge of practical life, and little strength to perform its duties.

As I have seen these evils, I have inquired, Must our sons and daughters become moral and physical weaklings, in order to obtain an education in the schools? This should not be; it need not be, if teachers and students will but be true to the laws of nature, which are also the laws of God. All the powers of mind and body should be called into active exercise, that the youth may become strong, well-balanced men and women.

Many students are in so great haste to complete their education that they are not thorough in anything which they undertake. Few have sufficient courage and self-control to act from principle. Most students fail to understand the true object of education, and hence fail to take such a course as to secure this object. They apply themselves to the study of mathematics or the languages, while they neglect a study far more essential to the happiness and success of life. Many who can explore the depths of the earth with the geologist, or traverse the heavens with the astronomer, show not the slightest interest in the wonderful mechanism of their own bodies. Others can tell just how many bones there are in the human frame, and correctly describe every organ of the body, and yet they are as ignorant of the laws of health, and the cure of disease, as though life were controlled by blind fate, instead of definite and unvarying law.

Physical health lies at the very foundation of all the student's ambitions and his hopes. Hence the pre-eminent importance of gaining a knowledge of those laws by which health is secured and preserved. Every youth should learn how to regulate his dietetic habits,--what to eat, when to eat, and how to eat. He should learn how many hours to give to study, and how much time to spend in physical exercise. The human body may be compared to nicely adjusted machinery, which needs care to keep it in running order. One part should not be subjected to constant wear and pressure, while another part is rusting from inaction. While the mind is tasked, the muscles also should have their proportion of exercise.

The proper regulation of his habits of eating, sleeping, study, and exercise, is a duty which every student owes to himself, to society, and to God.

The education which will make the young a blessing to the world, is that which enables them to attain a true and noble manhood or womanhood. That student who is studying hard, sleeping little, exercising little, and eating irregularly of an improper or inferior quality of food, is obtaining mental training at the expense of health and morals, of spirituality, and, it may be, of life.

The young naturally desire activity, and if they find no legitimate scope for their pent-up energies after the confinement of the schoolroom, they become restless and impatient of control, and thus are led to engage in the rude, unmanly sports that disgrace so many schools and colleges, and even to plunge into scenes of actual dissipation. Many of the youth who left their homes innocent, are corrupted by their associations at school.

Every institution of learning should make provision for the study and practice of agriculture and the mechanic arts. Competent teachers should be employed to instruct the youth in the various industrial pursuits, as well as in the several branches of study. While a part of each day is devoted to mental improvement, let a stated portion be given to physical labor, and a suitable time to devotional exercises and the study of the Scriptures.

This training would encourage habits of self-reliance, firmness, and decision. Graduates of such institutions would be prepared to engage successfully in the practical duties of life. They would have courage and perseverance to surmount obstacles, and firmness of principle that would not yield to evil influences.

If the youth can have but a one-sided education, which is of the greatest importance, the study of the sciences, with all the disadvantages to health and morals, or a thorough training in practical duties, with sound morals and good physical development? We unhesitatingly say, the latter. But with proper effort both may, in most cases, be secured.

Those who combine useful labor with study have no need of gymnastic exercises. And work performed in the open air is tenfold more beneficial to health than in-door labor. Both the mechanic and the farmer have physical exercise, yet the farmer is the healthier of the two. Nothing short of nature's invigorating air and sunshine will fully meet the demands of the system. The tiller of the soil finds in his labor all the movements that were ever practiced in the gymnasium. His movement-room is the open fields. The canopy of heaven is its roof, the solid earth its floor. Here he plows and hoes, sows and reaps. Watch him, as in "haying time" he mows and rakes, pitches and tumbles, lifts and loads, throws off, treads down, and stows away. These various movements call into action the bones, joints, muscles, sinews, and nerves of the body. His vigorous exercise causes full, deep, strong inspirations and exhalations, which expand the lungs and purify the blood, sending the warm current of life bounding through arteries and veins. A farmer who is temperate in all his habits usually enjoys health. His work is pleasant to him. He has a good appetite. He sleeps well, and may be happy.

The Importance of Physical Training 47

Contrast the condition of the active farmer with that of the student who neglects physical exercise. He sits in a close room, bending over his desk or table, his chest contracted, his lungs crowded. He cannot take full, deep inspirations. His brain is tasked to the utmost, while his body is as inactive as though he had no particular use for it. His blood moves sluggishly through the system. His feet are cold, his head hot. How can such a person have health?

Let the student take regular exercise that will cause him to breathe deep and full, taking into his lungs the pure invigorating air of heaven, and he will be a new being. It is not hard study that is destroying the health of students, so much as it is their disregard of nature's laws.

In institutions of learning, experienced teachers should be employed to instruct young ladies in the mysteries of the kitchen. A knowledge of domestic duties is beyond price to every woman. There are families without number whose happiness is wrecked by the inefficiency of the wife and mother. It is not so important that our daughters learn painting, fancy work, music, or even "cube root," or the figures of rhetoric, as that they learn how to cut, make, and mend their own clothing, or to prepare food in a wholesome and palatable manner. When a little girl is nine or ten years old, she should be required to take her regular share in household duties, as she is able, and should be held responsible for the manner in which she does her work. That was a wise father, who, when asked what he intended to do with his daughters, replied, "I intend to apprentice them to their excellent mother, that they may learn the art of improving time, and be fitted to become wives and mothers, heads of families, and useful members of society."

Washing clothes upon the old-fashioned rubbing-board, sweeping, dusting, and a variety of other duties in the kitchen and the garden, will be valuable exercise for young ladies. Such useful labor will supply the place of croquet, archery, dancing, and other amusements which benefit no one.

Many ladies, accounted well-educated, having graduated with honors at some institution of learning, are shamefully ignorant of the practical duties of life. They are destitute of the qualifications necessary for the proper regulation of the family, and hence essential to its happiness. They may talk of woman's elevated sphere, and of her rights, yet they themselves fall far below the true sphere of woman. It is the right of every daughter of Eve to have a thorough knowledge of household duties, to receive training in every department of domestic labor. Every young lady should be so educated that if called to fill the position of wife and mother, she may preside as a queen in her own domain. She should be fully competent to guide and instruct her children and to direct her servants, or, if need be, to minister with her own hands to the wants of her household. It is her right to understand the mechanism of the human body and the principles of hygiene, the matters of diet and dress, labor and recreation, and countless others that intimately concern the well-being of her household. It is her right to obtain such a knowledge of the best methods of treating disease that she can care for her children in sickness, instead of leaving her precious treasures in the hands of stranger nurses and physicians.

The idea that ignorance of useful employment is an essential characteristic of the true gentleman or lady, is contrary to the design of God in the creation of man. Idleness is a sin, and ignorance of common duties is the result of folly, which afterlife will give ample occasion to bitterly regret.

Those who make it their rule of life to serve and honor God will give heed to the apostle's injunction, "Whether ye eat, or drink, or whatsoever ye do, do all to the glory of God." Such students will preserve their integrity in the face of temptation, and will come from school with well-developed intellects, and with health of body and health of soul.--Signs of the Times, June 29, 1882.

FOR ADDITIONAL READING

The Primal Object of Education, The Review and Herald, July 11, 1882

Daniel's Integrity Under Test

The prophet Daniel was an illustrious character. He was a bright example of what men may become when united with the God of wisdom. A brief account of the life of this holy man of God is left on record for the encouragement of those who should afterward be called to endure trial and temptation.

When the people of Israel, their king, nobles, and priests, were carried into captivity, four of their number were selected to serve in the court of the king of Babylon. One of these was Daniel, who early gave promise of the remarkable ability developed in later years. These youth were all of princely birth, and are described as "children in whom was no blemish, but well-favored, and skillful in all wisdom, and cunning in knowledge, and understanding science, and such as had ability in them." Perceiving the superior talents of these youthful captives, King Nebuchadnezzar determined to prepare them to fill important positions in his kingdom. That they might be fully qualified for their life at court, according to Oriental custom, they were to be taught the language of the Chaldeans, and to be subjected for three years to a thorough course of physical and intellectual discipline.

The youth in this school of training were not only to be admitted to the royal palace, but it was provided that they should eat of the meat, and drink of the wine, which came from the king's table. In all this the king considered that he was not only bestowing great honor upon them, but securing for them the best physical and mental development that could be obtained.

Among the viands placed before the king were swine's flesh and other meats which were declared unclean by the law of Moses, and which the Hebrews had been expressly forbidden to eat. Here Daniel was brought to a severe test. Should he adhere to the teachings of his fathers concerning meats and drinks, and offend the king, and probably lose not only his position but his life? or should he disregard the commandment of the Lord, and retain the favor of the king, thus securing great intellectual advantages and the most flattering worldly prospects?

Daniel did not long hesitate. He decided to stand firm in his integrity, let the result be what it might. He "purposed in his heart that he would not defile himself with the portion of the king's meat, nor with the wine which he drank."

There are many among professed Christians today who would decide that Daniel was too particular, and would pronounce him narrow and bigoted. They consider the matter of eating and drinking as of too little consequence to require such a decided stand,--one involving the probable sacrifice of every earthly advantage. But those who reason thus will find in the day of judgment that they turned from God's express requirements, and set up their own opinion as a standard of right and wrong. They will find that what seemed to them unimportant was not so regarded of God. His requirements should be sacredly obeyed. Those who accept and obey one of His precepts because it is convenient to do so, while they reject another because its observance would require a sacrifice, lower the standard of right, and by their example lead others to lightly regard the holy law of God. "Thus saith the Lord" is to be our rule in all things.

Daniel was subjected to the severest temptations that can assail the youth of today; yet he was true to the religious instruction received in early life. He was surrounded with influences calculated to subvert those who would vacillate between principle and inclination; yet the word of God presents him as a faultless character. Daniel dared not trust to his own moral power. Prayer was to him a necessity. He made God his strength, and the fear of God was continually before him in all the transactions of his life.

Daniel possessed the grace of genuine meekness. He was true, firm, and noble. He sought to live in peace with all, while he was unbending as the lofty cedar wherever principle was involved. In everything that did not come in collision with his allegiance to God, he was respectful and obedient to those who had authority over him; but he had so high a sense of the claims of God that the requirements of earthly rulers were held subordinate. He would not be induced by any selfish consideration to swerve from his duty.

The character of Daniel is presented to the world as a striking example of what God's grace can make of men fallen by nature and corrupted by sin. The record of his noble, self-denying life is an encouragement to our common humanity. From it we may gather strength to nobly resist temptation, and firmly, and in the grace of meekness, stand for the right under the severest trial.

Daniel might have found a plausible excuse to depart from his strictly temperate habits; but the approval of God was dearer to him than the favor of the most powerful earthly potentate--dearer even than life itself. Having by his courteous conduct obtained favor with Melzar, the officer in charge of the Hebrew youth, Daniel made a request that they might not eat of the king's meat or drink of his wine. Melzar feared that should he comply with this request, he might incur the displeasure of the king, and thus endanger his own life. Like many at the present day, he thought that an abstemious diet would render these youth pale and sickly in appearance, and deficient in muscular strength, while the luxurious food from the king's table would make them ruddy and beautiful, and would promote physical and mental activity.

Daniel requested that the matter be decided by a ten days' trial, the Hebrew youth during this brief period being permitted to eat of simple food, while their companions partook of the king's dainties. The request was finally granted, and then Daniel felt assured that he had gained his case. Although but a youth, he had seen the injurious effects of wine and luxurious living upon physical and mental health.

Daniel's Integrity Under Test

At the end of the ten days the result was found to be quite the opposite of Melzar's expectations. Not only in personal appearance, but in physical activity and mental vigor, those who had been temperate in their habits exhibited a marked superiority over their companions who had indulged appetite. As a result of this trial, Daniel and his associates were permitted to continue their simple diet during the whole course of their training for the duties of the kingdom.

The Lord regarded with approval the firmness and self-denial of these Hebrew youth, and His blessing attended them. He "gave them knowledge and skill in all learning and wisdom; and Daniel had understanding in all visions and dreams." At the expiration of the three years of training, when their ability and acquirements were tested by the king, he "found none like Daniel, Hananiah, Mishael, and Azariah; therefore stood they before the king. And in all matters of wisdom and understanding, that the king inquired of them, he found them ten times better than all the magicians and astrologers that were in all his realm."

The life of Daniel is an inspired illustration of what constitutes a sanctified character. It presents a lesson for all, and especially for the young. A strict compliance with the requirements of God is beneficial to the health of body and mind. In order to reach the highest standard of moral and intellectual attainments, it is necessary to seek wisdom and strength from God, and to observe strict temperance in all the habits of life. In the experience of Daniel and his companions we have an instance of the triumph of principle over temptation to indulge the appetite. It shows us that through religious principle young men may triumph over the lusts of the flesh, and remain true to God's requirements, even though it cost them a great sacrifice.

What if Daniel and his companions had made a compromise with those heathen officers, and had yielded to the pressure of the occasion, by eating and drinking as was customary with the Babylonians? That single instance of departure from principle would have weakened their sense of right and their abhorrence of wrong. Indulgence of appetite would have involved the sacrifice of physical vigor, clearness of intellect, and spiritual power. One wrong step would probably have led to others, until, their connection with Heaven being severed, they would have been swept away by temptation.

God has said, "Them that honor Me, I will honor." While Daniel clung to his God with unwavering trust, the spirit of prophetic power came upon him. While he was instructed of man in the duties of court life, he was taught of God to read the mysteries of future ages, and to present to coming generations, through figures and similitudes, the wonderful things that would come to pass in the last days.--Signs of the Times, Sept. 28, 1882.

FOR ADDITIONAL READING

Holiday Gifts, Signs of the Times, December 14, 1882
Young Men as Missionary Workers, The Review and Herald, July 17, 1883
Science and Revelation, Signs of the Times, March 13, 1884
Science and the Bible in Education, Signs of the Times, March 20, 1884
The Training of Children, Signs of the Times, April 10, 1884
Important Duties in Home Life, Signs of the Times, April 17, 1884

The Importance of Education

The true object of education should be carefully considered. God has entrusted to each one capacities and powers, that they may be returned to Him enlarged and improved. All His gifts are granted to us to be used to the utmost. He requires everyone of us to cultivate our powers, and attain the highest possible capacity for usefulness, that we may do noble work for God, and bless humanity. Every talent that we possess, whether of mental capacity, money, or influence, is of God, so that we may say with David, "All things come of Thee, and of Thine own have we given Thee."

Dear youth, what is the aim and purpose of your life? Are you ambitious for education that you may have a name and position in the world? Have you thoughts that you dare not express, that you may one day stand upon the summit of intellectual greatness; that you may sit in deliberative and legislative councils, and help to enact laws for the nation? There is nothing wrong in these aspirations. You may everyone of you make your mark. You should be content with no mean attainments. Aim high, and spare no pains to reach the standard.

The fear of the Lord lies at the foundation of all true greatness. Integrity, unswerving integrity, is the principle that you need to carry with you into all the relations of life. Take your religion into your school-life, into your boarding-house, into all your pursuits. The important question with you now is, how to so choose and perfect your studies that you will maintain the solidity and purity of an untarnished Christian character, holding all temporal claims and interests in subjection to the higher claims of the gospel of Christ. You want now to build as you will be able to furnish, to so relate yourself to society and to life that you may answer the purpose of God in your creation. As disciples of Christ, you are not debarred from engaging in temporal pursuits; but you should carry your religion with you. Whatever the business you may qualify yourself to engage in, never entertain the idea that you cannot make a success of it without sacrificing principle.

Balanced by religious principle, you may climb to any height you please. We would be glad to see you rising to the noble elevation God designs that you shall reach. Jesus loves the precious youth; and He is not pleased to see them grow up with uncultivated, undeveloped talents. They may become strong men of firm principle, fitted to be entrusted with high responsibilities, and to this end they may lawfully strain every nerve.

But never commit so great a crime as to pervert your God-given powers to devil and destroy others. There are gifted men who use their ability to spread moral ruin and corruption; but all such are sowing seed that will produce a harvest which they will not be proud to reap. It is a fearful thing to use God-given abilities in such a way as to scatter blight and woe instead of blessing in society. It is also a fearful thing to fold the talent entrusted to us in a napkin, and hide it away in the world; for this is casting away the crown of life. God claims our service. There are responsibilities for everyone to bear; and we can fulfill life's grand mission only when these responsibilities are fully accepted, and faithfully and conscientiously discharged.

Says the wise man, "Remember now thy Creator in the days of thy youth." But do not for a moment suppose that religion will make you sad and gloomy and will block up the way to success. The religion of Christ does not obliterate or even weaken a single faculty. It in no way incapacitates you for the enjoyment of any real happiness; it is not designed to lessen your interest in life, or to make you indifferent to the claims of friends and society. It does not mantle the life in sackcloth; it is not expressed in deep-drawn sighs and groans. No, no; those who in everything make God first and last and best, are the happiest people in the world. Smiles and sunshine are not banished from their countenance. Religion does not make the receiver coarse and rough, untidy and uncourteous; on the contrary, it elevates and ennobles him, refines his taste, sanctifies his judgment, and fits him for the society of heavenly angels and for the home that Jesus has gone to prepare.

Let us never lose sight of the fact that Jesus is a wellspring of joy. He does not delight in the misery of human beings, but loves to see them happy. Christians have many sources of happiness at their command, and they may tell with unerring accuracy what pleasures are lawful and right. They may enjoy such recreations as will not dissipate the mind or debase the soul, such as will not disappoint, and leave a sad after influence to destroy self-respect or bar the way to usefulness. If they can take Jesus with them, and maintain a prayerful spirit, they are perfectly safe.

The Psalmist says: "The entrance of Thy words giveth light; it giveth understanding to the simple." As an educating power the Bible is without a rival. No scientific works are so well adapted to develop the mind as a contemplation of the great and vital truths and practical lessons of the Bible. No other book has ever been printed which is so well calculated to give mental power. Men of the greatest intellects, if not guided by the word of God in their research, become bewildered; they cannot comprehend the Creator or His works. But set the mind to grasp and measure eternal truth, summon it to effort by delving for the jewels of truth in the rich mine of the word of God, and it will never become dwarfed and enfeebled, as when left to dwell upon commonplace subjects.

The Bible is the most instructive and comprehensive history that has ever been given to the world. Its sacred pages contain the only authentic account of the creation. Here we behold the power that "stretched forth the heavens, and laid the foundations of the earth." Here we have a truthful history of the human race, one that is unmarred by human prejudice or human pride.

In the word of God we find subject for the deepest thought; its truths arouse to the loftiest aspiration. Here we hold communion with patriarchs and prophets, and listen to the voice of the Eternal as He speaks with men.

The Importance of Physical Training

Here we behold what the angels contemplate with wonder,--the Son of God, as He humbled Himself to become our substitute and surety, to cope single-handed with the powers of darkness, and to gain the victory in our behalf.

Our youth have the precious Bible; and if all their plans and purposes are tested by the Holy Scriptures, they will be led into safe paths. Here we may learn what God expects of the beings formed in His image. Here we may learn how to improve the present life, and how to secure the future life. No other book can satisfy the questionings of the mind, and the cravings of the heart. By giving heed to the teachings of God's word, men may rise from the lowest depths of ignorance and degradation to become sons of God, associates of sinless angels.

The more the mind dwells upon these themes, the more it will be seen that the same principles run through natural and spiritual things. There is harmony between nature and Christianity; for both have the same Author. The book of nature and the book of revelation indicate the working of the same divine mind. There are lessons to be learned in nature; and there are lessons, deep, earnest, and all-important lessons, to be learned from the book of God.

Young friends, the fear of the Lord lies at the very foundation of all progress; it is the beginning of wisdom. Your Heavenly Father has claims upon you; for without solicitation or merit on your part He gives you the bounties of His providence; and more than this, He has given you all heaven in one gift, that of His beloved Son. In return for this infinite gift, He claims of you willing obedience. As you are bought with a price, even the precious blood of the Son of God, He requires that you make a right use of the privileges you enjoy. Your intellectual and moral faculties are God's gifts, talents entrusted to you for wise improvement, and you are not at liberty to let them lie dormant for want of proper cultivation, or be crippled and dwarfed by inaction. It is for you to determine whether or not the weighty responsibilities that rest upon you shall be faithfully met, whether or not your efforts shall be well directed and your best.

We are living in the perils of the last days. All heaven is interested in the characters you are forming. Every provision has been made for you, that you should be a partaker of the divine nature, having escaped the corruption that is in the world through lust. Man is not left alone to conquer the powers of evil by his own feeble efforts. Help is at hand, and will be given every soul who really desires it. Angels of God, that ascend and descend the ladder that Jacob saw in vision, will help every soul who wills to climb even to the highest heaven. They are guarding the people of God, and watching how every step is taken. Those who climb the shining way will be rewarded; they will enter into the joy of their Lord.

Importance of Education

With Daniel, the fear of the Lord was the beginning of wisdom. He was placed in a position where temptation was strong. In king's courts, dissipation was on every side; selfish indulgence, gratification of appetite, intemperance and gluttony, were the order of each day. Daniel could join in the debilitating, corrupting practices of the courtiers, or he could resist the influence that tended downward. He chose the latter course. He purposed in his heart that he would not be corrupted by the sinful indulgences with which he was brought in contact, let the consequences be what they might. He would not even defile himself with the king's meat, or with the wine that he drank. The Lord was pleased with the course that Daniel pursued. He was greatly beloved and honored of heaven; and to him the God of wisdom gave skill in the learning of the Chaldeans, and understanding in all visions and dreams.

If the students who attend our colleges would be firm, and maintain integrity, if they would not associate with those who walk in the paths of sin, nor be charmed by their society, like Daniel they would enjoy the favor of God. If they would discard unprofitable amusements and indulgence of appetite, their minds would be clear for the pursuit of knowledge. They would thus gain a moral power that would enable them to remain unmoved when assailed by temptation. It is a continual struggle to be always on the alert to resist evil; but it pays to obtain one victory after another over self and the powers of darkness. And if the youth are proved and tested, as was Daniel, what honor can they reflect to God by their firm adherence to the right.

A spotless character is as precious as the gold of Ophir. Without pure, unsullied virtue, none can ever rise to any honorable eminence. But noble aspirations and the love of righteousness are not inherited. Character cannot be bought; it must be formed by stern efforts to resist temptation. The formation of a right character is the work of a lifetime, and is the outgrowth of prayerful meditation united with a grand purpose. The excellence of character that you possess must be the result of your own effort. Friends may encourage you, but they cannot do the work for you. Wishing, sighing, dreaming, will never make you great or good. You must climb. Gird up the loins of your mind, and go to work with all the strong powers of your will. It is the wise improvement of your opportunities, the cultivation of your God-given talents, that will make you men and women that can be approved of God, and a blessing to society. Let your standard be high, and with indomitable energy, make the most of your talents and opportunities, and press to the mark.

Will our youth consider that they have battles to fight? Satan and his hosts are arrayed against them, and they have not the experience that those of mature age have gained.

Satan has an intense hatred for Christ, and the purchase of His blood, and he works with all deceivableness of unrighteousness. He seeks by every artifice to enlist the young under his banner; and he uses them as his agents to suggest doubts of the Bible. When one seed of doubt is sown, Satan nourishes it until it produces an abundant harvest. If he can unsettle one youth in regard to the Scripture, that one will not cease to work until other minds are leavened with the same skepticism.

Those who cherish doubts will boast of their independence of mind; but they are far enough from possessing genuine independence. Their minds are filled with slavish fear, lest someone as weak and superficial as themselves should ridicule them. This is weakness, and slavery to the veriest tyrant. True liberty and independence are found in the service of God. His service will place upon you no restriction that will not increase your happiness. In complying with His requirements, you will find a peace, contentment, and enjoyment that you can never have in the path of wild license and sin. Then study well the nature of the liberty you desire. Is it the liberty of the sons of God, to be free in Christ Jesus? or do you call the selfish indulgence of base passions freedom? Such liberty carries with it the heaviest remorse; it is the cruelest bondage.

True independence of mind is not stubbornness. It leads the youth to form their opinions on the word of God, irrespective of what others may say or do. If in the company of the unbelieving, the atheist, or the infidel, it leads them to acknowledge and defend their belief in the sacred truths of the gospel against the cavilings and witticisms of their ungodly associates. If they are with those who think it is a virtue to parade the faults of professed Christians, and then scoff at religion, morality, and virtue, real independence of mind will lead them courteously yet boldly to show that ridicule is a poor substitute for sound argument. It will enable them to look beyond the caviler to the one who influences him, the adversary of God and man, and to resist him in the person of his agent.

Stand up for Jesus, young friends, and in your time of need Jesus will stand up for you. "By their fruits ye shall know them." Either God or Satan controls the mind; and the life shows so clearly that none need mistake to which power you yield allegiance. Everyone has an influence either for good or for evil. Is your influence on the side of Christ or on that of Satan? Those who turn away from iniquity enlist the power of Omnipotence in their favor. The atmosphere that surrounds them is not of earth. By the silent power of a well-ordered life and a godly conversation, they may present Jesus to the world. They may reflect Heaven's light, and win souls to Christ.

I am glad that we have institutions where our youth can be separated from the corrupting influences so prevalent in the schools of the present day. Our brethren and sisters should be thankful that in the providence of God our colleges have been established, and should stand ready to sustain them by their means. Every influence should be brought to bear to educate the youth and to elevate their morals. They should be trained to have moral courage to resist the tide of moral pollution in this degenerate age. With a firm hold upon divine power, they may stand in society to mold and fashion, rather than to be fashioned after the world's model.

There can be no more important work than the proper education of our youth. We must guard them, fighting back Satan, that he shall not take them out of our arms. When the youth come to our colleges, they should not be made to feel that they have come among strangers, who do not care for their souls. There should be fathers and mothers in Israel who will watch for their souls, as they that must give account. Brethren and sisters, do not hold yourselves aloof from the dear youth, as though you have no particular concern or responsibility for them. You who have long professed to be Christians have a work to do to patiently and kindly lead them in the right way. You should show them that you love them because they are younger members of the Lord's family, the purchase of His blood.

The future of society will be determined by the youth of today. Satan is making earnest, persevering efforts to corrupt the mind and debase the character of every young person; and shall we who have more experience stand as mere spectators, and see him accomplish his purpose without hindrance? Let us stand at our post as minute men, to work for these youth, and through the help of God hold them back from the pit of destruction. In the parable, while men slept, the enemy sowed tares; and while you, my brethren and sisters, are unconscious of his work, he is gathering an army of youth under his banner; and he exults, for through them he carries on his warfare against God.

The teachers in our schools have a heavy responsibility to bear. They must be in words and character what they wish their students to be,--men and women that fear God and work righteousness. If they are acquainted with the way themselves, they can train the youth to walk in it. They will not only educate them in the sciences, but train them to have moral independence, to work for Jesus, and to take up burdens in His cause.

Teachers, what opportunities are yours? What a privilege is within your reach of molding the minds and characters of the youth under your charge! What a joy it will be to you to meet them around the great white throne, and know that you have done what you could to fit them for immortality! If your work stands the test of the great day, how like sweetest music will fall upon your ear the benediction of the Master, "Well done, good and faithful servant; enter thou into the joy of thy Lord."

In the great harvest field there is abundance of work for all, and those who neglect to do what they can, will be found guilty before God. Let us work for time and for eternity. Let us work for the youth with all the powers God has bestowed upon us, and He will bless our well-directed efforts. Our Saviour longs to save the young. He would rejoice to see them around His throne clothed in the spotless robes of His righteousness. He is waiting to place upon their heads the crown of life, and hear their happy voices join in ascribing honor and glory and majesty to God and the Lamb in the song of victory that shall echo and re-echo throughout the courts of heaven.--Review and Herald, August 19, 26, 1884.

Danger of Reading Fictitious or Infidel Books

Every Christian, whether old or young, will be assailed by temptations; and our only safety is in carefully studying our duty, and then doing it at any cost to ourselves. Everything has been done for us to secure our salvation, and we must be not only willing but anxious to learn the will of God, and do all things to His glory. This is the Christian's life work. He will not try to see how far he can venture in the path of indifference and unbelief, and yet be called a child of God; but he will study to see how closely he can imitate the life and character of Christ.

Young friends, a knowledge of the Bible will help you to resist temptation. If you have been in the habit of reading storybooks, will you consider whether it is right to spend your time with these books, which merely occupy your time and amuse you, but give you no mental or moral strength? If you are reading them, and find that they create a morbid craving for exciting novels, if they lead you to dislike the Bible, and cast it aside, if they involve you in darkness and backsliding from God,--if this is the influence they have over you, stop right where you are. Do not pursue this course of reading until your imagination is fired, and you become unfitted for the study of the Bible, and the practical duties of real life.

Cheap works of fiction do not profit. They impart no real knowledge; they inspire no great and good purpose; they kindle in the heart no earnest desires for purity; they excite no soul hunger for righteousness. On the contrary, they take time which should be given to the practical duties of life and to the service of God,--time which should be devoted to prayer, to visiting the sick, caring for the needy, and educating yourself for a useful life. When you commence reading a storybook, how frequently the imagination is so excited that you are betrayed into sin. You disobey your parents, and bring confusion into the domestic circle by neglecting the simple duties devolving upon you. And worse than this, prayer is forgotten, and the Bible is read with indifference or entirely neglected.

There is another class of books that you should avoid,--the productions of such infidel writers as Paine and Ingersoll. These are often urged upon you with the taunt that you are a coward, and afraid to read them. Frankly tell these enemies who would tempt you--for enemies they are, however much they may profess to be your friends--that you will obey God, and take the Bible as your guide. Tell them that you are afraid to read these books; that your faith in the word of God is now altogether too weak, and you want it increased and strengthened instead of diminished; and that you do not want to come in such close contact with the father of lies.

I warn you to stand firm, and never do a wrong action rather than be called a coward. Allow no taunts, no threats, no sneering remarks, to induce you to violate your conscience in the least particular, and thus open a door whereby Satan can come in and control the mind.

Suffer not yourselves to open the lids of a book that is questionable. There is a hellish fascination in the literature of Satan. It is the powerful battery by which he tears down a simple religious faith. Never feel that you are strong enough to read infidel books; for they contain a poison like that of asps. They can do you no good, and will assuredly do you harm. In reading them, you are inhaling the miasmas of hell. They will be to your soul like a corrupt stream of water, defiling the mind, keeping it in the mazes of skepticism, and making it earthly and sensual. These books are written by men whom Satan employs as his agents; and by this means he designs to confuse the mind, withdraw the affections from God, and rob your Creator of the reverence and gratitude which His works demand.

94 The mind needs to be trained, and its desires controlled and brought into subjection to the will of God.

Instead of being dwarfed and deformed by feeding on the vile trash which Satan provides, it should have wholesome food, which will give strength and vigor.

Young Christian, you have everything to learn. You must be an interested student of the Bible; you must search it, comparing scripture with scripture. If you would do your Master good and acceptable service, you must know what He requires. His word is a sure guide; if it is carefully studied, there is no danger of falling under the power of the temptations that surround the youth, and crowd in upon them.--The Youth's Instructor, September 10, 1884.

FOR ADDITIONAL READING

The True Object of Education, Signs of the Times, September 18, 1884

The Benefits of Industry, Signs of the Times, October 9, 1884

Science Falsely So—Called, Signs of the Times, November 6, 1884, November 13, 1884

The Schools of the Ancient Hebrews

The institutions of human society find their best models in the word of God. For those of instruction, in particular, there is no lack of both precept and example. Lessons of great profit, even in this age of educational progress, may be found in the history of God's ancient people.

The Lord reserved to Himself the education and instruction of Israel. His care was not restricted to their religious interests. Whatever affected their mental or physical well-being, became also an object of divine solicitude, and came within the province of divine law.

God commanded the Hebrews to teach their children His requirements, and to make them acquainted with all His dealings with their people. The home and the school were one. In the place of stranger lips, the loving hearts of the father and mother were to give instruction to their children. Thoughts of God were associated with all the events of daily life in the home dwelling. The mighty works of God in the deliverance of His people were recounted with eloquence and reverential awe. The great truths of God's providence and of the future life were impressed on the young mind. It became acquainted with the true, the good, the beautiful.

By the use of figures and symbols the lessons given were illustrated, and thus more firmly fixed in the memory. Through this animated imagery the child was, almost from infancy, initiated into the mysteries, the wisdom, and the hopes of his fathers, and guided in a way of thinking and feeling and anticipating, that reached beyond things seen and transitory, to the unseen and eternal.

From this education many a youth of Israel came forth vigorous in body and mind, quick to perceive and strong to act, the heart prepared like good ground for the growth of the precious seed, the mind trained to see God in the words of revelation and the scenes of nature. The stars of heaven, the trees and flowers of the field, the lofty mountains, the babbling brooks, all spoke to him, and the voices of the prophets, heard throughout the land, met a response in his heart.

Such was the training of Moses in the lowly cabin home in Goshen; of Samuel, by the faithful Hannah; of David, in the hill-dwelling at Bethlehem; of Daniel, before the scenes of the captivity separated him from the home of his fathers. Such, too, was the early life of Christ, in the humble home at Nazareth; such the training by which the child Timothy learned from the lips of his mother Eunice, and his grandmother Lois, the truths of Holy Writ.

Further provision was made for the instruction of the young, by the establishment of the "school of the prophets." If a youth was eager to obtain a better knowledge of the Scriptures, to search deeper into the mysteries of the kingdom of God, and to seek wisdom from above, that he might become a teacher in Israel, this school was open to him.

By Samuel the schools of the prophets were established to serve as a barrier against the widespread corruption resulting from the iniquitous course of Eli's sons, and to promote the moral and spiritual welfare of the people. These schools proved a great blessing to Israel, promoting that righteousness which exalteth a nation, and furnishing it with men qualified to act, in the fear of God, as leaders and counselors. In the accomplishment of this object, Samuel gathered companies of young men who were pious, intelligent and studious. These were called the sons of the prophets. The instructors were men not only versed in divine truth, but those who had themselves enjoyed communion with God, and had received the special endowment of His Spirit. They enjoyed the respect and confidence of the people, both for learning and piety.

In Samuel's day there were two of these schools,--one at Ramah, the home of the prophet, and the other at Kirjath-jearim, where the ark then was. Two were added in Elijah's time, at Jericho and Bethel, and others were afterward established at Samaria and Gilgal.

The pupils of these schools sustained themselves by their own labor as husbandmen and mechanics. In Israel this was not considered strange or degrading; it was regarded a crime to allow children to grow up in ignorance of useful labor. In obedience to the command of God, every child was taught some trade, even though he was to be educated for holy office. Many of the religious teachers supported themselves by manual labor. Even so late as the time of Christ, it was not considered anything degrading that Paul and Aquila earned a livelihood by their labor as tent-makers.

The chief subjects of study were the law of God with the instructions given to Moses, sacred history, sacred music, and poetry. It was the grand object of all study to learn the will of God and the duties of His people. In the records of sacred history were traced the footsteps of Jehovah. From the events of the past were drawn lessons of instruction for the future. The great truths set forth by the types and shadows of the Mosaic law were brought to view, and faith grasped the central object of all that system, the Lamb of God that was to take away the sins of the world.

The Hebrew language was cultivated as the most sacred tongue in the world. A spirit of devotion was cherished. Not only were students taught the duty of prayer, but they were taught how to pray, how to approach their Creator, how to exercise faith in Him, and how to understand and obey the teachings of His Spirit. Sanctified intellects brought forth from the treasure house of God things new and old.

The art of sacred melody was diligently cultivated. No frivolous waltz was heard, nor flippant song that should extol man and divert the attention from God; but sacred, solemn psalms of praise to the Creator, exalting His name and recounting His wondrous works. Thus music was made to serve a holy purpose, to lift the thoughts to that which was pure and noble and elevating, and to awaken in the soul devotion and gratitude to God.

How wide the difference between the schools of ancient times, under the supervision of God himself, and our modern institutions of learning. Even from theological schools many students graduate with less real knowledge of God and of religious truth than when they entered. Few schools are to be found that are not governed by the maxims and customs of the world. There are few in which a Christian parent's love for his children will not meet with bitter disappointment.

In what consists the superior excellence of our systems of education? Is it in the classical literature which is crowded into our sons? Is it in the ornamental accomplishments which our daughters obtain at the sacrifice of health or mental strength? Is it in the fact that modern instruction is so generally separated from the word of truth, the gospel of our salvation? Does the chief excellence of popular education consist in treating the individual branches of study, apart from that deeper investigation which involves the searching of the Scriptures, and a knowledge of God and the future life? Does it consist in imbuing the minds of the young with heathenish conceptions of liberty, morality, and justice? Is it safe to trust our youth to the guidance of those blind leaders who study the sacred oracles with far less interest than they manifest in the classical authors of ancient Greece and Rome?

"Education," remarks a writer, "is becoming a system of seduction." There is deplorable lack of proper restraint and judicious discipline. The most bitter feelings, the most ungovernable passions, are excited by the course of unwise and ungodly teachers. The minds of the young are easily excited, and drink in insubordination like water.

The existing ignorance of God's word, among the people professedly Christian, is alarming. The youth in our public schools have been robbed of the blessings of holy things. Superficial talk, mere sentimentalism, passes for instruction in morals and religion; but it lacks the vital characteristics of real godliness. The justice and mercy of God, the beauty of holiness, and the sure reward of rightdoing, the heinous character of sin, and the certainty of punishment, are not impressed upon the minds of the young.

Skepticism and infidelity, under some pleasing disguise, or as a covert insinuation, too often find their way into schoolbooks. In some instances, the most pernicious principles have been inculcated by teachers. Evil associates are teaching the youth lessons of crime, dissipation, and licentiousness that are horrible to contemplate. Many of our public schools are hotbeds of vice.

How can our youth be shielded from these contaminating influences? There must be schools established upon the principles, and controlled by the precepts, of God's word. Another spirit must be in our schools, to animate and sanctify every branch of education. Divine co-operation must be fervently sought. And we shall not seek in vain. The promises of God's word are ours. We may expect the presence of the heavenly teacher. We may see the Spirit of the Lord diffused as in the schools of the prophets, and every object partake of a divine consecration. Science will then be, as she was to Daniel, the handmaid of religion; and every effort, from first to last, will tend to the salvation of man, soul, body, and spirit, and the glory of God through Christ.--Signs of the Times, August 13, 1885.

FOR ADDITIONAL READING

Christian Courtesy, The Review and Herald, September 1, 1885

The Teacher and His Work, The Review and Herald, September 22, 1885

Courtship and Marriage

In these days of peril and corruption, the young are exposed to many trials and temptations. Many are sailing in a dangerous harbor. They need a pilot; but they scorn to accept the much needed help, feeling that they are competent to guide their own bark, and not realizing that it is about to strike a hidden rock that may cause them to make shipwreck of faith and happiness. They are infatuated with the subject of courtship and marriage, and their principal burden is to have their own way. In this, the most important period of their lives, they need an unerring counselor, and infallible guide. This they will find in the word of God. Unless they are diligent students of that word, they will make grave mistakes, which will mar their happiness and that of others, both for the present and the future life.

There is a disposition with many to be impetuous and headstrong. They have not heeded the wise counsel of the word of God; they have not battled with self, and obtained precious victories; and their proud, unbending will has driven them from the path of duty and obedience. Look back over your past life, young friends, and faithfully consider your course in the light of God's word. Have you cherished that conscientious regard for your obligations to your parents that the Bible enjoins? Have you treated with kindness and love the mother who has cared for you from infancy? Have you regarded her wishes, or have you brought pain and sadness to her heart by carrying out your own desires and plans? Has the truth you profess sanctified your heart, and softened and subdued your will? If not, you have close work to do to make past wrongs right.

The Bible presents a perfect standard of character. This sacred book, inspired by God, and written by holy men, is a perfect guide under all circumstances of life. It sets forth distinctly the duties of both young and old. If made the guide of life, its teachings will lead the soul upward. It will elevate the mind, improve the character, and give peace and joy to the heart. But many of the young have chosen to be their own counselor and guide, and have taken their cases in their own hands. Such need to study more closely the teachings of the Bible. In its pages they will find revealed their duty to their parents and to their brethren in the faith. The fifth commandment reads, "Honor thy father and thy mother: that thy days may be long upon the land which the Lord thy God giveth thee." Again we read, "Children, obey your parents in the Lord: for this is right." One of the signs that we are living in the last days is that children are disobedient to parents, unthankful, unholy. The word of God abounds in precepts and counsels enjoining respect for parents. It impresses upon the young the sacred duty of loving and cherishing those who have guided them through infancy, childhood, and youth, up to manhood and womanhood, and who are now in great degree dependent upon them for peace and happiness. The Bible gives no uncertain sound on this subject; nevertheless, its teachings have been greatly disregarded.

The young have many lessons to learn, and the most important one is to learn to know themselves. They should have correct ideas of their obligations and duties to their parents, and should be constantly learning in the school of Christ to be meek and lowly of heart. While they are to love and honor their parents, they are also to respect the judgment of men of experience with whom they are connected in the church. A young man who enjoys the society and wins the friendship of a young lady unbeknown to her parents, does not act a noble Christian part toward her or toward her parents. Through secret communications and meetings he may gain an influence over her mind; but in so doing he fails to manifest that nobility and integrity of soul which every child of God will possess. In order to accomplish their ends, they act a part that is not frank and open and according to the Bible standard, and prove themselves untrue to those who love them and try to be faithful guardians over them. Marriages contracted under such influences are not according to the word of God. He who would lead a daughter away from duty, who would confuse her ideas of God's plain and positive commands to obey and honor her parents, is not one who would be true to the marriage obligations.

The question is asked, "Wherewithal shall a young man cleanse his way?" and the answer is given, "By taking heed thereto according to Thy word." The young man who makes the Bible his guide, need not mistake the path of duty and of safety. That blessed book will teach him to preserve his integrity of character, to be truthful, to practice no deception. "Thou shalt not steal" was written by the finger of God upon the tables of stone; yet how much underhand stealing of affections is practiced and excused. A deceptive courtship is maintained, private communications are kept up, until the affections of one who is inexperienced, and knows not whereunto these things may grow, are in a measure withdrawn from her parents and placed upon him who shows by the very course he pursues that he is unworthy of her love. The Bible condemns every species of dishonesty, and demands right-doing under all circumstances. He who makes the Bible the guide of his youth, the light of his path, will obey its teachings in all things. He will not transgress one jot or tittle of the law in order to accomplish any object, even if he has to make great sacrifices in consequence. If he believes the Bible, he knows that the blessing of God will not rest upon him if he departs from the strict path of rectitude. Although he may appear for a time to prosper, he will surely reap the fruit of his doings.

The curse of God rests upon many of the ill-timed, inappropriate connections that are formed in this age of the world. If the Bible left these questions in a vague, uncertain light, then the course that many youth of today are pursuing in their attachments for one another, would be more excusable. But the requirements of the Bible are not halfway injunctions; they demand perfect purity of thought, of word, and of deed. We are grateful to God that His word is a light to the feet, and that none need mistake the path of duty. The young should make it a business to consult its pages and heed its counsels; for sad mistakes are always made in departing from its precepts.

If there is any subject that should be considered with calm reason and unimpassioned judgment, it is the subject of marriage. If ever the Bible is needed as a counselor, it is before taking a step that binds persons together for life. But the prevailing sentiment is that in this matter the feelings are to be the guide; and in too many cases lovesick sentimentalism takes the helm, and guides to certain ruin. It is here that the youth show less intelligence than on any other subject; it is here that they refuse to be reasoned with. The question of marriage seems to have a bewitching power over them. They do not submit themselves to God. Their senses are enchained, and they move forward in secretiveness, as if fearful that their plans would be interfered with by someone.

This underhand way in which courtships and marriages are carried on, is the cause of a great amount of misery, the full extent of which is known only to God. On this rock thousands have made shipwreck of their souls. Professed Christians, whose lives are marked with integrity, and who seem sensible upon every other subject, make fearful mistakes here. They manifest a set, determined will that reason cannot change. They become so fascinated with human feelings and impulses that they have no desire to search the Bible and come into close relationship with God. Satan knows just what elements he has to deal with, and he displays his infernal wisdom in various devices to entrap souls to their ruin. He watches every step that is taken, and makes many suggestions, and often these suggestions are followed rather than the counsel of God's word. This finely woven, dangerous net is skillfully prepared to entangle the young and unwary. It may often be disguised under a covering of light; but those who become its victims, pierce themselves through with many sorrows. As the result, we see wrecks of humanity everywhere.

When will our youth be wise? How long will this kind of work go on? Shall children consult only their own desires and inclinations irrespective of the advice and judgment of their parents? Some seem never to bestow a thought upon their parents' wishes or preferences, nor to regard their matured judgment. Selfishness has closed the door of their hearts to filial affection. The minds of the young need to be aroused in regard to this matter. The fifth commandment is the only commandment to which is annexed a promise, but it is held lightly, and is even positively ignored by the lover's claim. Slighting a mother's love, dishonoring a father's care, are sins that stand registered against many youth.

One of the greatest errors connected with this subject is that the young and inexperienced must not have their affections disturbed, that there must be no interference in their love experience. If there ever was a subject that needed to be viewed from every standpoint, it is this. The aid of the experience of others, and a calm, careful weighing of the matter on both sides, is positively essential. It is a subject that is treated altogether too lightly by the great majority of people. Take God and your God-fearing parents into your counsel, young friends. Pray over the matter. Weigh every sentiment, and watch every development of character in the one with whom you think to link your life destiny. The step you are about to take is one of the most important in your life, and should not be taken hastily. While you may love, do not love blindly.

Examine carefully to see if your married life would be happy, or inharmonious and wretched. Let the questions be raised, Will this union help me heavenward? will it increase my love for God? and will it enlarge my sphere of usefulness in this life? If these reflections present no drawback, then in the fear of God move forward. But even if an engagement has been entered into without a full understanding of the character of the one with whom you intend to unite, do not think that the engagement makes it a positive necessity for you to take upon yourself the marriage vow, and link yourself for life to one whom you cannot love and respect. Be very careful how you enter into conditional engagements; but better, far better, break the engagement before marriage than separate afterward, as many do.

True love is a plant that needs culture. Let the woman who desires a peaceful, happy union, who would escape future misery and sorrow, inquire before she yields her affections, Has my lover a mother? What is the stamp of her character? Does he recognize his obligations to her? Is he mindful of her wishes and happiness? If he does not respect and honor his mother, will he manifest respect and love, kindness and attention, toward his wife? When the novelty of marriage is over, will he love me still? Will he be patient with my mistakes, or will he be critical, overbearing, and dictatorial? True affection will overlook many mistakes; love will not discern them.

The youth trust altogether too much to impulse. They should not give themselves away too easily, nor be captivated too readily by the winning exterior of the lover. Courtship, as carried on in this age, is a scheme of deception and hypocrisy, with which the enemy of souls has far more to do than the Lord. Good common sense is needed here if anywhere; but the fact is, it has little to do in the matter.

If children would be more familiar with their parents, if they would confide in them, and unburden to them their joys and sorrows, they would save themselves many a future heartache. When perplexed to know what course is right, let them lay the matter just as they view it before their parents, and ask advice of them. Who are so well calculated to point out their dangers as godly parents? Who can understand their peculiar temperaments so well as they? Children who are Christians will esteem above every earthly blessing the love and approbation of their God-fearing parents. The parents can sympathize with the children, and pray for and with them that God will shield and guide them. Above everything else they will point them to their never-failing Friend and Counselor, who will be touched with the feeling of their infirmities. He who was tempted in all points like as we are, yet without sin, knows how to succor those who are tempted, and who come to Him in faith.--Review and Herald, January 26, 1886.

FOR ADDITIONAL READING

Home Education, The Youth's Instructor, April 21, 1886

Christian Recreation, The Review and Herald, May 25, 1886

Importance of Training in the Work of God

The work of the laborer is not small or unimportant. If he gives himself to any branch of the work, his first business is to take heed to himself, afterward to the doctrine. He is to search his own heart and to put away sin; then he is to keep the Pattern, Christ Jesus, ever before him as his example. He is not to feel at liberty to shape his course as best pleases his own inclination. He is the property of Jesus. He has chosen a high vocation, and from it his whole future life must take its coloring and mold. He has entered the school of Christ, and he may obtain a knowledge of Christ and His mission, and of the work he has to perform. All his powers must be brought under control of the great Teacher. Every faculty of mind, every organ of the body, must be kept in as healthy a condition as possible, so that the work of God shall not bear the marks of his defective character.

Before a person is prepared to become a teacher of the truth to those who are in darkness, he must become a learner. He must be willing to be counseled. He cannot place his foot on the third, fourth, or fifth round of the ladder of progress before he has begun at the first round. Many feel that they are fitted for the work when they know scarcely anything about it. If such are allowed to start out to labor in self-confidence, they will fail to receive that knowledge which it is their privilege to obtain, and will be doomed to struggle with many difficulties for which they are entirely unprepared.

Now, to every worker is granted the privilege of improvement, and he should make everything bend to that object. Whenever a special effort is to be made in an important place, a well arranged system of labor should be established, so that those who wish to become colporteurs and canvassers, and those who are adapted to give Bible readings in families, may receive the necessary instruction. Those who are workers should also be learners, and while the minister is laboring in word and doctrine they should not be wandering listlessly about, as though there was nothing in the discourse which they needed to hear. They should not regard the speaker simply as an orator, but as a messenger from God to men. Personal preferences and prejudices must not be allowed to influence them in hearing. If all would imitate the example of Cornelius, and say, "Now therefore are we all here present before God, to hear all things that are commanded thee of God," they would receive much more profit from the sermons which they hear.

There should be connected with our missions training-schools for those who are about to enter the fields as laborers. They should feel that they must become as apprentices to learn the trade of laboring for the conversion of souls. The labor in these schools should be varied. The study of the Bible should be made of primary importance, and at the same time there should be a systematic training of the mind and manners that they may learn to approach people in the best possible way. All should learn how to labor with tact and with courtesy, and with the Spirit of Christ. They should never cease to become learners, but should ever continue to dig for truth and for the best ways of working, as they would dig for buried gold.

Let all who are commencing in the work decide that they will not rest short of becoming first-class workers. In order to do this, their minds must not be allowed to drift with circumstances and to follow impulse, but they must be chained to the point, tasked to the utmost to comprehend the truth in all its bearings.

Men of ability have labored at a great disadvantage because their minds were not disciplined for the work. Seeing the need of laborers, they stepped into the gap, and although they may have accomplished much good, it is in many cases not a tithe of what they could have accomplished, had they had the proper training at the start.

Many who contemplate giving themselves to the service of God, do not feel the need of any special training. But those who feel thus are the very ones who stand in greatest need of a thorough drill. It is when they have little knowledge of themselves and of the work that they feel best qualified. When they know more, then they feel their ignorance and inefficiency. When they subject their hearts to close examination, they will see so much in them unlike the character of Christ, that they will cry out, "Who is sufficient for these things?" and in deep humility they will strive daily to put themselves in close connection with Christ. By crucifying self they are placing their feet in the path in which He can lead them.

There is danger that the inexperienced worker, while seeking to qualify himself for the work, will feel competent to place himself in any kind of a position, where various winds of doctrines are blowing about him. This he cannot do without peril to his own soul. If trials and temptations come upon him, the Lord will give strength to overcome them; but when one places himself in the way of temptation, it often happens that Satan through his agents advances his sentiments in such a manner as to confuse and unsettle the mind. By communion with God and close searching of the Scriptures, the worker should become thoroughly established himself before he enters regularly upon the work of teaching others. John, the beloved disciple, was exiled to lonely Patmos, that he might be separated from all strife, and even from the work he loved, and that the Lord might commune with him and open before him the closing scenes in this earth's history. It was in the wilderness that John the Baptist learned the message that he was to bear, to prepare the way for the coming One.

Importance of Training in the Work of God

But above everything else it should be impressed upon the individuals who have decided to become God's servants, that they must be converted men. The heart must be pure. Godliness is essential for this life and the life which is to come. The man without a solid, virtuous character will surely be no honor to the cause of truth. The youth who contemplates laboring together with God, should be pure in heart. In his lips, in his mouth, should be no guile. The thoughts should be pure. Holiness of life and character is a rare thing, but this the worker must have or he cannot yoke up with Christ. Christ says, "Without Me ye can do nothing." If those who purpose to work for others' good and for the salvation of their fellow men rely on their own wisdom, they will fail. If they are entertaining humble views of themselves, then they are simple enough to believe in God and expect His help. "Lean not unto thine own understanding. In all thy ways acknowledge Him, and He shall direct thy paths." Then we have the privilege of being directed by a wise counselor, and increased understanding is given to the true, sincere seeker for truth and for knowledge.

The reason why we have no more men of great breadth and extended knowledge, is because they trust to their own finite wisdom, and seek to place their own mold upon the work, in the place of having the mold of God. They do not earnestly pray and keep the communication open between God and their souls, that they can recognize His voice. Messengers of light will come to the help of those who feel that they are weakness itself, without the guardianship of Heaven. The word of God must be studied more, and be brought into the life and character, fashioned after the standard of righteousness God has laid down in His word. Then the mind will expand and strengthen, and be ennobled by grasping the things that are eternal. While the world are careless and indifferent to the message of warning and mercy given them in the Bible, God's people, who see the end near, should be more decided and more devoted, and work more earnestly, that they may show forth the praises of Him who hath called them out of darkness into His marvelous light.

Knowledge is power, either for good or for evil. Bible religion is the only safeguard for human beings. Much attention is given to the youth in this age, that they may enter a room gracefully, dance, and play on instruments of music. But this education is denied them, to know God and to answer to His claims. The education that is lasting as eternity, is almost wholly neglected as old-fashioned and undesirable. The educating of the children to take hold of the work of character building in reference to their present good, their present peace and happiness, and to guide their feet in the path cast up for the ransomed of the Lord to walk in, is considered not fashionable, and, therefore, not essential. In order to have your children enter the gates of the city of God as conquerors, they must be educated to fear God and keep His commandments in the present life. It is these that Jesus has pronounced blessed: "Blessed are they that do

His commandments, that they may have right to the tree of life, and may enter in through the gates into the city."

The blessing is pronounced upon those who are familiar with the revealed will of God in His word. The Bible is the great agent in the hands of its Author to strengthen the intellect. It opens the garden of the mind to the cultivation of the heavenly Husbandman. It is because there is so little attention given to what God says and to that which God requires, that there are so few who have any burden to do missionary work, so few who have been passing under drill, calling into service every power to be trained and strengthened to do higher service for God.

Altogether too feeble efforts are being made to connect those with our schools of different nationalities who ought to be connected with them, that they may receive an education and become fitted for the work so noble, so elevated, and far-reaching in its influence. The days of ignorance God winked at. But increased light is shining; the light and privileges of understanding Bible truth are abundant, if workers will only open the eyes of their understanding. The truth must be diffusive. Foreign and home missions call for thorough Christian characters to engage in missionary enterprises. The missions in our cities at home and abroad call for men who are imbued with the Spirit of Christ, who will work as Christ worked.--Review and Herald, June 14, 1887.

Proper Education of the Young

The third angel is represented as flying in the midst of the heavens, showing that the message is to go forth throughout the length and breadth of the earth. It is the most solemn message ever given to mortals, and all who connect with the work should first feel their need of an education, and a most thorough training process for the work, in reference to their future usefulness; and there should be plans made and efforts adopted for the improvement of that class who anticipate connecting with any branch of the work. Ministerial labor cannot and should not be entrusted to boys, neither should the work of giving Bible readings be entrusted to inexperienced girls, because they offer their services, and are willing to take responsible positions, but who are wanting in religious experience, without a thorough education and training. They must be proved to see if they will bear the test; and unless there is developed a firm, conscientious principle to be all that God would have them to be, they will not correctly represent our cause and work for this time. There must be with our sisters engaged in the work in every mission, a depth of experience, gained from those who have had an experience, and who understand the manners and ways of working. The missionary operations are constantly embarrassed for the want of workers of the right class of minds, and the devotion and piety that will correctly represent our faith.

There are numbers that ought to become missionaries who never enter the field, because those who are united with them in church capacity or in our colleges, do not feel the burden to labor with them, to open before them the claims that God has upon all the powers, and do not pray with them and for them; and the eventful period which decides the plans and course of life passes, convictions with them are stifled; other influences and inducements attract them, and the temptations to seek worldly positions that will, they think, bring them money, take them into the worldly current. These young men might have been saved to the ministry through well-organized plans. If the churches in the different places do their duty, God will work with their efforts by His Spirit, and will supply faithful men to the ministry.

Our schools are to be educating schools and training schools; and if men and women come forth from them fitted in any sense for the missionary field, they must have impressed upon them the greatness of the work, and that practical godliness must be brought into their daily experience, to be fitted for any place of usefulness in our world, or in the church, or in God's great moral vineyard, now calling for laborers in foreign lands.

The youth must be impressed with the idea that they are trusted. They have a sense of honor, and they want to be respected, and it is their right. If pupils receive the impression that they cannot go out or come in, sit at the table, or be anywhere, even in their rooms, except they are watched, a critical eye is upon them to criticize and report, it will have the influence to demoralize, and pastime will have no pleasure in it. This knowledge of a continual oversight is more than a parental guardianship, and far worse; for wise parents can, through tact, often discern beneath the surface and see the working of the restless mind under the longings of youth, or under the forces of temptations, and set their plans to work to counteract evils. But this constant watchfulness is not natural, and produces evils that it is seeking to avoid. The healthfulness of youth requires exercise, cheerfulness, and a happy, pleasant atmosphere surrounding them for the development of physical health and symmetrical, character.

God's word must be opened to the youth, but a youth should not be placed in the position to do this. Those who must have an eye upon them constantly to insure their good behavior, will require to be watched in any position where they may be. Therefore the mold given the character in youth by such a system of training, is wholly deleterious. Aim for mental discipline and the formation of right moral sentiments and habits.

Studies should generally be few and well chosen, and those who attend our colleges are to have a different training from that of the common schools of the day. They have been generally taught upon Christian principles, if they have wise and God-fearing parents. The word of God has been respected in their homes, and its teachings made the law of the home. They have been brought up in the nurture and admonition of the gospel, and when they come to the schools, this same education and training is to go on. The world's maxims, the world's customs and practices, are not the teaching they need; but they are to see that the teachers in the schools care for their souls, that they will take a decided interest in their spiritual welfare, and religion is to be the great principle inculcated; for the love and fear of God are the beginning of wisdom. Youth removed from the domestic atmosphere, from the home rule and guardianship of parents, if left to themselves to pick and choose their companions, meet with a crisis in their history not generally favorable to piety or principle.

Then, wherever a school is established, there should be warm hearts to take a lively interest in our youth. Fathers and mothers are needed with warm sympathy, and with kindly admonitions, and all the pleasantness possible should be brought into the religious exercises. If there are those who prolong religious exercises to weariness, they are leaving impressions upon the mind of the youth, that would associate religion with all that is dry, unsocial, and uninteresting. And these youth make their own standard not the highest, but weak principles and a low standard spoil those who if properly taught, would be not only qualified to be a blessing to the cause, but to the church and to the world. Ardent, active piety in the teacher is essential. Morning and evening service in the chapel, and the Sabbath meetings, may be, without constant care and unless vitalized by the Spirit

Proper Education of the Young

of God, the most formal, dry, and bitter mixture, and, to the youth, the most burdensome and the least pleasant and attractive of all the school exercises. The social meetings should be managed with plans and devices to make them not only seasons of pleasantness, but positively attractive.

Let those who are competent to teach youth, study themselves in the school of Christ, and learn lessons to communicate to youth. Sincere, earnest, heartfelt devotion is needed. All narrowness should be avoided. Let teachers so far unbend from their dignity as to be one with the children in their exercises and amusements, without leaving the impression that you are watching them, and without going round and round in stately dignity, as though you were like a uniformed soldier on guard over them. Your very presence gives a mold to their course of action. Your unity with them causes your heart to throb with new affection. The youth need sympathy, affection, and love, else they will become discouraged. A spirit of "I care for nobody and nobody cares for me" takes possession of them, and although they profess to be followers of Christ, they have a tempting devil on their track, and they are in danger of becoming disheartened, and lukewarm, and backslidden from God. Then some feel it a duty to blame them, and to treat them coldly, as if they were a great deal worse than they really are, and but few, and perhaps none, feel it a special duty to make personal effort to reform them, and to remove the baleful impressions that have been made upon them.

The teacher's obligations are weighty and sacred, but no part of the work is more important than to look after the youth with tender, loving solicitude, that they may feel that we have a friend in them. Once gain their confidence, and you can lead them, control them, and train them easily. The holy motives of our Christian principles must be brought into our life. The salvation of our pupils is the highest interest entrusted to the God-fearing teacher. He is Christ's worker, and his special and determined effort should be to save souls from perdition and win them to Jesus Christ. God will require this at the hands of teachers. Everyone should lead a life of piety, of purity, of painstaking effort in the discharge of every duty. If the heart is glowing with the love of God, there will be pure affection, which is essential; prayers will be fervent, and faithful warnings will be given. Neglect these, and the souls under your charge are endangered. Better spend less time in long speeches, or in absorbing study, and attend to these neglected duties.

After all these efforts, teachers may find that some under their charge will develop unprincipled characters. They are lax in morals as the result, in many cases, of vicious example and neglected parental discipline. And teachers doing all they can will fail to bring these youth to a life of purity and holiness; and after patient discipline, affectionate labor, and fervent prayer, they will be disappointed by those from whom they have hoped so much. And in addition to this, the reproaches of the parents will come to them, because they did not have power to counteract the influence of their own example and unwise training. The teacher will have these discouragements after doing his duty. But he must work on, trusting in God to work with him, standing at his post manfully, and laboring on in faith. Others will be saved to God, and their influence will be exerted in saving others. Let the minister, the Sabbath school teacher, and the teachers in our colleges unite heart and soul and purpose in the work of saving our youth from ruin.

Many have felt, "Well, it doesn't matter if we are not so particular to become thoroughly educated," and a lower standard of knowledge has been accepted. And now when suitable men are wanted to fill various positions of trust, they are rare; when women are wanted with well-balanced minds, with not a cheap style of education, but with an education fitting them for any position of trust, they are not easily found. What is worth doing at all, is worth doing well. While religion should be the pervading element in every school, it will not lead to a cheapening of the literary attainments. While a religious atmosphere should pervade the school, diffusing its influence, it will make all who are truly Christians feel more deeply their need of thorough knowledge, that they may make the best use of the faculties that God has bestowed upon them. While growing in grace and in the knowledge of our Lord Jesus Christ, they will groan under a sense of their imperfections, and will seek constantly to put to the stretch their powers of mind, that they may become intelligent Christians.

The Lord Jesus is dishonored by low ideas or designs on our part. He who does not feel the binding claims of God's law, and neglects to keep every requirement, violates the whole law. He who is content to partially meet the standard of righteousness, and who does not triumph over every spiritual foe, will not meet the designs of Christ. He cheapens the whole plan of his religious life, and weakens his religious character, and under the force of temptation his defects of character gain the supremacy, and evil triumphs. We need to be persevering and determined, to meet the highest standard possible. Pre-established habits and ideas must be overcome in many cases, before we can make advancement in religious life. The faithful Christian will bear much fruit; he is a worker; he will not lazily drift, but will put on the whole armor to fight the battles of the Lord. The essential work is to conform the tastes, the appetite, the passions, the motives, the desires, to the great moral standard of righteousness. The work must begin at the heart. That must be pure, wholly conformed to Christ's will, else some master passion, or some habit or defect, will become a power to destroy. God will accept of nothing short of the whole heart.

God wants the teachers in our schools to be efficient. If they are advanced in spiritual understanding, they will feel that it is important that they should not be deficient in the knowledge of the sciences. Piety and a religious experience lie at the very foundation of true education. But let none feel that having an earnestness in religious matters is all that is essential in order to become educators. While they need no less of piety, they also need a thorough knowledge of the sciences. This will make them not only good, practical Christians, but will enable them to educate the youth, and at the same time they will have heavenly wisdom to lead them to the fountain of living waters. He is a Christian who aims to reach the highest attainments for the purpose of doing others good. Knowledge harmoniously blended with a Christlike character will make a person truly a light to the world. God works with human efforts. All those who give all diligence to make their calling and election sure, will feel that a superficial knowledge will not fit them for positions of usefulness. Education balanced by a solid religious experience, fits the child of God to do his appointed work steadily, firmly, understandingly. If one is learning of Jesus, the greatest educator the world ever knew, he will not only have a symmetrical Christian character, but a mind trained to effectual labor. Minds that are quick to discern will go deep beneath the surface.

God does not want us to be content with lazy, undisciplined minds, dull thoughts, and loose memories. He wants every teacher to be efficient, not to feel satisfied with some measure of success, but to feel his need of perpetual diligence in acquiring knowledge. Our bodies and souls belong to God, for He has bought them. He has given us talents, and has made it possible for us to acquire more, in order that we may be able to help ourselves and others onward in the way to life. It is the work of each individual to develop and strengthen the gifts which God has lent him, with which to do most earnest, practical work, both in temporal and religious things. If all realized this, what a vast difference we should see in our schools, in our churches, and in our missions! But the larger number are content with a meager knowledge, a few attainments, just to be passable; and the necessity of being men like Daniel and Moses, men of influence, men whose characters have become harmonious by their working to bless humanity and glorify God,--such an experience but few have had, and the result is, there are but few now fitted for the great want of the times.

God does not ignore ignorant men, but if they are connected with Christ, if they are sanctified through the truth, they will be constantly gathering knowledge. By exerting every power to glorify God, they will have increased power with which to glorify Him. But those who are willing to remain in a narrow channel because God condescended to accept them when they were there, are very foolish; and yet there are hundreds and thousands who are doing this very thing. God has given them the living machinery, and this needs to be used daily in order for the mind to reach higher and still higher attainments. It is a shame that many link ignorance with humility, and that with all the qualities God has given us for education, so great a number are willing to remain in the same low position that they were in when the truth first reached them. They do not grow mentally; they are no better fitted and prepared to do great and good works than when they first heard the truth.

Many who are teachers of the truth cease to be students, digging, ever digging for truth as for hidden treasures. Their minds reach a common, low standard; but they do not seek to become men of influence,--not for the sake of selfish ambition, but for Christ's sake, that they may reveal the power of the truth upon the intellect. It is no sin to appreciate literary talent, if it is not idolized; but no one is to strive for vainglory to exalt self. When this is the case, there is an absence of the wisdom that cometh from above, which is first pure, then peaceable, easy to be entreated, full of love and of good fruits.

The established missions in our cities, if conducted by men who have ability to wisely manage such missions, will be steady lights, shining amid the moral darkness. The opening of the Scriptures by means of Bible readings is an essential part of the work connected with these missions; but workers cannot take hold of this work unless they are prepared for it. Many ought to be trained in school before they even know how to study to bring their minds and thoughts under the control of the will, and how to use wisely their mental powers.

There is much to be learned by us as a people before we are qualified to engage in the great work of preparing a people to stand in the day of the Lord. Our Sabbath schools which are to instruct the children and youth are too superficial. The managers of these need to plow deeper. They need to put more thought and more hard work upon the work they are doing. They need to be more thorough students of the Bible, and to have a deeper religious experience, in order to know how to conduct Sabbath schools after the Lord's order, and how to lead children and youth to their Saviour. This is one of the branches of the work that is crippling along for the want of efficient, discerning men and women who feel their accountability to God to use their powers, not to exhibit self, not for vainglory, but to do good.

How broad and extended the command is, "Go ye therefore, and teach all nations, baptizing them in the name of the Father, and of the Son, and of the Holy Ghost: teaching them to observe all things whatsoever I have commanded you: and, lo, I am with you alway, even unto the end of the world"! What honor is here conferred upon man, and yet how large a number hug the shore! How few will launch out into the deep, and let down their nets for a draught! Now, if this is done, if men are laborers together with God, if men are called to act in city missions, and to meet all classes of minds, there should be special preparations for this kind of work.--Review and Herald, June 21, 1887.

FOR ADDITIONAL READING

Divine Wisdom, The Review and Herald, April 17, 1888

The Value of Bible Study

"All Scripture is given by inspiration of God, and is profitable for doctrine, for reproof, for correction, for instruction in righteousness: that the man of God may be perfect, thoroughly furnished unto all good works." The word of God is like a treasure house, containing everything that is essential to perfect the man of God. We do not appreciate the Bible as we should. We do not have a proper estimate of the richness of its stores, nor do we realize the great necessity of searching the Scriptures for ourselves. Men neglect the study of the word of God in order to pursue some worldly interest, or to engage in the pleasures of the time. Some trivial affair is made an excuse for ignorance of the Scriptures given by inspiration of God. But anything of an earthly character might better be put off, than this all-important study, that is to make us wise unto eternal life.

My heart aches as I see men--even those who profess to be looking for Christ's coming--devoting their time and talents to circulating books that contain nothing concerning the special truths for our time,--books of narrative, books of biography, books of men's theories and speculations. The world is full of such books; they can be had anywhere; but can the followers of Christ engage in so common a work when there is crying need for God's truth on every hand? It is not our mission to circulate such works. There are thousands of others to do this, who have as yet no knowledge of anything better. We have a definite mission, and we ought not to turn from it to side issues, employing men and means to bring to the attention of the people books that have no bearing upon the present truth.

Do you pray for the advancement of the truth? Then work for it, and show that your prayers rise from sincere and earnest hearts. God does not work miracles where He has provided means by which the work may be accomplished. Use your time and talents in His service, and He will not fail to work with your efforts. If the farmer fails to plow and sow, God does not work a miracle to undo the results of his neglect. Harvest time finds his fields barren--there are no sheaves to be reaped, no grain to be garnered. God provided the seed and the soil, the sun and the rain; and if the agriculturist had employed the means that were at his hand, he would have received according to his sowing and his labor.

There are great laws that govern the world of nature, and spiritual things are controlled by principles equally certain; the means for an end must be employed, if the desired results are to be obtained. Those who make no decided efforts themselves, are not working in harmony with the laws of God. They are not using the provisions of the heavenly Father, and they can expect nothing but meager returns. The Holy Spirit will not compel men to take a certain course of action. We are free moral agents; and when sufficient evidence has been given us as to our duty, it is left with us to decide our course.

You who are waiting in idle expectation that God will perform some wonderful miracle to enlighten the world in regard to the truth, I want to ask you if you have employed the means God has provided for the advancement of His cause? You who pray for light and truth from heaven, have you studied the Scriptures? Have you desired "the sincere milk of the word," that you may grow thereby? Have you submitted yourselves to the revealed command? "Thou shalt," and "thou shalt not," are definite requirements, and there is no place for idleness in the Christian life. You who mourn your spiritual dearth, do you seek to know and to do the will of God? Are you striving to enter in at the strait gate? There is work, earnest work, to be done for the Master. The evils condemned in God's word, must be overcome. You must individually battle against the world, the flesh and the devil. The word of God is called "the sword of the Spirit," and you should become skillful in its use, if you would cut your way through the hosts of opposition and darkness.

Wrench yourself away from hurtful associations. Count the cost of following Jesus, and make it, with a determined purpose to cleanse yourselves from all filthiness of the flesh and spirit. Eternal life is worth your all, and Jesus has said, "Whosoever he be of you that forsaketh not all that he hath, he cannot be My disciple." He who does nothing, but waits to be compelled by some supernatural agency, will wait on in lethargy and darkness. God has given His word. God speaks in unmistakable language to your soul. Is not the word of His mouth sufficient to show you your duty, and to urge its fulfillment?

Those who humbly and prayerfully search the Scriptures, to know and to do God's will, will not be in doubt of their obligations to God. For "if any man will do His will, he shall know of the doctrine." If you would know the mystery of godliness, you must follow the plain word of truth,-- feeling or no feeling, emotion or no emotion. Obedience must be rendered from a sense of principle, and the right must be pursued under all circumstances. This is the character that is elected of God unto salvation. The test of a genuine Christian is given in the word of God. Says Jesus, "If ye love Me, keep My commandments." "He that hath My commandments, and keepeth them, he it is that loveth Me: and he that loveth Me shall be loved of My Father, and I will love him, and will manifest Myself to him. . . . If a man love Me, he will keep My words: and My Father will love him, and we will come unto him, and make our abode with him. He that loveth Me not keepeth not My sayings: and the word which ye hear is not Mine, but the Father's which sent Me."

Here are the conditions upon which every soul will be elected to eternal life. Your obedience to God's commandments will prove your right to an inheritance with the saints in light. God has elected a certain excellence of character; and everyone who, through the grace of Christ, shall reach

The Value of Bible Study

the standard of His requirement, will have an abundant entrance into the kingdom of glory. All who would reach this standard of character, will have to employ the means that God has provided to this end. If you would inherit the rest that remaineth for the children of God, you must become a co-laborer with God. You are elected to wear the yoke of Christ,--to bear His burden, to lift His cross. You are to be diligent "to make your calling and election sure." Search the Scriptures, and you will see that not a son or a daughter of Adam is elected to be saved in disobedience to God's law. The world makes void the law of God; but Christians are chosen to sanctification through obedience to the truth. They are elected to bear the cross, if they would wear the crown.

The Bible is the only rule of faith and doctrine. And there is nothing more calculated to energize the mind, and strengthen the intellect, than the study of the word of God. No other book is so potent to elevate the thoughts, to give vigor to the faculties, as the broad, ennobling truths of the Bible. If God's word were studied as it should be, men would have a breadth of mind, a nobility of character, and a stability of purpose, that is rarely seen in these times. Thousands of men who minister in the pulpit are lacking in essential qualities of mind and character, because they do not apply themselves to the study of the Scriptures. They are content with a superficial knowledge of the truths that are full of rich depths of meaning; and they prefer to go on, losing much in every way, rather than to search diligently for the hidden treasure.

The search for truth will reward the seeker at every turn, and each discovery will open up richer fields for his investigation. Men are changed in accordance with what they contemplate. If commonplace thoughts and affairs take up the attention, the man will be commonplace. If he is too negligent to obtain anything but a superficial understanding of God's truth, he will not receive the rich blessings that God would be pleased to bestow upon him. It is a law of the mind, that it will narrow or expand to the dimensions of the things with which it becomes familiar. The mental powers will surely become contracted, and will lose their ability to grasp the deep meanings of the word of God, unless they are put vigorously and persistently to the task of searching for truth. The mind will enlarge, if it is employed in tracing out the relation of the subjects of the Bible, comparing scripture with scripture, and spiritual things with spiritual. Go below the surface; the richest treasures of thought are waiting for the skilful and diligent student.

Those who are teaching the most solemn message ever given to the world, should discipline the mind to comprehend its significance. The theme of redemption will bear the most concentrated study, and its depth will never be fully explored. You need not fear that you will exhaust this wonderful theme. Drink deep of the well of salvation. Go to the fountain for yourself, that you may be filled with refreshment, that Jesus may be in you a well of water, springing up unto everlasting life. Only Bible truth and

Bible religion will stand the test of the judgment. We are not to pervert the word of God to suit our convenience, and worldly interests, but to honestly inquire, "What wilt Thou have me to do?" "Ye are not your own, for ye are bought with a price." And what a price! Not "with corruptible things, as silver and gold, . . . but with the precious blood of Christ." When man was lost, the Son of God said, I will redeem him, I will become his surety and substitute. He laid aside His royal robes, clothed His divinity with humanity, stepped down from the royal throne, that He might reach the very depth of human woe and temptation, lift up our fallen natures, and make it possible for us to be overcomers, the sons of God, the heirs of the eternal kingdom. Shall we then allow any consideration of earth to turn us away from the path of truth? Shall we not challenge every doctrine and theory, and put it to the test of God's word?

We should not allow any argument of man's to turn us away from a thorough investigation of Bible truth. The opinions and customs of men are not to be received as of divine authority. God has revealed in His word what is the whole duty of man, and we are not to be swayed from the great standard of righteousness. He sent His only-begotten Son to be our example, and bade us to hear and follow Him. We must not be influenced from the truth as it is in Jesus, because great and professedly good men urge their ideas above the plain statements of the word of God.

The work of Christ is to draw men from the false and spurious to the true and genuine. "He that followeth Me shall not walk in darkness, but shall have the light of life." There is no danger of going into error while we follow in the footsteps of "the Light of the world." We are to work the works of Christ. We must engage heart and soul in His service; we must search the word of life, and present it to others. We must educate the people to realize the importance of its teaching, and the danger of deviating from its plain commands.

The Jews were led into error and ruin, and to the rejection of the Lord of glory, because they knew not the Scriptures, nor the power of God. A great work is before us,--to lead men to take God's word as the rule of their lives, to make no compromise with tradition and custom, but to walk in all the commandments and ordinances of the Lord.--Review and Herald, July 17, 1888.

The Book of Books

The study of the Bible will give strength to the intellect. Says the Psalmist, "The entrance of Thy words giveth light; it giveth understanding unto the simple." The question has often been asked me, "Should the Bible become the important book in our schools?" It is a precious book, a wonderful book. It is a treasury containing jewels of precious value. It is a history that opens to us the past centuries. Without the Bible we should have been left to conjectures and fables in regard to the occurrences of past ages. Of all the books that have flooded the world, be they ever so valuable, the Bible is the Book of books, and is most deserving of the closest study and attention. It gives not only the history of the creation of this world, but a description of the world to come. It contains instruction concerning the wonders of the universe, and it reveals to our understanding the Author of the heavens and the earth. It unfolds a simple and complete system of theology and philosophy. Those who are close students of the word of God, and who obey its instructions, and love its plain truths, will improve in mind and manners. It is an endowment of God that should awaken in every heart the most sincere gratitude; for it is the revelation of God to man.

If the truths of the Bible are woven into practical life, they will bring the mind up from its earthliness and debasement. Those who are conversant with the Scriptures, will be found to be men and women who exert an elevating influence. In searching for the heaven-revealed truths, the Spirit of God is brought into close connection with the sincere searcher of the Scriptures. An understanding of the revealed will of God, enlarges the mind, expands, elevates, and endows it with new vigor, by bringing its faculties in contact with stupendous truths. If the study of the Scriptures is made a secondary consideration, great loss is sustained. The Bible was for a time excluded from our schools, and Satan found a rich field, in which he worked with marvelous rapidity, and gathered a harvest to his liking.

The understanding takes the level of the things with which it becomes familiar. If all would make the Bible their study, we should see a people further developed, capable of thinking more deeply, and showing a greater degree of intelligence, than the most earnest efforts in studying merely the sciences and histories of the world could make them. The Bible gives the true seeker an advanced mental discipline, and he comes from contemplation of divine things with his faculties enriched; self is humbled, while God and His revealed truth are exalted. It is because men are unacquainted with the precious Bible histories, that there is so much lifting up of man, and so little honor given to God. The Bible contains just that quality of food that the Christian needs in order that he may grow strong in spirit and intellect. The searching of all books of philosophy and science cannot do for the mind and morals what the Bible can do, if it is studied and practiced. Through the study of the Bible, converse is held with patriarchs and prophets. The truth is clothed in elevated language, which exerts a fascinating power over the mind; the thought is lifted up from the things of earth, and brought to contemplate the glory of the future immortal life. What wisdom of man can compare with the grandeur of the revelation of God? Finite man, who knows not God, may seek to lessen the value of the Scriptures, and may bury the truth beneath the supposed knowledge of science.

[131] Those who boast of wisdom beyond the teaching of the word of God, need to drink deeper of the fountain of knowledge, that they may learn their real ignorance. There is a boasted wisdom of men, that is foolishness in the sight of God. "Let no man deceive himself. If any man among you seemeth to be wise in this world, let him become a fool, that he may be wise. For the wisdom of this world is foolishness with God. For it is written, He taketh the wise in their own craftiness." Those who have only this wisdom, need to become fools in their own estimation. The greatest ignorance that now curses the human race is in regard to the binding claims of the law of God; and this ignorance is the result of neglecting the study of the word of God. It is Satan's determined plan to so engage and absorb the mind, that God's great guidebook shall not be the Book of books, and that the sinner may not be led from the path of transgression to the path of obedience.

The Bible is not exalted to its place, and yet of what infinite importance it is to the souls of men. In searching its pages, we move through scenes majestic and eternal. We behold Jesus, the Son of God, coming to our world, and engaging in the mysterious conflict that discomfited the powers of darkness. O how wonderful, how almost incredible it is, that the infinite God would consent to the humiliation of His own dear Son! Let every student of the Scriptures contemplate this great fact, and he will not come from such a contemplation without being elevated, purified, and ennobled.

The Bible is a book which discloses the principles of right and truth. It contains whatever is needful for the saving of the soul, and at the same time it is adapted to strengthen and discipline the mind. If used as a textbook in our schools, it will be found far more effective than any other book in the world, in guiding wisely in the affairs of this life, as well as in aiding the soul up the ladder of progress which reaches to heaven. God cares for us as intellectual beings, and He has given us His word as a lamp to our feet and a light to our pathway. "The entrance of Thy words giveth light; it giveth understanding unto the simple." It is not the mere reading of the word that will accomplish the result that is designed by Heaven, but the truth revealed in the word of God must find an entrance into the heart, if the good intended is obtained.

[132] The best educated in the sciences are not always the most effective instruments for God's use. There are many who find themselves laid aside, and those who have had fewer advantages of obtaining knowledge of books, taking their places, because the latter have a knowledge of practical things that is essential to the uses of everyday life; while those who

consider themselves learned, often cease to be learners, are self-sufficient, and above being taught, even by Jesus, who was the greatest teacher the world ever knew. Those who have grown and expanded, whose reasoning faculties have been improved by deep searching of the Scriptures, that they may know the will of God, will come into positions of usefulness; for the word of God has had an entrance into their life and character. It must do its peculiar work, even to the piercing asunder of the joints and marrow, and discerning the thoughts and intents of the heart. God's word is to become the nourishment by which the Christian must grow strong in spirit and in intellect, that he may battle for truth and righteousness.

Why is it that our youth, and even those of maturer years, are so easily led into temptation and sin? It is because the word of God is not studied and meditated upon as it should be. If it were appreciated, there would be an inward rectitude, a strength of spirit, that would resist the temptations of Satan to do evil. A firm, decided will-power is not brought into the life and character because the sacred instruction of God is not made the study, and the subject of meditation. There is not the effort put forth that there should be to associate the mind with pure, holy thoughts and to divert it from what is impure and untrue. There is not the choosing of the better part, the sitting at the feet of Jesus, as did Mary, to learn the most sacred lessons of the divine Teacher, that they may be laid up in the heart, and practiced in the daily life. Meditation upon holy things will elevate and refine the mind, and will develop Christian ladies and gentlemen.

God will not accept one of us who is belittling his powers in lustful, [133] earthly debasement, by thought, or word, or action. Heaven is a pure and holy place, where none can enter unless they are refined, spiritualized, cleansed, and purified. There is a work for us to do for ourselves, and we shall be capable of doing it only by drawing strength from Jesus. We should make the Bible our study above every other book; we should love it, and obey it as the voice of God. We are to see and to understand His restrictions and requirements, "thou shalt" and "thou shalt not," and realize the true meaning of the word of God.

When God's word is made the man of our counsel, and we search the Scriptures for light, angels of heaven come near to impress the mind, and enlighten the understanding, so that it can truly be said, "The entrance of Thy words giveth light; it giveth understanding unto the simple." It is no marvel that there is not more heavenly-mindedness shown among the youth who profess Christianity, when there is so little attention given to the word of God. The divine counsels are not heeded; the admonitions are not obeyed; grace and heavenly wisdom are not sought, that past sins may be avoided, and every taint of corruption be cleansed from the character. David's prayer was, "Make me to understand the way to Thy precepts: so shall I talk of Thy wondrous works."

If the minds of our youth, as well as those of more mature age, were directed aright when associated together, their conversation would be upon exalted themes. When the mind is pure, and the thoughts elevated by the truth of God, the words will be of the same character, "like apples of gold in pictures of silver." But with the present understanding, with the present practices, with the low standard which even Christians are content to reach, the conversation is cheap and profitless. It is "of the earth, earthy," and savors not of the truth, or of heaven, and does not come up, even to the standard of the more cultured class of worldlings. When Christ and heaven are the themes of contemplation, the conversation will give evidence of the fact. The speech will be seasoned with grace, and the speaker will show that he has been obtaining an education in the school of the divine Teacher. Says the psalmist, "I have chosen the way of truth: Thy judgments have I laid before me." He treasured the word of God. It found an entrance to his understanding, not to be disregarded, but to be practiced in his life.

Unless the sacred word is appreciated, it will not be obeyed as a sure and safe and precious textbook. Every besetting sin must be put away. Warfare must be waged against it until it is overcome. The Lord will work with your efforts. As finite, sinful man works out his own salvation with fear and trembling, it is God who works in him, to will and to do of His own good pleasure. But God will not work without the co-operation of man. He must exercise his powers to the very utmost; he must place himself as an apt, willing student in the school of Christ; and as he accepts the grace that is freely offered to him, the presence of Christ in the thought and in the heart will give him decision of purpose to lay aside every weight of sin, that the heart may be filled with all the fullness of God, and of His love.

The students of our schools should consider that through the contemplation of sin, the sure result has followed, and their God-given faculties have been weakened and unfitted for moral advancement, because they have been misapplied. There are many who admit this as the truth. They have cherished pride and self-conceit, until these evil traits of character have become a ruling power, controlling their desires and inclinations. While they have had a form of godliness, and have performed many acts of self-righteousness, there has been no real heart change. They have not brought their life practices into definite and close measurement with the great standard of righteousness, the law of God. Should they critically compare their life with this standard, they could not but feel that they were deficient, sinsick, and in need of a physician. They can only understand the depth to which they have fallen, by beholding the infinite sacrifice that has been made by Jesus Christ, to lift them out of their degradation.

There are but few who have an appreciation of the grievous character of sin, and who comprehend the greatness of the ruin that has resulted from the transgression of God's law. By examining the wonderful plan of redemption to restore the sinner to the moral image of God, we see that the only means for man's deliverance was wrought out by the self-sacrifice, and the unparalleled condescension and love of the Son of God. He alone had the strength to fight the battles with the great Adversary of God and man, and, as our substitute and surety, He has given power to those who lay hold of Him by faith, to become victors in His name, and through His merits.

We can see in the cross of Calvary what it has cost the Son of God to bring salvation to a fallen race. As the sacrifice in behalf of man was complete, so the restoration of man from the defilement of sin must be thorough and complete. The law of God has been given to us, that we may have rules to govern our conduct. There is no act of wickedness that the law will excuse; there is no unrighteousness that will escape its condemnation. The life of Christ is a perfect fulfillment of every precept of this law. He says, "I have kept My Father's commandments." The knowledge of the law would condemn the sinner, and crush hope from his breast, if he did not see Jesus as his substitute and surety, ready to pardon his transgression, and to forgive his sin. When, through faith in Jesus Christ, man does according to the very best of his ability, and seeks to keep the way of the Lord by obedience to the ten commandments, the perfection of Christ is imputed to cover the transgression of the repentant and obedient soul.

There will be an effort made on the part of many pretended friends of education to divorce religion from the sciences, in our schools. They would spare no pains or expense to impart secular knowledge; but they would not mingle with it a knowledge of what God has revealed as constituting perfection of character. And yet a training in the truth of God would develop the mind, and impart secular knowledge as well; for the very foundation of true education is in the fear of the Lord. Says the psalmist, "The fear of the Lord is the beginning of wisdom." The living oracles of God reveal the deceptions of the father of lies. Who of our youth can know anything of what is truth, in comparison with error, unless they are acquainted with the Scriptures? The simplicity of true godliness must be brought into the education of our young people, if they are to have divine knowledge to escape the corruptions that are in the world through lust. Those who are truly the followers of Christ, will not serve God only when it is in accordance with their inclination, but, as well, when it involves self-denial and cross-bearing. The earnest counsel given by the apostle Paul to Timothy, that he might not fail in doing his duty, should be set before the youth of today: "Let no man despise thy youth; but be thou an example of the believers, in word, in conversation, in charity, in spirit, in faith, in purity." Besetting sins must be battled with and overcome. Objectionable traits of character, whether hereditary or cultivated, should be taken up separately, and compared with the great rule of righteousness; and in the light reflected from the word of God, they should be firmly resisted and overcome, through the strength of Christ. "Follow peace with all men, and holiness, without which no man shall see the Lord."

Day by day, and hour by hour, there must be a vigorous process of self-denial and of sanctification going on within; and then the outward works will testify that Jesus is abiding in the heart by faith. Sanctification does not close the avenues of the soul to knowledge, but it comes to expand the mind, and to inspire it to search for truth, as for hidden treasure; and the knowledge of God's will advances the work of sanctification. There is a heaven, and O, how earnestly we should strive to reach it. I appeal to you students of our schools and colleges, to believe in Jesus as your Saviour. Believe that He is ready to help you by His grace, when you come to Him in sincerity. You must fight the good fight of faith. You must be wrestlers for the crown of life. Strive, for the grasp of Satan is upon you; and if you do not wrench yourselves from him, you will be palsied and ruined. The foe is on the right hand, and on the left, before you, and behind you; and you must trample him under your feet. Strive, for there is a crown to be won. Strive, for if you win not the crown, you lose everything in this life and in the future life. Strive, but let it be in the strength of your risen Saviour.

Will the students of our schools study, and endeavor to copy the life and character of Him who came down from heaven to show them what they must be, if they would enter the kingdom of God? I have borne you a message of the near coming of the Son of God in the clouds of heaven with power and great glory. I have not presented before you any definite time, but have repeated to you the injunction of Christ himself, to watch unto prayer, "For in such an hour as ye think not, the Son of man cometh." The warning has come echoing down the ages to our time, "Behold, I come quickly; and My reward is with Me, to give every man according as his work shall be. I am Alpha and Omega, the beginning and the end, the first and the last. Blessed are they that do His commandments, that they may have right to the tree of life, and may enter in through the gates into the city."--Review and Herald, August 21, 1888.

FOR ADDITIONAL READING

The Work of Reform, Signs of the Times, June 3, 1889

Proper Education, The Review and Herald, July 14, 1889

Home Training, Signs of the Times, July 22, 1889

Religion and Scientific Education, Testimonies for the Church, 5: 501-504

The Education of Our Children, Idem, 5: 505-507

Dangers to the Young, Idem, 5: 508-516

Suitable Reading for Our Children, Idem, 5: 516-520

Advice to the Young, Idem, 5: 520-529

Needs of Our Institutions, Idem, 5: 549-554

Our Institution at Battle Creek, Testimonies for the Church, 5: 555-567

Education of Workers, Testimonies for the Church, 5: 580-586

Parental Responsibility

God has permitted the light of health reform to shine upon us in these last days, that by walking in the light we may escape many of the dangers to which we shall be exposed. Satan is working with great power to lead men to indulge appetite, gratify inclination, and spend their days in heedless folly. He presents attractions in a life of selfish enjoyment and of sensual indulgence. Intemperance saps the energies of both mind and body. He who is thus overcome has placed himself upon Satan's ground, where he will be tempted and annoyed, and finally controlled at pleasure by the enemy of all righteousness. Parents need to be impressed with their obligation to give to the world children having well-developed characters,--children who will have moral power to resist temptation, and whose life will be an honor to God and a blessing to their fellow men. Those who enter upon active life with firm principles, will be prepared to stand unsullied amid the moral pollutions of this corrupt age. Let mothers improve every opportunity to educate their children for usefulness.

The work of the mother is sacred and important. She should teach her children, from the cradle up, habits of self-denial and self-control. Her time, in a special sense, belongs to her children. But if it is mostly occupied with the follies of this degenerate age, if society, dress, and amusements absorb her attention, her children will fail to be suitably educated.

Many mothers who deplore the intemperance that exists everywhere, do not look deep enough to see the cause. Too often it may be traced to the home table. Many a mother, even among those who profess to be Christians, is daily setting before her household, rich and highly seasoned food, which tempts the appetite and encourages overeating. In some families, flesh-meats constitute the principal article of diet, and in consequence, the blood is filled with cancerous and scrofulous humors. Then when suffering and disease follow, Providence is charged with that which is the result of a wrong course. I repeat: Intemperance begins at the table, and, with the majority, appetite is indulged until indulgence becomes second nature.

Whoever eats too much, or of food which is not healthful, is weakening his power to resist the clamors of other appetites and passions. Many parents, to avoid the task of patiently educating their children to habits of self-denial, indulge them in eating and drinking whenever they please. The desire to satisfy the taste and to gratify inclination, does not lessen with the increase of years; and these indulged youth, as they grow up, are governed by impulse, slaves to appetite. When they take their places in society, and begin life for themselves, they are powerless to resist temptation. In the glutton, the tobacco devotee, the winebibber, and the inebriate, we see the evil results of erroneous education and of self-indulgence.

When we hear the sad lamentation of Christian men and women over the terrible evils of intemperance, the questions at once arise: Who have educated the youth? who have fostered in them these unruly appetites? who have neglected the solemn responsibility of forming their characters for usefulness in this life, and for the society of heavenly angels in the next?

When parents and children meet at the final reckoning, what a scene will be presented! Thousands of children who have been slaves to appetite and debasing vice, whose lives are moral wrecks, will stand face to face with the parents who made them what they are. Who but the parents must bear this fearful responsibility? Did the Lord make these youth corrupt?--Oh, no! Who, then, has done this fearful work? Were not the sins of the parents transmitted to the children in perverted appetites and passions? and was not the work completed by those who neglected to train them according to the pattern which God has given? Just as surely as they exist, all these parents will pass in review before God.

Satan is ready to do his work; he will not neglect to present allurements which the children have no will or moral power to resist. I saw that, through his temptations, he is instituting ever-changing fashions, and attractive parties and amusements, that mothers may be led to devote their time to frivolous matters, instead of to the education and training of their children. Our youth need mothers who will teach them from the cradle, to control passion, to deny appetite, and to overcome selfishness. They need line upon line, precept upon precept, here a little and there a little.

The Hebrews were taught how to train their children so that they might avoid the idolatry and wickedness of the heathen nations: "Therefore shall ye lay up these My words in your heart and in your soul, and bind them for a sign upon your hand, that they may be as frontlets between your eyes. And ye shall teach them your children, speaking of them when thou sittest in thine house, and when thou walkest by the way, when thou liest down, and when thou risest up."

Woman should fill the position which God originally designed for her, as her husband's equal. The world needs mothers who are mothers not merely in name, but in every sense of the word. We may safely say that the distinctive duties of woman are more sacred, more holy, than those of man. Let woman realize the sacredness of her work, and in the strength and fear of God take up her life mission. Let her educate her children for usefulness in this world, and for a home in the better world.

The position of a woman in her family is more sacred than that of the king upon his throne. Her great work is to make her life an example such as she would wish her children to copy. And precept as well as example, she is to store their minds with useful knowledge, and lead them to self-sacrificing labor for the good of others. The great stimulus to the toiling, burdened mother should be that every child who is trained aright, and who has the inward adorning, the ornament of a meek and quiet spirit, will shine in the courts of the Lord.

I entreat Christian mothers to realize their responsibility, and to live, not to please themselves, but to glorify God. Christ pleased not Himself, but took upon Him the form of a servant. He left the royal courts, and clothed His divinity with humanity, that by His own example He might teach us how we may be exalted to the position of sons and daughters in the royal family, children of the heavenly King. But what are the conditions upon which we may obtain this great blessing?--"Come out from among them, and be ye separate, saith the Lord, and touch not the unclean thing; and I will receive you, and will be a Father unto you, and ye shall be My sons and daughters."

Christ humbled Himself from the position of one equal with God to that of a servant. His home was in Nazareth, a place proverbial for its wickedness. His parents were among the lowly poor. His trade was that of a carpenter, and He labored with His hands to do His part in sustaining the family. For thirty years He was subject to His parents. The life of Christ points out our duty to be diligent in labor, and to provide for those entrusted to our care.

In His lessons of instruction to His disciples, Jesus taught them that His kingdom is not a worldly kingdom, where all are striving for the highest position; but He gave them lessons in humility and self-sacrifice for the good of others. His humility did not consist in a low estimate of His own character and qualifications, but in adapting Himself to fallen humanity, in order to raise them up with Him to a higher life. Yet how few see anything attractive in the humility of Christ! Worldlings are constantly striving to exalt themselves one above another; but Jesus, the Son of God, humbled Himself in order to uplift man. The true disciple of Christ will follow His example. Would that the mothers of this generation might feel the sacredness of their mission, not trying to vie with their wealthy neighbors in appearance, but seeking to honor God by the faithful performance of duty. If right principles in regard to temperance were implanted in the youth who are to form and mold society, there would be little necessity for temperance crusades. Firmness of character, moral control, would prevail, and in the strength of Jesus the temptations of these last days would be resisted.

It is a most difficult matter to unlearn the habits which have been indulged through life. The demon of intemperance is of giant strength, and is not easily conquered. But if parents begin the crusade against it at their own firesides, in their own families, in the principles they teach their children from very infancy, then they may hope for success. It will pay you, mothers, to use the precious hours which are given you by God in forming the characters of your children, and in teaching them to adhere strictly to the principles of temperance in eating and drinking.

A sacred trust is committed to parents, to guard the physical and moral constitutions of their children, so that the nervous system may be well balanced, and the soul not endangered. Fathers and mothers should understand the laws of life, that they may not, through ignorance, allow wrong tendencies to develop in their children. The diet affects both physical and moral health. How carefully, then, should mothers study to supply the table with most simple, healthful food, in order that the digestive organs may not be weakened, the nerves unbalanced, or the instruction which they give their children counteracted.

Satan sees that he cannot have so great power over minds when the appetite is kept under control as when it is indulged, and he is constantly working to lead men to indulgence. Under the influence of unhealthful food, the conscience becomes stupefied, the mind is darkened, and its susceptibility to impressions is impaired. But the guilt of the transgressor is not lessened because the conscience has been violated till it has become insensible.

Since a healthy state of mind depends upon the normal condition of the vital forces, what care should be exercised that neither stimulants nor narcotics be used! Yet we see that a large number of those who profess to be Christians are using tobacco. They deplore the evils of intemperance; yet while speaking against the use of liquors, these very men will eject the juice of tobacco. There must be a change of sentiment with reference to tobacco-using before the root of the evil will be reached. We press the subject still closer. Tea and coffee are fostering the appetite for stronger stimulants. And then we come still closer home, to the preparation of food, and ask, Is temperance practiced in all things? are the reforms which are essential to health and happiness carried out here?

Every true Christian will have control of his appetites and passions. Unless he is free from the bondage of appetite, he cannot be a true, obedient servant of Christ. The indulgence of appetite and passion blunts the effect of truth upon the heart. It is impossible for the spirit and power of the truth to sanctify a man, soul, body, and spirit, when he is controlled by sensual desires.--"Christian Temperance and Bible Hygiene," pp. 75-80, 1890.

Education and Health

For generations the prevailing system of education has been destructive to health, and even to life itself. Many parents and teachers fail to understand that in the child's early years the greatest attention needs to be given to the physical constitution, that a healthy condition of body and brain may be secured. It has been the custom to encourage sending children to school when they were mere babies, needing a mother's care. In many instances the little ones are crowded into ill-ventilated schoolrooms, where they sit in improper positions, upon poorly constructed benches, and as the result, the young and tender frames often become deformed. Little children, whose limbs and muscles are not strong, and whose brains are undeveloped, are kept confined, to their injury. Many have but a slight hold on life to begin with, and confinement in school from day to day makes them nervous, and they become diseased. Their bodies are dwarfed in consequence of the exhausted condition of the nervous system. Yet when the lamp of life goes out, parents and teachers do not realize that they were in any way responsible for quenching the vital spark. Standing by the grave of their child, the afflicted parents look upon their bereavement as a special dispensation of Providence, when it was their own inexcusable, ignorant course that destroyed the young life. Under such circumstances, to charge the death to Providence, savors of blasphemy. God wants the little ones to live, and receive a right education, that they may develop a beautiful character, glorify Him in this world, and praise Him in the better world.

Parents and teachers take the responsibility of training these children, yet how few of them realize their duty before God to become acquainted with the physical organism, that they may know how to preserve the life and health of those who are placed in their charge. Thousands of children die because of the ignorance of those who care for them.

Many children have been ruined for life, and some have died, as the result of the injudicious course of parents and teachers, in forcing the young intellect while neglecting the physical nature. The children were too young to be in a schoolroom. Their minds were taxed with lessons when they should have been left untasked until the physical strength was sufficient to support mental effort. Small children should be as free as lambs to run out-of-doors. They should be allowed the most favorable opportunity to lay the foundation for a sound constitution.

Youth who are kept in school, and confined to close study, cannot have sound health. Mental effort without corresponding physical exercise, calls an undue proportion of blood to the brain, and thus the circulation is unbalanced. The brain has too much blood, while the extremities have too little. The hours of study and recreation should be carefully regulated, and a portion of the time should be spent in physical labor. When the habits of students in eating and drinking, dressing and sleeping are in accordance with physical law, they can obtain an education without sacrificing health. The lesson must be often repeated, and pressed home to the conscience, that education will be of little value if there is no physical strength to use it after it is gained.

Students should not be permitted to take so many studies that they will have no time for physical training. The health cannot be preserved unless some portion of each day is given to muscular exertion in the open air. Stated hours should be devoted to manual labor of some kind, anything which will call into action all parts of the body. Equalize the taxation of the mental and physical powers, and the mind of the student will be refreshed. If he is diseased, physical exercise will often help the system to recover its normal condition. When students leave college, they should have better health and a better understanding of the laws of life than when they entered it. The health should be as sacredly guarded as the character.

Many students are deplorably ignorant of the fact that diet exerts a powerful influence upon the health. Some have never made a determined effort to control the appetite, or to observe proper rules in regard to diet. They eat too much, even at their meals, and some eat between meals whenever the temptation is presented. If those who profess to be Christians desire to solve the questions so perplexing to them, why their minds are so dull, why their religious aspirations are so feeble, they need not, in many instances, go farther than the table; here is cause enough, if there were no other.

Many separate themselves from God by their indulgence of appetite. He who notices the fall of a sparrow, who numbers the very hairs of the head, marks the sin of those who indulge perverted appetite at the expense of weakening the physical powers, benumbing the intellect, and deadening the moral perceptions.

The teachers themselves should give proper attention to the laws of health, that they may preserve their own powers in the best possible condition, and by example as well as by precept, may exert a right influence upon their pupils. The teacher whose physical powers are already enfeebled by disease or overwork, should pay special attention to the laws of life. He should take time for recreation. He should not take upon himself responsibility outside of his school work, which will so tax him, physically or mentally, that his nervous system will be unbalanced; for in this case he will be unfitted to deal with minds, and cannot do justice to himself or to his pupils.

Our institutions of learning should be provided with every facility for instruction regarding the mechanism of the human system. Students should be taught how to breathe, how to read and speak so that the strain will not come on the throat and lungs, but on the abdominal muscles. Teachers need to educate themselves in this direction. Our students should have a thorough training, that they may enter upon active life with an intelligent knowledge of the habitation which God has given them. Teach them that they must be learners as long as they live. And while you are teaching them, remember that they will teach others. Your lesson will be repeated for the benefit of many more than sit before you day by day.--"Christian Temperance and Bible Hygiene," pp. 81-84, 1890.

Home Education

The work of the mother is an important one. Amid the homely cares and trying duties of everyday life, she should endeavor to exert an influence that will bless and elevate her household. In the children committed to her care, every mother has a sacred charge from the heavenly Father; and it is her privilege, through the grace of Christ, to mold their characters after the divine pattern, to shed an influence over their lives that will draw them toward God and heaven. If mothers had always realized their responsibility, and made it their first purpose, their most important mission, to fit their children for the duties of this life and for the honors of the future immortal life, we would not see the misery that now exists in so many homes in our land. The mother's work is such that it demands continual advancement in her own life, in order that she may lead her children to higher and still higher attainments. But Satan lays his plans to secure the souls of both parents and children. Mothers are drawn away from the duties of home and the careful training of their little ones, to the service of self and the world. Vanity, fashion, and matters of minor importance are allowed to absorb the attention, and the physical and moral education of the precious children is neglected.

If she makes the customs and practices of the world her criterion, the mother will become unfitted for the responsible duties of her lot. If fashion holds her in bondage, it will weaken her powers of endurance, and make life a wearing burden instead of a blessing. Through physical weakness she may fail to appreciate the value of the opportunities that are hers, and her family may be left to grow up without the benefit of her thought, her prayers, and her diligent instruction. If mothers would only consider the wonderful privileges that God has given them, they would not be so easily turned aside from their sacred duties to the trivial affairs of the world.

The mother's work begins with the babe in her arms. I have often seen the little one throw itself and scream, if its will was crossed in any way. This is the time to rebuke the evil spirit. The enemy will try to control the minds of our children, but shall we allow him to mold them according to his will? These little ones cannot discern what spirit is influencing them, and it is the duty of the parents to exercise judgment and discretion for them. Their habits must be carefully watched. Evil tendencies are to be restrained, and the mind stimulated in favor of the right. The child should be encouraged in every effort to govern itself.

Regularity should be the rule in all the habits of children. Mothers make a great mistake in permitting them to eat between meals. The stomach becomes deranged by this practice, and the foundation is laid for future suffering. Their fretfulness may have been caused by unwholesome food, still undigested; but the mother feels that she cannot spend time to reason upon the matter and correct her injurious management. Neither can she stop to soothe their impatient worrying. She gives the little sufferers a piece of cake or some other dainty to quiet them, but this only increases the evil. Some mothers, in their anxiety to do a great amount of work, get wrought up into such nervous haste that they are more irritable than the children, and by scolding and even blows they try to terrify the little ones into quietude.

Mothers often complain of the delicate health of their children, and consult the physician, when, if they would but exercise a little common sense, they would see that the trouble is caused by errors in diet.

We are living in an age of gluttony, and the habits to which the young are educated, even by many Seventh-day Adventists, are in direct opposition to the laws of nature. I was seated once at the table with several children under twelve years of age. Meat was plentifully served, and then a delicate, nervous girl called for pickles. A bottle of chow-chow, fiery with mustard and pungent with spices, was handed her, from which she helped herself freely. The child was proverbial for her nervousness and irritability of temper, and these fiery condiments were well calculated to produce such a condition. The oldest child thought he could not eat a meal without meat, and showed great dissatisfaction, and even disrespect, if it was not provided for him. The mother had indulged him in his likes and dislikes till she had become little better than a slave to his caprices. The lad had not been provided with work, and he spent the greater portion of his time in reading that which was useless or worse than useless. He complained almost constantly of headache, and had no relish for simple food.

Parents should provide employment for their children. Nothing will be a more sure source of evil than indolence. Physical labor that brings healthful weariness to the muscles, will give an appetite for simple, wholesome food, and the youth who is properly employed will not rise from the table grumbling because he does not see before him a platter of meat and various dainties to tempt his appetite.

Jesus, the Son of God, in laboring with His hands at the carpenter's trade, gave an example to all youth. Let those who scorn to take up the common duties of life remember that Jesus was subject to His parents, and contributed His share toward the sustenance of the family. Few luxuries were seen on the table of Joseph and Mary, for they were among the poor and lowly.

Parents should be an example to their children in the expenditure of money. There are those who, as soon as they get money, spend it for dainties to eat, or for needless adornments of dress, and when the supply of money becomes reduced, they feel the need of that which they have wasted. If they have an abundant income, they use every dollar of it; if small, it is not sufficient for the habits of extravagance they have acquired, and they borrow to supply the demand. They gather from any source possible to meet their fancied necessities. They become dishonest and untruthful, and the record that stands against them in the books of heaven is such as they will not care to look upon in the day of judgment. The desire of the eye must be gratified, the craving of the appetite indulged, and they keep themselves poor by their improvident habits, when they might have learned to live within their means. Extravagance is one of the sins to which youth are prone. They despise economical habits, for fear they shall be thought niggardly and mean. What will Jesus, the Majesty of heaven, who has given them an example of patient industry and economy, say to such?

It is not necessary to specify here how economy may be practiced in every particular. Those whose hearts are fully surrendered to God, and who take His word as their guide, will know how to conduct themselves in all the duties of life. They will learn of Jesus, who is meek and lowly of heart; and in cultivating the meekness of Christ they will close the door against innumerable temptations.

They will not be studying how to gratify appetite and the passion for display, while so many cannot even keep hunger from the door. The amount daily spent in needless things, with the thought, "It is only a nickel," "It is only a dime," seems very little; but multiply these littles by the days of the year, and as the years go by, the array of figures will seem almost incredible.

The Lord has been pleased to present before me the evils which result from spendthrift habits, that I might admonish parents to teach their children strict economy. Teach them that money spent for that which they do not need, is perverted from its proper use. He that is unfaithful in that which is least, would be unfaithful in much. If men are unfaithful with earthly goods, they cannot be entrusted with the eternal riches. Set a guard over the appetite; teach your children by example as well as by precept to use a simple diet. Teach them to be industrious, not merely busy, but engaged in useful labor. Seek to arouse the moral sensibilities. Teach them that God has claims upon them, even from the early years of their childhood. Tell them that there are moral corruptions to be met on every hand, that they need to come to Jesus and give themselves to Him, body and spirit, and that in Him they will find strength to resist every temptation. Keep before their minds that they were not created merely to please themselves, but to be the Lord's agents for noble purposes. Teach them, when temptations urge into paths of selfish indulgence, when Satan is seeking to shut out God from their sight, to look to Jesus, pleading, "Save, Lord, that I be not overcome." Angels will gather about them in answer to their prayers, and lead them into safe paths.

Christ prayed for His disciples, not that they should be taken out of the world, but that they should be kept from evil,--that they might be kept from yielding to the temptations they would meet on every hand. This is a prayer that should be offered up by every father and mother. But should they thus plead with God in behalf of their children, and then leave them to do as they please? Should they pamper the appetite until it gets the mastery, and then expect to restrain the children?--No; temperance and self-control should be taught from the very cradle up. Upon the mother must rest largely the responsibility of this work. The tenderest earthly tie is that between the mother and her child. The child is more readily impressed by the life and example of the mother than by that of the father, because of this stronger and more tender bond of union. Yet the mother's responsibility is a heavy one, and should have the constant aid of the father.

Intemperance in eating and drinking, intemperance in labor, intemperance in almost everything, exists on every hand. Those who make great exertions to accomplish just so much work in a given time, and continue to labor when their judgment tells them they should rest, are never gainers. They are living on borrowed capital. They are expending the vital force which they will need at a future time. And when the energy they have so recklessly used is demanded, they fail for want of it. The physical strength is gone, the mental powers fail. They realize that they have met with a loss, but do not know what it is. Their time of need has come, but their physical resources are exhausted. Everyone who violates the laws of health must some time be a sufferer to a greater or less degree. God has provided us with constitutional force, which will be needed at different periods of our lives. If we recklessly exhaust this force by continual overtaxation, we shall sometime be losers. Our usefulness will be lessened, if not our life itself destroyed.

As a rule the labor of the day should not be prolonged into the evening. If all the hours of the day are well improved, the work extended into the evening is so much extra, and the overtaxed system will suffer from the burden imposed upon it. I have been shown that those who do this, often lose much more than they gain, for their energies are exhausted, and they labor on nervous excitement. They may not realize any immediate injury, but they are surely undermining their constitutions.

Let parents devote the evenings to their families. Lay off care and perplexity with the labors of the day. The husband and father would gain much if he would make it a rule not to mar the happiness of his family by bringing his business troubles home to fret and worry over. He may need the counsel of his wife in difficult matters, and they may both obtain relief in their perplexities by unitedly seeking wisdom of God; but to keep the mind constantly strained upon business affairs will injure the health of both mind and body.

Let the evenings be spent as happily as possible. Let home be a place where cheerfulness, courtesy, and love exist. This will make it attractive to the children. If the parents are continually borrowing trouble, are irritable and faultfinding, the children partake of the same spirit of dissatisfaction and contention, and home is the most miserable place in the world. The children find more pleasure among strangers, in reckless company, or in the street, than at home. All this might be avoided if temperance in all things were practiced, and patience cultivated. Self-control on the part of all the members of the family will make home almost a paradise. Make your rooms as cheerful as possible. Let the children find home the most attractive place on earth. Throw about them such influences that they will not seek for street companions, nor think of the haunts of vice except with horror. If the home life is what it should be, the habits formed there will be a strong defense against the assaults of temptation when the young shall leave the shelter of home for the world.

Do we build our houses for the happiness of the family, or merely for display? Do we provide pleasant, sunny rooms for our children, or do we keep them darkened and closed, reserving them for strangers who are not dependent on us for happiness? There is no nobler work that we can do, no greater benefit that we can confer upon society, than to give to our children a proper education, impressing upon them, by precept and example, the important principle that purity of life and sincerity of purpose will best qualify them to act their part in the world.

Our artificial habits deprive us of many privileges and much enjoyment, and unfit us for usefulness. A fashionable life is a hard, thankless life. How often time, money, and health are sacrificed, the patience sorely tried, and self-control lost, merely for the sake of display. If parents would cling to simplicity, not indulging in expense for the gratification of vanity, and to follow fashion; if they would maintain a noble independence in the right, unmoved by the influence of those who, while professing Christ, refuse to lift the cross of self-denial, they would by this example itself give their children an invaluable education. The children would become men and women of moral worth, and, in their turn, would have courage to stand bravely for the right, even against the current of fashion and popular opinion.

Every act of the parents tells on the future of the children. In devoting time and money to the outward adorning and the gratification of perverted appetite, they are cultivating vanity, selfishness, and lust in the children. Mothers complain of being so burdened with care and labor that they cannot take time patiently to instruct their little ones, and to sympathize with them in their disappointments and trials. Young hearts yearn for sympathy and tenderness, and if they do not obtain it from their parents, they will seek it from sources that may endanger both mind and morals. I have heard mothers refuse their children some innocent pleasure, for lack of time and thought, while their busy fingers and weary eyes were diligently engaged on some useless piece of adorning, something which could only serve to encourage vanity and extravagance in the children. "As the twig is bent, the tree is inclined." As the children approach manhood and womanhood, these lessons bear fruit in pride and moral worthlessness. The parents deplore the children's faults, but are blind to the fact that they are but reaping the crop from seed of their own planting.

Christian parents, take up your life burden, and think candidly of the sacred obligations that rest upon you. Make the word of God your standard, instead of following the fashions and customs of the world, the lust of the eye, and the pride of life. The future happiness of your families and the welfare of society depend largely upon the physical and moral education which your children receive in the first years of their life. If their tastes and habits are as simple in all things as they should be, if the dress is tidy, without extra adornment, mothers will find time to make their children happy, and teach them loving obedience.

Do not send your little ones away to school too early. The mother should be careful how she trusts the molding of the infant mind to other hands. Parents ought to be the best teachers of their children until they have reached eight or ten years of age. Their schoolroom should be the open air, amid the flowers and birds, and their textbook the treasure of nature. As fast as their minds can comprehend it, the parents should open before them God's great book of nature. These lessons, given amid such surroundings, will not soon be forgotten. Great pains should be taken to prepare the soil of the heart for the Sower to scatter the good seed. If half the time and labor that is now worse than wasted in following the fashions of the world, were devoted to the cultivation of the minds of the children, to the formation of correct habits, a marked change would be apparent in families.

Not long since I heard a mother say that she liked to see a house fitly constructed, that defects in the arrangement and mismatched woodwork in the finishing annoyed her. I do not condemn nice taste in this respect, but as I listened to her, I regretted that this nicety could not have been brought into her methods of managing her children. These were buildings for whose framing she was responsible; yet their rough, uncourteous ways, their passionate, selfish natures, and uncontrolled wills, were painfully apparent to others. Ill-formed characters, mismatched pieces of humanity, indeed they were, yet the mother was blind to it all. The arrangement of her house was of more consequence to her than the symmetry of her children's character.

Cleanliness and order are Christian duties, yet even these may be carried too far, and made the one essential, while matters of greater importance are neglected. Those who neglect the interests of the children for these considerations are tithing the mint and cumin, while they neglect the weightier matters of the law,--justice, mercy, and the love of God.

Those children who are the most indulged become willful, passionate, and unlovely. Would that parents could realize that upon judicious, early training depends the happiness of both the parents and the children. Who are these little ones that are committed to our care? They are the younger members of the Lord's family. "Take this son, this daughter," He says, "nurse them for me, and fit them up 'that they may be polished after the similitude of a palace,' that they may shine in the courts of the Lord." Precious work! Important work! Yet we see mothers sighing for a wider field of labor, for some missionary work to do. If they could only go to Africa or India, they would feel that they were doing something. But to take up the little daily duties of life, and to carry them forward faithfully, perseveringly, seems to them an unimportant thing. Why is this? Is it not often because the mother's work is so rarely appreciated? She has a thousand cares and burdens of which the father seldom has any knowledge. Too often he returns home bringing with him his cares and business perplexities to overshadow the family, and if he does not find everything just to his mind at home, he gives expression to his feelings in impatience and faultfinding. He can boast of what he has achieved through the day, but the mother's work, to his mind, amounts to little, or is at least undervalued. To him her cares appear trifling. She has only to cook the meals, look after the children, sometimes a large family of them, and keep the house in order. She has tried all day to keep the domestic machinery running smoothly. She has tried, though tired and perplexed, to speak kindly and cheerfully, and to instruct the children and keep them in the right path. All this has cost effort, and much patience on her part. She cannot, in her turn, boast of what she has done. It seems to her as though she has accomplished nothing. But it is not so. Though the results of her work are not apparent, angels of God are watching the careworn mother, noting the burdens she carries from day to day. Her name may never appear upon the records of history, or receive the honor and applause of the world, as may that of the husband and father; but it is immortalized in the book of God. She is doing what she can, and her position in God's sight is more exalted than that of a king upon his throne; for she is dealing with character, she is fashioning minds.

The mothers of the present day are making the society of the future. How important that their children be so brought up that they shall be able to resist the temptations they will meet on every side in later life!

Whatever may be his calling and its perplexities, let the father take into his home the same smiling countenance and pleasant tones with which he has all day greeted visitors and strangers. Let the wife feel that she can lean upon the large affections of her husband,--that his arms will strengthen and uphold her through all her toils and cares, that his influence will sustain hers, and her burden will lose half its weight. Are the children not his as well as hers?

Let the father seek to lighten the mother's task. In the time that he would devote to selfish enjoyment of leisure, let him seek to become acquainted with his children--associate with them in their sports, in their work. Let him point them to the beautiful flowers, the lofty trees, in whose very leaves they can trace the work and love of God. He should teach them that the God who made all these things loves the beautiful and the good. Christ pointed His disciples to the lilies of the field and the birds of the air, showing how God cares for them, and presented this as an evidence that He will care for man, who is of higher consequence than birds and flowers. Tell the children that however much time may be wasted in attempts at display, our appearance can never compare, for grace and beauty, with that of the simplest flowers of the field. Thus their minds may be drawn from the artificial to the natural. They may learn that God has given them all these beautiful things to enjoy, and that He wants them to give Him the heart's best and holiest affections.

Parents should seek to awaken in their children an interest in the study of physiology. Youth need to be instructed in regard to their own bodies. There are but few among the young who have any definite knowledge of the mysteries of life. The study of the wonderful human organism, the relation and dependence of all its complicated parts, is one in which most mothers take little if any interest. They do not understand the influence of the body upon the mind, or of the mind upon the body. They occupy themselves with needless trifles, and then plead that they have no time to obtain the information which they need in order to care properly for the health of their children. It is less trouble to trust them to the doctors. Thousands of children die through ignorance of the laws of their being.

If parents themselves would obtain knowledge upon this subject and feel the importance of putting it to a practical use, we should see a better condition of things. Teach your children to reason from cause to effect. Show them that if they violate the laws of their being, they must pay the penalty by suffering. If you cannot see as rapid improvement as you desire, do not be discouraged, but instruct them patiently, and press on until victory is gained. Continue to teach them in regard to their own bodies, and how to take care of them. Recklessness in regard to bodily health tends to recklessness in morals.

Do not neglect to teach your children how to prepare healthful food. In giving them these lessons in physiology and in good cooking, you are giving them the first steps in some of the most useful branches of education, and inculcating principles which are needful elements in a religious education.

All the lessons of which I have spoken in this article are needed. If properly heeded, they will be like a bulwark that will preserve our children from the evils which are flooding the world. We want temperance at our tables. We want houses where the God-given sunlight and the pure air of heaven are welcomed. We want a cheerful, happy influence in our homes. We must cultivate useful habits in our children, and must instruct them in the things of God. It costs something to do all this. It costs prayers and tears, and patient, oft-repeated instruction. We are sometimes put to our wit's end to know what to do; but we can take the children to God in our prayers, pleading that they may be kept from evil, praying, "Now, Lord, do Thy work; soften and subdue the hearts of our children," and He will hear us. He hearkens to the prayers of the weeping, careworn mothers. When Christ was on earth, the burdened mothers brought their children to Him; they thought that if He would lay His hands upon them, they would have better courage to bring them up as they ought to go. The Saviour knew why these mothers came to Him with their little ones, and He rebuked the disciples, who would have kept them away, saying, "Suffer the little children to come unto Me, and forbid them not; for of such is the kingdom of God." Jesus loves the little ones, and He is watching to see how parents are doing their work.

Iniquity abounds on every hand, and if the children are saved, earnest, persevering effort must be put forth. Christ has said, "I sanctify Myself, that they also might be sanctified." He wanted His disciples to be sanctified, and He made Himself their example, that they might follow Him. What if fathers and mothers should take this same position, saying, "I want my children to have steadfast principles, and I will give them an example of this in my life"? Let the mother think no sacrifice too great, if made for the salvation of her household. Remember, Jesus gave His life for the purpose of rescuing you and yours from ruin. You will have His sympathy and help in this blessed work, and will be a laborer together with God.

In whatever else we may fail, let us be thorough in the work for our children. If they go forth from the home training, pure and virtuous, if they fill the least and lowest place in God's great plan of good for the world, our life work can never be called a failure.--"Christian Temperance and Bible Hygiene," pp. 60-72, 1890.

Mental Inebriates

What shall our children read? is a serious question, and demands a serious answer. I am troubled to see, in Christian families, periodicals and newspapers containing continued stories that leave no impress of good upon the mind. I have watched those whose taste for fiction has been thus cultivated. They have had the privilege of listening to the truths of God's word, of becoming acquainted with the reasons of our faith; but they have grown to mature years destitute of true piety. These dear youth need so much to put into their character building the very best material,--the love and fear of God and a knowledge of Christ. But many have not an intelligent understanding of the truth as it is in Jesus. The mind is feasted upon sensational stories. They live in an unreal world, and are unfitted for the practical duties of life. I have observed children allowed to come up in this way. Whether at home or abroad, they are either restless or dreamy, and are unable to converse, save upon the most commonplace subjects. The nobler faculties, those adapted to higher pursuits, have been degraded to the contemplation of trivial or worse than trivial subjects, until their possessor has become satisfied with such topics, and scarcely has power to reach anything higher. Religious thought and conversation has become distasteful. The mental food for which he has acquired a relish, is contaminating in its effects, and leads to impure and sensual thoughts. I have felt sincere pity for these souls as I have considered how much they are losing by neglecting opportunities to gain a knowledge of Christ, in whom our hopes of eternal life are centered. How much precious time is wasted, in which they might be studying the Pattern of true goodness.

I am personally acquainted with some who have lost the healthy tone of the mind through wrong habits of reading. They go through life with a diseased imagination, magnifying every little grievance. Things which a sound, sensible mind would not notice, become to them unendurable trials, insurmountable obstacles. To them, life is in constant shadow.

Those who have indulged the habit of racing through exciting stories, are crippling their mental strength, and disqualifying themselves for vigorous thought and research. There are men and women now in the decline of life who have never recovered from the effects of intemperate reading. The habit, formed in early years, has grown with their growth and strengthened with their strength; and their efforts to overcome it, though determined, have been only partially successful. Many have never recovered their original vigor of mind. All attempts to become practical Christians end with the desire. They cannot be truly Christlike, and continue to feed the mind upon this class of literature. Nor is the physical effect less disastrous. The nervous system is unnecessarily taxed by this passion for reading. In some cases, youth, and even those of mature age, have been afflicted with paralysis from no other cause than excess in reading. The mind was kept under constant excitement, until the delicate machinery of the brain became so weakened that it could not act, and paralysis was the result.

When an appetite for exciting, sensational stories is cultivated, the moral taste becomes perverted, and the mind is unsatisfied unless constantly fed upon this trashy, unwholesome food. I have seen young ladies, professed followers of Christ, who were really unhappy unless they had on hand some new novel or story-paper. The mind craved stimulation as the drunkard craves intoxicating drink. These youth manifested no spirit of devotion; no heavenly light was shed upon their associates, to lead them to the fount of knowledge. They had no deep, religious experience. If this class of reading had not been constantly before them, there might have been some hope of their reforming; but they craved it, and would have it.

I am pained to see young men and women thus ruining their usefulness in this life, and failing to obtain an experience that will prepare them for an eternal life in heavenly society. We can find no more fit name for them than "mental inebriates."

Intemperate habits of reading exert a pernicious influence upon the brain as surely as does intemperance in eating and drinking.

The best way to prevent the growth of evil is to preoccupy the soil. The greatest care and watchfulness is needed in cultivating the mind and sowing therein the precious seeds of Bible truth. The Lord, in His great mercy, has revealed to us in the Scriptures the rules of holy living. He tells us the sins to shun; He explains to us the plan of salvation, and points out the way to heaven. He has inspired holy men to record, for our benefit, instruction concerning the dangers that beset the path, and how to escape them. Those who obey His injunction to search the Scriptures will not be ignorant of these things. Amid the perils of the last days, every member of the church should understand the reasons of his hope and faith,--reasons which are not difficult of comprehension. There is enough to occupy the mind, if we would grow in grace and in the knowledge of our Lord Jesus Christ.

We are finite, but we are to have a sense of the infinite. The mind must be brought into exercise in contemplating God, and His wonderful plan for our salvation. The soul will thus be lifted above the mere earthly and commonplace, and fixed upon that which is ennobling and eternal. The thought that we are in God's world, in the presence of the great Creator of the universe, who made man after His own likeness, will lead the mind into broad, exalted fields for meditation. The thought that God's eye is watching over us, that He loves us, and cared so much for us to give His dearly beloved Son to redeem us, that we might not miserably perish, is a great one; and he who opens his heart to the acceptance and contemplation of themes like these, will never be satisfied with trivial, sensational subjects.

If the Bible were studied as it should be, men would become strong in intellect. The subjects treated upon in the word of God, the dignified simplicity of its utterance, the noble themes which it presents to the mind, develop faculties in man which cannot otherwise be developed. In the Bible, a boundless field is opened for the imagination. The student will come from a contemplation of its grand themes, from association with its lofty imagery, more pure and elevated in thought and feeling than if he had spent the time in reading any work of mere human origin, to say nothing of those of a trifling character. Youthful minds fail to reach their noblest development when they neglect the highest source of wisdom,--the word of God. The reason why we have so few men of good mind, of stability and solid worth, is that God is not feared, God is not loved, the principles of religion are not carried out in the life as they should be.

God would have us avail ourselves of every means of cultivating and strengthening our intellectual powers. We were created for a higher, nobler existence than the life that now is. This time is one of preparation for the future, immortal life. Where can be found grander themes for contemplation, a more interesting subject for thought, than the sublime truths unfolded in the Bible? These truths will do a mighty work for man, if he will but follow what they teach. But how little the Bible is studied! Every unimportant thing is dwelt upon in preference to its themes. If the Bible were read more, if its truths were better understood, we should be a far more enlightened and intelligent people. Angels from the world of light stand by the side of the earnest seeker after truth, to impress and illuminate his mind. He who is dark of understanding may find light through an acquaintance with the Scriptures.--"Christian Temperance and Bible Hygiene," pp. 123-26, 1890. [166]

FOR ADDITIONAL READING

The Literal Week, Patriarchs and Prophets, 111-116

The Schools of the Prophets, Patriarchs and Prophets, 592-602

Teach by Precept and Example, The Review and Herald, March 31, 1891

The Mother's Work, The Review and Herald, September 15, 1891

A Knowledge of God, Steps to Christ, 89-96

Books in Our Schools

In the work of educating the youth in our schools, it will be a difficult matter to retain the influence of God's Holy Spirit and at the same time hold fast to erroneous principles. The light shining upon those who have eyes to see, cannot be mingled with the darkness of heresy and error found in many of the textbooks recommended to the students in our colleges. Both teachers and pupils have thought that in order to obtain an education, it was necessary to study the productions of writers who teach infidelity, because their works contain some bright gems of thought. But who was the originator of these gems of thought?--It was God and God alone; for He is the source of all light. Are not all things essential for the health and growth of the spiritual and moral nature found in the pages of Holy Writ? Is not Christ our living head? And are not we to grow up in Him to the full stature of men and women? Can an impure fountain send forth sweet waters? Why should we wade through the mass of error contained in the works of pagans and infidels, for the sake of obtaining the benefit of a few intellectual truths, when all truth is at our command?

Man can accomplish nothing good without God. He is the originator of every ray of light that has pierced the darkness of the world. All that is of value comes from God, and belongs to Him. There is a reason that the agents of the enemy sometimes display remarkable wisdom. Satan himself was educated and disciplined in the heavenly courts, and he has a knowledge of good as well as of evil. He mingles the precious with the vile, and this is what gives him his power of deceiving the sons of men. But because Satan has stolen the livery of heaven in order that he may exercise an influence in his usurped dominions, shall those who have been sitting in darkness and have seen a great light, turn from the light to recommend darkness? Shall those who have known the oracles of God recommend our students to study the books that express pagan or infidel sentiments, that they may become intelligent? Satan has his agents, educated after his methods, inspired by his spirit, and adapted to his works; but shall we co-operate with them? Shall we as Christians, recommend the works of his agents as valuable, even essential to the attainment of an education?

The Lord himself has signified that schools should be established among us in order that true knowledge may be obtained. No teacher in our schools should suggest the idea that, in order to have the right discipline, it is essential to study textbooks expressing pagan and infidel sentiments. Students who are thus educated, are not competent to become educators in their turn; for they are filled with the subtle sophistries of the enemy. The study of works that in any way express infidel sentiments is like handling black coals; for a man cannot be undefiled in mind who thinks along the line of skepticism. In going to such sources for knowledge, are we not turning away from the snow of Lebanon to drink from the turbid water of the valley?

Men who turn away from the knowledge of God, have placed their minds under control of their master, Satan, and he trains them to be his servants. The less the productions expressing infidel views are brought before the youth, the better. Evil angels are ever on the alert that they may exalt before the minds of the youth that which will do them injury, and as books expressing infidel and pagan sentiments are read, these unseen agents of evil seek to impress those who study them with the spirit of questioning and unbelief. Those who drink from these polluted channels do not thirst for the waters of life; for they are satisfied with the broken cisterns of the world. They think they have the treasures of knowledge, when they are hoarding that which is but wood and hay and stubble, not worth gaining, not worth keeping. Their self-esteem, their idea that a superficial knowledge of things constitutes education, make them boastful and self-satisfied, when they are, as were the Pharisees, ignorant of the Scriptures and the power of God.

O that our youth would treasure up the knowledge that is imperishable, that they can carry with them into the future, immortal life, the knowledge that is represented as gold and silver and precious stones! The class of educators and learners who deem themselves wise, know nothing as they ought to know it. They need to learn meekness and lowliness in the school of Christ, that they may esteem highly that which Heaven regards as excellent. Those who receive a valuable education, one that will be as enduring as eternity, will not be regarded as the world's best educated men. But the Scriptures declare that "the fear of the Lord is the beginning of wisdom." This kind of knowledge is below par in the estimation of the world, and yet it is essential for every youth to become wise in the Scriptures, if he would have eternal life. The apostle says, "All Scripture is given by inspiration of God, and is profitable for doctrine, for reproof, for correction, for instruction in righteousness: that the man of God may be perfect, throughly furnished unto all good works." This is broad enough. Let all seek to comprehend, to the full extent of their powers, the meaning of the word of God. A mere superficial reading of the inspired word will be of little advantage; for every statement made in the sacred pages requires thoughtful contemplation. It is true that some passages do not require as earnest concentration as do others; for their meaning is more evident. But the student of the word of God should seek to understand the bearing of one passage upon another until the chain of truth is revealed to his vision. As veins of precious ore are hidden beneath the surface of the earth, so spiritual riches are concealed in the passage of Holy Writ, and it requires mental effort and prayerful attention to discover the hidden meaning of the word of God. Let every student who values the heavenly treasure put to the stretch his mental and spiritual powers, and sink the shaft deep into the mine of truth, that he may obtain the celestial gold,--that wisdom which will make him wise unto salvation.

If half the zeal manifested in seeking to comprehend the bright ideas of infidels, was manifested in studying the plan of salvation, thousands who are now in darkness, would be charmed with the wisdom, the purity, the elevation of the provisions of God in our behalf; they would be lifted out of and away from themselves in wonder and amazement at the love and condescension of God in giving His only-begotten Son for a fallen race. How is it that many are satisfied to drink at the turbid streams that flow in the murky valley, when they might refresh their souls at the living streams of the mountains? The prophet asks, "Will a man leave the snow of Lebanon which cometh from the rock of the field? or shall the cold flowing waters that come from another place be forsaken?" The Lord answers, "My people hath forgotten Me, they have burned incense to vanity, and they have caused them to stumble in their ways from the ancient paths, in a way not cast up."

It is a sad fact that men who have been entrusted with fine capabilities to be employed in the service of God, have prostituted their powers in the service of evil, and laid their talents at the feet of the enemy. They submitted in the most servile bondage to the prince of evil, while rejecting the service of Christ as humiliating and undesirable. They looked upon the work of the follower of Christ as a work below their ambition, that required a stepping down from their greatness, a species of slavery, that would enthrall their powers, and narrow the circle of their influence. He who had made an infinite sacrifice that they might be set free from the bondage of evil, was set aside as unworthy their best efforts and most exalted service.

These men had received their talents from God, and every gem of thought by which they had been esteemed worthy of the attention of scholars and thinkers, belongs not to them, but to the God of all wisdom, whom they did not acknowledge. Through tradition, through false education, these men are exalted as the world's educators; but in going to them students are in danger of accepting the vile with the precious; for superstition, specious reasoning, and error are mingled with portions of true philosophy and instruction. This mingling makes a potion that is poisonous to the soul,--destructive of faith in the God of all truth. Those who have a thirst for knowledge need not go to these polluted fountains; for they are invited to come to the fountain of life and drink freely. Through searching the word of God, they may find the hidden treasure of truth that has long been buried beneath the rubbish of error, human tradition, and opinions of men.

The Bible is the great educator; for it is not possible prayerfully to study its sacred pages without having the intellect disciplined, ennobled, purified, and refined. "Thus saith the Lord, Let not the wise man glory in his wisdom, neither let the mighty man glory in his might, let not the rich man glory in his riches: but let him that glorieth glory in this, that he understandeth and knoweth Me, that I am the Lord which exercise lovingkindness, judgment, and righteousness, in the earth: for in these things I delight, saith the Lord. Behold, the days come, saith the Lord, that I will punish all them which are circumcised with the uncircumcised."

Those who claim to be Christians, who profess to believe the truth, and yet drink at the polluted fountains of infidelity, and by precept and example draw others away from the cold, snow-waters of Lebanon, are fools, though they profess themselves to be wise. "Hear ye the word which the Lord speaketh unto you, O house of Israel: Thus saith the Lord, Learn not the way of the heathen, and be not dismayed at the signs of heaven; for the heathen are dismayed at them. . . . But the Lord is the true God, He is the living God, and an everlasting King: at His wrath the earth shall tremble, and the nations shall not be able to abide His indignation. Thus shall ye say unto them, The gods that have not made the heavens and the earth, even they shall perish from the earth, and from under these heavens. He hath made the earth by His power, He hath established the world by His wisdom, and hath stretched out the heavens by His discretion. When He uttereth His voice, there is a multitude of waters in the heavens, and He causeth the vapors to ascend from the ends of the earth; He maketh lightnings with rain, and bringeth forth the wind out of His treasures. Every man is brutish in his knowledge: every founder is confounded by the graven image: for his molten image is falsehood, and there is no breath in them. They are vanity, and the work of errors: in the time of their visitation they shall perish. The Portion of Jacob is not like them: for He is the former of all things; and Israel is the rod of His inheritance: the Lord of hosts is His name."

"Thus saith the Lord; Cursed be the man that trusteth in man, and maketh flesh his arm, and whose heart departeth from the Lord. For he shall be like the heath in the desert, and shall not see when good cometh; but shall inhabit the parched places in the wilderness, in a salt land and not inhabited. Blessed is the man that trusteth in the Lord, and whose hope the Lord is. For he shall be as a tree planted by the waters, and that spreadeth out her roots by the river, and shall not see when heat cometh, but her leaf shall be green; and shall not be careful in the year of drought, neither shall cease from yielding fruit. . . . O Lord, the Hope of Israel, all that forsake Thee shall be ashamed, and they that depart from Me shall be written in the earth, because they have forsaken the Lord, the fountain of living waters. Heal me, O Lord, and I shall be healed; save me, and I shall be saved: for Thou art my praise."

Let believers in the truth for this time, turn away from authors that teach infidelity. Let not the works of skeptics appear on your library shelves, where your children can have access to them. Let those who have tasted the good word of God, and the powers of the world to come, no longer deem it an essential feature of a good education to have a knowledge of the writings of those who deny the existence of God, and pour contempt upon His holy word. Give no place to the agents of Satan, since there is nothing by which to vindicate their doings; a clean thing cannot come out of an unclean.--Review and Herald, Nov. 10, 1891.

The Teacher of Truth the Only Safe Educator

There are two classes of educators in the world. One class are those whom God makes channels of light, and the other class are those whom Satan uses as his agents, who are wise to do evil. One class contemplates the character of God, and increases in the knowledge of Jesus, whom God hath sent into the world. This class becomes wholly given up to those things which bring heavenly enlightenment, heavenly wisdom, to the uplifting of the soul. Every capability of their nature is submitted to God, and their thoughts are brought into captivity to Christ. The other class is in league with the prince of darkness, who is ever on the alert that he may find an opportunity to teach others the knowledge of evil. If place is made for him, he will not be slow to press his way into heart and mind.

There is great need of elevating the standard of righteousness in our schools, to give instruction after God's order. Should Christ enter our institutions for the education of the youth, He would cleanse them as He cleansed the temple, banishing many things that have a defiling influence. Many of the books which the youth study would be expelled, and their places would be filled with others that would inculcate substantial knowledge, and abound in sentiments which might be treasured in the heart, in precepts that might govern the conduct. Is it the Lord's purpose that false principles, false reasoning, and the sophistries of Satan should be kept before the mind of our youth and children? Shall pagan and infidel sentiments be presented to our students as valuable additions to their store of knowledge? The works of the most intellectual skeptic are works of a mind prostituted to the service of the enemy, and shall those who claim to be reformers, who seek to lead the children and youth in the right way, in the path cast up, imagine that God will be pleased with having them present to the youth that which will misrepresent His character, placing Him in a false light before the young? Shall the sentiments of unbelievers, the expressions of dissolute men, be advocated as worthy of the student's attention, because they are the productions of men whom the world admires as great thinkers? Shall men professing to believe in God, gather from these unsanctified authors their expressions and sentiments, and treasure them up as precious jewels to be stored away among the riches of the mind?--God forbid.

The Lord bestowed upon these men whom the world admires, priceless intellectual gifts; He endowed them with master minds; but they did not use them to the glory of God. They separated themselves from Him as did Satan; but while they separated themselves from Him, they still retained many of the precious gems of thought which He had given them, and these they placed in a framework of error to give luster to their own human sentiments, to make attractive the utterances inspired by the prince of evil. It is true that in the writings of pagans and infidels there are found thoughts of an elevated character, which are attractive to the mind. But there is a reason for this. Was not Satan the lightbearer, the sharer of God's glory in heaven, and next to Jesus in power and majesty? In the words of inspiration, he is described as one who seals up "the sum, full of wisdom, and perfect in beauty." The prophet says, "Thou hast been in Eden the garden of God; every precious stone was thy covering. . . . Thou art the anointed cherub that covereth; and I have set thee so: thou wast upon the holy mountain of God; thou hast walked up and down in the midst of the stones of fire. Thou wast perfect in thy ways from the day that thou wast created, till iniquity was found in thee. . . . Thine heart was lifted up because of thy beauty, thou hast corrupted thy wisdom by reason of thy brightness: I will cast thee to the ground, I will lay thee before kings, that they may behold thee. Thou hast defiled thy sanctuaries by the multitude of thine iniquities, by the iniquity of thy traffic; therefore will I bring forth a fire from the midst of thee, it shall devour thee, and I will bring thee to ashes upon the earth in the sight of all them that behold thee. All they that know thee among the people shall be astonished at thee: thou shalt be a terror, and never shalt thou be any more."

The greatness and power with which the Creator endowed Lucifer he has perverted; and yet, when it suits his purpose, he can impart to men sentiments that are enchanting. Everything in nature comes from God; yet Satan can inspire his agents with thoughts that appear elevating and noble. Did he not come to Christ with quotations of Scripture when he designed to overthrow Him with his specious temptations? This is the way in which he comes to man, as an angel of light disguising his temptations under an appearance of goodness, and making men believe him to be the friend rather than the enemy of humanity. It is in this way that he has deceived and seduced the race,--beguiling them with subtle temptations, bewildering them with specious deceptions.

Satan has ascribed to God all the evils to which flesh is heir. He has represented Him as a God who delights in the sufferings of His creatures, who is revengeful and implacable. It was Satan who originated the doctrine of eternal torment as a punishment for sin, because in this way he could lead men into infidelity and rebellion, distract souls, and dethrone the human reason.

Heaven, looking down, and seeing the delusions into which men were led, knew that a divine Instructor must come to earth. Men in ignorance and moral darkness must have light, spiritual light; for the world knew not God, and He must be revealed to their understanding. Truth looked down from heaven and saw not the reflection of her image; for dense clouds of moral darkness and gloom enveloped the world, and the Lord Jesus alone was able to roll back the clouds: for He was the Light of the world. By

His presence He could dissipate the gloomy shadow that Satan had cast between man and God. Darkness covered the earth, and gross darkness the people. Through the accumulated misrepresentations of the enemy, many were so deceived that they worshiped a false god, clothed with the attributes of the satanic character.

The Teacher from heaven, no less a personage than the Son of God, came to earth to reveal the character of the Father to men, that they might worship Him in spirit and in truth. Christ revealed to men the fact that the strictest adherence to ceremony and form would not save them; for the kingdom of God was spiritual in its nature. Christ came to the world to sow it with truth. He held the keys to all the treasures of wisdom, and was able to open doors to science, and to reveal undiscovered stores of knowledge, were it essential to salvation. He presented to men that which was exactly contrary to the representations of the enemy in regard to the character of God, and sought to impress upon men the paternal love of the Father, who "so loved the world, that He gave His only-begotten Son, that whosoever believeth in Him should not perish but have everlasting life." He urged upon men the necessity of prayer, repentance, confession, and the abandonment of sin. He taught them honesty, forbearance, mercy, and compassion, enjoining upon them to love not only those who loved them, but those who hated them, who treated them despitefully. In this He was revealing to them the character of the Father, who is long-suffering, merciful, and gracious, slow to anger, and full of goodness and truth. Those who accepted His teaching were under the guardian care of angels, who were commissioned to strengthen, to enlighten, that the truth might renew and sanctify the soul.

Christ declares the mission He had in coming to the earth. He says in His last public prayer, "O righteous Father, the world hath not known Thee: but I have known Thee, and these have known that Thou hast sent Me. And I have declared unto them Thy name, and will declare it; that the love wherewith Thou hast loved Me may be in them, and I in them." When Moses asked the Lord to show him His glory, the Lord said, "I will make all My goodness pass before thee." "And the Lord passed by before him, and proclaimed, The Lord, The Lord God, merciful and gracious, longsuffering, and abundant in goodness and truth, keeping mercy for thousands, forgiving iniquity and transgression and sin, and that will by no means clear the guilty. . . . And Moses made haste, and bowed his head toward the earth, and worshiped." When we are able to comprehend the character of God as did Moses, we too shall make haste to bow in adoration and praise. Jesus contemplated nothing less than "that the love wherewith Thou hast loved Me" should be in the hearts of His children, that they might impart the knowledge of God to others.

O what an assurance is this, that the love of God may abide in the hearts of all who believe in Him! O what salvation is provided; for He is able to save unto the uttermost all that come unto God by Him. In wonder we exclaim, How can these things be? But Jesus will be satisfied with nothing less than this. Those who are partakers of His sufferings here, of His humiliation, enduring for His name's sake, are to have the love of God bestowed upon them as it was upon the Son. One who knows, has said, "The Father himself loveth you." One who has had an experimental knowledge of the length, and breadth, and height, and depth of that love, has declared unto us this amazing fact. This love is ours through faith in the Son of God, therefore a connection with Christ means everything to us. We are to be one with Him as He is one with the Father, and then we are beloved by the infinite God as members of the body of Christ, as branches of the living Vine. We are to be attached to the parent stock, and to receive nourishment from the Vine. Christ is our glorified Head, and the divine love flowing from the heart of God, rests in Christ, and is communicated to those who have been united to Him. This divine love entering the soul inspires it with gratitude, frees it from its spiritual feebleness, from pride, vanity, and selfishness, and from all that would deform the Christian character.

Look, O look to Jesus and live! You cannot but be charmed with the matchless attractions of the Son of God. Christ was God manifest in the flesh, the mystery hidden for ages, and in our acceptance or rejection of the Saviour of the world are involved eternal interests.

To save the transgressor of God's law, Christ, the one equal with the Father, came to live heaven before men, that they might learn to know what it is to have heaven in the heart. He illustrated what man must be to be worthy of the precious boon of the life that measures with the life of God.

The life of Christ was a life charged with a divine message of the love of God, and He longed intensely to impart this love to others in rich measure. Compassion beamed from His countenance, and His conduct was characterized by grace, humility, truth, and love. Every member of His church militant must manifest the same qualities, if He would join the church triumphant. The love of Christ is so broad, so full of glory, that in comparison to it, everything that men esteem as great, dwindles into insignificance. When we obtain a view of it, we exclaim, O the depth of the riches of the love that God bestowed upon men in the gift of His only-begotten Son!

When we seek for appropriate language in which to describe the love of God, we find words too tame, too weak, too far beneath the theme, and we lay down our pen and say, "No, it cannot be described." We can only do as did the beloved disciple, and say, "Behold, what manner of love the Father hath bestowed upon us, that we should be called the sons of God." In attempting any description of this love, we feel that we are as infants lisping their first words. Silently we may adore; for silence in this matter is the only eloquence. This love is past all language to describe. It is the mystery of God in the flesh, God in Christ, and divinity in humanity. Christ bowed down in unparalleled humility, that in His exaltation to the throne of God, He might also exalt those who believe in Him, to a seat with Him upon His throne. All who look upon Jesus in faith that the wounds and bruises that sin has made will be healed in Him, shall be made whole.

The themes of redemption are momentous themes, and only those who are spiritually minded can discern their depth and significance. It is our safety, our life, our joy, to dwell upon the truths of the plan of salvation. Faith and prayer are necessary in order that we may behold the deep things of God. Our minds are so bound about with narrow ideas, that we catch but limited views of the experience it is our privilege to have. How little do we comprehend what is meant by the prayer of the apostle, when he says, "That He would grant you, according to the riches of His glory, to be strengthened with might by His Spirit in the inner man; that Christ may dwell in your hearts by faith; that ye, being rooted and grounded in love, may be able to comprehend with all saints what is the breadth, and length, and depth, and height; and to know the love of Christ, which passeth knowledge, that ye might be filled with all the fullness of God. Now unto Him that is able to do exceeding abundantly above all that we ask or think, according to the power that worketh in us, unto Him be glory in the church by Christ Jesus throughout all ages, world without end. Amen."--Review and Herald, Nov. 17, 1891.

The Treasures With Which to Store the Mind

Jesus beheld the human race, ignorant, apostate from God, standing under the penalty of the broken law; and He came to bring deliverance, to offer a complete pardon, signed by the Majesty of heaven. If man will accept this pardon, he may be saved; if he rejects it, he will be lost. The wisdom of God alone can unfold the mysteries of the plan of salvation. The wisdom of men may or may not be valuable, as experience shall prove, but the wisdom of God is indispensable; and yet many who profess to be wise are willingly ignorant of the things that pertain to eternal life. Miss what you may in the line of human attainments, but you must have faith in the pardon brought to you at infinite cost, or all of wisdom attained in earth, will perish with you.

Were the Sun of Righteousness to withdraw His beams of light from the world, we should be left in the darkness of eternal night. Jesus spake as never man spake. He poured out to men the whole treasure of heaven in wisdom and knowledge. He is the light that lighteth every man who cometh into the world. Every phase of truth was evident to Him. He did not come to utter uncertain sentiments and opinions; but only to speak truth established upon eternal principles. Then why take the unstable words of men as exalted wisdom, when a greater and certain wisdom is at your command? Men take the writings of scientists, falsely so-called, and seek to make their deductions harmonize with the statements of the Bible. But where there is no agreement, there can be no harmony. Christ declares, "No man can serve two masters." Their interests are sure to clash. Again and again men have attempted to put the Bible and the writings of men upon a common basis; but the attempt has proved a failure; for we cannot serve God and mammon.

We are in the world, but we are not to be of the world. Jesus entreats that those for whom He died, may not lose their eternal reward by lavishing their affections on the things of this perishing earth, and so cheat themselves out of unending happiness. An enlightened judgment compels us to acknowledge that heavenly things are superior to the things of earth, and yet the depraved heart of man leads him to give precedence to the things of the world. The opinions of great men, the theories of science, falsely so-called, are blended with the truths of Holy Writ.

But the heart that is surrendered to God, loves the truth of God's word; for through the truth the soul is regenerated. The carnal mind finds no pleasure in contemplating the word of God, but he who is renewed in the spirit of his mind, sees new charms in the living oracles; for divine beauty and celestial light seem to shine in every passage. That which was to the carnal mind a desolate wilderness, to the spiritual mind becomes a land of living streams. That which to the unrenewed heart appeared a barren waste, to the converted soul becomes the garden of God, covered with fragrant buds and blooming flowers.

The Bible has been placed in the background, while the sayings of great men, so-called, have been taken in its stead. May the Lord forgive us the slight we have put upon His word. Through inestimable treasures are in the Bible, and it is like a mine full of precious ore, it is not valued, it is not searched, and its riches are not discovered. Mercy and truth and love are valuable beyond our power to calculate; we cannot have too great a supply of these treasures, and it is in the word of God we find out how we may become possessors of these heavenly riches, and yet why is it that the word of God is uninteresting to many professed Christians? Is it because the word of God is not spirit and is not life? Has Jesus put upon us an uninteresting task, when He commands us to "search the Scriptures"? Jesus says, "The words that I speak unto you, they are spirit and they are life." But spiritual things are spiritually discerned, and the reason of your lack of interest is that you lack the Spirit of God. When the heart is brought into harmony with the word, a new life will spring up within you, a new light will shine upon every line of the word, and it will become the voice of God to your soul. In this way you will take celestial observations, and know whither you are going, and be able to make the most of your privileges today.

We should ask the Lord to open our understanding, that we may comprehend divine truth. If we humble our hearts before God, empty them of vanity and pride and selfishness, through the grace abundantly bestowed upon us; if we sincerely desire and unwaveringly believe, the bright beams of the Sun of Righteousness will shine into our minds, and illuminate our darkened understanding. Jesus is the Light that lighteth every man that cometh into the world. He is the Light of the world, and He bids us come unto Him, and learn of Him. Jesus was the great Teacher. He could have made disclosures on the sciences that would have placed the discoveries of the greatest men in the background as utter littleness; but this was not His mission or His work. He had come to seek and to save that which was lost, and He could not permit Himself to be turned from His one object. He allowed nothing to divert Him. This work He has given into our hands. Shall we do it?

In the days of Christ the established teachers instructed men in the traditions of the fathers, in childish fables, mingled with the opinions of those who they thought were high authorities. Yet neither high nor low could discern any ray of light in their teaching. What wonder was it that crowds followed in the footsteps of the Lord, and gave Him homage as they listened to His words! He revealed truths that had been buried under the rubbish of error, and He freed them from the exactions and traditions of men, and bade them stand fast forever. He rescued truth from its obscurity, and set it in its proper framework, to shine in its original luster. He addressed men in His own name; for authority was vested in Himself, and why should men, professing to be His followers, not speak with authority concerning subjects on which He has given light? Why take inferior sources of instruction when Christ is the great Teacher who knows all things? Why present inferior authors to the attention of students, when He whose words are spirit and life invites, "Come, . . . and learn of Me"?

Shall we not be intensely interested in the lessons of Christ? Shall we not be charmed with the new and glorious light of heavenly truth? This light is above everything that man can present. We can receive light only as we come to the cross and present ourselves at the altar of sacrifice. Here man's weakness is made manifest; here His strength is revealed. Here men see there is power in Christ to save to the uttermost all that come unto God by Him.

Shall we not be doers of the words of Him who knows all things? Shall we not make the Bible the man of our counsel in the education and training of our youth? The word of God is the foundation of all true knowledge, and Christ teaches what men must do in order to be saved. Hitherto the designs of the enemy have been carried out in bringing before our students such books as have taught specious errors, and presented fables that have tempted their carnal appetites. Shall we bring into our schools the sower of tares? Shall we permit men who are called great, and yet who have been taught by the enemy of all truth, to have the education of our youth? Or shall we take the word of God as our guide, and have our schools conducted more after the order of the ancient schools of the prophets?

If the Bible was studied and obeyed; if we had the spirit of Christ, we should make determined efforts to be laborers together with God. We should better appreciate the worth of the soul; for every soul converted to God means a vessel dedicated to a holy use, a depositary of truth, a bearer of light to others. God expects more of the schools than has yet been brought forth. Christ has said, "Labor not for the meat which perisheth, but for that meat which endureth unto everlasting life; which the Son of man shall give unto you; for Him hath God the Father sealed."

Then we shall rightly understand the teaching of God's word, and esteem the truth as the most valuable treasure with which to store the mind. We shall have a constant wellspring of the waters of life. We shall pray as did the psalmist, "Open Thou mine eyes, that I may behold wondrous things out of Thy law," and shall find as he did that "the judgments of the Lord are true and righteous altogether. More to be desired are they than gold, yea, than much fine gold: sweeter also than honey and the honeycomb. Moreover by them is Thy servant warned: and in keeping of them there is great reward."--Review and Herald, Nov. 24, 1891.

The Science of Salvation the First of Sciences

The schools established among us are matters of grave responsibility; for important interests are involved. In a special manner our schools are a spectacle unto angels and to men. A knowledge of science of all kinds is power, and it is in the purpose of God that advanced science shall be taught in our schools as a preparation for the work that is to precede the closing scenes of earth's history. The truth is to go to the remotest bounds of the earth, through agents trained for the work. But while the knowledge of science is a power, the knowledge which Jesus in person came to impart to the world was the knowledge of the gospel. The light of truth was to flash its bright rays into the uttermost parts of the earth, and the acceptance or rejection of the message of God involved the eternal destiny of souls.

The plan of salvation had its place in the counsels of the Infinite from all eternity. The gospel is the revelation of God's love to men, and means everything that is essential to the happiness and well-being of humanity. The work of God in the earth is of immeasurable importance, and it is Satan's special object to crowd it out of sight and mind, that he may make his specious devices effectual in the destruction of those for whom Christ died. It is his purpose to cause the discoveries of men to be exalted above the wisdom of God. When the mind is engrossed with the conceptions and theories of men to the exclusion of the wisdom of God, it is stamped with idolatry. Science, falsely so called, has been exalted above God, nature above its Maker, and how can God look upon such wisdom?

In the Bible the whole duty of man is defined. Solomon says, "Fear God, and keep His commandments: for this is the whole duty of man." The will of God is revealed in His written word, and this is the essential knowledge. Human wisdom, familiarity with the languages of different nations, is a help in the missionary work. An understanding of the customs of the people, of the location and time of events, is practical knowledge; for it aids in making the figures of the Bible clear, in bringing out the force of Christ's lessons; but it is not positively necessary to know these things. The wayfaring man may find the pathway cast up for the ransomed to walk in, and there will be no excuse found for anyone who perishes through misapprehension of the Scriptures.

In the Bible every vital principle is declared, every duty made plain, every obligation made evident. The whole duty of man is summed up by the Saviour. He says, "Thou shalt love the Lord thy God with all thy heart, and with all thy soul, and with all thy mind. . . . Thou shalt love thy neighbor as thyself." In the word the plan of salvation is plainly delineated. The gift of eternal life is promised on condition of saving faith in Christ. The drawing power of the Holy Spirit is pointed out as an agent in the work of man's salvation. The rewards of the faithful, the punishment of the guilty, are all laid out in clear lines. The Bible contains the science of salvation for all those who will hear and do the words of Christ.

The apostle says, "All Scripture is given by inspiration of God, and is profitable for doctrine, for reproof, for correction, for instruction in righteousness: that the man of God may be perfect, thoroughly furnished unto all good works." The Bible is its own expositor. One passage will prove to be a key that will unlock other passages, and in this way light will be shed upon the hidden meaning of the word. By comparing different texts treating on the same subject, viewing their bearing on every side, the true meaning of the Scriptures will be made evident.

Many think that they must consult commentaries on the Scriptures in order to understand the meaning of the word of God, and we would not take the position that commentaries should not be studied; but it will take much discernment to discover the truth of God under the mass of the words of men. How little has been done by the church as a body professing to believe the Bible, to gather up the scattered jewels of God's word into one perfect chain of truth! The jewels of truth do not lie upon the surface, as many suppose. The master mind in the confederacy of evil is ever at work to keep the truth out of sight, and to bring into full view the opinions of great men. The enemy is doing all in his power to obscure heaven's light through educational processes; for he does not mean that men shall hear the voice of the Lord, saying, "This is the way, walk ye in it."

The jewels of truth lie scattered over the field of revelation; but they have been buried beneath human traditions, beneath the sayings and commandments of men, and the wisdom from heaven has been practically ignored; for Satan has succeeded in making the world believe that the words and achievements of men are of great consequence. The Lord God, the Creator of the worlds, at infinite cost has given the gospel to the world. Through this divine agent, glad, refreshing springs of heavenly comfort and abiding consolation have been opened for those who will come to the fountain of life. There are veins of truth yet to be discovered; but spiritual things are spiritually discerned. Minds beclouded with evil cannot appreciate the value of the truth as it is in Jesus. When iniquity is cherished, men do not feel the necessity of making diligent effort, with prayer and reflection, to understand what they must know or lose heaven. They have so long been under the shadow of the enemy, that they view the truth as men behold objects through a smoked and imperfect glass; for all things are dark and perverted in their eyes. Their spiritual vision is feeble and untrustworthy; for they look upon the shadow, and turn away from the light.

But those who profess to believe in Jesus, should ever press to the light. They should daily pray for the light of the Holy Spirit to shine upon the pages of the sacred book, that they may be enabled to comprehend the things of the Spirit of God. We must have implicit trust in God's word, or we are lost. The words of men, however great they may be, are not able to make us perfect, to thoroughly furnish unto all good works. "God hath from the beginning chosen you to salvation through sanctification of the Spirit and belief of the truth." In this text the two agencies in the salvation of man are revealed,--the divine influence, the strong, living faith of those who follow Christ. It is through the sanctification of the Spirit and the belief of the truth, that we become laborers together with God. God waits for the co-operation of His church. He does not design to add a new element of efficiency to His word; He has done His great work in giving His inspiration to the world. The blood of Jesus, the Holy Spirit, the divine word, are ours. The object of all this provision of heaven is before us,--the souls for whom Christ died,--and it depends upon us to lay hold of the promises God has given, and become laborers together with Him; for divine and human agencies must co-operate in this work.

The reason that many professed Christians do not have a clear, well-defined experience, is that they do not think it is their privilege to understand what God has spoken through His word. After the resurrection of Jesus, two of His disciples were journeying toward Emmaus, and Jesus joined them. But they did not recognize their Lord, and thought He was some stranger, although "beginning at Moses and all the prophets, He expounded unto them in all the Scriptures the things concerning Himself. And they drew nigh unto the village, whither they went: and He made as though He would have gone further. But they constrained Him, saying, Abide with us: for it is toward evening, and the day is far spent. And He went in to tarry with them. And it came to pass, as He sat at meat with them, He took bread, and blessed it, and brake, and gave to them. And their eyes were opened, and they knew Him; and He vanished out of their sight. And they said one to another, Did not our hearts burn within us, while He talked with us by the way, and while He opened to us the Scriptures? . . . Then opened He their understanding, that they might understand the Scriptures." This is the work that we may look to Christ to do for us; for what the Lord has revealed, is for us and our children forever.

Jesus knew that whatever was presented that was out of harmony with what He came to earth to unfold, was false and delusive. But He said, "Everyone that is of the truth heareth My voice." Having stood in the counsels of God, having dwelt in the everlasting heights of the sanctuary, all elements of truth were in Him, and of Him; for He was one with God. "Verily, verily, I say unto thee, We speak what we do know, and testify that we have seen; and ye receive not our witness. If I have told you earthly things, and ye believe not, how shall ye believe, if I tell you of heavenly things? And no man hath ascended up to heaven, but He that came down from heaven, even the Son of man which is in heaven." "Every word of God is pure: He is a shield unto them that put their trust in Him. Add thou not unto His words, lest He reprove thee, and thou be found a liar."--Review and Herald, Dec. 1, 1891.

Christian Character Exemplified in Teachers and Students

In the name of my Master I appeal to the young men and women who claim to be sons and daughters of God, to obey the word of God. I appeal to teachers in our schools to set a right example to those with whom they are associated. Those who would be qualified to mold the character of the youth, must be learners in the school of Christ, that they may be meek and lowly of heart, as was the divine Pattern. In dress, in deportment, in all their ways, they should exemplify the Christian character, revealing the fact that they are under wise disciplinary rules of the great Teacher. The Christian youth should be in earnest, trained to bear responsibilities with brave heart and willing hand. He should be ready to encounter the trials of life with patience and fortitude. He should seek to form a character after the model of the divine One, following maxims of worth, confirming himself in habits that will enable him to win the victor's crown.

In school life the youth may sow seeds which will bear a harvest, not of thorns, but of precious grain for the heavenly garner. There is no time more favorable than the time spent in school in which to acknowledge the power of Christ's saving grace, to be controlled by the principles of the divine law, and it is for the student's interest to live a godly life. The crowning glory of life results from a connection with Christ. No man liveth unto himself. Your life is interwoven with all others in the common web of humanity, and you are to be laborers together with God for the salvation of those who perish in degradation and woe. You are to be instruments in influencing all those with whom you associate to a better life, to direct the mind to Jesus.

John writes: "I have written unto you, young men, because ye are strong, and the word of God abideth in you, and ye have overcome the wicked one." And Paul exhorts Titus to bid the young men to "be sober-minded." Elevate your soul to be as was Daniel, a loyal, steadfast servant of the Lord of hosts. Ponder well the path of your feet; for you are standing on holy ground, and the angels of God are about you. It is right that you should feel that you must climb to the highest round of the educational ladder. Philosophy and history are important studies; but your sacrifice of time and money will avail nothing, if you do not use your attainments for the honor of God and the good of humanity. Unless the knowledge of science is a steppingstone to the attainment of the highest purposes, it is worthless. The education that does not furnish knowledge as enduring as eternity, is of no purpose. Unless you keep heaven and the future, immortal life before you, your attainments are of no permanent value. But if Jesus is your teacher, not simply on one day of the week, but every day, every hour, you may have His smile upon you in the pursuit of literary acquirements.

Daniel ever kept before him the glory of God, and you should also say, Lord, I desire knowledge, not for the glorification of self, but to meet the expectation of Jesus, that I may perfect an intelligent Christian character, through the grace He has given unto me. Will the students be true to principle as was Daniel?

In the future there will be more pressing need of men and women of literary qualifications than there has been in the past; for broad fields are opening out before us, white already for harvest. In these fields you may be laborers together with God. But if you are lovers of pleasure more than lovers of God, if you are filled with levity, if you allow the golden opportunities to pass without acquiring knowledge, without placing solid timbers in your character building, you will be dwarfed and crippled in any line of occupation you may undertake.

While a good education is a great benefit if combined with consecration in its possessor, still those who do not have the privilege of gaining high literary attainments need not think they cannot advance in intellectual and spiritual life. If they will make the most of the knowledge they have, if they will seek to gather something to their store every day, and will overcome all perverseness of temper through the studious cultivation of Christlike traits of character, God will open channels of wisdom to them, and it may be said of them as it was said of old, concerning the Hebrew children, God gave them wisdom and understanding.

It is not true that brilliant young men always make the greatest success. How often men of talent and education have been placed in positions of trust, and have proved failures. Their glitter had the appearance of gold, but when it was tried, it proved to be but tinsel and dross. They made a failure of their work through unfaithfulness. They were not industrious and persevering, and did not go to the bottom of things. They were not willing to begin at the bottom of the ladder, and with patient toil, ascend round after round till they reached the top. They walked in the sparks (their bright flashes of thought) of their own kindling. They did not depend on the wisdom which God alone can give. Their failure was not because they did not have a chance, but because they were not sober-minded. They did not feel that their educational advantages were of value to them, and so did not advance as they might have advanced in the knowledge of religion and science. Their mind and character were not balanced by high principles of right.

Let our young men be sober, and ponder the ways of their feet. Let them shun sin because it is destructive in its tendencies and displeasing to God. Let them discern what possibilities are within their reach, and seek God for grace to keep in the paths of righteousness. Let them seek the

Christian Character Exemplified in Teachers and Students

counsel and guidance of the Lord, that they may spend their lives for His glory in the world.

In obtaining an education, success is not to be regarded as a matter of chance or destiny; it is from that God who read the heart of Daniel, who looked with pleasure upon his purity of motive, his determination of purpose to honor the Lord. Daniel did not walk in sparks of his own kindling, but made the Lord his wisdom. Divine philosophy was made the foundation of his education. He welcomed the counsel of the Lord. Would that all students were as was Daniel; but many do not see the importance of submitting to divine discipline.

O that all might realize that without Christ they can do nothing! Those who do not gather with Him scatter abroad. Their thoughts and actions will not bear the right character, and their influence will be destructive of good. Our actions have a twofold influence; for they affect others as well as ourselves. This influence will either be a blessing or a curse to those with whom we associate. How little we appreciate this fact. Actions make habits, and habits, character, and if we do not guard our habits, we shall not be qualified to unite with heavenly agencies in the work of salvation, nor be prepared to enter the heavenly mansions that Jesus has gone to prepare; for no one will be there except those who have surrendered their will and way to God's will and way. He whose character is proved, who has stood the test of trial, who is a partaker of the divine nature, will be among those whom Christ pronounces blessed.

Without Christ we can do nothing. The pure principles of uprightness, virtue, and goodness are all from God. A conscientious discharge of duty, Christlike sympathy, love for souls and love for your own soul, because you belong to God, and have been bought with the precious blood of Christ, will make you a laborer together with God, and endow you with persuasive, drawing power. You must respect your own faith in order successfully to introduce it to others. By example as well as precept, you must show that you reverence your faith, speaking reverently of sacred things. Never allow one expression of lightness and trifling to escape your lips when quoting Scripture. As you take the Bible in your hands, remember that you are on holy ground. Angels are around you, and could your eyes be opened, you would behold them. Let your conduct be such that you will leave the impression upon every soul with whom you associate that a pure and holy atmosphere surrounds you. One vain word, one trifling laugh, may balance a soul in the wrong direction. Terrible are the consequences of not having a constant connection with God.

Abstain from all evil. Common sins, however insignificant they may be regarded, will impair your moral sense, and extinguish the inward impression of the Spirit of God. The character of the thoughts leaves its imprint upon the soul, and all low conversation pollutes the mind. All evil works ruin to those who commit it. God may and will forgive the repenting sinner, but though forgiven, the soul is marred; the power of the elevated thought possible to the unimpaired mind is destroyed. Through all time the soul bears the scars. Then let us seek for that faith which works by love and purifies the heart, that we may represent the character of Christ to the world.--Review and Herald, Dec. 8, 1891.

The World By Wisdom Knew Not God

The truth of God is infinite, capable of measureless expansion, and the more we contemplate it, the more will its glory appear. The truth has been opened before us, and yet the words of Paul to the Galatians are applicable to us. He says: "O foolish Galatians, who hath bewitched you, that ye should not obey the truth, before whose eyes Jesus Christ hath been evidently set forth, crucified among you? This only would I learn of you, Received ye the Spirit by the works of the law, or by the hearing of faith? are ye so foolish? having begun in the Spirit, are ye now made perfect by the flesh? have ye suffered so many things in vain? if it be yet in vain."

"Without Me," Christ says, "ye can do nothing." Those who undertake to carry forward the work in their own strength will certainly fail. Education alone will not fit a man for a place in the work, will not enable him to obtain a knowledge of God. Hear what Paul has to say on this matter: "For Christ sent me not to baptize, but to preach the gospel: not with wisdom of words, lest the cross of Christ should be made of none effect. For the preaching of the cross is to them that perish foolishness; but unto us which are saved it is the power of God. For it is written, I will destroy the wisdom of the wise, and will bring to nothing the understanding of the prudent. Where is the wise? where is the scribe? where is the disputer of this world? hath not God made foolish the wisdom of this world? For after that in the wisdom of God the world by wisdom knew not God, it pleased God by the foolishness of preaching to save them that believe."

Through successive ages of darkness, in the midnight of heathenism, God permitted men to try the experiment of finding out God by their own wisdom, not to demonstrate their inability to His satisfaction, but that men themselves might see that they could not obtain a knowledge of God and of Jesus Christ His Son, save through the revelation of His word by the Holy Spirit. When Christ came to the world, the experiment had been fully tried, and the result made it evident that the world by wisdom knew not God. Even in the church God has allowed men to test their own wisdom in this matter, but when a crisis has been brought about through human fallibility, God has risen mightily to defend His people. When the church has been brought low, when trial and oppression have come upon His people, He more abundantly exalted them by signal deliverance. When unfaithful teachers came among the people, weakness followed, and the faith of God's people seemed to wane; but God arose and purged His floor, and the tried and true were lifted up.

There are times when apostasy comes into the ranks, when piety is left out of the heart by those who should have kept step with their divine

Leader. The people of God separate from the source of their strength, and pride, vanity, extravagance, and display follow. There are idols within and idols without; but God sends the Comforter as a reprover of sin, that His people may be warned of their apostasy and rebuked for their backsliding. When the more precious manifestations of His love shall be gratefully acknowledged and appreciated, the Lord will pour in the balm of comfort and the oil of joy.

When men are led to realize that their human calculations come far short, and are convinced that their wisdom is but foolishness, then it is that they turn to the Lord to seek Him with all the heart, that they may find Him.

It has been shown me that every church among us needs the deep movings of the Spirit of God. O we would point men to the cross of Calvary. We would bid them look upon Him whom their sins have pierced. We would bid them to behold the Redeemer of the world suffering the penalty of their transgression of the law of God. The verdict is that "the soul that sinneth it shall die." But on the cross the sinner sees the only-begotten of the Father, dying in his stead, and giving the transgressor life. All the intelligences in earth and heaven are called upon to behold what manner of love the Father hath bestowed upon us, that we should be called the sons of God. Every sinner may look and live. Do not survey that scene of Calvary with careless, thoughtless mind. Can it be that angels shall look down upon us, the recipients of God's love, and see us cold, indifferent, unimpressible, when heaven in amazement beholds the stupendous work of redemption to save a fallen world, and desires to look into the mystery of Calvary's love and woe? Angels in wonder and amazement look upon those for whom so great salvation has been provided, and marvel that the love of God does not awaken them, and lead them to pour forth melodious strains of gratitude and adoration. But the result which all heaven looks to behold is not seen among those who profess to be followers of Christ. How readily do we speak in endearing words of our friends and relatives, and yet how slow we are to speak of Him whose love has no parallel, set forth in Christ crucified among you.

The love of our heavenly Father in the gift of His only-begotten Son to the world, is enough to inspire every soul, to melt every hard, loveless heart into contrition and tenderness; and yet shall heavenly intelligences see in those for whom Christ died, insensibility to His love, hardness of heart, and no response of gratitude and affection to the Giver of all good things? Shall affairs of minor importance absorb the whole power of the being, and the love of God meet no return? Shall the Sun of Righteousness shine in vain? In view of what God has done, could His claims be less upon you? Have we hearts that can be touched, that can be impressed with divine love? Are we willing to be chosen vessels? Has not God His eye upon us, and has He not bidden us to send forth His message of light? We need an increase of faith. We must wait, we must watch, we must pray, we must work, pleading that the Holy Ghost may be poured out upon us abundantly, that we may be lights in the world.

Jesus looked upon the world in its fallen state with infinite pity. He took humanity upon Himself that He might touch and elevate humanity. He came to seek and to save that which was lost. He reached to the very depth of human misery and woe, to take man as He found him, a being tainted with corruption, degraded with vice, depraved by sin, and united with Satan in apostasy, and elevate him to a seat upon His throne. But it was written of Him that "He shall not fail nor be discouraged," and He went forth in the path of self-denial and self-sacrifice, giving us an example that we should follow in His steps. We should work as did Jesus, departing from our own pleasure, turning away from Satan's bribes, despising ease, and abhorring selfishness, that we may seek and save that which is lost, bringing souls from darkness into light, into the sunshine of God's love. We have been commissioned to go forth and preach the gospel to every creature. We are to bring to the lost the tidings that Christ can forgive sin, can renew the nature, can clothe the soul in the garments of His righteousness, bring the sinner to His right mind, and teach him and fit him up to be a laborer together with God.

The converted soul lives in Christ. His darkness passes away, and a new and heavenly light shines into his soul. "He that winneth souls is wise." "And they that be wise shall shine as the brightness of the firmament; and they that turn many to righteousness as the stars forever and ever." What is done through the co-operation of men with God is a work that shall never perish, but endure through the eternal ages. He that makes God his wisdom, that grows up into the full stature of a man in Christ Jesus, will stand before kings, before the so-called great men of the world, and show forth the praises of Him who hath called him out of darkness into His marvelous light. Science and literature cannot bring into the darkened mind of men the light which the glorious gospel of the Son of God can bring. The Son of God alone can do the great work of illuminating the soul. No wonder Paul exclaims, "For I am not ashamed of the gospel of Christ; for it is the power of God unto salvation to everyone that believeth." The gospel of Christ becomes personality in those who believe, and makes them living epistles, known and read of all men. In this way the leaven of godliness passes into the multitude. The heavenly intelligences are able to discern the true elements of greatness in character; for only goodness is esteemed as efficiency with God.

"Without Me," Christ says, "ye can do nothing." Our faith, our example, must be held more sacred than they have been held in the past. The word of God must be studied as never before; for it is the precious offering that we must present to men, in order that they may learn the way of peace, and obtain that life which measures with the life of God. Human wisdom so highly exalted among men sinks into insignificance before that wisdom which points out the way cast up for the ransomed of the Lord to walk in. The Bible alone affords the means of distinguishing the path of life from the broad road that leads to perdition and death.--Review and Herald, Dec. 15, 1891.

The Relation of Education to the Work of God

Say not ye, There are yet four months, and then cometh harvest? Behold, I say unto you, Lift up your eyes, and look on the fields; for they are white already to harvest. And he that reapeth receiveth wages, and gathereth fruit unto life eternal; that both he that soweth and he that reapeth may rejoice together."

There is a great dearth of laborers to go forth into missionary fields, endowed with the true missionary spirit, ready to shed forth the light of truth amid the moral darkness of the world. The enemies of God are daily plotting for the suppression of the truth, and the enslaving of the souls of men. They are seeking to exalt the false Sabbath, and by fastening men in error, deepen the darkness that covers the earth, and the gross darkness that covers the people. In a time like this, shall those who know the truth be inactive, and allow the powers of darkness to prevail? Shall not those who believe the truth for this time be wide awake, and work with an energy consistent with the profession of faith they make? Shall not those who understand the truth of God make every sacrifice to win souls to Christ, to yield allegiance to the law of God? The day is far spent, the night is at hand, and it is essential to work while it is day; for the night cometh, in which no man can work. In a time like this, we should have but this object in view,--the employing of every means that God has provided by which the truth may be planted in the hearts of men. It is for this very purpose that the word of God was sent to the world, that it might control the life, and transform the character. It is the duty of every Christian to strive to the utmost of his ability to spread abroad the knowledge of the truth. Christ has commissioned His disciples to go forth into all the world and preach the gospel to all nations.

With the great work before us of enlightening the world, we who believe the truth should feel the necessity of thorough education in the practical branches of knowledge, and especially our need of an education in the truths of the Scriptures. Error of every character is now exalted as truth, and it is our duty earnestly to search the sacred word, that we may know what is truth, and be able intelligently to present it to others. We shall be called upon to make known the reasons of our faith. We shall have to stand before magistrates to answer for our allegiance to the law of God. The Lord has called us out from the world that we may be witnesses for His truth; and all through our ranks, young men and women should be trained for positions of usefulness and influence. They are privileged to become missionaries for God; but they cannot be mere novices in education and in the knowledge of the word of God, and do justice to the sacred work to which they are appointed. In every land the want of education among our workers is painfully apparent. We realize that education is not only necessary to the proper fulfillment of the duties of domestic life, but necessary for success in all branches of usefulness.

In view of the need of education for the work of God, and for the successful fulfillment of the various responsibilities of life, how thankful should we be that a school is about to be opened in Melbourne under the direction of earnest believers in the truth for this time. For the success of this new enterprise, for the benefit it will bring to you and your children, let all our brethren and sisters now take hold heartily to cooperate with those who have come to bear the burden of the work. Teachers have come to you from America in the fear and love of God, not without sacrifice, to aid you in your efforts to lift up the standard of truth among the people. They desire to educate the youth to understand the word of God, that your children may be able to open the Scriptures to others. It now remains for those who have already been enlightened by the truth in these colonies, to co-operate with the efforts of their American brethren, knowing that in Christ all race prejudices, all national distinctions, are laid aside, and we are all brethren, engaged in the work of advancing the Redeemer's kingdom. We are all one in Christ, and should unite heartily in an effort to educate and train an army of young men and women in such a way that they will be consistent, well-balanced Christians, able to understand and explain the Scriptures. The purity, faith, zeal, and consistency of character in those who go forth to work for the Lord, should be so evident that others may see their good works, and be led to glorify our Father who is in heaven. If our profession of faith is sustained by heartfelt piety, it will be a means of good; for thereby souls will be influenced to comply with the terms of salvation. God designs that His grace should be made manifest in the believer, that through the Christlike character of individual members, the church may become the light of the world.

Let parents make every possible effort to send their children to the school that will soon open in Melbourne; for through this very means, it may be that members of your own family will be qualified of the Lord to become workers in His cause. There are many openings for missionaries in Australia, New Zealand, and the islands of the sea. And it will not be possible to supply laborers from America to fill all the many openings. Workers must be educated in these fields, who can take up the work, and go forth as light-bearers to the dark places of these lands. Not many can go to America to obtain an education; and even if they could go, it might not be best for them, or for the advancement of the work. The Lord would have schools established in this country to educate workers, to give character to the work of present truth in these new fields, and to awaken an interest in unbelievers. He would have you make a center for education in your own country, where students of promise may be educated in practical branches, and in the truths of the Bible, that they may be prepared to work in these lands, rescuing souls from the bondage of Satan. Teachers may come from America, until the work is fairly established, and by this means a new bond of union may be formed between America and Australia, New Zealand, and the islands of the sea.

There are youth in these countries whom God has graciously endowed with mental ability; but in order to do their best work, their powers must be properly directed. They should use their God-given talents for the attainment of high scholarship, becoming workmen that need not to be ashamed, rightly dividing the word of truth, wise unto salvation. This talent needs developing, and since a school is about to be established here, it certainly is not wisdom to send pupils at so great expense to America. The work is to be done here. This is missionary ground, and every individual who is thought worthy of the education that our American schools could give, should obtain an education right here on the ground of their future labors. Those who have ability can be trained here so that they can put their knowledge into practical use at the earliest opportunity, and become agents in the hands of the Lord for the dissemination of light and truth.

But were none of these responsibilities laid upon you, were there no missionary fields to enter, it would yet be necessary that your children should be educated. Whatever business parents might think suitable for their children, whether they desired them to become manufacturers, agriculturists, mechanics, or to follow some professional calling, they would reap great advantages from the discipline of an education. Your children should have an opportunity to study the Bible in the school. They need to be thoroughly furnished with the reasons of our faith, to understand the Scriptures for themselves. Through understanding the truths of the Bible, they will be better fitted to fill positions of trust. They will be fortified against the temptations that will beset them on the right hand and on the left. But if they are thoroughly instructed and consecrated, they may be called, as was Daniel, to fill important responsibilities. Daniel was a faithful statesman in the courts of Babylon; for he feared, loved, and trusted God; and in time of temptation and peril he was preserved by the power of God. We read that God gave Daniel wisdom, and endowed him with understanding.

Those who obtain a knowledge of God's will, and practice the teaching of His word, will be found faithful in whatever position of trust they may be placed. Consider this, parents, and place your children where they will be educated in the principles of truth, where every effort will be made to help them to maintain their consecration, if converted, or if unconverted, to influence them to become the children of God, and thus fit them to go forth to win others to the truth.

Let those who have the love of truth in their hearts, estimate the value of a soul for whom Christ has died, in the light reflected from the cross of Calvary. There are many who feel moved by the Spirit of God to go forth into the vineyard of the Lord. They long to seek and save that which is lost.

But because of lack of knowledge and discipline, they are not qualified to go forth to the work of elevating and ennobling their fellow men. Those who teach others must themselves be taught. They need to learn how to deal with human minds. They are to become colaborers with Christ, improving every opportunity to impart to men a knowledge of God. In order to be agents for God in the work of elevating men's minds from the earthly and sensual to the spiritual and heavenly, the workers must be educated and trained. By becoming learners themselves, they will better understand how to instruct others. They must acquire mental discipline, by putting into exercise their God-given ability, bringing the whole heart and mind to the task of acquiring knowledge. With the glory of God in view, they must put their whole energy into the work, learning all they can, and becoming intelligent, that they may impart knowledge to others.

There is a great work to be done in these countries; and the love of Christ, and love for souls for whom He has died, should constrain us to put forth every effort in our power to seek and to save that which was lost. Let everyone stand as a faithful soldier of Christ to work for and with your brethren, that the work may be a success in your hands. Let everyone who enlists in this much-needed enterprise remember that the school is established not merely for the benefit of ourselves and our children; but that the knowledge of the truth may be imparted, and perishing souls saved in the eternal kingdom. Let everyone take hold of this work, determined not to fail nor be discouraged, and the Lord will work wonders among us. If at this time we fail to make a determined effort to enlarge and uplift the work, and draw back because matters are not managed according to our own ideas, the Lord will surely pass us by, and choose other agencies who will take hold of His work in His way, and follow the leadings of His Spirit. O that everyone would do his duty, that our influence might be united to advance the cause of God!

The eye of God is upon these lands; for here He would set up His standard and unfurl His banner. Here on this missionary soil, He would see souls won to Jesus Christ. He would have every professed Christian a true missionary, ready to wheel into line, to do his individual work in his place, and all join in systematic effort. He would have men forget their own notions and prejudices, which bring only darkness and doubt upon their souls, and engage in work for those who are ready to perish. He would have them realize that no man liveth unto himself. It is through inattention to unselfish effort for others, that many have become dwarfed and crippled in their religious experience. Some who are in the background might have been far advanced in the knowledge of God, if they had not stood apart from their brethren, withdrawing from association with believers who did not work according to their limited ideas. O, if these hinderers would lose sight of themselves and interest themselves in the salvation of souls, their petty differences would be forgotten, and alienation from their brethren could not exist. If when they came together, they would not speak concerning the things to which they see objections, but would hold their mouth as with a bridle, and would seek the Lord in earnest prayer that His Holy Spirit might rest upon them, that they might have a burden for souls for whom Christ died, they would find that their darkness would flee away, and light and hope would come into their souls. Self-esteem would vanish, and they would become teachable as children. Stubbornness would melt away in contemplation of the love of God, and their hearts would glow, touched with a coal from off the altar. Sorrow would be banished, and cheerfulness take its place; for the infinite love and goodness of God would be the theme of their testimony.

Those who would be overcomers must be drawn out of themselves; and the only thing which will accomplish this great work, is to become intensely interested in the salvation of others. This does not mean that you are to convert men to your way of doing, or to compel them to view things in the same light as you do; but you are to seek to present the truth as it is in Jesus, and laboring to be a blessing to others, you will be blessed of God abundantly. That you have done and are doing something to enlarge the boundaries of the kingdom of God in rescuing poor souls from Satan's yoke of superstition and error, will rejoice the heart, and broaden your ideas and plans. As you identify your interest with that of Christ, you will sanctify to God your talent of ability, influence, and means. Some of you will consider it your privilege to leave your homes that you may labor in the islands of the sea, and rescue souls from the bondage of sin and error. As you gain a new and deeper experience, you will learn what it is to pray in the Holy Spirit; and those who are backslidden from God will be reclaimed, and there will be more anxiety manifested to learn of Jesus to be meek and lowly of heart, than to point out the mistakes and errors of your brethren; for by faith you accept Christ as your personal Saviour. You will not then come to meeting to tell your doubts and fears. You will have something better to talk about; for your hearts will be enlarged, having the peace of Christ, which passeth understanding. This is the experience that God would have you understand in this country.

But in order to reach this experience, definite steps must be taken. The methods and plans by which the work is to be done must be after the Lord's order, not after your individual ideas, and the results will more than compensate for the outlay. Missionary effort will become more general, and the example of one zealous worker, working in the right direction, will influence others, and they also will go forth to preach the gospel. The missionary spirit will pass from house to house, and the brethren will find something to talk about of more interest than their grievances. They will be interested in displaying the jewels of truth which the Bible contains, and churches will be established, meetinghouses erected, and many will come to the help of the Lord. The brethren will be united in bonds of love, and will realize their unity with experienced Christians in all parts of the world, as they are one in their plans, one in the object of their interest. An advance step taken by those at the head of the work will be felt by those in this country and in all lands, and those in foreign countries will respond to the effort made at the center of the work in following our great Leader; and so, through the conversion of souls to the truth, a volume of praise will rise to Him who sitteth upon the throne.

The missionary work in Australia and New Zealand is yet in its infancy; but the same work must be accomplished in Australia, New Zealand, in Africa, India, China, and the islands of the sea, as has been accomplished in the home field. Under the appropriate symbol of an angel flying through the midst of heaven is represented the work of the people of God. In this work heavenly intelligences co-operate with human agencies in extending the last message to the inhabitants of the world. But the plans and work of men are not keeping pace with the providence of God; for while some in these countries who claim to believe the truth declare by their attitude, "We want not Thy way, O Lord, but our own way," there are many who are pleading with God that they may understand what is truth. In secret places they are weeping and praying that they may see light in the Scriptures; and the Lord of heaven has commissioned His angels to co-operate with human agencies in carrying forward His vast design, that all who desire light may behold the glory of God. We are to follow where God's providence opens the way; and as we advance, we shall find that Heaven has moved before us, enlarging the field for labor far beyond the proportion of our means and ability to supply. The great want of the field open before us, should appeal to all to whom God has entrusted talents of means or ability, that they may devote themselves and their all to God. We are to be as faithful stewards, not only of our means, but of the grace given unto us, that many souls may be brought under the blood-stained banner of Prince Immanuel. The purposes and ends to be attained by consecrated missionaries are very comprehensive. The field for missionary operation is not limited by caste or nationality. The field is the world, and the light of truth is to go to all the dark places of the earth in a much shorter time than many think possible.

God purposes to set in operation agencies in your own country to aid in this great work of enlightening the world. He designs to employ you and your children as soldiers to act a part in this aggressive warfare against the powers of darkness, and you surely will not ignore God's blessing, and regard lightly the privilege extended to you! He would have you engage in the conflict, striving together for His glory, not seeking for the supremacy, not striving to exalt self by depreciating others. He would endow you with the true missionary spirit, which elevates, purifies, and ennobles whatever it touches, making pure and good and noble all who voluntarily come under its influence; for every agent who co-operates with the heavenly intelligences will be endued with power from on high, and represent the character of Christ. The missionary spirit enables us to appreciate more fully the words of the Lord's prayer, when He directs us to pray, "Thy kingdom come. Thy will be done in earth, as it is in heaven." The missionary spirit broadens our thoughts, and brings us into union with all who have a comprehension of the expanding influence of the Holy Spirit.

God would disperse the clouds that have gathered about souls in these colonies, and unite all our brethren in Christ Jesus. He would have us bound in bands of Christian fellowship, filled with love for souls for whom Christ has died. Said Christ, "This is My commandment, That ye love one another, as I have loved you." He would have us united in heart and plans to do the great work committed to us. Brethren should stand shoulder to shoulder, uniting their prayers at the throne of grace, that they may move the arm of the Omnipotent. Heaven and earth will then be closely connected in the work, and there will be joy and gladness in the presence of the angels of God, when the lost sheep is found and restored.

The Holy Spirit, that melts and subdues the human heart will lead men to do the works of Christ. They will heed the injunction, "Sell that ye have, and give alms; provide yourselves bags which wax not old, a treasure in the heavens that faileth not." Christ gave Himself for us, and His followers are required to give themselves, with their talents of means and ability, to Him. What more could the Lord do for man than that which He has done? And shall we not render unto Him all that we have and are, practicing self-sacrifice, and self-denial? If we are the disciples of Christ, it will be made manifest to the world through our love for those for whom He died.

It was through the spirit of love that the gospel was brought to you, and to all men who have a knowledge of God. We are required not merely to admire men whom God has used, to wish that we had such men now, but to yield ourselves to be used of God as His human agents. It was His Spirit that inspired their efforts, and He can abundantly bestow upon His workers today the same courage, zeal, earnestness, and devotion. It was Jesus who gave these men grace, power, fortitude, and perseverance, and He is willing to do the same for everyone who would be a true missionary.

God has begun to work in this country, and the church must unite with heavenly intelligences, manifesting holy activity, and by exercising their powers become more efficient to save souls and glorify God. We who have seen the light of truth, are called upon to aid in its advancement, to waken to the large responsibility of the missionary work to be accomplished in our borders; and it is the duty of every soul to co-operate with those who would advance the work. Let everyone seek to draw in even cords with Christ. Let us hide our ways in God's ways, that all variance may cease, that Christ's character may be represented in kindness, forbearance, self-denial, meekness, humility, and love. Let all join heartily to do the utmost of their ability to support the school that is now to be established; for in the hands of God it may be the means of educating workers to shed forth the light of truth upon the people. Who will be on the Lord's side? Who will now see the work to be done, and do it?--Supplement to The Bible Echo, Sept. 1, 1892.

The Need of Trained Workers

I have been deeply interested in the relation of a recent experience of Elder Daniells, who, on his way from Melbourne to Adelaide, stopped at a town called Nhill, to visit some young men who have been sending in orders to the Echo office for our papers and books. He found here a young man by the name of Hansen, a Dane, who chanced upon the Echo at a public library, and became an interested reader of the paper. The subjects of truth presented in its columns found a place in his heart, and he began to talk about them to a friend at the hotel where he was in service. This man, Mr. Williams, also became interested, and they sent in orders for other publications, becoming regular subscribers to the paper. Elder Daniells found them eager for a better knowledge of the truth. Upon the table of Mr. Williams was found "Thoughts on Daniel and the Revelation," and several other books published by our people. They had seen but one man who was of our faith. They bought from Elder Daniells three copies of "Steps to Christ," so that they might have one apiece, and another to give to a minister. Elder Daniells was pleased with his visit, and encouraged by his conversation with these inquirers after truth.

These men had studied the truth from the printed page and the Bible, and had accepted all points of doctrine as far as they could understand them without the aid of the living preacher. A great work is going silently on through the distribution of our publications; but what a great amount of good might be done if some of our brethren and sisters from America would come to these colonies, as fruit growers, farmers, or merchants, and in the fear and love of God, would seek to win souls to the truth. If such families were consecrated to God, He would use them as His agents. Ministers have their place and their work, but there are scores that the minister cannot reach, who might be reached by families who could visit with the people and impress upon them the truth for these last days. In their domestic or business relations they could come in contact with a class who are inaccessible to the minister, and they could open to them the treasures of the truth, and impart to them a knowledge of salvation. There is altogether too little done in this line of missionary work; for the field is large, and many workers could labor with success in this line of effort. If those who have received a knowledge of the truth had realized the necessity of studying the Scriptures for themselves, if they had felt the weight of responsibility that rests upon them, as faithful stewards of the grace of God, they would have brought light to many who sit in darkness, and what a harvest of souls would have been gathered for the Master. If each one realized his accountability to God for his personal influence, he would in no case be an idler, but would cultivate his ability, and train every power that he might serve Him who has purchased him with His own blood.

The youth especially should feel that they must train their minds, and take every opportunity to become intelligent, that they may render acceptable service to Him who has given His precious life for them. And let no one make the mistake of regarding himself as so well educated as to have no more need of studying books or nature. Let everyone improve every opportunity with which in the providence of God he is favored, to acquire all that is possible in revelation or science. We should learn to place the proper estimate on the powers that God has given us. If a youth has to begin at the lowest round of the ladder, he should not be discouraged, but be determined to climb round after round until he shall hear the voice of Christ saying, "Child, come up higher. Well done, thou good and faithful servant: thou hast been faithful over a few things, I will make thee ruler over many things: enter thou into the joy of thy Lord."

We are to compare our characters with the infallible standard of God's law. In order to do this, we must search the Scriptures, measuring our attainments by the word of God. Through the grace of Christ, the highest attainments in character are possible; for every soul who comes under the molding influence of the Spirit of God, may be transformed in mind and heart. In order to understand your condition, it is necessary to study the Bible, and to watch unto prayer. The apostle says, "Examine yourselves, whether ye be in the faith; prove your own selves. Know ye not your own selves, how that Jesus Christ is in you, except ye be reprobates?" Let not those who are ignorant remain in ignorance. They cannot remain in ignorance, and meet the mind of God. They are to look to the cross of Calvary, and estimate the soul by the value of the offering there made. Jesus says to all believers, "Ye are My witnesses." "Ye are laborers together with God." This being true, how earnestly should each one strive to make use of every power to improve every opportunity for becoming efficient that he may be "not slothful in business; fervent in spirit; serving the Lord."

Every talent that has been given to men is to be exercised that it may increase in value, and all the improvement must be rendered back to God. If you are defective in manner, in voice, in education, you need not always remain in this condition. You must continually strive that you may reach a higher standard both in education and in religious experience, that you may become teachers of good things. As servants of the great King, you should individually realize that you are under obligation to improve yourselves by observation, study, and by communion with God. The word of God is able to make you wise, to guide and make you perfect in Christ. The blessed Saviour was a faultless pattern for all His followers to imitate. It is the privilege of the child of God to understand spiritual things, to be able wisely to manage that which may be entrusted to his charge. God does not provide a way whereby anyone may have an excuse for doing slipshod work; and yet a great deal of this kind of work has been offered to Him by those who work in His cause, but it is not acceptable unto Him.

Young men and women, have you, as individuals purchased at infinite cost, sought to study to show yourselves approved unto God, workmen which need not be ashamed? Have you brought to God the precious talent of your voice, and put forth painstaking effort to speak clearly, distinctly, and readily? However imperfect may be your manner of utterance, you may correct your faults, and refuse to allow yourself to have a nasal tone, or to speak in a thick, indistinct way. If your articulation is distinct and intelligible, your usefulness will be greatly increased. Then do not leave one defective habit of speech uncorrected. Pray about the matter, and co-operate with the Holy Spirit that is working for your perfection. The Lord, who made man perfect in the beginning, will help you to cultivate your physical and mental powers, and fit you to bear burdens and responsibilities in the cause of God.

There are thousands today who are unqualified for the work of the ministry, who cannot take a position of sacred trust, and are lost to the cause, because they have failed to value the talents given them of God, and have not cultivated their powers of mind and body, so that they may fill positions of trust in the Master's work. Individually we are here as probationers, and the Lord is testing and proving our fidelity to Him.

He would employ us as agents to communicate the light of His word to the world. If we improved the light given us of God by diffusing it to others, we shall have increased light; for to him "that hath shall be given, and he shall have abundance: but from him that hath not shall be taken away even that which he hath." It is at our own option as to what we shall do with the light God has given. We may walk in it, or refuse to follow in the steps of Christ, and thus extinguish our light.

Considering the light that God has given, it is marvelous that there are not scores of young men and women inquiring, "Lord, what wilt Thou have me to do?" It is a perilous mistake to imagine that unless a young man has decided to give himself to the ministry, no special effort is required to fit him for the work of God. Whatever may be your calling, it is essential that you improve your abilities by diligent study. Young men and women should be urged to appreciate the heaven-sent blessings of opportunities to become well disciplined and intelligent. They should take advantage of the schools that have been established for the purpose of imparting the best of knowledge. It is sinful to be indolent and negligent in regard to obtaining an education. Time is short, and therefore because the Lord is soon to come to close the scenes of earth's history, there is all the greater necessity of improving present opportunities and privileges.

Young men and young women should place themselves in our schools, in the channel where knowledge and discipline may be obtained. They should consecrate their ability to God, become diligent Bible students, that they may be fortified against erroneous doctrine, and not be led away by the error of the wicked; for it is by diligent searching of the Bible that we obtain a knowledge of what is truth. But the practice of the truth we already know, increased light will shine upon us from the holy Scriptures. As we surrender our will to the will of God, as we humble our hearts before Him, we shall earnestly desire to become colaborers with Him, going forth to save those who perish. Those who are truly consecrated to God will not enter the work prompted by the same motive which leads men to engage in worldly business, merely for the sake of a livelihood, but they will enter the work allowing no worldly consideration to control them, realizing that the cause of God is sacred.

The world is to be warned, and no soul should rest satisfied with a superficial knowledge of truth. You know not to what responsibility you may be called. You know not where you may be called upon to give your witness of truth. Many will have to stand in the legislative courts; some will have to stand before kings and before the learned of the earth, to answer for their faith. Those who have only a superficial understanding of truth will not be able clearly to expound the Scriptures, and give definite reasons for their faith. They will become confused, and will not be workmen that need not to be ashamed. Let no one imagine that he has no need to study, because he is not to preach in the sacred desk. You know not what God may require of you. It is a lamentable fact that the advancement of the cause is hindered by the dearth of educated laborers who have fitted themselves for positions of trust. The Lord will accept of thousands to labor in His great harvest field, but many have failed to fit themselves for the work. But everyone who has espoused the cause of Christ, who has offered himself as a soldier in the Lord's army, should place himself where he may have faithful drill. Religion has meant altogether too little to the professed followers of Christ; for it is not the will of God that anyone should remain ignorant when wisdom and knowledge have been placed within reach.

How few have qualified themselves in the science of saving souls! How few understand the work that should be done in building up the church, in communicating light to those who sit in darkness! Yet God has given to every man his work. We are to work out our own salvation with fear and trembling; for it is God that worketh in us, both to will and to do of His good pleasure. In the work of salvation there is a co-operation of human and divine agencies. There is much said concerning the inefficiency of human effort, and yet the Lord does nothing for the salvation of the soul without the co-operation of man. The word of God is clear and distinct on this point, and yet when so much depends upon our co-operation with the heavenly agencies, men conduct themselves as though they could afford to set aside the claims of God, and let the things of eternal importance wait their convenience. They act as though they could manage spiritual things to suit themselves, and they place eternal interests in subordination to earthly and temporal matters. But how presumptuous is this to deal thus with that which is most essential, and most easily lost.

Where are those who would be wise laborers together with God? The apostle says, "Ye are God's husbandry, ye are God's building." But will men trust that they may be able under pressure of circumstances to step into some important position, when they have neglected to train and discipline themselves for the work? Will they imagine that they may be polished instruments in the hands of God for the salvation of souls for whom Christ died, when they have neglected to use the opportunities placed at their command for obtaining a fitness for the work? "We wrestle not against flesh and blood, but against principalities, against powers, against the rulers of the darkness of this world, against spiritual wickedness in high places. Wherefore take unto you the whole armor of God, that ye may be able to withstand in the evil day, and having done all, to stand." Everyone needs to improve his God-given faculties and opportunities, that individually we may be laborers together with God.

God is continually working for us that we may come behind in no gift. He has given us our physical, mental, and moral powers, and if we improve as we should, we shall be able to meet the supernatural powers of darkness and conquer them. Jesus has pointed out the way of life, He has made manifest the light of truth, He has given the Holy Spirit, and endowed us richly with everything essential to our perfection. But these advantages are not acknowledged, and we overlook our privileges and opportunities, and fail to co-operate with the heavenly intelligences, and thus fail to become noble, intelligent workers for God. Those to whom their own way looks more attractive than does the way of the Lord, cannot be used in His service, for they would misrepresent the character of Christ, and lead souls away from acceptable service to God.

Those who work for the Master must be well-disciplined, that they may stand as faithful sentinels. They must be men and women who will carry out the plans of God for the wise improvement of the minds of those who come under their influence. They must unite with all the agencies who are seeking to fulfill the will of God in saving a lost world. Christ has given Himself, the just for the unjust, He has died on Calvary's cross, and He has entrusted to human agencies the work of completing the great measure of redeeming love; for man co-operates with God in His effort to save the perishing. In the neglected duties of the church we read the retarding of the fulfillment of the purpose of God; but if men fail to accomplish their work, it would be better had they never been born. Great evil will follow the neglect of co-operating with God; for eternal life will be lost. Our success as candidates for heaven will depend on our earnestness in fulfilling the conditions upon which eternal life is granted. We must receive and obey the word of God, we cannot be idlers, and float with the current. We must be diligent students of the word of God. We must train and educate ourselves as good soldiers of Christ. We must advance the work, becoming laborers together with God.--Review and Herald, February 14, 1893.

To Teachers and Students

To the Teachers and Students in Our College at Battle Creek, and in All Our Educational Institutions

In the night seasons messages have been given to me to give to you in Battle Creek, and to all our schools. While it is in the order of God that the physical powers shall be trained as well as the mental, yet the physical exercise should in character be in complete harmony with the lessons given by Jesus Christ to His disciples. That which is given to the world should be seen in the lives of Christians, so that in education and in self-training the heavenly intelligences should not record in the books that the students and the teachers in our schools are "lovers of pleasures more than lovers of God." This is the record now being made of a large number. "Lovers of pleasures more than lovers of God." Thus Satan and his angels are laying their snares for your souls, and he is working in a certain way upon teachers and pupils to induce them to engage in exercises and amusements which become intensely absorbing, but which are of a character to strengthen the lower powers, and create appetites and passions that will take the lead, and counteract most decidedly the operations and working of the Holy Spirit of God upon the human heart.

What saith the Holy Spirit to you? What was its power and influence upon your hearts during the General Conference, and the Conferences in other states? Have you taken special heed to yourselves? Have the teachers in the school felt that they must take heed? If God has appointed them as educators of the youth, they are also "overseers of the flock." They are not in the school work to invent plans for exercises and games to educate pugilists; not there to bring down sacred things on a level with the common.

I was speaking to the teachers in messages of reproof. All the teachers need exercise, a change of employment. God has pointed out that this should be useful, practical work; but you have turned away from God's plan, to follow human inventions, and that to the detriment of spiritual life. Not a jot or tittle of the after-influence of an education in that line will fit you to meet the severe conflicts in these last days. What kind of education are our teachers and students receiving? Has God devised and planned this kind of exercise for you, or is it brought in by the human inventions and human imaginations? How is the mind prepared for contemplation and meditation, and serious thoughts, and the earnest, contrite prayer, coming from hearts subdued by the Holy Spirit of God? "As it was in the days of Noe, so shall it be also in the days of the Son of Man." "And God saw that the wickedness of man was great in the earth, and that every imagination of the thoughts of his heart was only evil continually."

The Lord opened before me the necessity of establishing a school at Battle Creek that should not pattern after any school in existence. We were to have teachers who would keep their souls in the love and fear of God. Teachers were to educate in spiritual things, to prepare a people to stand in the trying crisis before us; but there has been a departure from God's plan in many ways. The amusements are doing more to counteract the working of the Holy Spirit than anything else, and the Lord is grieved.

"Wash you, make you clean; put away the evil of your doings from before Mine eyes; cease to do evil [but do not rest here; move onward in following the Light of the world]; learn to do well; seek judgment, relieve the oppressed, judge the fatherless, plead for the widow. Come now, and let us reason together, saith the Lord: though your sins be as scarlet, they shall be as white as snow; though they be red like crimson, they shall be as wool." Here is your field in which to exercise your intellect and give you change of exercise. "If ye be willing and obedient, ye shall eat the good of the land."

How is the faithful city become an harlot! it was full of judgment; righteousness lodged in it; but now murderers. Thy silver is become dross, thy wine mixed with water: thy princes are rebellious, and companions of thieves: everyone loveth gifts, and followeth after rewards: they judge not the fatherless, neither doth the cause of the widow come unto them."

"O house of Jacob, come ye, and let us walk in the light of the Lord." "Cease ye from man, whose breath is in his nostrils: for wherein is he to be accounted of?" "Put not your trust in princes, nor in the son of man, in whom there is no help. His breath goeth forth, he returneth to his earth; in that very day his thoughts perish. Happy is he that hath the God of Jacob for his help, whose hope is in the Lord his God." "O my people, they which lead thee cause thee to err, and destroy the way of thy paths."

I am alarmed for you at Battle Creek. Teachers are very exact in visiting with denunciation and punishments those students who violate the slight rules, not from any vicious purpose, but heedlessly; or circumstances occur which make it no sin for them to deviate from rules which have been made, and which should not be held with inflexibility if transgressed, and yet the person in fault is treated as if he had grievously sinned. Now I want you to consider, teachers, where you stand, and deal with yourselves and pronounce judgment against yourselves; for you have not only infringed the rules, but you have been so sharp, so severe upon students; and more than this, there is a controversy between you and God. You have not made straight paths for your feet lest the lame be turned out of the way. You have departed from safe paths. I say "teachers"; I do not specify names. I leave that to your own consciences to appropriate. The Lord God of Israel has wrought in your midst again and again. You have had great evidences of the stately steppings of the Most High. But a period of great light, of the wonderful revealings of the Spirit and power of God, is a period of great peril, lest the light shall not be improved. Will you consider

Jeremiah 17:5-10; 18:12-15? For you are most surely coming under the rebuke of God. Light has been shining in clear and steady rays upon you. What has this light done for you? Christ, the Chief Shepherd, is looking upon you with displeasure, and is inquiring, "Where is the flock that was given thee, thy beautiful flock?" "Wherefore I take you to record this day, that I am pure from the blood of all men. For I have not shunned to declare unto you all the counsel of God. Take heed therefore unto yourselves, and to all the flock, over which the Holy Ghost hath made you overseers, to feed the church of God, which He hath purchased with His own blood." "Feed the flock of God which is among you, taking the oversight thereof, not by constraint, but willingly; not for filthy lucre, but of a ready mind."

Those teachers who have not a progressive religious experience, who are not learning daily lessons in the school of Christ, that they may be ensamples to the flock, but who accept their wages as the main thing, are not fit for the solemn, awfully solemn, position they occupy. For this scripture is appropriate to all our schools established as God designed they should be, after the order or example of the schools of the prophets, imparting a higher class of knowledge--mingling not dross with the silver, and wine with water--which is a representation of precious principles. False ideas and unsound practices are leavening the pure, and corrupting that which should ever be kept pure, and looked upon by the world, by angels, and by men, as the Lord's institution--schools where the education to love and fear God is made first. "And this is life eternal, that they might know Thee the only true God, and Jesus Christ, whom Thou hast sent." "Neither as being lords over God's heritage, but being ensamples to the flock."

Let the teachers who claim to be Christians be learning daily in the school of Christ His lessons. "Take my yoke upon you, and learn of Me; for I am meek and lowly in heart: and ye shall find rest unto your souls." I ask you, Is every educator in the school wearing the yoke of Christ, or manufacturing yokes of his own to place upon the necks of others, yokes which they themselves will not wear, sharp, severe, exacting; and this, too, while they are carrying themselves very loosely toward God, offending every day in little and larger matters, and making it evident in words, in spirit, and in actions, that they are not a proper example for the students, and are not having a sense that they are under discipline to the greatest Teacher the world ever knew? There needs to be a higher, holier mold on the school in Battle Creek, and on other schools which have taken their mold from it. The customs and practices of the Battle Creek school go forth to all the churches, and the pulse heartbeats of that school are felt throughout the body of believers.

It is not in God's order that thousands of dollars shall be expended in enlargements and additions in institutions in Battle Creek. There is altogether too much there now. Take that extra means and establish the work in suffering portions of other fields, to give character to the work. I have spoken the word of God upon this point. There are reasons many do not see, that I have no liberty to open before you now; but I tell you in the name of the Lord, you will make a mistake in your adding building to building; for there are being centered in Battle Creek responsibilities that are altogether too much for one location. If these responsibilities were divided and placed in other localities, it would be far better than crowding so much into Battle Creek, robbing other destitute fields of the advantages God would have them privileged with.

There are too many lords in the school who love to rule over God's heritage. There is altogether too little of Christ and too much of self. But those who are under the dictation of the Spirit of God, who are under rule to Christ, are ensamples to the flock; and when the Chief Shepherd shall appear, they shall receive a crown of glory that fadeth not away.

"Likewise, ye younger, submit yourselves unto the elder. Yea, all of you be subject one to another, and be clothed with humility: for God resisteth the proud, and giveth grace to the humble. Humble yourselves therefore under the mighty hand of God, that He may exalt you in due time." All your self-uplifting works out the natural result, and makes you in character such as God will not for a moment approve. "Without Me," says Christ, "ye can do nothing." Work and teach, work in Christ's lines, and then you will never work in your own weak ability, but will have the co-operation of the divine, combined with the God-given human ability. "Casting all your care upon Him; for He careth for you. Be sober, be vigilant" [not in kicking football and in educating yourselves in the objectionable games which ought to make every Christian blush with mortification at the afterthoughts] "be sober, be vigilant; because your adversary the devil, as a roaring lion, walketh about, seeking whom he may devour." Yes, he is on your playground watching your amusements, catching every soul that he finds off his guard, sowing his seeds in human minds, and controlling the human intellect. For Christ's sake call a halt at the Battle Creek College, and consider the after-workings upon the heart and the character and principles, of these amusements copied after the fashion of other schools. You have been steadily progressing in the ways of the Gentiles, and not after the example of Jesus Christ. Satan is on the schoolground; he is present in every exercise in the schoolroom. The students that have had their minds deeply excited in their games, are not in the best condition to receive the instruction, the counsel, the reproof, most essential for them in this life and for the future immortal life.

Of Daniel and his fellows the Scripture states: "As for these four children, God gave them knowledge and skill in all learning and wisdom: and Daniel had understanding in all visions and dreams." In what manner are you fitting yourselves to co-operate with God? "Draw nigh to God, and He will draw nigh to you." "Resist the devil, and he will flee from you." Let the diet be carefully studied; it is not healthful. The various little dishes concocted for desserts are injurious instead of helpful and healthful, and from the light given me, there should be a decided change in the preparation of food. There should be a skillful, thorough cook, that will give ample supplies of substantial dishes to the hungry students. The education in this line of table supplies is not correct, healthful, or satisfying, and a decided reform is essential. These students are God's inheritance, and the most sound and healthful principles are to be brought into the boarding-school in regard to diet. The dishes of soft foods, the soups and liquid foods, or the free use of meat, are not the best to give healthful muscles, sound digestive organs, or clear brains. O how slow we are to learn! And of all institutions in our world the school is the most important! Here the diet question is to be studied; no one person's appetite, or tastes, or fancy or notion is to be followed; but there is need of great reform; for lifelong injury will surely be the result of the present manner of cooking. Of all the positions of importance in that college, the first is that of the one who is employed to direct in the preparation of the dishes to be placed before the hungry students; for if this work is neglected, the mind will not be prepared to do its work, because the stomach has been treated unwisely and cannot do its work properly. Strong minds are needed. The human intellect must gain expansion and vigor and acuteness and activity. It must be taxed to do hard work, or it will become weak and inefficient. Brain power is required to think most earnestly; it must be put to the stretch to solve hard problems and master them, else the mind decreases in power and aptitude to think. The mind must invent, work, and wrestle, in order to give hardness and vigor to the intellect; and if the physical organs are not kept in the most healthful condition by substantial, nourishing food, the brain does not receive its portion of nutrition to work. Daniel understood this, and he brought himself to a plain, simple, nutritious diet, and refused the luxuries of the king's table. The desserts which take so much time to prepare, are, many of them, detrimental to health. Solid foods requiring mastication will be far better than mush or liquid foods. I dwell upon this as essential. I send my warning to the College at Battle Creek, to go from there to all our institutions of learning. Study up on these subjects, and let the students obtain a proper education in the preparation of wholesome, appetizing, solid foods that nourish the system. They do not have now, and have not had in the past, the right kind of training and education as to the most healthful food to make healthful sinews and muscle, and give nourishment to the brain and nerve powers.

The intellect is to be kept thoroughly awake with new, earnest, whole-hearted work. How is it to be done? The power of the Holy Spirit must purify the thoughts and cleanse the soul of its moral defilement. Defiling habits not only abase the soul, but debase the intellect. Memory suffers, laid on the altar of base, hurtful practices. "He that soweth to his flesh shall of the flesh reap corruption; but he that soweth to the Spirit shall of the Spirit reap life everlasting." When teachers and learners shall consecrate soul, body, and spirit of God, and purify their thoughts by obedience to the laws of God, they will continually receive a new endowment of physical and mental power. Then will there be heart-yearnings after God, and earnest prayer for clear perception to discern. The office and work of the Holy Spirit is not for them to use it, as many suppose, but for the Holy Spirit to use them, molding, fashioning, and sanctifying every power. The giving of the faculties to lustful practices disorders the brain and nerve power, and though professing religion, they are not now and never will be agents whom God can use; for He despises the practices of impurity, which destroy the vital nerve energies. This sin of impurity is lessening physical vigor and mental capabilities, so that everything like mental taxation will after a short time become irksome. Memory is fitful; and, O what a loathsome offering is thus presented to God!

Then when I look upon the scenes presented before me; when I consider the schools established in different places, and see them falling so far below anything like the schools of the prophets, I am distressed beyond measure. The physical exercise was marked out by the God of wisdom. Some hours each day should be devoted to useful education in lines of work that will help the students in learning the duties of practical life, which are essential for all our youth. But this has been dropped out, and amusements introduced, which simply give exercise, without being any special blessing in doing good and righteous actions, which is the education and training essential.

The students, everyone, need a most thorough education in practical duties. The time employed in physical exercise, which, step by step, leads on to excess, to intensity in the games and the exercise of the faculties, ought to be used in Christ's lines, and the blessing of God would rest upon them in so doing. All should go forth from the schools with educated efficiency, so that when thrown upon their own resources, they would have a knowledge they could use which is essential to practical life. The seeking out of many inventions to employ the God-given faculties most earnestly in doing nothing good, nothing you can take with you in future life, no record of good deeds, of merciful actions, stands registered in the book of heaven,--"Weighed in the balances and found wanting."

Diligent study is essential, and diligent hard work. Play is not essential. The influence has been growing among students in their devotion to amusements, to a fascinating, bewitching power, to the counteracting of the influence of the truth upon the human mind and character. A well-balanced mind is not usually obtained in the devotion of the physical powers to amusements. Physical labor that is combined with mental taxation for usefulness, is a discipline in practical life, sweetened always by the reflection that it is qualifying and educating the mind and body better to perform the work God designs men shall do in various lines. The more perfectly youth understand how to perform the duties of practical life, the more keen and the more healthful will be their enjoyment day by day in being of use to others.

The mind thus educated to enjoy physical taxation in practical life becomes enlarged, and through culture and training, well disciplined and richly furnished for usefulness, and acquires a knowledge essential to be a help and blessing to themselves and to others. Let every student consider, and be able to say, I study, I work, for eternity. They can learn to be patiently industrious and persevering in their combined efforts of physical and mental labor. What force of powers is put into your games of football and your other inventions after the way of the Gentiles--exercises which bless no one! Just put the same powers into exercise in doing useful labor, and would not your record be more pleasing to meet in the great day of God?

Whatever is done under the sanctified stimulus of Christian obligation, because you are stewards in trust of talents to use to be a blessing to yourself and to others, gives you substantial satisfaction; for all is done to the glory of God. I cannot find an instance in the life of Christ where He devoted time to play and amusement. He was the great Educator for the present and the future life. I have not been able to find one instance where He educated His disciples to engage in amusement of football or pugilistic games, to obtain physical exercise, or in theatrical performances; and yet Christ was our pattern in all things. Christ, the world's Redeemer, gave to every man his work and bids them "occupy till I come." And in doing His work, the heart warms to such an enterprise, and all the powers of the soul are enlisted in a work assigned of the Lord and Master. It is a high and important work. The Christian teacher and student are enabled to become stewards of the grace of Christ, and be always in earnest.

All they can do for Jesus is to be in earnest, having a burning desire to show their gratitude to God in the most diligent discharge of every obligation that is laid upon them, that, by their fidelity to God, they may respond to the great and wonderful gift of the only-begotten Son of God, that through faith in Him they should not perish, but have everlasting life.

There is need of each one in every school and in every institution, being, as was Daniel, in such close connection with the Source of all wisdom, that his prayers will enable him to reach the highest standard of his duties in every line, that he may be able to fulfill his scholastic requirements not only under able teachers, but also under the supervision of heavenly intelligences, knowing that the All-seeing, the Ever-sleepless Eye was upon him. The love and fear of God was before Daniel, and he educated and trained all his powers to respond as far as possible to the loving care of the Great Teacher, conscious of his amenability to God. The four Hebrew children would not allow selfish motives and love of amusements to occupy the golden moments of this life. They worked with a willing heart and ready mind. This is no higher standard than every Christian may attain. God requires of every Christian scholar more than has been given him. Ye are "a spectacle unto the world, and to angels, and to men."--"Special Testimonies on Education," October, 1893.

The Best Education and Its Purpose

The best education that can be given to children and youth is that which bears the closest relation to the future, immortal life. This kind of education should be given by godly parents, by devoted teachers, and by the church, to the end that the youth in turn may become zealous missionaries for either home or foreign fields. They are to be earnestly instructed in the truths of the Bible, that they may become pillars in the church, champions for truth, rooted and grounded in the faith. They are to know whereof they believe, and to have such an experience in divine things that they will never become betrayers of sacred trusts.

The youth should be educated by precept and example that they are to be agents for God, messengers of mercy, ready for every good word and work, that they are to be blessings to those who are ready to perish. We are in great need of educated ability, and the talents entrusted to our youth should be consecrated to the service of God, and employed in His work. There should be men and women who are qualified to work in the churches and to train our young people for special lines of work, that souls may be brought to see Jesus. The schools established by us should have in view this object, and not be after the order of the denominational schools established by other churches, or after the order of worldly seminaries and colleges. They are to be of an altogether higher order, where no phase of infidelity shall be originated, or countenanced. The students are to be educated in practical Christianity, and the Bible must be regarded as the highest, the most important textbook.

There is a great demand in all parts of the world for Christian teachers and for medical missionaries. In all parts of the field both at home and abroad, are open doors for those who can do good to body and soul, presenting the precious light of truth. The past neglect in this direction must not be perpetuated. Great light has shone upon our pathway in some directions more than others, and yet our advance along these very lines has been far behind the light we have had. Many of our most promising young men and women have offered their best ability at the shrine of idols, and have given themselves as a sacrifice to the prince of evil. O that the youth in our schools, one and all, might yield to the precious strivings of the Spirit of the Lord, that they might know the indications of His providence, and wait upon God, that they might know and do His will! In this way they would open the door of the heart to Jesus.

In surrendering ourselves to God, we reap great advantages; for if we have weaknesses of character, as we all have, we unite ourselves to One who is mighty to save. Our ignorance will be united to infinite wisdom, our frailty to enduring might, and, like Jacob, we may each become a prince with God. Connected with the Lord God of Israel, we shall have power from above which will enable us to be overcomers; and by the impartation of divine love, we shall find access to the hearts of men. We shall have fastened our trembling grasp upon the throne of the Infinite, and shall say, "I will not let Thee go, except Thou bless me." The assurance is given that He will bless us and make us a blessing; and this is our light, our joy, our triumph. When the youth understand what it is to have the favor and love of God in the heart, they will begin to realize the value of their blood-bought privileges, and will consecrate their ability to God, and strive with all their God-given powers to increase their talents to use in the Master's service.

The only safety for our youth in this age of sin and crime is to have a living connection with God. They must learn how to seek God, that they may be filled with His Holy Spirit, and act as though they realized that the whole host of heaven was looking upon them with interested solicitude, ready to minister unto them in danger and in time of need. The youth should be barricaded by warning and instruction against temptation. They should be taught what are the encouragements held out to them in the word of God. They should have delineated before them the peril of taking a step into the by-paths of evil. They should be educated to revere the counsels of God in His sacred oracles. They should be so instructed that they will set their resolution against evil, and determine that they will not enter into any path where they could not expect Jesus to accompany them, and His blessing to abide upon them. They should be taught practical, daily religion that will sanctify them in every relation of life, in their homes, in business, in the church, in society. They must be so educated that they will realize that it is a perilous thing to trifle with their privileges, but that God expects them reverently and earnestly to seek daily for His blessing. The blessing of God is a precious gift, and it is to be counted of such worth that it will not be surrendered at any cost. The blessing of God maketh rich, and it addeth no sorrow.

My heart is stirred to its depths as I read of the prostitution of noble powers to the service of Satan. In governmental departments, in positions of high responsibility, in official trusts, men are tempted by the evil one; and corruption and crime, embezzlements, robberies, and extortions are the result. There are terrible sinks of corruption, pouring out upon our world poisonous influences that corrupt the community. In every place Satan has set his traps that he may catch men of education, of good natural endowments, men who are capable of becoming laborers together with God, companions of angels, inhabitants of heaven, that he may bind them to his car as his slaves. And yet Jesus has ransomed them from the bondage of the enemy, and they refuse to be at liberty, and will not become the sons of God, heirs of God, and joint heirs with Jesus Christ to an immortal inheritance. They live as though the earth, money, position, houses, and lands were the main objects of their creation. Through the tender mercy of God their life is prolonged; but is it not a pitiable sight to see men of high ability living on so low a plane?

The Best Education and Its Purpose

The ransom has been paid, and it is possible for all to come to God, and through a life of obedience to attain unto everlasting life. Then how sad it is that men turn from the immortal inheritance, and live for the gratification of pride, for selfishness and display, and through submission to the rule of Satan, lose the blessing which they might have both in this life and in the life to come. They might enter into the palaces of heaven, and associate on terms of freedom and equality with Christ and heavenly angels, and with the princes of God; and yet, incredible as it may seem, they turn from heavenly attractions. The Creator of all worlds proposes to love those who believe in His only-begotten Son as their personal Saviour, even as He loves His Son. Even here and now His gracious favor is bestowed upon us to this marvelous extent. He has given to men the gift of the Light and Majesty of heaven, and with Him He has bestowed all the treasures of heaven. Much as He has promised us for the life to come, He also bestows princely gifts upon us in this life, and as subjects of His grace, He would have us enjoy everything that will ennoble, expand, and elevate our characters. It is His design to fit us for the heavenly courts above.

But Satan is contending for the souls of men, and casts his hellish shadow athwart their path, in order that they shall not behold the light. He would not have them catch a glimpse of the future honor, the eternal glories, laid up for those who shall be inhabitants of heaven, or have a taste of the experience that gives a foretaste of the happiness of heaven. But with the heavenly attractions set before the mind to inspire hope, to awaken desire, to spur to effort, how can we turn from the prospect, and choose sin and its wages, which is death?

Those who accept Christ as their Saviour have the promise of the life that now is, and that which is to come. The human agent owes no part of his ability to the service of Satan; but his entire allegiance is due to the infinite and eternal God. The lowliest disciple of Christ may become an inhabitant of heaven, an heir of God to an inheritance incorruptible, and that fadeth not away. O that everyone might make choice of the heavenly gift, become an heir of God to that inheritance whose title is secure from any destroyer, world without end! O, choose not the world, but choose the better inheritance! Press, urge your way toward the mark for the prize of your high calling in Christ Jesus. For Christ's sake, let the aim of your education be shaped by the inducements of the better world.--Review and Herald, Nov. 21, 1893.

Christ as Teacher

For His own wise purpose the Lord veils spiritual truths in figures and symbols. Through the use of figures of speech the plainest and most telling rebuke was often given to His accusers and enemies, and they could find in His words no occasion to condemn Him. In parables and comparisons He found the best method of communicating divine truth. In simple language, using figures and illustrations drawn from the natural world, He opened spiritual truth to His hearers, and gave expression to precious principles that would have passed from their minds, and left scarcely a trace, had He not connected His words with stirring scenes of life, experience, or nature. In this way He called forth their interest, aroused inquiry, and when He had fully secured their attention, He decidedly impressed upon them the testimony of truth. In this way He was able to make sufficient impression upon the heart so that afterward His hearers could look upon the thing with which He connected His lesson, and recall the words of the divine Teacher.

The teaching of Jesus was of an entirely different order from that of the learned scribes. They professed to be expositors of the law, both written and traditional. But the formal tone of their instruction would indicate that they saw nothing in the doctrines of the sacred oracles which possessed vital power. They presented nothing new, uttered no words that reached the longing of the soul. They offered no food for the hungry sheep and lambs. Their custom was to dwell upon the obscurities of the law, and the result of their reasoning was a jargon of absurdities, which neither the learned could fathom nor the common people understand.

Christ came to unveil divine truth to the world. He taught as one having authority. He spake as never man spake. There was no hesitancy in His manner, not the shadow of a doubt in His utterances. He spake as one who understood every part of His subject. He could have opened mysteries which patriarchs and prophets desired to look into, which human curiosity had been impatiently desirous of understanding. But when men could not discern the most simple, plainly stated truths, how could they understand mysteries which were hid from mortal eyes? Jesus did not disdain to repeat old, familiar truths; for He was the author of these truths. He was the glory of the temple. Truths which had been lost sight of, which had been misplaced, misinterpreted, and disconnected from their pure position, He separated from the companionship of error; and showing them as precious jewels in their own bright luster, He reset them in their proper framework, and commanded them to stand fast forever. What a work was this! It was of such a character that no finite man could comprehend or do it. Only the divine Hand could take the truth which, from its connection with error, had been serving the cause of the enemy of God and man, and place it where it would glorify God, and be the salvation of humanity. The work of Christ was to give again to the world the truth in its original freshness and beauty. He represented the spiritual and the heavenly, by the things of nature and experience. He gave fresh manna to the hungry soul, presented a new kingdom which was to be set up among men.

The Jewish rabbis presented the requirements of the law as a wearing round of exactions. They did just what Satan is doing in our day,--presented the law before the people as a cold, rigid code of commands and traditions. Superstitions buried the light, the glory, the dignity, and far-reaching claims of the law of God. They professed to speak to the people in the place of God. After the transgression of Adam, the Lord spoke no longer directly with man; the human race was given into the hands of Christ, and all communication came through Him to the world. It was Christ who spoke the law on Mount Sinai, and He knew the bearing of all its precepts, the glory and majesty of the law of heaven. In His sermon on the mount, Christ defines the law, and seeks to inculcate in the minds of His hearers the far-reaching claims of the precepts of Jehovah. His instructions came as a new revelation to the people; and the teachers of the law, the scribes and the Pharisees, as well as the common people, were astonished at His doctrine. The words of Christ were not new, and yet they came with the force of revelation; for they presented the truth in its proper light, and not in the light in which the teachers had set it before the people. He showed no regard for the traditions and commandments of men, but opened the eyes of their understanding to behold wondrous things out of the law of God, which is the foundation of His throne from the beginning of the world; and as long as the heavens and the earth remain, through the ceaseless ages of eternity, it will be the great standard of righteousness, holy and just and good.

The system of Jewish economy was the gospel in figure, a presentation of Christianity which was to be developed as fast as the minds of the people could comprehend spiritual light. Satan ever seeks to make obscure the truths that are plain, and Christ ever seeks to open the mind to comprehend every essential truth concerning the salvation of fallen man. To this day there are still aspects of truth which are dimly seen, connections that are not understood, and far-reaching depths in the law of God that are uncomprehended. There is immeasurable breadth, dignity, and glory in the law of God; and yet the religious world has set aside this law, as did the Jews, to exalt the traditions and commandments of men. Before the days of Christ, men asked in vain, "What is truth?" Darkness covered the earth, and gross darkness the people. Even Judea was shrouded in gloom, although the voice of God spoke to them in His oracles. The truth of God had been silenced by the superstition and traditions of its professed interpreters, and contention, jealousy, and prejudice divided the professed children of God. Then was a Teacher sent from God, even Him who was the Way, the Truth, and the Life. Jesus presented to view the pure, rich truth of heaven to shine amid the moral darkness and gloom of earth. God had said, "Let there be spiritual light," and the light of the glory of God was revealed in the face of Jesus Christ.

Christ was manifested as the Saviour of men. The people were not to trust in their own works, in their own righteousness, or in themselves in any way, but in the Lamb of God which taketh away the sins of the world. In Him the Advocate with the Father was revealed. Through Him the invitation was given, "Come now, and let us reason together, saith the Lord: though your sins be as scarlet, they shall be as white as snow; though they be red like crimson, they shall be as wool." This invitation comes sounding down along the lines to us today. Let not pride, or self-esteem, or self-righteousness keep anyone from confessing his sins, that he may claim the promise: "He that covereth his sins shall not prosper: but whoso confesseth and forsaketh them shall have mercy." Keep nothing back from God, and neglect not the confession of your faults to the brethren when they have a connection with them. "Confess your faults one to another, and pray one for another, that ye may be healed." Many a sin is left unconfessed, to be confronted in the day of final accounts; better far to see your sins now, to confess them, and put them away, while the atoning Sacrifice pleads in your behalf. Do not dislike to learn the will of God on this subject. The health of your soul, the unity of your brethren, may depend upon the course you pursue in these things. Humble yourselves, therefore, under the mighty hand of God, that He may exalt you in due time, "casting all your care upon Him; for He careth for you."

It is a lamentable fact that the erring heart is unwilling to be criticised, or to subject itself to humiliation by the confession of sin. Some see their faults, but thinking confession will detract from their dignity, they excuse their wrong, and shield themselves from the discipline that confession would give to the soul. The thought of their manifest error will remain to embitter their enjoyments and embarrass their movements; for in passing out of the path of confession, they fail to be faithful examples to the people. They see the errors of others; but how can they have courage to give the advice, "Confess your faults one to another, and pray one for another, that ye may be healed," when they have failed to follow this instruction in their own lives? How much will ministers or people learn of a truth which they thrust aside, and forget if possible, because it is not agreeable; because it does not flatter their pride, but reproves and pains? Ministers and people, if saved at all, must be saved day by day, hour by hour. They must hunger and thirst for the righteousness of Christ, the illumination of the Holy Spirit. Church members,--those placed in positions of trust,--must be baptized with the Spirit of God, or they will not be qualified for the positions they accept.

A man may have a knowledge of the Scriptures which will not make him wise unto salvation, although he may be able to master his opponents in public controversy. If he does not have a yearning of soul after God; if he does not search his own heart as with a lighted candle, fearing that any wrong should lurk there; if he is not possessed with a desire to answer the prayer of Christ, that His disciples may be one as He is one with the Father, that the world may believe that Jesus is the Christ,--he flatters himself in vain that he is a Christian. His knowledge, begun in ambition, is carried forward in pride; but his soul is destitute of the divine love, the gentleness and meekness of Christ. He is not a wise man in the sight of God. He may have wisdom to overcome an opponent; but wise unto salvation, he cannot possibly be without the agency of the Holy Spirit. And the "fruit of the Spirit is love, joy, peace, longsuffering, gentleness, goodness, faith, meekness, temperance." Neither talent, eloquence, nor selfish study of the Scriptures, will produce love to God or conformity to the image of Christ. Nothing but divine power can regenerate the human heart and character, and imbue the soul with the love of Christ, which will ever manifest itself in love to those for whom He died.--Review and Herald, Nov. 28, 1893.

The Education Most Essential for Gospel Workers

There are Christian workers who have not received a collegiate education because it was impossible for them to secure this advantage; but God has given evidence that He has chosen them. He has ordained them to go forth and labor in His vineyard. He has made them effectual co-workers with Himself. They have a teachable spirit; they feel their dependence upon God, and the Holy Spirit is with them to help their infirmities. It will quicken and energize the mind, direct their thoughts, and aid in the presentation of truth. When the laborer stands before the people to hold forth the words of life, there is heard in his voice the echo of the voice of Christ.

It is evident that he walks with God; that he has been with Jesus and learned of Him. He has brought the truth into the inner sanctuary of the soul; it is to him a living reality, and he presents the truth in the demonstration of the Spirit and of power. The people hear the joyful sound. God speaks to their hearts through the man consecrated to His service. As the worker lifts up Jesus through the Spirit, he becomes really eloquent. He is earnest and sincere, and is beloved by those for whom he labors.

What a sin would rest upon anyone who should listen to such a man merely to criticize, to notice bad grammar, or incorrect pronunciation, and hold these errors up to ridicule. The Pharisees scoffed at Christ; they criticized the simplicity of His language, which was so plain that the child, the aged, the common people heard Him gladly, and were charmed by His words. The Sadducees also derided Him because His discourses were so unlike anything delivered by their rulers and scribes. Those Jewish teachers spoke in monotonous tones, and the plainest and most precious scriptures were made uninteresting and unintelligible, buried under such a mass of tradition and learned lore that after the rabbis had spoken, the people knew less of the meaning of the Scriptures than before they listened. There were many souls starving for the Bread of Life, and Jesus fed them with pure, simple truth. In His teaching He drew illustrations from the things of nature and the common transactions of life, with which they were familiar. Thus the truth became to them a living reality; the scenes of nature and the affairs of daily life were ever repeating to them the Saviour's precious teachings. Christ's manner of teaching was just what He desires His servants to follow.

The speaker who has not a thorough education may sometimes fall into errors of grammar or pronunciation; he may not employ the most eloquent expressions or the most beautiful imagery, but if he has himself eaten of the Bread of Life; if he has drunk of the Fountain of Life, he can feed the hungry souls; he can give of the Water of Life to him that is athirst.

His defects will be forgiven and forgotten. His hearers will not become weary or disgusted, but will thank God for the message of grace sent them through His servant.

If the worker has consecrated himself fully to God and is diligent in prayer for strength and heavenly wisdom, the grace of Christ will be his teacher, and he will overcome great defects and become more and more intelligent in the things of God. But let none take license from this to be indolent, to squander time and opportunities, and neglect the training that is essential for him in order to become efficient. The Lord is in no wise pleased with those who have opportunities to obtain knowledge but who excuse themselves in neglecting to improve all the privileges He has placed within their reach that they may become intelligent, well qualified workers, of whom He will not be ashamed.

Above all other people upon the earth, the man whose mind is enlightened by the opening of the word of God to his understanding, will feel that he must give himself to greater diligence in the perusal of the word of God, and to a diligent study of the sciences, for his hope and calling are greater than any other. The more closely connected man is with the Source of all knowledge and wisdom, the more he can be advantaged intellectually as well as spiritually through his relation to God. The knowledge of God is the essential education, and this knowledge every true worker will make it his constant study to obtain.--"Christian Education," 1893.

FOR ADDITIONAL READING

City Missions, the Trianing of Workers, etc., General Conference Bulletin, pp. 161-163 (1893)

Christian Education (1893)

Students Deciding Their Eternal Destiny

Let the students remember that to form characters that will stand the test of the judgment, is very serious business. You yourselves are responsible for the kind of character you build. No professor in an institution of learning can make your character. You yourselves decide your own eternal destiny. It is necessary to contemplate such characters as are worthy of imitation. We refer you to Joseph in Egypt, and to Daniel in Babylon. These youths were tried and proved; and because they stood firm to principle, they became representative men, and patterns of integrity. I would say to the youth at our institutions of learning, whether you profess to believe or not, that you are now in probationary time, and a second probation will not come to any of you. This is the only opportunity you will have of standing the test and proving of God.

With the deepest interest the angels of God in the heavenly courts are watching the development of character; and from the records in the books of heaven, actions are weighed, and moral worth is measured. Every day the record of your life is passed unto God, just as it is, whether it is one of merit or of demerit. You are lacking in true elevation and nobility of soul, and no man can give you the character you need. The only way you can attain to the standard of moral worth by which you are to be measured, is to depend upon Christ, and co-operate with Him in steadfast, earnest, determined purpose.

Those who do this will not bring into their work a spirit of lightness, of frivolity, and of love of amusement. They will consider that at no small cost to their parents or to themselves, they have come to the school to obtain a better knowledge of the sciences, and to get a more comprehensive understanding of both the Old and New Testament. I would address you as those who have reasoning minds, and who have an intelligent understanding of your privileges and duties. Would it not be best for you to co-operate with your teachers, in order that you may reach the very highest standard that it is possible for you to attain? Time is more valuable to you than gold, and you should improve every precious moment. You should consider what will be your influence upon others. If one pupil is reckless, and indulges an excessive love of amusements, he should bring himself under the control of principle, lest he may become a working agent for Satan, to counteract, by his wrong influence, the work which teachers are trying to do, and mar that which heavenly intelligences are seeking to accomplish through human agents. He may frustrate the design of God, and fail to accept Christ and to become indeed a son of God.

Obligations between teachers and pupils are mutual. Teachers should make diligent effort that their own souls may be sanctified through the grace of Christ, and that they may labor in Christ's lines for the salvation of their pupils. On the other hand, students should not pursue such a course of action as will make it hard and trying to their teachers, and bring upon them temptations hard to resist. Pupils should not, by a wrong course of action, lower the high standing and reputation of the school, and give reason for the report to go abroad among believers and unbelievers, that Seventh-day Adventist schools, though purporting to be established for giving the best of education to those who attend, are no better than the common schools throughout the world. This is not the character nor the reputation that God would have our schools bear; and those who have lent the influence with which God has entrusted them, to give such a character or reputation to the school, have lent it in a wrong direction. Those who have shown disrespect for rules, and who have sought to break down authority, whether they are believers or unbelievers, are registered in the books of heaven as those who cannot be trusted as members of the royal family, children of the heavenly King. The teachers who carry the burden of the work that they should, will have sufficient responsibility, care, and burden, without having the added burden of your disobedience. They will appreciate every effort that is made on the part of the students to co-operate with them in the work.

One careless, insubordinate student, who does not cultivate self-respect, who is not well disposed, and who does not try to do his best, is doing himself great injury. He is deciding what shall be the tone of his character, and is inducing others to depart from truth and uprightness, who, if it were not for his pernicious influence, would dare to be true and noble. One student who feels his accountability to be faithful in helping his instructors, will help himself more than he helps all others. Heaven looks down with approbation upon the students who strive to do right, and have a firm purpose to be true to God. They will receive help from God. Of Daniel and his companions who stood firm as a rock to truth, it is written, "As for these four children, God gave them knowledge and skill in all learning and wisdom: . . . and in all matters of wisdom and understanding, that the king inquired of them, he found them ten times better than all the magicians and astrologers that were in all his realm."

If you do not intend to improve your opportunities and privileges, why do you spend, in attending the school, money that your parents have worked hard to obtain? They have sent you away from the home roof, with high hopes that you would be educated and benefited by your sojourn at college. They have followed you with letters and with prayers, and every line you have written them has been read with eagerness. They have thanked God for every indication that you would make a success of your Christian life, and they have wept for gladness at the indications of your advancement in scientific and spiritual knowledge. O I want to beseech of you to do nothing that is questionable. Consider in what light your parents would regard your actions, and forbear to do anything that would put thorns in their pillows. Do not be thoughtless, careless, and lawless. Your actions do not end with yourselves; they reflect credit or discredit upon the school, according as they are good or bad. If you do evil, you grieve Jesus Christ, who bought you with the price of His own blood, hurt the soul of your principal, wound the hearts of your teachers, and injure and mar your own soul. You make a blot upon your record, of which you will be ashamed. Will it pay? It is always best and safe to do right because it is right. Will you not now do some serious thinking? Right thinking lies at the foundation of right action. Make up your mind that you will respond to the expectations your parents have of you, that you will make faithful efforts to excel, that you will see to it that the money expended for you has not been misapplied and misused. Have a determined purpose to co-operate with the efforts made by parents and teachers, and reach a high standard of knowledge and character. Be determined not to disappoint those who love you well enough to trust you. It is manly to do right, and Jesus will help you to do right, if you seek to do it because it is right.

Those interested in your behalf have flattering hopes for you, that you will become useful men, who will be filled with moral worth and unswerving integrity. For the youth who have gone from New Zealand to America, much has been ventured; and I will say to these students, Set your aim high, and then step by step ascend to reach the standard, even though it may be by painful effort, through self-denial and self-sacrifice. Christ will be to you a present help in every time of need, if you call upon Him, that you may be like Daniel, whom no temptation could corrupt. Do not disappoint your parents and your friends; but above all, do not disappoint Him who so loved you that He gave His own life in order to cancel your sins and become your personal Saviour. Jesus said, "Without Me ye can do nothing." Bear this in mind. If you have made mistakes, you may gain a victory by discerning these mistakes, and by regarding them as beacons of warning, to enable you to shun their repetition. I need not tell you that this will be turning your defeat into victory, disappointing the enemy, and honoring your Redeemer, whose property you are.

We feel sorry indeed that any weakness of character should have marred the record of the past, because we know it is an evidence that you did not watch unto prayer. We feel sorry that mistakes have been made, because they have placed upon the teachers burdens which they ought not to have borne. Teachers have their own natural weaknesses of character to contend with, and they are capable of moving unwisely under the stress of temptation. They may think they are doing right when they are enforcing strict discipline, and yet they may be making mistakes in the case with which they are dealing. How much better would it be for both pupils and teachers, if students would place themselves upon their honor, and act from pure and noble motives, so that their very course of action would recommend them to those who were their teachers and educators. If in every possible way and under every circumstance, they would treat those who are in positions of trust, and bearing responsibility, as they themselves would like to be treated, what peace and success would attend the school.

Why should students link themselves with the great apostate, to become his agents in tempting others, and through others causing the fall of many? Every human being has his own individual trials, peculiar to himself, and no one is free from temptation. If teachers are disciples of Christ, and are engaging in the work in a way which is approved of God, Satan will surely assail them with his temptations. If the great deceiver can stir up evil elements of character in the students, and through them bring perplexity and discouragement upon the educators, he has succeeded in gaining his purpose. If under the temptation the teacher reveals weakness, in any respect, then his influence is marred; but he who proves an agent for the great adversary of souls, must render an account to God for the part he acted in causing the teacher to stumble. Let students carefully consider this phase of the subject, and let them rather study how to encourage and sustain their teachers, than how to bring discouragement and temptation upon them. In so doing, they will not be sowing tares that will spring up among the wheat. "Be not deceived; God is not mocked: for whatsoever a man soweth, that shall he also reap. For he that soweth to his flesh shall of the flesh reap corruption; but he that soweth to the Spirit shall of the Spirit reap life everlasting. And let us not be weary in well doing: for in due season we shall reap, if we faint not. As we have therefore opportunity, let us do good unto all men, especially unto them who are of the household of faith." Galatians 6:7-10.

Students will be tempted to do lawless things, when it is only to please themselves and to have what they call "fun." If they will put themselves upon their honor, and consider the fact that in doing these things they bless no one, they benefit no one, but involve others as well as themselves in difficulty, they will be more likely to take a manly and honorable course, and put their will on the side of Christ's will. They will work in Christ's lines, and help their teachers to carry their burdens, which Satan would make more discouraging by employing thoughtless minds in vain tricks. They will seek to make an atmosphere in the school, which, instead of being depressing and enfeebling to the moral powers, will be healthful and exhilarating. In thus doing, students can have a consciousness that they have acted their part on Christ's side of the question, and have not given one jot of influence or ability to the great adversary of all that is good. With how much more satisfaction can students recall such a course of action, than a course of action where they have sanctioned secret plans to disrespect and disregard authority. They will have reason to praise God that they have resisted the clamorings of inclination, and have put their influence on the side of order, diligence, and obedience. Let every student remember that it is in his power to help, and not hinder, the cause of education.

Students in our institutions of learning may either form characters after the divine similitude, or degrade their God-given powers, and bring themselves down to a low level, and they will have no one to blame but themselves if they degrade themselves. Everything that God could do has been done in behalf of man. Every want has been anticipated; every difficulty, every emergency, has been provided for. The crooked places have been made straight, the rough places smooth, and therefore no one will be excused in the day of judgment, if he has cherished unbelief and resisted the workings of the Holy Spirit.

Jesus Christ has given Himself as a complete offering in behalf of every fallen son and daughter of Adam. O what humiliation He bore! How He descended, step after step, lower and lower in the path of humiliation, yet He never degraded His soul with one foul blot of sin! All this He suffered, that He might lift you up, cleanse, refine, and ennoble you, and place you as a joint heir with Himself upon His throne. How shall you make your calling and election sure? What is the way of salvation? Christ says, "I am the way, the truth, and the life." However sinful, however guilty you may be, you are called, you are chosen. "Draw nigh to God, and He will draw nigh to you." Not one will be forced against his will to come to Jesus Christ. The Majesty of heaven, the only-begotten Son of the true and living God, opened the way for you to come to Him, by giving His life as a sacrifice on Calvary's cross. But while He suffered all this for you, He is too pure, He is too just, to behold iniquity. But even this need not keep you away from Him; for He says, "I came not to call the righteous, but sinners to repentance." Let perishing souls come to Him just as they are, without one plea, and plead the atoning blood of Christ, and they will find acceptance with God, who dwelleth in glory between the cherubim above the mercy seat. The blood of Jesus is a never-failing passport, by which all your petitions may find access to the throne of God.--"Christian Education" (Supplement), 1893.

Formality, Not Organization, an Evil

Evil does not result because of organization, but because of making organization everything, and vital godliness of little moment. When form and machinery take the pre-eminence, and a laborious task is made of carrying on the work that should be done with simplicity, evil will result, and little will be accomplished in proportion to the effort put forth. The object of organization is just the reverse of this; and should we disorganize, it would be like tearing down that which we have built up. Evil results have been seen, both in the Sabbath school work and in the missionary society, because of making much of machinery while vital experience was lost sight of. In many of the imagined improvements that have been brought in, the mold of man has been placed upon the work. In the Sabbath school, men and women have been accepted as officers and teachers, who have not been spiritually minded, and had no live interest in the work committed to their care; but matters can be set in order only through the aid of the Holy Spirit. The same evil has existed for years as now exists in our churches. Formality, pride, and love of display have taken the place of true piety and humble godliness. We might see a different order of things should a number consecrate themselves wholly to God, and then devote their talents to the Sabbath school work, ever advancing in knowledge, and educating themselves so that they would be able to instruct others as to the best methods to employ in the work; but it is not for the workers to seek for methods by which they can make a show, consuming time in theatrical performances and musical display, for this benefits no one. It does no good to train the children to make speeches for special occasions. They should be won to Christ, and instead of expending time, money, and effort to make a display, let the whole effort be made to gather sheaves for the harvest.

Many have seemed to think that all that was essential in Sabbath school work was to organize the school, and drill the scholars so that they would act in harmony with a set of ceremonies and forms; and that if persons could be secured as teachers, the Sabbath school would run itself. Teachers are often secured who cannot lead souls to Christ because they know not what it is to find Him precious to their own souls; but all those who do not value the soul so that they will work as Christ would have them, will scatter away from Christ. "He that [mark these words] gathereth not with Me, scattereth abroad." If teachers have no burden to lead souls to Jesus, they will grow indifferent to the truth; they will become careless, and the atmosphere with which they surround their souls will work to scatter away from Christ. And with such elements in the Sabbath school, there will be a perpetual conflict with difficulties; for when the teachers engage in the work and have no interest in it, the pupils will partake of the same spirit.

But although these difficulties exist, will it abolish them to put an end to organization? I am sure that the Lord has wrought in the organization that has been perfected, and the fact that there are discouraging features in the work should not be thought a sufficient reason for disorganization. Much light was given to us in reference to the organization of churches, and yet we had a hard battle to fight in perfecting organization; but the victory was gained at last, and now shall the church be disorganized because of indifference, formality, and pride? Shall we go back to disorder because unconsecrated members of the church have placed upon the work the mold of man, and sought to fashion the church to meet a popular standard?

It is true that the simplicity of true godliness has to a large degree been lost from the church, and many of those who profess to be followers of Christ have become so blinded that they think that gain is godliness, and they devote their powers to the things of time. They do not realize that all their intellectual ability has been purchased by Christ, and that they should devote to Him the best results of their thought, that His cause may be advanced. But instead of giving their sharp, clear ideas to advance the cause, to strengthen and bless the church, they devote all their powers to the advancement of their own interests. They do not gather with Christ, but lead away from Him by their words and acts. They surround their souls with an atmosphere that is deleterious to spirituality. They profess to be followers of Christ, but they do not know Him by an experimental knowledge. They do not practice religion. They do not seek to be Christians in the same way in which they would learn a trade. They profess to believe advanced truth; but it is evident that they keep it in the outer court; for it has no sanctifying power on life and character. They do not realize how much is at stake; for the salvation of their own souls and that of others is imperiled. They do not realize that in order to be a savor of life unto life they must be under spiritual discipline and training, learning in the school of Christ. Without this spiritual discipline, they become inefficient, ignorant, and undeveloped, and see no necessity for the spiritual training and knowledge which would qualify them to hold positions of influence and usefulness. If they do not consecrate themselves wholly to God, becoming learners in His school, they will do haphazard work that will result in injury to the church.

But because of these unconsecrated influences, shall we take backward steps, and tear down those methods which it has cost us much to build, and declare that organization is all a mistake? We dare not do this. There are many things that need adjusting; for some things of little importance are made much of, while other things of vast importance are neglected, and looked upon as unessential. The minds of men need literary as well as spiritual training that they may be harmoniously developed; for without literary training, men cannot fill acceptably various positions of trust.

The great educating book is the Bible, and yet it is little read or practiced. O that every individual would seek to make of himself all that he could, improving his opportunities to the very best of his ability, purposing to use every power which God has given him, not simply to advance his temporal affairs, but to advance his spiritual interests. O that all might search diligently to know what is truth, to study earnestly that they might have correct language and cultivated voices, that they might present the truth in all its elevated and ennobling beauty. Let no one imagine that he will drift into some position of usefulness. If men would be used to work for God, let them put to the stretch their powers, and concentrate their minds in earnest application. It is Satan that would keep men in ignorance and inefficiency, that they may be developed in a one-sided way which they may never be able to correct. He would have men exercise one set of faculties to the exclusion of the exercise of another set, so that the mind will lose its vigor, and when there is a real necessity, be unable to rise to the emergency. God wants men to do their best, and while Satan is pulling the mind in one direction, Jesus is drawing it in another.

When the truth is received into the heart, it begins the work of refining and sanctifying the receiver. He who cherishes the truth, will not feel that he has no more need of enlightenment, but will realize as he carries out the truth in his practical life, that he is in need of continual light that he may increase in knowledge. As he brings the truth into his life, he will feel his real ignorance, and realize the necessity of having a more thorough education, that he may understand how to use his ability to the best account.

There is a dearth of educated ability among us, and we have not men who are sufficiently trained to do justice to the work of managing our Sabbath schools and churches. Many who know the truth, still do not understand it in such a way that they could hold their own in its presentation. They are not prepared to present it in such a way that its sacred, majestic character will be clear to the people. Instead of less discipline, they need more thorough training. It is impossible for anyone to foresee to what he may be called. He may be placed in situations where he will need quick discernment and well balanced arguments, and therefore it is for the honor of Christ that well educated workers should be multiplied among us; they will be better able to communicate the truth in a clear, intelligent way, and the truth should be presented in a way that will be as free as possible from defects.

True education, when the mind is under the controlling influence of the Holy Spirit, is of great importance, and each individual should learn to rightly appreciate the capabilities that God has given; and by the practice of the knowledge he gains, he may, by the influence of his own character, impress upon others the value of obtaining a training for the service of Christ, and lead them to follow His example. There is much to be done in the world, and it is not profitable to set novices to work upon those matters that are of the highest importance. The apathy, the indolence, the inattention that has been manifested in regard to education is marvelous, but it is well pleasing to Satan. God would have us arouse from our indifference, and no longer allow the intellectual powers to run to waste, and degenerate into imbecility. Men are to appreciate the talents entrusted to them, and take advantage of the opportunities placed within their reach. Let the mental powers be girded for work, and by vigorous exertion let the mind be enlarged and developed.

There is more need now than ever before that our young men and women shall be intellectually qualified for the work. Our Sabbath schools not only need intellectual, but spiritual workers, and the mind receives its tone and efficiency by thorough discipline. By superficial study, the mind gradually loses its tone, and degenerates into imbecility, and is not capable of any taxing effort. But education prepares men to know and to do the very line of work that must at this time be done. Thorough discipline, under a wise teacher, is of more value than the natural aptitude and endowment, where there is no discipline.

The Lord has made manifest His appreciation of man, in that He gave His only-begotten Son to redeem him. Satan has also manifested his appreciation of well trained and sanctified ability, by the ingenious methods by which he seeks to divert the mind and heart of such an one from the service of God, that he may lead him to join in the ranks of apostasy. Like an angel of light, he comes with his insinuations to draw men into his service; for he knows that an educated man or woman, when not under the control of the Spirit of God, can be of great advantage to him. He will pursue the student with specious temptations, seeking to induce him to take pride in his attainments, and to imagine that he is some great one, that he may trust in himself, and walk in the sparks of his own kindling. Thus he is led to separate his soul from God, the source of all light and knowledge, and, in order that he may exalt himself, unite with Satan, the originator of all sin.

The fear of the Lord is the beginning of all wisdom; and when God is not depended upon, the result of education is only to elevate ungodliness. The reason that the church is weak and inefficient is that there is a want of the grace of Christ among those who profess the truth for these last days. If the Lord has ever spoken by me, there is sin of almost every character cherished by many who claim to be children of God; and unless they separate themselves from Satan and cling to Jesus our righteousness, the woe of God will be upon those who have had great light, and yet have chosen to walk in darkness. "Then began He to upbraid the cities wherein most of His mighty works were done, because they repented not: Woe unto thee, Chorazin; woe unto thee, Bethsaida; for if the mighty works, which were done in you, had been done in Tyre and Sidon, they would have repented long ago in sackcloth and ashes. But I say unto you, It shall be more tolerable for Tyre and Sidon at the day of judgment, than for you. And thou, Capernaum, which art exalted unto heaven, shalt be brought down to hell: for if the mighty works, which have been done in thee, had been done in Sodom, it would have remained until this day. But I say unto you, That it shall be more tolerable for the land of Sodom in the day of judgment, than for thee."

It is a fearful thing to have great light and blessing, to have many opportunities and privileges, and yet make no saving use of them. Those who do not make a saving use of their opportunities, will be condemned by the privileges God has granted to them; but those who walk in the light will have increased light. Those who have had the light of truth, and yet have failed to walk in the light, are under the same sentence of condemnation as were Chorazin and Bethsaida. Shall not these warnings be heeded? Shall not these admonitions have weight with us? In the near future it will be seen just who have been walking humbly with God, and who have been obeying His orders. Those who have been walking in the sparks of their own kindling will lie down in sorrow. It will be seen that they have made a terrible mistake. O let us awake! Light is now shining; let the windows of the mind and heart be opened to welcome the heaven-sent rays. Shall Jesus say of those who profess to obey the truth, and yet who fail to walk in its light, "In them is fulfilled the prophecy of Esaias, which saith, By hearing ye shall hear, and shall not understand; and seeing ye shall see, and shall not perceive: for this people's heart is waxed gross, and their ears are dull of hearing, and their eyes they have closed; lest at any time they should see with their eyes, and hear with their ears, and should understand with their heart, and should be converted, and I should heal them"?--"Christian Education," 1893.

To Teachers

Everyone who has to do with educating the younger class of students, should consider that these children are affected by, and feel the impressions of, the atmosphere, whether it be pleasant or unpleasant.

If the teacher is connected with God, if he has Christ abiding in his heart, the spirit that is cherished by him is felt by the children. When a teacher manifests impatience or fretfulness toward a child, the fault may not be with the child one half as much as with the teacher. Teachers become tired with their work, then something the children say or do does not accord with their feelings, but will they let Satan's spirit enter into them, and lead them to create feelings in the children very unpleasant and disagreeable, through their own lack of tact and wisdom from God? There should not be a teacher employed, unless you have evidence by test and trial, that he loves, and fears to offend God. If teachers are taught of God, if their lessons are daily learned in the school of Christ, they will work in Christ's lines. They will win and draw with Christ; for every child and youth is precious.

Every teacher needs Christ abiding in his heart by faith, and to possess a true, self-denying, self-sacrificing spirit for Christ's sake. One may have sufficient education and knowledge in science to instruct; but has it been ascertained that he has tact and wisdom to deal with human minds? If instructors have not the love of Christ abiding in the heart, they are not fit to be brought into connection with children, and to bear the grave responsibilities placed upon them, of educating these children and youth. They lack the higher education and training in themselves, and they know not how to deal with human minds. There is the spirit of their own insubordinate, natural hearts that is striving for the control, and to subject the plastic minds and characters of children to such a discipline, is to leave scars and bruises upon the mind that will never be effaced.

If a teacher cannot be made to feel the responsibility and the carefulness he should ever reveal in dealing with human minds, his education has in some cases been very defective. In the home life the training has been harmful to the character, and it is a sad thing to reproduce this defective character and management in the children brought under his control. We are standing before God on test and trial to see if we can individually be trusted to be of the number of the family who shall compose the redeemed in heaven. "And I saw the dead, small and great, stand before God; and the books were opened: and another book was opened, which is the book of life: and the dead were judged out of those things which were written in the books, according to their works."

Here are represented the great white throne and He that sat on it, from whose face the earth and heaven fled away. Let every teacher consider that he is doing his work in the sight of the universe of heaven. Every child with whom the teacher is brought in contact has been purchased by the blood of God's only-begotten Son, and He who has died for these children would have them treated as His property. Be sure that your contact, teachers, with everyone of these children shall be of that character that will not make you ashamed when you meet them in that great day when every word and action is brought in review before God, and with its burden of results laid open before you individually. "Bought with a price,"--O what a price, eternity alone will reveal!

The Lord Jesus Christ has infinite tenderness for those whom He has purchased at the cost of His own sufferings in the flesh, that they should not perish with the devil and his angels, but that He may claim them as His chosen ones. They are the claim of His love, of His own property; and He looks upon them with unutterable affection, and the fragrance of His own righteousness He gives to His loved ones who believe in Him. It requires tact and wisdom and human love, and sanctified affection for the precious lambs of the flock, to lead them to see and appreciate their privilege in yielding themselves up to the tender guidance of the faithful shepherds. The children of God will exercise the gentleness of Jesus Christ.

Teachers, Jesus is in your school every day. His great heart of infinite love is drawn out, not only for the best-behaved children, who have the most favorable surroundings, but for children who have by inheritance objectionable traits of character. Even parents have not understood how much they are responsible for the traits of character developed in their children, and have not had the tenderness and wisdom to deal with these poor children, whom they have made what they are. They fail to trace back the cause of these discouraging developments which are a trial to them. But Jesus looks upon these children with pity and with love, for He sees, He understands from cause to effect.

The teacher may bind these children to his or her heart by the love of Christ abiding in the soul-temple as a sweet fragrance, a savor of life unto life. The teachers may, through the grace of Christ imparted to them, be the living human agency--be laborers together with God--to enlighten, lift up, encourage, and help to purify the soul from its moral defilement; and the image of God shall be revealed in the soul of the child, and the character become transformed by the grace of Christ.

The gospel is the power and wisdom of God, if it is correctly represented by those who claim to be Christians. Christ crucified for our sins should humble every soul before God in his own estimation. Christ risen from the dead, ascended on high, our living Intercessor in the presence of God, is the science of salvation which we need to learn and teach to children and youth. Said Christ, "I sanctify Myself, that they also might be sanctified." This is the work that ever devolves upon every teacher. There must not be any haphazard work in this matter, for even the work of educating the children in the day schools requires very much of the grace of

Christ and the subduing of self. Those who naturally are fretful, easily provoked, and have cherished the habit of criticism, of thinking evil, should find some other kind of work that will not reproduce any of their unlovely traits of character in the children and youth, for they have cost too much. Heaven sees in the child, the undeveloped man or woman, with capabilities and powers that, if correctly guided and developed with heavenly wisdom, will become the human agencies through whom the divine influences can co-operate to be laborers together with God. Sharp words, and continual censure bewilder the child, but never reform him. Keep back that pettish word; keep your own spirit under discipline to Jesus Christ; then will you learn how to pity and sympathize with those brought under your influence. Do not exhibit impatience and harshness, for if these children did not need educating, they would not need the advantages of the school. They are to be patiently, kindly, and in love brought up the ladder of progress, climbing step by step in obtaining knowledge.

It is a daily working agency that is to be brought into exercise, a faith that works by love, and purifies the soul of the educator. Is the revealed will of God placed as your highest authority? If Christ is formed within, the hope of glory, then the truth of God will so act upon your natural temperament, that its transforming agency will be revealed in a changed character, and you will not by your influence through the revealings of an unsanctified heart and temper, turn the truth of God into a lie before any of your pupils; nor in your presentation of a selfish, impatient, unchristlike temper in dealing with any human mind, reveal that the grace of Christ is not sufficient for you at all times and in all places. Thus you will show that the authority of God over you is not merely in name but in reality and truth. There must be a separation from all that is objectionable or unchristlike, however difficult it may be to the true believer.

Inquire, teachers, you who are doing your work not only for time but eternity, Does the love of Christ constrain my heart and my soul, in dealing with the precious souls for whom Jesus has given His own life? Under His constraining discipline, do old traits of character, not in conformity to the will of God, pass away and the opposite take their place? "A new heart also will I give you." Have all things become new through your conversion to the Lord Jesus Christ? In words and by painstaking effort are you sowing such seed in these young hearts that you can ask the Lord to water it, that it shall, with His imputed righteousness, ripen into a rich harvest? Ask yourselves, Am I by my own unsanctified words and impatience and want of that wisdom that is from above, confirming these youth in their own perverse spirit, because they see that their teacher has a spirit unlike Christ? If they should die in their sins, shall I not be accountable for their souls? The soul who loves Jesus, who appreciates the saving power of His grace, will feel such a drawing near to Christ, that he will desire to work in His lines. He cannot, dare not, let Satan control his spirit and poisonous miasma surround his soul. Everything will be placed one side that will corrupt his influence, because it opposes the will of God and endangers the souls of the precious sheep and lambs; and he is required to watch for souls as they that must give an account. Wherever God has, in providence, placed us, He will keep us; as our day our strength shall be.

Whoever shall give way to his natural feelings and impulses makes himself weak and untrustworthy, for he is a channel through which Satan can communicate to taint and corrupt many souls, and these unholy fits that control the person unnerve him, and shame and confusion are the sure result. The spirit of Jesus Christ ever has a renewing, restoring power upon the soul that has felt its own weakness and fled to the unchanging One who can give grace and power to resist evil. Our Redeemer had a broad comprehensive humanity. His heart was ever touched with the known helplessness of the little child that is subject to rough usage; for He loved children. The feeblest cry of human suffering never reached His ear in vain. And everyone who assumes the responsibility of instructing the youth will meet obdurate hearts, perverse dispositions, and his work is to co-operate with God in restoring the moral image of God in every child. Jesus, precious Jesus,--a whole fountain of love was in His soul. Those who instruct the children should be men and women of principle.

The religious life of a large number who profess to be Christians is such as to show that they are not Christians. They are constantly misrepresenting Christ, falsifying His character. They do not feel the importance of this transformation of character, and that they must be conformed to His divine likeness; and at times they will exhibit a false phase of Christianity to the world, which will work ruin to the souls of those who are brought into association with them, for the very reason that they are, while professing to be Christians, not under the control of Jesus Christ. Their own hereditary and cultivated traits of character are indulged as precious qualifications when they are death-dealing in their influence over other minds. In plain, simple words, they walk in the sparks of their own kindling. They have a religion subject to, and controlled by, circumstances. If everything happens to move in a way that pleases them, and there are no irritating circumstances that call to the surface their unsubdued, unchristlike natures, they are condescending and pleasant, and will be very attractive. When there are things that occur in the family or in their association with others which ruffle their peace and provoke their tempers, if they lay every circumstance before God, and continue their request, supplicating His grace before they shall engage in their daily work as teachers, and know for themselves the power and grace and love of Christ abiding in their own hearts before entering upon their labors, angels of God are brought with them into the schoolroom. But if they go in a provoked, irritated spirit into the schoolroom, the moral atmosphere surrounding their souls is leaving its impression upon the children who are under their care, and in the place of being fitted to instruct the children, they need one to teach them the lessons of Jesus Christ.

Let every teacher who accepts the responsibility of educating the children and youth, examine himself, and study critically from cause to effect. Has the truth of God taken possession of my soul? Has the wisdom which cometh from Jesus Christ, which is first "pure, then peaceable, gentle, and easy to be entreated, full of mercy and good fruits, without partiality and without hypocrisy" been brought into my character? While I stand in the responsible position of an educator, do I cherish the principle that "the fruit of righteousness is sown in peace of them that make peace"? The truth is not to be kept to be practiced when we feel just like it, but at all times and in all places.

Well balanced minds and symmetrical characters are required as teachers in every line. Give not this work into the hands of young women and young men who know not how to deal with human minds. They know so little of the controlling power of grace upon their own hearts and characters that they have to unlearn, and learn entirely new lessons in Christian experience. They have never learned to keep their own soul and character under discipline to Jesus Christ, and bring even the thoughts into captivity to Jesus Christ. There are all kinds of characters to deal with in the children and youth. Their minds are impressible. Any thing like a hasty, passionate exhibition on the part of the teacher may cut off her influence for good over the students whom she is having the name of educating. And will this education be for the present and future eternal good of the children and youth? There is the correct influence to be exerted upon them for their spiritual good. Instruction is to be constantly given to encourage the children in the formation of correct habits in speech, in voice, in deportment.

Many of those children have not had proper training at home. They have been sadly neglected. Some have been left to do as they pleased; others have been found fault with and discouraged. But little pleasantness and cheerfulness have been shown toward them, and but few words of approval have been spoken to them. The defective characters of the parents have been inherited, and the discipline given by these defective characters has been objectionable in the formation of characters. Solid timbers have not been brought into the character building. There is no more important work that can be done than the educating and training of these youth and children. The teachers who work in this part of the Lord's vineyard need to learn first how to be self-possessed, keeping their own temper and feelings under control, in subjection to the Holy Spirit of God. They should give evidence of having not a one-sided experience, but a well balanced mind, a symmetrical character so that they can be trusted because they are conscientious Christians, themselves under the chief Teacher, who has said, "Learn of Me, for I am meek and lowly of heart, and ye shall find rest unto your souls." Then learning in Christ's school daily they can educate children and youth.

Self-cultured, self-controlled, under discipline in the school of Christ, having a living connection with the great Teacher, they will have an intelligent knowledge of practical religion; and keeping their own souls in the love of God, they will know how to exercise the grace of patience and Christlike forbearance. The patience, love, long forbearance, and tender sympathies are called into activity. They will discern that they have a most important field in the Lord's vineyard to cultivate. They must lift up their hearts unto God in sincere prayer, Be Thou my pattern, and then by beholding Jesus they will do the work of Jesus Christ. Jesus said, "The Son can do nothing of Himself, but what He seeth the Father do." So with the sons and daughters of God; they steadfastly and teachably look to Jesus, doing nothing in their own way and after their own will and pleasure; but that which they have, in the lessons of Christ, seen Him, their Pattern, do, they do also. Thus they represent to the students under their instruction at all times and upon all occasions the character of Jesus Christ. They catch the bright rays of the Sun of Righteousness and reflect these precious beams upon the children and youth whom they are educating. The formation of correct habits is to leave its impress upon the mind and characters of the children, that they may practice the right way. It means much to bring these children under the direct influence of the Spirit of God, training and disciplining them in the nurture and admonition of the Lord. The formation of correct habits, the exhibition of a right spirit, will call for earnest efforts in the name and strength of Jesus. The instructor must persevere, giving line upon line, precept upon precept, here a little and there a little, in all long-suffering and patience, sympathy and love, binding these children to his heart by the love of Christ revealed in himself.

This truth can in the highest sense be acted, and exemplified before the children. "Who can have compassion on the ignorant, and on them that are out of the way; for that he himself also is compassed with infirmity. And by reason hereof he ought, as for the people, so also for himself, to offer for sins."

Let teachers bear this in mind, and never lose sight of it when they are inclined to have their feelings stirred against the children and youth for any misbehavior; let them remember that the angels of God are looking upon them sorrowfully; for if the children do err and misbehave, then it is all the more essential that those who are placed over them as teachers should be able to teach them by precept and example. In no case are they to lose self-control, to manifest impatience and harshness, and want of sympathy and love; for these children are the property of Jesus Christ, and teachers must be very careful and God-fearing in regard to the spirit they cherish and the words they utter, for the children will catch the spirit manifested, be it good or evil. It is a heavy and a sacred responsibility.

There need to be teachers who are thoughtful, considerate of their own weakness and infirmities and sins, and who will not be oppressive and discourage the children and youth. There needs to be much praying, much faith, much forbearance and courage, which the Lord is ready to bestow. For God sees every trial, and a wonderful influence can be exerted by teachers, if they will practice the lessons which Christ has given them. But will these teachers consider their own wayward course, that they make very feeble efforts to learn in the school of Christ and practice Christlike meekness and lowliness of heart? The teachers should be themselves in obedience to Jesus Christ, and ever practicing His words, that they may exemplify the character of Jesus Christ to the students. Let your light shine in good works, in faithful watching and caring for the lambs of the flock, with patience, with tenderness, and the love of Jesus in your own hearts.

To place young men and young women in such a field, who have not developed a deep, earnest love for God and the souls for whom Christ died, is making a mistake which will result in the loss of many precious souls. The teacher needs to be susceptible to the influences of the Spirit of God. Not one who will become impatient and irritated, should be an educator. Teachers must consider that they are dealing with children, not men and women. They are children who have everything to learn, and it is much more difficult for some to learn than others. The dull scholar needs much more encouragement than he receives. If teachers are placed over these varied minds, who naturally love to order and dictate and magnify themselves in their authority, who will deal with partiality, having favorites to whom they will show preferences, while others are treated with exactitude and severity, it will create a state of confusion and insubordination. Teachers who have not been blessed with a pleasant and well balanced experience may be placed to take charge of children and youth, but a great wrong is done to those whom they instruct. Parents must come to view this matter in a different light. They must feel it their duty to co-operate with the teacher, to encourage wise discipline, and to pray much for the one who is teaching their children. You will not help the children by fretting, censuring, or discouraging them; neither will you act a good part to help them to rebel, and to be disobedient and unkind and unlovable, because of the spirit you develop. If you are Christians indeed, you will have an abiding Christ, and the spirit of Him who gave His life for sinners; and the wisdom of God will teach you in every emergency the course to pursue.

Children are in need of having a steady, firm, living principle of righteousness exercised over them and practiced before them. Be sure you let the true light shine before your pupils. The light of heaven is wanted. Never let the world have the impression that your spirit and taste and longings are of no higher and purer order than that of worldlings. If you in your actions leave this impression upon them, you let a false, deceptive light lead them to ruin. The trumpet must give a certain sound. There is a broad, clear, and deep line drawn by the eternal God between the righteous and unrighteous, the godly and the ungodly; between those who are obedient to God's commandments and those who are disobedient.

The ladder which Jacob saw in the night vision, the base of it resting upon the earth and the topmost round reaching unto the highest heavens; God himself above the ladder, and His glory shining upon every round; angels ascending and descending upon this ladder of shining brightness, is a symbol of constant communication kept up between this world and heavenly places. God accomplishes His will through the instrumentality of heavenly angels in continual intercourse with humanity. This ladder reveals a direct and important channel of communication with the inhabitants of this earth. The ladder represented to Jacob the world's Redeemer, who links earth and heaven together. Everyone who has seen the evidence and light of truth and accepts the truth, professing his faith in Jesus Christ, is a missionary in the highest sense of the word. He is the receiver of heavenly treasures, and it is his duty to impart them, to diffuse that which he has received.

Then to those who are accepted as teachers in our schools is opened a field for labor and cultivation, for the sowing of the seed and for the harvesting of the ripening grain. What can give greater satisfaction than to be laborers together with God in educating and training the children and youth to love God and keep His commandments? Lead the children whom you are instructing in the day school and the Sabbath school to Jesus. What can give you greater joy than to see children and youth following Christ, the great Shepherd, who calls, and the sheep and lambs hear His voice and follow Him? What can spread more sunshine through the soul of the interested, devoted worker than to know that his persevering patient labor is not in vain in the Lord, and to see his pupils have the sunshine of joy in their souls because Christ has forgiven their sins? What can be more satisfying to the worker together with God, than to see children and youth receiving the impressions of the Spirit of God in true nobility of character and in the restoration of the moral image of God--the children seeking the peace coming from the Prince of peace? The truth a bondage? Yes, in one sense; it binds the willing souls in captivity to Jesus Christ, bowing their hearts to the gentleness of Jesus Christ. O it means so much more than finite minds can comprehend, to present in every missionary effort Jesus Christ and Him crucified. "But He was wounded for our transgressions, He was bruised for our iniquities: the chastisement of our peace was upon Him, and with His stripes we are healed." "For He hath made Him to be sin for us, who knew no sin; that we might be made the righteousness of God in Him." This is to be the burden of our work. If anyone thinks he is capable of teaching in the Sabbath school or in the day school the science of education, he needs first to learn the fear of the Lord, which is the beginning of wisdom, that he may teach this the highest of all sciences.

"And this is life eternal, that they might know Thee the only true God, and Jesus Christ, whom Thou hast sent." "I have given unto them the words which Thou gavest Me; and they have received them, and have known surely that I came out from Thee, and they have believed that Thou didst send Me." Here is the work laid before us, to be representatives of Christ, as He in our world was the representative of the Father. We are to teach the words given us in the lessons of Christ. "I have given unto them the words which Thou gavest Me." We have our work, and every instructor of the youth in any capacity is to receive in a good and honest heart what God has unfolded and recorded in His holy word in the lessons of Christ, meekly to accept the words of life. We are in the antitypical day of atonement, and not only are we to humble our hearts before God and confess our sins but we are, by all our educating talent, to seek to instruct those with whom we are brought in contact, and to bring them by precept and example to know God and Jesus Christ whom He hath sent.

O I so much wish that the Lord of heaven would open many eyes that are now blind, that they might see themselves as God sees them, and give to them a sense of the work to be done in the fields of labor. But I have no hope that all the appeals I make will avail, unless the Lord speaks to the soul and writes His requirements upon the tablets of the heart. Cannot every living human agent have a high and elevated sense of what it means to have a large and important field of home missionary work appointed to him, without the necessity of going to far-off lands? And while some must proclaim the message of mercy to them that are afar off, there are many who have to proclaim the message to those who are nigh. Our schools are to be educating schools to qualify youth to become missionaries both by precept and example. Let the one who is acting in the capacity of teacher ever bear in mind that these children and youth are the purchase of the blood of the Son of God. They must be led to believe in Christ as their personal Saviour. The name of each separate believer is graven on the palms of His hands. The Chief Shepherd is looking down from the heavenly sanctuary upon the sheep of His pasture. "He calleth His own sheep by name, and leadeth them out." "If any man sin, we have an advocate with the Father, Jesus Christ the righteous." O precious, blessed truth! He does not treat one case with indifference.

His impressive parable of the good shepherd represents the responsibility of every minister and of every Christian who has accepted a position as teacher of children and youth and a teacher of old and young, in opening to them the Scriptures. If one strays from the fold, he is not followed with harsh words and with a whip, but with winning invitations to return. The ninety and nine that had not strayed do not call for the sympathy and tender, pitying love of the shepherd. But the shepherd follows the sheep and lambs that have caused him the greatest anxiety and have engrossed his sympathies. The disinterested, faithful shepherd leaves all the rest of the sheep, and his whole heart and soul and energies are taxed to seek the one that is lost. And then the figure--praise God--the shepherd returns with the sheep, carrying him in his arms, rejoicing at every step; he says, "Rejoice with me; for I have found my sheep which was lost." I am so thankful we have in the parable, the sheep found. And this is the very lesson the shepherd is to learn,--success in bringing the sheep and lambs back.

There is no picture presented before our imagination of a sorrowful shepherd returning without the sheep. And the Lord Jesus declares the pleasure of the shepherd and his joy in finding the sheep causes pleasure and rejoicing in heaven among the angels. The wisdom of God, His power and His love, are without a parallel. It is the divine guarantee that not one, even, of the straying sheep and lambs is overlooked and not one left unsuccored. A golden chain--the mercy and compassion of divine power--is passed around everyone of these imperiled souls. Then shall not the human agent cooperate with God? Shall he be sinful, failing, defective in character himself, regardless of the soul ready to perish? Christ has linked him to His eternal throne by offering His own life.

Zechariah's description of Joshua, the high priest, is a striking representation of the sinner for whom Christ is mediating that he may be brought to repentance. Satan is standing at the right hand of the Advocate, resisting the work of Christ, and pleading against Him that man is his property, since he has chosen him as his ruler. But the Defender of man, the Restorer, mightier than the mightiest, hears the demands and claims of Satan, and answers him: "The Lord rebuke thee, O Satan; even the Lord that hath chosen Jerusalem rebuke thee: is not this a brand plucked out of the fire? Now Joshua was clothed with filthy garments and stood before the angel. And He answered and spake unto those that stood before Him, saying, Take away the filthy garments from him. And unto him He said, Behold I have caused thine iniquity to pass from thee, and I will clothe thee with change of raiment. And I said, Let them set a fair miter upon his head. So they set a fair miter upon his head, and clothed him with garments. And the angel of the Lord stood by."

Bear in mind, every teacher who takes the responsibility of dealing with human minds, that every soul who is inclined to err and is easily tempted, is the special object for whom Christ is solicitor. They that are whole need not a physician, but those that are sick. The compassionate Intercessor is pleading, and will sinful, finite men and women repulse a single soul?

Shall any man or woman be indifferent to the very souls for whom Christ is pleading in the courts of heaven? Shall you in your course of action, imitate the Pharisees, who would be merciless, and Satan, who would accuse and destroy? O will you individually humble your own souls before God, and let that stern nerve and iron will be subdued and broken?

Step away from Satan's voice and from acting his will, and stand by the side of Jesus, possessing His attributes, the possessor of keen and tender sensibilities, who can make the cause of afflicted, suffering ones His own. The man who has had much forgiven will love much. Jesus is a compassionate intercessor, a merciful and faithful high priest. He, the Majesty of heaven--the King of glory--can look upon finite man, subject to the temptations of Satan, knowing that He has felt the power of Satan's wiles. "Wherefore in all things it behooved Him to be made like unto His brethren [clothing His divinity with humanity], that He might be a merciful and faithful high priest in things pertaining to God, to make reconciliation for the sins of the people. For in that He himself hath suffered being tempted, He is able to succor them that are tempted."

Then I call upon you, my brethren, to practice working in lines in which Christ worked. You must never put on the cloak of severity and condemn and denounce and drive away from the fold poor, tempted mortals; but as laborers together with God, heal the spiritually diseased. This you will do if you have the mind of Christ. "For we have not an high priest which cannot be touched with the feeling of our infirmities; but was in all points tempted like as we are, yet without sin." "Hast thou not known? hast thou not heard, that the everlasting God, the Lord, the Creator of the ends of the earth, fainteth not, neither is weary? There is no searching of His understanding."--"Christian Education," 1893.

Suspension of Students

One thing I wish you to understand, that I have not been in harmony with the expelling of students from the school, unless human depravity and gross licentiousness make it necessary, that others shall not be corrupted. There has been an error in sending students from the school as in the case of--, of--, and other cases, which has been a great evil, and souls thus treated have opened before them a course of action that has secured them in the ranks of the enemy as armed and equipped enemies. Again as to making public the errors of the students to the school,--I have been brought in to see and hear some of these exposures, and then been shown the after-influence. It has been harmful in every respect, and has no beneficial influence upon the school. Had those who acted a part in these things had the spirit and wisdom of Christ, they would have seen a way to remedy the existing difficulties more after the likeness of Jesus Christ. It never helps a student to be humiliated before the whole school. It creates a wound that mortifies. It heals nothing, cures nothing. There are students who are suspended from school. They are in this action thrust upon Satan's battle ground to cope with principalities and powers without armor or defense, to become an easy prey to Satan's devices. Let me speak a word to you in the name of the Lord. When there is a proper course taken, in cases where students seem so easily led astray, there will be found no necessity for suspension or expulsion. There is a right way, and the Spirit of the Lord must move the human agent or else there will be grave mistakes made. It is the nicest work that was ever entered upon by the human agent, the dealing with human minds. Teachers are to consider that they are not dealing with angels, but human beings with like passions as they themselves have. Characters are not formed in one mold. There is every phase of character received by children as an inheritance. The defects and the virtues in traits of character are thus revealed. Let every instructor take this into consideration. Hereditary and cultivated deformity of human character, as also beauty of character, will have to be met, and much grace cultivated in the instructor to know how to deal with the erring for their present and eternal good. Impulse, impatience, pride, selfishness, and self-esteem, if cherished, will do a great amount of evil which may thrust the soul upon Satan's battle ground without wisdom to navigate his bark, but he will be in danger of being tossed about at the sport of Satan's temptations until shipwrecked. Every teacher has his own peculiar traits of character to watch lest Satan should use him as his agent to destroy souls, by his own unconsecrated traits of character. The only safety for teachers is to learn daily in the school of Christ, His meekness, His lowliness of heart, then self will be hid in Christ, and he will meekly wear the yoke of Christ, and consider that he is dealing with His heritage. I must state to you, that I have been shown that the best methods have not always been practiced in dealing with the errors and mistakes of students, and the result has been that souls have been imperiled and some lost. Evil tempers in the teachers, unwise movements, self-dignity have done a bad work. There is no form of vice, worldliness, or drunkenness, that will do a more baleful work upon the character, embittering the soul, and setting in train evils that overbear good, than human passions not under the control of the Spirit of God. Anger, getting touched, stirred up, will never pay. How many prodigals are kept out of the kingdom of God by the unlovely character of those who claim to be Christians. Jealousy, envy, pride, and uncharitable feelings, self-righteousness, easily provoked, thinking evil, harshness, cold, unsympathetic, these are the attributes of Satan. Teachers will meet with these things in the students' characters. It is a terrible thing to have these things to deal with; but in seeking to cast out these evils, the worker has in many instances developed similar attributes which have marred the soul of the one with whom he is dealing.

There is really no place in heaven for these dispositions. A man with such a character will only make heaven miserable, because he himself is miserable. "Except ye be born again," said Christ, "ye cannot enter the kingdom of heaven." To enter heaven, a man must have Christ formed within, the hope of glory, and take heaven with him. The Lord Jesus alone can fashion and change the character. For want of patience, kindness, forbearance, unselfishness, and love, the revealings of the traits flash forth involuntarily when off guard, and unchristian words, unchristlikeness of character burst forth sometimes to the ruin of the soul. "Rejoiceth not in iniquity." Mark it. The apostle meant where there is a cultivation of genuine love for precious souls, it will be exhibited for those most in need of that patience which suffereth long and is kind, and will not be ready to magnify a small indiscretion or direct wrong into large unpardonable offenses, and will not make capital of others' misdoings. The love for souls for whom Christ died will not do that which has been done through misconceptions of that which was due to the erring, exposing their errors and weakness before a whole school. How do you think Jesus has looked upon such transactions? Had He been present He would have said to those doing these things, "Ye know not the Scriptures nor the power of God." For in the Scriptures it is plainly shown how to deal with the erring. Forbearance, kindly consideration, "Consider thyself lest thou also be tempted," would meet the stubborn, obdurate heart. Love of Jesus will cover a multitude of sins, that they shall not prey upon the offender neither be exposed to create feelings of every stripe and character in the human breast of those to whom these errors and mistakes are laid open, and in the one thus dealt with. He is too often driven to desperation. His mind is beyond the healing. Now the work is to have the grace of Christ in the soul which will never, never be guilty of exposing another's wrongs, unless it is a positive necessity. Practice in the line of Christ. The true witness speaks in Revelation 21:5. Practice love. There is nothing in Christianity that is capricious.

If a man will not exercise his arm, it becomes weak and deficient in muscular strength. Unless the Christian exercises his spiritual powers, he acquires no strength of character, no moral vigor. Love is a very precious plant and must be cultivated if it flourishes. The precious plant of love is to be treated tenderly (practiced), and it will become strong and vigorous and rich in fruit-bearing, giving expression to the whole character. A Christlike nature is not selfish, not unkind, and will not hurt the souls of those who are struggling with Satan's temptations. It will enter into the feelings of those who are tempted that the trials and temptations shall be so managed as to bring out the gold and consume the dross. This is the practice which God appoints to all. In this, Christ's school, all may learn their lessons daily, both teachers and pupils, to be patient, humble, generous, noble. You will all have to seek God most earnestly in prayer mingled with living faith, and the molding hand of God will bring out His own image in your character. Temptations will come, but not overcome. But through grace found in opening the heart to the knock and voice of Jesus, Christian character and experience are growing more and more beautiful and heavenly. Let us bear in mind that we are dealing with souls that Christ has purchased with infinite cost to Himself. O tell the erring, God loves you, God died for you. Weep over them, pray with them. Shed tears over them, but do not get angry with them. They are Christ's purchased possession. Let everyone seek a character that will express love in all his actions. "Whoso shall offend one of these little ones which believe in Me, it were better for him that a millstone were hanged about his neck, and that he were drowned in the depths of the sea." It were better not to live than to exist day by day devoid of that love [281] which Christ has revealed in His character, and has enjoined upon His children. Said Christ, "Love one another as I have loved you." We live in a hard, unfeeling, uncharitable world. Satan and his confederacy are plying every art to seduce the souls for whom Christ has given His precious life. Everyone who loves God in sincerity and truth, will love the souls for whom Christ has died. If we wish to do good to souls, our success with these souls will be in proportion to their belief in our belief in, and appreciation of, them. Respect shown to the struggling human soul is the sure means through Christ Jesus of the restoration of the self-respect the man has lost. Our advancing ideas of what he may become is a help we cannot ourselves fully appreciate. We have need of the rich grace of God every hour, then we will have a rich, practical experience, for God is love. He that dwelleth in love, dwelleth in God. Give love to them that need it most. The most unfortunate, those who have the most disagreeable temperaments need our love, our tenderness, our compassion. Those who try our patience need most love. We pass through the world only once; any good thing we can do, we should do most earnestly, untiringly, with the same spirit as is stated of Christ in His work. He will not fail nor be discouraged. The rough, stubborn, sullen dispositions are the ones who need help the most. How can they be helped? Only by that love practiced in dealing with them which Christ revealed to fallen man. Treat them, you may, as they deserve. What if Christ had treated us thus? He, the undeserving, was treated as we deserve. Still we are treated by Christ with grace and love as we did not deserve, but as He deserved. Treat some characters, as you think they richly deserve, and you will cut off from them the last thread of hope, spoil your influence and ruin the soul. Will it pay? No, I say no, a hundred times no. Bind these souls who need all the help it is possible for you to give them close to a loving, sympathizing, pitying heart, overflowing with Christlike love, and you will save a soul from death and hide a multitude of sins. Had we not better try the love process?

Be careful what you do in the line of suspending students. This is a solemn business. It should be a very grave fault which requires this discipline. Then there should be a careful consideration of all the circumstances connected with the case. Students sent from home a short distance or a long distance, thousands and thousands of miles, are away from and deprived of the advantages of home, and if expelled are refused the privileges of school. All their expenses have to be met by someone who has had hope and confidence in these subjects that their money would not be invested in vain. The student enters into, or falls into, temptation, and he is to be disciplined for his wrong. He feels keenly that his record is marred, and he disappoints those who have trusted him to develop a character under the influence of his training in his scholastic life, which will pay all that has been invested in his behalf. But he is suspended for his foolish course of action. What will he do? Courage is at the lowest ebb, courage and even manliness are not cherished. He is on expense, and precious time is lost. Who is tender and kind, and feels the burden of these souls? What wonder that Satan takes advantage of the circumstances. They are thrust on Satan's battle ground and the very worst feelings of the human heart are called into exercise and strengthened and become confirmed. I put the case as it has been presented to me. I wish all could view this as it has in all its bearings been shown me. I think there would be radical changes made in many rules and methods of dealing with human minds. There would be more physicians to heal human souls, who understand how to deal with human minds. There would be far more forgiveness and sympathy and love practiced, and far less discouraging, tearing down influences exercised. Supposing that Christ should deal with all His sons and daughters who learn of Him, as the human agent, as teachers, deal with those under their charge that when the law of the Lord, His rules, His injunctions have been disregarded by us, the guilty are expelled or suspended, turning the erring away from His saving, uplifting, educating influences, leaving him to pick and choose his own way and course of action without His divine assistance, what would become of our souls? His constant forgiving love is binding up our soul's interest with Himself. O the mightiness of the love of Jesus overwhelms me as I consider it. The yoke of Christ is easy and His burden is light. When we enter more entirely into the love of Jesus by practice, we shall see far different results in our own advancement as Christians, and in the molding of the character of those brought in relationship with us. The most difficult business for individuals is the giving up that which one thinks is his right. Love seeketh not her own. Heaven-born love strikes deeper than the surface. Love vaunteth not itself, is not puffed up. Fortified with the grace of Christ love doth not behave itself unseemly. He that dwelleth in love, dwelleth in God. God is love. We all need love, gentleness, tenderness, compassion, and forbearance. Expel from the soul every vestige of selfishness or human dignity.

When all hope was excluded from Adam and Eve in consequence of transgression and sin, when justice demanded the death of the sinner, Christ gave Himself to be a sacrifice for the sin of the world. The world was under condemnation. Christ became substitute and surety for man. He would give His life for the world, which is represented as the one lost sheep that had strayed from the fold, whose guilt as well as helplessness was charged against them and stood in the way, hindering their return. "Herein is love, not that we loved God, but that He loved us, and sent His Son to be a propitiation for our sins." "All we like sheep have gone astray; we have turned everyone to his own way; and the Lord hath laid on Him the iniquity of us all." Every son and daughter of God, if they have an abiding Saviour will act out Christ. Every soul that has not an abiding Saviour will reveal the same in unchristlikeness in character. Love is not cherished and put in exercise. "Lift Him up, the risen Saviour," in our words, in our conversation, in our dealing with the erring.

I know by the burden which is rolled upon me, that many who are officiating in our schools need themselves to learn in the school of Christ His meekness, His tender dealing with the erring, His compassion and love. Until they are melted over and the dross separated from the character they will work at cross purposes. I am deeply grieved in my heart for serious results which have followed unwise dealings, more serious than many are willing to admit to their own conscience or to God. Self is so large in many, ever striving for the mastery. There are those who profess to be followers of Jesus Christ who have never died to self. They have never fallen on the rock and been broken. Until this shall be, they will live unto self, and if they die as they are, it is forever too late for their wrongs to be righted. I love their souls. Jesus loves their souls and He will do a good work for them, if they will humble themselves under His mighty hand, repent and be converted, surrender every day to God. It must be a constant, daily surrender. We must be minute men and women, ever on guard over self, and watching to improve every opportunity to do good and only good for the souls for whom Christ has given His life to make them His own. When the human agents deal with these souls in a hard spirit they grieve the heart of Christ, and put Him to open shame, for they misrepresent in their own character the character of Christ. Said one, "Thy gentleness hath made me great." I pray to our heavenly Father that all connected with our schools may be in Christ as the branch is united to the living vine.--MS., 1893.

To the Students at Battle Creek College

I have a very deep interest in the educational institution at Battle Creek. For years my husband and myself were greatly exercised in reference to establishing a school in which our youth and children should have advantages of a superior character to those found in the common public schools, or in the colleges of the world. The Lord plainly specified what should be the character of the influence and instruction the school should maintain, in order that the important work might be accomplished for which the school was designed. As the knowledge and fear of the Lord is the beginning of wisdom, it was necessary that the study of the Bible should have a prominent place among the various branches of scientific education. The standard of the school was to be of high order, and the principles of vital godliness were ever to be kept before the students as a most essential feature of education. "And this is life eternal, that they might know Thee the only true God, and Jesus Christ, whom Thou hast sent." The youth were to be instructed in regard to the times in which we live, and to be made to understand that which will come to pass before the closing up of the world's history.

One reason why it was necessary to establish institutions of our own was the fact that parents were not able to counteract the influence of the teaching their children were receiving in the public schools, and the error there taught was leading the youth into false paths. No stronger influence could be brought to bear upon the minds of the youth and children than that of those who were educating them in principles of science. For this reason it was evident that schools must be established in which our children should be instructed in the way of truth. In our schools it was specified that the youth were to be taught in the principles of Bible temperance, and every influence was to be brought to bear upon them that would tend to help them to shun the follies of this degenerate age, which were fast making the world as a second Sodom.

In our institutions of learning there was to be exerted an influence that would counteract the influence of the world, and give no encouragement to indulgence in appetite, in selfish gratification of the senses, in pride, ambition, love of dress and display, love of praise and flattery, and strife for high rewards and honors as a recompense for good scholarship. All this was to be discouraged in our schools. It would be impossible to avoid these things, and yet send them to the public schools, where they would daily be brought in contact with that which would contaminate their morals. All through the world there was so great a neglect of proper home training that the children found at the public schools, for the most part, were profligate, and steeped in vice.

The work that we as a people were to do in this matter, was to establish a school, and do the work that Jesus Christ, from the pillar of cloud, had directed as the work of His people,--to train and educate our children and youth to regard the commandments of God. The manifest disregard of the world for the law of God was contaminating the morals of those who professed to be keeping the law of God. But we are called upon to follow the example of Abraham. Of him the Lord has said, "I know him, that he will command his children and his household after him, and they shall keep the way of the Lord, to do justice and judgment."

Abraham had to leave his country and his father's house, and sojourn in a strange land, in order to introduce successfully the new order of things in his household. The providence of God was ever to open up new methods, and progress was to be made from generation to generation, in order to preserve in the world a knowledge of the true God, of His laws and commandments. This could be done only by cultivating home religion. But it was not possible for Abraham to do this while he was surrounded by his idolatrous kinsfolk and friends. He must at God's command go out alone, and listen to the voice of Christ, the leader of the children of Israel. Jesus was on the earth to instruct and educate the chosen people of God. Abraham decided to obey the law of God, and the Lord knew that there would be no betrayal of sacred trust on his part, no yielding to any other guide than Him whom he felt under responsibility to obey. He recognized that he was accountable for the instruction of his household and his children, and commanded them after him to do justice and judgment. In teaching them the laws of God, he taught them that the Lord is our judge, our lawgiver and king, and that parents and children were to be ruled by Him; that on the part of parents there was to be no oppression, and on the part of children no unfilial disobedience.

The Lord commanded Moses to go and speak unto Pharaoh, bidding him to allow Israel to leave Egypt. For four hundred years they had been in Egypt, and had been in slavery to the Egyptians. They had been corrupted by idolatry, and the time came when God called them forth from Egypt, in order that they might obey His laws and keep His Sabbath, which He had instituted in Eden. He spoke the ten commandments to them in awful grandeur from Mount Sinai, that they might understand the sacred and enduring character of the law, and build up the foundation of many generations, by teaching their children the binding claims of God's holy precepts.

This is the work that we are called upon to do. From the pulpits of the popular churches it is proclaimed that the first day of the week is the Sabbath of the Lord; but God has given us light, showing us that the fourth precept of the decalogue is as verily binding as are the other nine moral precepts. It is our work to make plain to our children that the first day of the week is not the true Sabbath, and that its observance after light has come to us as to what is the true Sabbath, is idolatry, and in plain contradiction to the law of God. In order to give them instruction in regard to the claims of the law of Jehovah, it is necessary that we separate our children from worldly associations and influences, and keep before them the Scriptures of truth, by educating them line upon line, and precept upon precept, that they may not prove disloyal to God.

The Protestants have accepted the spurious Sabbath, the child of the papacy, and have exalted it above God's holy, sanctified day; and our institutions of learning have been established for the express purpose of counteracting the influence of those who do not follow the word of God. These are sufficient reasons to show the necessity of having educational institutions of our own; for we must teach truth rather than fiction and falsehood. The school is to supplement the home training, and both at home and at school, simplicity of dress, diet, and amusement must be maintained. An atmosphere must be created that will not be deleterious to the moral nature. Line upon line, precept upon precept, our children and households must be educated to keep the way of the Lord, to stand firmly for truth and righteousness. We must maintain a position against every species of sophistry that bewilders in this degenerate age, when error is glossed over, and so mingled with truth that it is almost impossible for those who are not familiar with the distinctions that the Scriptures make between the traditions of men and the word of God, to distinguish truth from error. It has been plainly stated that in this age "some shall depart from the faith, giving heed to seducing spirits, and doctrines of devils."

As the truth is brought into practical life, the standard is to be elevated higher and higher, to meet the requirements of the Bible. This will necessitate opposition to the fashions, customs, practices, and maxims of the world. Worldly influences, like the waves of the sea, beat against the followers of Christ to sweep them away from the true principles of the meekness and grace of Christ; but they are to stand as firm as a rock to principle. It will require moral courage to do this, and those whose souls are not riveted to the eternal Rock, will be swept away by the worldly current. We can stand firm only as our life is hid with Christ in God. Moral independence will be wholly in place when opposing the world. By conforming entirely to the will of God, we shall be placed upon vantage ground, and shall see the necessity of decided separation from the customs and practices of the world. We are not to elevate our standard just a little above the world's standard; but we are to make the line of demarcation decidedly apparent.

There are many in the church who at heart belong to the world, but God calls upon those who claim to believe the advanced truth, to rise above the present attitude of the popular churches of today. Where is the self-denial, where is the cross-bearing that Christ has said should characterize His followers? The reason we have had so little influence upon unbelieving relatives and associates is that we have manifested little decided difference in our practices from those of the world. Parents need to awake, and purify their souls by practicing the truth in their home life. When we reach the standard that the Lord would have us reach, worldlings will regard Seventh-day Adventists as odd, singular, strait-laced extremists. "We are made a spectacle unto the world, and to angels, and to men."

We are under solemn, sacred covenant to God to bring up our children, not for the world, not to put their hands into the hands of the world, but to love and fear God, and to keep His commandments. We are to instruct them to work intelligently in Christ's lines, to present a noble, elevated Christian character to those with whom they associate. For this reason our schools have been established, that youth and children may be so educated as to exert an influence for God in the world. Then shall our schools become converted to the world, and follow its customs and fashions? "I beseech you therefore, brethren, by the mercies of God, that ye present your bodies a living sacrifice, holy, acceptable unto God, which is your reasonable service. And be not conformed to this world: but be ye transformed by the renewing of your mind, that ye may prove what is that good, and acceptable, and perfect, will of God."

When those who have reached the years of youth and manhood see no difference between our schools and the colleges of the world, and have no preference as to which they attend, though error is taught by precept and example in the schools of the world, then there is need of closely examining the reasons that lead to such a conclusion. Our institutions of learning may swing into worldly conformity. Step by step they may advance to the world; but they are prisoners of hope, and God will correct and enlighten them, and bring them back to their upright position of distinction from the world. I am watching with intense interest, hoping to see our schools thoroughly imbued with the spirit of true and undefiled religion. When the students are thus imbued, they will see that there is a great work to be done in the lines in which Christ worked, and the time they have given to amusements will be given up to doing earnest missionary work. They will endeavor to do good to all about them, to lift up souls that are bowed down in discouragement, and to enlighten those who are in the darkness of error. They will put on the Lord Jesus Christ, and make no provision for the flesh to fulfill the lusts thereof.--Review and Herald, Jan. 9, 1894.

Students Required to be Workers with God

Jesus died for mankind, and in giving His life He exalted humanity in the scale of moral value with God. The Son of the infinite God clothed His divinity with humanity, and submitted to the death of the cross, that He might become a steppingstone by which humanity might meet with divinity. He made it possible for man to become a partaker of the divine nature, and escape the corruptions that are in the world through lust. Christ is continually working to uplift and ennoble man, and He requires that every soul whom He has redeemed from hopeless misery, shall co-operate with Him in the great work of saving the lost. We are not to lay snares and make secret plans to draw souls into temptation.

O, if everyone could see this matter as it is presented before me in all its bearings, how soon would they quit with the enemy in his artful work! How they would despise his measures to bring sin upon the human family! How they would hate sin with a perfect hatred, as they consider the fact that it cost the life of heaven's Commander, in order that they should not perish, that man should not be bound a hopeless captive to Satan's chariot, a degraded slave to his will, a trophy of his victory and his kingdom.

Who will link up with Satan? Who will wear his badge? Who will choose him as a captain, and refuse to stand under the blood-stained banner of the Captain of our salvation? Christ died for every son and daughter of Adam; and when the Son of God has expressed such amazing love, making this great sacrifice for the sinner, in order that through faith in Him he need not perish but have everlasting life, how can the subject of this great love be indifferent and stand in sin and disobedience, and not heartily confess Christ without one moment's delay? How can anyone love to do evil? How can the youth prostitute their reasoning faculties to Satan, and give their influence to that which will weaken their own moral power and efficiency? In doing the will of Him who loves the world, and who gave His only-begotten Son to die for them, they strengthen every faculty of the soul, and increase their own happiness and peace.

The Lord has greatly honored men, by giving Jesus Christ to recover them from Satan's claims. Will you be recovered? Will you have the precious gift of Christ? or will you refuse His service? Jesus has said, "He that gathereth not with Me scattereth abroad." He has said, "Without Me ye can do nothing," and, "My grace is sufficient for thee." Everyone who seeks to do well in his own finite strength, will find his efforts a failure; but those who accept Christ by faith, will find him a personal Saviour. They will enlist in His army, they will become His soldiers, and fight the good fight of faith. If they are students in the school, they will feel that they are enlisted to make the school the most orderly, elevated, and praiseworthy institution in the world. They will put every jot of their influence on the side of God, on the side of Christ, and on the side of heavenly intelligences. They will feel it to be their duty to form a Christian endeavor society, that they may help every student to see the inconsistency of a course of action that God will not approve. They will draw with Christ, and do their utmost to perfect Christian characters. They will take upon themselves the work of leading the lame and the weak into the safe, upward path. They will form Christian endeavor meetings to make plans that will be a blessing to the institution of learning, and do all in their power to make the school what God designed and signified that it should be. They will have in mind the value and efficiency of Christian endeavor meetings, in preparing missionaries to go forth to give the warning to the world.

Students should have their own seasons of prayer, where they may offer fervent, simple petitions that God shall bless the president of the school with physical strength, mental clearness, moral power, and spiritual discernment, and that every teacher shall be qualified by the grace of Christ to do his work with fidelity and with fervent love. They should pray that teachers may be the agents through whom God shall work to make good prevail over evil, through a knowledge of Jesus Christ whom He hath sent. May God give the students who attend our institutions of learning, grace and courage to act up to the principles revealed in the law of God, which is an expression of His character. Never be found disparaging the schools which God has established. If you have failed at any time, falling into temptation, it is because you did not make God your strength, because you did not have the faith that works by love and purifies the soul.

Let every sincere Christian who has a connection with our schools, be determined to be a faithful servant in the cause of Christ, and help every student to be faithful, pure, and holy in life. Let everyone who loves God seek to win those who have not yet confessed Christ. Every day they may exert a silent, prayerful influence, and co-operate with Jesus Christ, the missionary-in-chief to our world. Let every--man, woman, and youth--grow in excellence of character and devotion, in purity and holiness, and live with an eye single to the glory of God, that the enemies of our faith may not triumph. Let there be such a binding together in the bonds of our holy faith, that our united influence may be wholly on the Lord's side, and may work for the transformation of those with whom we associate. Let it be made manifest that you have a living connection with God, and are ambitious for the Master's glory, seeking to cultivate in yourselves every grace of character by which you may honor Him who gave His life for you. May the love of Christ exercise a constraining power to draw others into the path cast up for the ransomed of the Lord to walk in. When the students in our schools shall learn to like God's will, they will find it comparatively easy to do it.

If students see defects of character in others, let them be thankful that they have discerned these defects, and therefore may be put on their guard against them. You will, no doubt, see persons who are not learning the meekness and lowliness of Christ, but who love display, and are vain, frivolous, and worldly. The only remedy for such is to behold Jesus, and by studying His character they will come to despise everything that is vain and frivolous, weak and mean. The character of Christ is full of forbearance, patience, goodness, mercy, and unexampled love. By beholding such a character, they will rise above the littleness of that which has fashioned and molded them, and made them unholy and unlovely. They will say, "I have not sat with vain persons, neither will I go in with dissemblers." They will realize that "he that walketh with wise men shall be wise: but a companion of fools shall be destroyed."

Let everyone who is seeking to live a Christian life, remember that the church militant is not the church triumphant. Those who are carnally minded will be found in the church. They are to be pitied more than blamed. The church is not to be judged as sustaining these characters, though they be found within her borders. Should the church expel them, the very ones who found fault with their presence there, would blame the church for sending them adrift in the world; they would claim that they were treated unmercifully. It may be that in the church there are those who are cold, proud, haughty, and unchristian, but you need not associate with this class. There are many who are warm-hearted, who are self-denying, self-sacrificing, who would, were it required, lay down their lives to save souls. Jesus saw the bad and the good in church relationship, and said, "Let both grow together until the harvest." None are under the necessity of becoming tares because every plant in the field is not wheat. If the truth were known, these complainers make their accusations in order to quiet a convicted, condemning conscience. Their own course of action is not wholly commendable. Even those who are striving for the mastery over the enemy, have sometimes been wrong and done wrong. Evil prevails over good when we do not trust wholly in Christ, and abide in Him. Inconsistencies of character will then be manifested that would not be revealed if we preserved the faith that works by love and purifies the soul.

We are not compelled to choose as familiar associates those who reject the love of God that has been expressed in giving His Son to our world, "that whosoever believeth in Him should not perish, but have everlasting life." Those who love God will not choose the enemies of God to be their friends. The question was asked, "Shouldest thou help the ungodly, and love them which hate the Lord?" Will you prefer the association of the irreligious and disloyal, to that of those who are obeying the commandments of God? Will you choose to separate yourself from those who love God, and place yourself as far as possible from the channel of light? You want to keep in an atmosphere of purity and faith, and bring into your character principles that will be as solid timbers. Christians will not choose and cultivate the society of non-Christians. If the Lord gives you a special position in the world, as He did Joseph and Daniel, then he will sustain and keep you in the midst of temptation. But you will never be where you will find too much light, in our world. Then how perilous it is to choose the association of those who love darkness rather than light, and will not come to the light, lest their deeds should be reproved.--Review and Herald, Jan. 16, 1894.

FOR ADDITIONAL READING

The Childhood of Jesus, The Youth's Instructor, August 30, 1894.

Words to Students

Every soul is surrounded with an atmosphere peculiar to the individual. This atmosphere may be full of spiritual malaria that is poisonous to the principles of righteousness. But when brought into association with others, it need not take us days or weeks to ascertain whether the atmosphere of the spirit is of Christ or of Satan. The influence of association is never stronger than in school life; but the student who comes to school with an earnest desire to be a help and a blessing to his fellows, will be careful to cast his influence on the right side, and seek companions who will join with him in cultivating right principles and practices.

Students should feel their responsibility in the matter of making their school life a success. They should bend every effort in the right direction, so that they may not disappoint their parents or guardians who work hard to keep them in school, and who are deeply anxious for their present and eternal welfare. Students should determine that they will make a record that they will not be ashamed to meet in the day of judgment. A student who is circumspect in his deportment, who will not be swayed to the right or left by wrong influences, will exercise a restraining power over those in the school who take pleasure in showing their independence, and in engaging in wicked sports in disobedience to the rules, and who fill the hearts of their teachers with sorrow and discouragement.

Life is a problem which we must individually work out for ourselves. No one can form a character for another; we each have a part to act in deciding our own destiny. We are God's free, responsible agents, and each one must work out his own salvation with fear and trembling, while God works in him to will and to do of His own good pleasure. Students may do good, or they may do evil, but "whatsoever a man soweth, that shall he also reap."

We are individually on trial under the proving of God. The intelligences of heaven are all enlisted to help every soul who will be drawn to Jesus, and every true lover of Jesus will co-operate with the heavenly agents in seeking to draw souls away from that which is foolish, low, and frivolous. The followers of Christ will not work on the side of Satan to weaken faith in true religion, to deprave others by casting about them an atmosphere which is ruinous to the morals and the character. But we are sorry to say that even in our schools there are persons who are Christians only in name. It will not take a long acquaintance with these professors to ascertain that they are successful agents of Satan. There are in our schools persons who are corrupt at heart, who yet have a pleasing address, and who are successful in fascinating a certain class of people, and before the unwary are aware of it, the influence of these persons has changed their sentiments, and fashioned them after the objectionable characters of these corrupt persons. But those who wear the garb of Christianity, and yet who are governed by the fashions and maxims of the world, are moral corrupters. They claim to be seeking heavenly treasures, but the atmosphere with which their souls are surrounded is one that is charged with a deadly spiritual miasma, and they should be shunned by those who would remain unspotted by the world.

The youth who has discernment can readily see what kind of persons these are, even though he lays no claim to Christianity; for he knows that they are not Christlike. But shall he allow them to be as stumbling blocks to him? He has a guidebook that describes those who are on the Lord's side. If he knows that their course is inconsistent with a profession of Christianity, if he understands what it means to live a godly life, he will be held accountable for the light and knowledge he has. He will be responsible for doing the Master's will, for showing to the world what is the true idea of Christianity--what it is to have a Christlike life and character.

We have a powerful enemy, and not only does he hate every human being made in the image of God, but with bitterest enmity he hates God and His only-begotten Son Jesus Christ. When men give themselves over to be the slaves of Satan, he does not manifest the enmity toward them which he does to those who bear the name of Christ, and give themselves to the service of God. He hates them with a deadly hatred. He knows that he can grieve Jesus by bringing them under the power of his deceptions, by injuring them, by weakening their faith, by making them incapable of doing God service as they are required to serve under their Captain Jesus Christ. Satan will permit those to have a degree of rest who are bound as slaves to his chariot, for they are his willing captives; but his enmity is aroused when the message of mercy reaches his bondslaves, and they seek to wrench themselves away from his power, that they may follow the true Shepherd. Then it is that he seeks to bind them with additional chains to hold them in their captivity. The conflict between the soul and Satan begins when the captive begins to tug at the chain, and longs to be free; for it is then that the human agent begins to co-operate with heavenly intelligences, when faith takes hold on Christ. Then it is that the Stronger than the strong man armed, is the helper of the soul, and the poor captive is strengthened by the Holy Spirit to obtain his freedom.

God has a deep and earnest love for every member of the human family; not one is forgotten, not one is left helpless and deceived to be overcome by the enemy. And if those who have enlisted in the army of Christ will put on the whole armor of God, and wear it, they will be proof against all the assaults of the enemy. Those who really desire to be taught of God, and to walk in His way, have the sure promise that if they feel their lack of wisdom and ask of God, He will give liberally, and upbraid not. The apostle says, "Let him ask in faith, nothing wavering. For he that wavereth is like a wave of the sea driven with the wind and tossed. For let not that man think that he shall receive anything of the Lord. A double-minded man is unstable in all his ways." God is behind every promise, and we cannot dishonor Him more than by questioning and hesitating, by asking and not believing, and then by talking doubt. If you do not immediately receive what you have asked for, will you go on in sullenness and unbelief? Believe; believe that God will do just what He has promised. Keep your prayers ascending, and watch, work, and wait. Fight the good fight of faith. Say to your heart, "God has invited me to come. He has heard my prayer. He has pledged His word that he will receive me, and He will fulfill His promise. I can trust God; for He so loved me that He gave His only-begotten Son to die for me. The Son of God is my Redeemer." "Ask, and it shall be given you; seek, and ye shall find; knock, and it shall be opened unto you." "If ye then, being evil, know how to give good gifts unto your children: how much more shall your heavenly Father give the Holy Spirit to them that ask Him?"

The youth who enter and continue their school life with the true object before them, will not be homesick or disappointed. They will not be restless and uneasy, not knowing what to do with themselves. They will find a helper in the Omnipotent One. They will have one aim in view, and that is to be men and women of principle, who will meet God's standard, and benefit humanity and glorify God. They will not regard their school life as a time for pleasure seeking, for idle amusement and foolish frolic, but will endeavor to make the most of their God-given opportunities and privileges, so that they shall not disappoint their parents and teachers, or grieve God and heavenly intelligences.

It is a solemn thing to die, but it is a far more solemn thing to live, and to form a character that will qualify us to enter the school in the heavenly courts above. We are living in an enemy's land, and we may expect difficulty and conflict. The youth will have to be able to endure hardness as good soldiers of Jesus Christ. It is not best that their path should be made perfectly smooth and easy, that they should be supplied with money, and not taught to feel the necessity of practicing self-denial and economy.

When a youth is making up his mind that he wants to obtain an education, he should carefully consider what is his motive in going to school? He should ask himself, How shall I best employ my time so as to reap all the benefit possible from my opportunities and privileges? Shall I put on the whole armor of God which has been provided for me by the gift of the only-begotten Son of God? Shall I open my heart to the Holy Spirit, that every faculty and energy may be aroused, which God has given me in trust? I am Christ's property, and am employed in His service. I am a steward of His grace.

Although, to your human judgment, some who profess Christianity do not meet your measurement of Christian character, you should not grieve the heart of Christ by living an inconsistent life; for others are in danger of being influenced by your wrong course of action. You are fighting for the crown of life, and should not rest satisfied in meeting a low standard.

The Lord accepts no halfway work; there must be on your part no blundering in the sacred work of God. Do not trust yourself, but surrender your will and ideas and ways to God, and do His will alone. Live to please Him who thought you of such value that He gave Jesus, His only-begotten

Son, to save you from your sins. Through His merit, you may be accepted. In your school life ever keep before you the thought that what is worth doing at all, is worth doing well. Depend upon God for wisdom, that you may not discourage one soul in right doing. Work with Christ in drawing souls to Him. But it will not do for you, while condemning half-hearted work in others, while pointing out their errors, to fail to do as well as they do, because you will not place yourself on the side of right and loyalty. Even though the rules and regulations seem needlessly exacting, be obedient to them; for you may err in your experience. Do your very best in everything you undertake. Jesus is your Saviour, and rely upon Him to help you day by day, that you may not sow tares, but the good seed of the kingdom.

"The light of the body is the eye: if therefore thine eye be single, thy whole body shall be full of light. But if thine eye be evil, thy whole body shall be full of darkness." As a student, you must learn to see with your brain as well as your eyes. You must educate your judgment so that it shall not be feeble and inefficient. You must pray for guidance, and commit your way unto the Lord. You must close your heart against all foolishness and sin, and open it to every heavenly influence. You must make the most of your time and opportunities, in order to develop a symmetrical character. Fun and folly and indolence cannot be entertained as your guests, if you copy the pattern, Christ Jesus, and become daily more intelligent as to what you shall do to be saved.

Youthful students, your life cannot be governed by impulse without proving an entire failure. You cannot follow your natural inclinations without meeting with a great loss. If you would move securely, you must keep the way of the Lord. Your understanding must be refined and purified; you must work according to God's plan, or fail to make a success. You must ever be growing and advancing in grace and knowledge. You will be able to do nothing acceptably in your school life without practicing habits of system and order. Haphazard work will bring certain failure.

You need to study carefully the question of amusements. Ask yourself, What is the influence of amusements on mind and character, and on the work which I have come to do? Ask yourself, What bearing has the question of amusements on my religious life, on my character as a Christian? Do the games in which you participate, fit you to engage in prayer and in the service of God? Do they aid you to bring as much zeal and earnestness into the Lord's work as you put into the games you play? Have not these amusements in which you have engaged, absorbed your interest so that you have not been able to put as much fervor into the learning of your lessons as you should have done? Which is to have the supremacy--the service of God, or the service of self? Let every student closely examine the ground on which he is standing.

Dear youth, you are now deciding your own eternal destiny. You must put persistent effort into your Christian life if you would perfect a right character. It will be to your eternal loss if you have a dwarfed, weakly, babyish religious experience. We are to be "complete in Him." "As ye have therefore received Christ Jesus the Lord, so walk ye in Him." This means that you are to study the life of Christ. You are to study it with as much more earnestness than you study secular lines of knowledge, as eternal interests are more important than temporal, earthly pursuits. If you appreciate the value and sacredness of eternal things, you will bring your sharpest thoughts, your best energies, to the solving of the problem that involves your eternal well-being; for every other interest sinks into nothingness in comparison with that.

You have the Pattern, Christ Jesus; walk in His footsteps, and you will be qualified to fill any and every position that you may be called upon to occupy. You will be "rooted and built up in Him, and stablished in the faith, as ye have been taught, abounding therein with thanksgiving." You are not to feel that you are a bondslave, but a son of God; that you are highly favored in that you have been regarded of so great value that God has made you His by paying an infinite ransom for your freedom. Jesus says, "I call you not servants; . . . but I have called you friends." When you appreciate His wondrous love, love and gratitude will be in your heart as a wellspring of joy.

Do not receive flattery, even in your religious life. Flattery is an art by which Satan lieth in wait to deceive and to puff up the human agent with high thoughts of himself. "Beware lest any man spoil you through philosophy and vain deceit, after the tradition of men, after the rudiments of the world, and not after Christ." Flattery has been the food upon which many of our youth have been nourished; and those who have praised and flattered have supposed that they were doing right; but they have been doing wrong. Praise, flattery, and indulgence have done more toward leading precious souls into false paths, than any other art that Satan has devised.

Flattery is a part of the world's policy, but it is no part of Christ's policy. Through flattery poor human beings, full of frailty and infirmities, come to think that they are efficient and worthy, and become puffed up in their fleshly mind. They become intoxicated with the idea that they possess ability beyond what they do have, and their religious experience becomes unbalanced. Unless in the providence of God they shall be turned from these deceptions, and become converted, and learn the A B C of religion in the school of Christ, they will lose their souls.

Many a youth has been flattered that he has ability as a natural gift; when the ability he thinks he has, can be attained only through diligent training and culture, learning the meekness and lowliness of Christ. Believing he is naturally gifted, he thinks there is no necessity of putting his mind to the task of mastering his lessons; and before he is aware, he is fast in the snare of Satan. God permits him to be attacked by the enemy, in order that he may understand his own weakness. He is permitted to make some decided blunder, and is plunged into painful humiliation. But when he is writhing under a sense of his own weakness, he is not to be judged harshly. This is the time above all others when he needs a judicious counselor, a true friend, who has discernment of character. This is the time when he needs a friend who is led by the Spirit of God, and who will deal patiently and faithfully with the erring, and lift up the soul that is bowed down. He is not to be lifted up by the aid of flattery. No one is authorized to deal out to the soul this delusive intoxicant of Satan. Rather he is to be pointed to the first rounds of the ladder, and his stumbling feet are to be placed on the lowest round of the ladder of progress. Peter says, "Add to your faith virtue; and to virtue knowledge; and to knowledge temperance; and to temperance patience; and to patience godliness; and to godliness brotherly kindness; and to brotherly kindness charity. For if these things be in you, and abound, they make you that ye shall neither be barren nor unfruitful in the knowledge of our Lord Jesus Christ."

Let the erring one be encouraged to climb step by step, round by round. The effort may be painful to him, but it will be by far the best lesson he has ever learned; for by so doing he will become acquainted with his own weakness, and thus be enabled to avoid in the future the errors of the past. Through the aid of wise counselors, his defeat will be turned into victory. But let no one attempt to begin at the top of the ladder. Let everyone start at the lowest round, and mount step by step, climbing up by Christ, clinging to Christ, ascending to the height of Christ. This is the only way to advance heavenward. Let nothing turn the attention away from the great work that is to be done. Let the thoughts, the aptitude, the keen exercise of the brain power, be put to the highest uses in studying the word and will of God. The Lord has a place for the very best ability He has entrusted to men. In the work of building up His kingdom, we may employ every capacity given of God, as faithfully and earnestly as did Daniel in Babylon, when he was found faithful to every duty to man, and loyal to his God.

God calls for far more tact, more wise generalship, than has yet been given Him by His human agents. There is need of sharp, sanctified thinking, and keen work to counteract the ingenious plans of Satan. There is a call for a higher standard to be met, a holier, more determined, self-sacrificing effort to be put forth in the Lord's work. Our youth must be educated to meet a higher standard, to understand that they are now deciding their own eternal destiny. There is no safeguard for anyone, save in having in the heart the truth as it is in Jesus. This must be planted in the heart by the Holy Spirit. Much that is now called religion will sink out of sight when it is assailed by the hosts of Satan. Nothing will stand but the truth,--the wisdom that is from above, which will sanctify the soul.

Let no one imagine that self-indulgence is religion. Let not selfishness be pampered. Let the youth learn to restrict their desires, and to beware of extravagance in the use of means. Let all look unto Jesus, contemplate His character, and follow in His footsteps. "For in Him dwelleth all the fullness of the Godhead bodily. And ye are complete in Him, which is the head of all principality and power."--Youth's Instructor, May 3, 10, 17, 24, 1894.

Study the Bible for Yourselves

Allow no one to be brains for you, allow no one to do your thinking, your investigating, and your praying. This is the instruction we need to take to heart today. Many of you are convinced that the precious treasure of the kingdom of God and of Jesus Christ is in the Bible which you hold in your hand. You know that no earthly treasure is attainable without painstaking effort. Why should you expect to understand the treasures of the word of God without diligently searching the Scriptures?

It is proper and right to read the Bible; but your duty does not end there; for you are to search its pages for yourselves. The knowledge of God is not to be gained without mental effort, without prayer for wisdom in order that you may separate from the pure grain of truth the chaff with which men and Satan have misrepresented the doctrines of truth. Satan and his confederacy of human agents have endeavored to mix the chaff of error with the wheat of truth. We should diligently seek for the hidden treasure, and seek wisdom from heaven in order to separate human inventions from the divine commands. The Holy Spirit will aid the seeker for great and precious truths which relate to the plan of redemption. I would impress upon all the fact that a casual reading of the Scriptures is not enough. We must search, and this means the doing of all the word implies. As the miner eagerly explores the earth to discover its veins of gold, so you are to explore the word of God for the hidden treasure that Satan has so long sought to hide from man. The Lord says, "If any man willeth to do His will, he shall know of the teaching." John 7:17 (R. V.)

The word of God is truth and light, and is to be a lamp unto your feet, to guide you every step of the way to the gates of the city of God. It is for this reason that Satan has made such desperate efforts to obstruct the path that has been cast up for the ransomed of the Lord to walk in. You are not to take your ideas to the Bible, and make your opinions a center around which truth is to revolve. You are to lay aside your ideas at the door of investigation, and with humble, subdued hearts, with self hid in Christ, with earnest prayer, you are to seek wisdom from God. You should feel that you must know the revealed will of God, because it concerns your personal, eternal welfare. The Bible is a directory by which you may know the way to eternal life. You should desire above all things that you may know the will and ways of the Lord. You should not search for the purpose of finding texts of Scripture that you can construe to prove your theories; for the word of God declares that this is wresting the Scriptures to your own destruction. You must empty yourselves of every prejudice, and come in the spirit of prayer to the investigation of the word of God.

The great error of the Romish Church is found in the fact that the Bible is interpreted in the light of the opinions of the "fathers." Their opinions are regarded as infallible, and the dignitaries of the church assume that it is their prerogative to make others believe as they do, and to use force to compel the conscience. Those who do not agree with them are pronounced heretics. But the word of God is not thus to be interpreted. It is to stand on its own eternal merits, to be read as the word of God, to be obeyed as the voice of God, which declares His will to the people. The will and voice of finite man are not to be interpreted as the voice of God.

The blessed Bible gives us a knowledge of the great plan of salvation, and shows us how every individual may have eternal life. Who is the author of the book?--Jesus Christ. He is the True Witness, and He says to His own, "I give unto them eternal life; and they shall never perish, neither shall any man pluck them out of My hand." The Bible is to show us the way to Christ, and in Christ eternal life is revealed. Jesus said to the Jews and to those who pressed about Him in great multitudes, "Search the Scriptures." The Jews had the word in the Old Testament, but they had so mingled it with human opinions, that its truths were mystified, and the will of God to man was covered up. The religious teachers of the people are following their example in this age.

Though the Jews had the Scriptures which testified of Christ, they were not able to discern Christ in the Scriptures; and although we have the Old and the New Testament, men wrest the Scriptures to evade their truths; and in their interpretations of the Scriptures, they teach, as did the Pharisees, the maxims and traditions of men for the commandments of God. In Christ's day the religious leaders had so long presented human ideas before the people, that the teaching of Christ was in every way opposed to their theories and practice. His sermon on the mount virtually contradicted the doctrines of the self-righteous scribes and Pharisees. They had so misrepresented God that He was looked upon as a stern judge, incapable of compassion, mercy, and love. They presented to the people endless maxims and traditions as proceeding from God, when they had no "Thus saith the Lord" for their authority. Though they professed to know and to worship the true and living God, they wholly misrepresented Him; and the character of God, as represented by His Son, was as an original subject, a new gift to the world. Christ made every effort so to sweep away the misrepresentations of Satan, that the confidence of man in the love of God might be restored. He taught man to address the Supreme Ruler of the universe by the new name--"Our Father." This name signifies His true relation to us, and when spoken in sincerity by human lips, it is music in the ears of God. Christ leads us to the throne of God by a new and living way, to present Him to us in His paternal love.--Review and Herald, Sept. 11, 1894.

Work and Education

Our minds have been much exercised day and night in regard to our schools. How shall they be conducted? And what shall be the education and training of the youth? Where shall our Australian Bible School be located? I was awakened this morning at one o'clock with a heavy burden upon my soul. The subject of education has been presented before me in different lines, in varied aspects, by many illustrations, and with direct specification, now upon one point, and again upon another. I feel, indeed, that we have much to learn. We are ignorant in regard to many things.

In writing and speaking upon the life of John the Baptist and the life of Christ, I have tried to present that which has been presented to me in regard to the education of our youth. We are under obligation to God to study this subject candidly; for it is worthy of close, critical examination upon every side. Of John the Baptist, Christ declared, "Of them that are born of women there hath not risen a greater." That prophet was led by the Spirit of God into the wilderness, away from the contaminating influences of the city, to obtain an education that would qualify him to receive instruction from God rather than from any of the learned scribes. He was not to connect himself with the rabbis; the less he became acquainted with their teachings, their maxims, and traditions, the more easily could the Lord impress his mind and heart, and give him the pure mold of truth that was to be given to the people to prepare the way of the Lord. The teachings of the scribes and Pharisees were of a character to turn the people away from the unadulterated truth that was to be presented by the Great Teacher when He should enter upon His mission. The only hope of the people was to open their hearts and minds to the light sent from heaven by His prophet, the forerunner of Christ.

These lessons are for us. Those who claim to know the truth and understand the great work to be done for this time are to consecrate themselves to God, soul, body, and spirit. In heart, in dress, in language, in every respect they are to be separate from the fashions and practices of the world. They are to be a peculiar and holy people. It is not their dress that makes them peculiar, but because they are a peculiar and holy people, they cannot carry the marks of likeness to the world.

As a people we are to prepare the way of the Lord. Every iota of ability God has given us must be put to use in preparing the people after God's fashion, after His spiritual mold, to stand in this great day of God's preparation; and the serious question may be awakened in world-loving hearts, "What is eternity to us? How will my case stand in the investigative judgment? What will be my lot and place?" Many who suppose they are going to heaven are blindfolded by the world. Their ideas of what constitutes a religious education and religious discipline are vague, resting only on probabilities; there are many who have no intelligent hope, and are running great risk in practicing the very things which Jesus has taught that they should not do, in eating, drinking, and dressing, binding themselves up with the world in a variety of ways. They have yet to learn the serious lessons so essential to growth in spirituality, to come out from the world and be separate. The heart is divided, the carnal mind craves conformity, similarity to the world in so many ways that the mark of distinction from the world is scarcely distinguishable. Money, God's money, is expended in order to make an appearance after the world's customs; the religious experience is contaminated with worldliness, and the evidence of discipleship--Christ's likeness in self-denial and cross-bearing--is not discernible by the world or by the universe of heaven.

In this country, Satan has in a most striking manner enthroned himself to control the leading men in the government of the nation. The education which they have received from childhood is erroneous. Many things are regarded as essential which have a most injurious effect upon the people. The many holidays have had a baleful influence upon the minds of the youth; their effect is demoralizing to the government, and they are entirely contrary to the will of God. They have a tendency to encourage an artificial excitement, a desire for amusement. The people are led to squander precious time which should be employed in useful labor to sustain their families honestly and keep clear of debt. The passion for amusements and the squandering of money in horse racing, in betting, and various similar lines, is increasing the poverty of the country, and deepening the misery that is the sure result of this kind of education.

Never can the proper education be given to the youth in this country, or any other country, unless they are separated a wide distance from the cities. The customs and practices in the cities unfit the minds of the youth for the entrance of truth. The liquor-drinking, the smoking and gambling, the horse racing, the theater going, the great importance placed upon holidays,--are all a species of idolatry, a sacrifice upon idol altars. If people conscientiously attend to their lawful business upon the holidays, they are regarded as mean-spirited and unpatriotic. The Lord cannot be served in this way. Those who multiply the days for pleasure and amusement are really giving patronage to liquor-sellers, and are taking from the poor the very means that should purchase food and clothing for their children, the very means that, used economically, would soon provide a dwelling place for their families. These evils we can only touch upon.

It is not the correct plan to locate school buildings where the students will have constantly before their eyes the erroneous practices that have molded their education during their lifetime, be it longer or shorter. These holidays, with all their train of evil, result in twentyfold more misery than good. In a large degree the observance of these days is really compulsory. Even persons who have been truly converted find it difficult to break away from these customs and practices. Should schools be located in the cities or within a few miles from them, it would be most difficult to counteract the influence of the former education which students have received in regard to these holidays and the practices connected with them, such as horse racing, betting, and the offering of prizes. The very atmosphere of these cities is full of poisonous malaria. The freedom of individual action is not respected; a man's time is not regarded as really his own; he is expected to do as others do. Should our school be located in one of these cities, or within a few miles of it, there would be a counterworking influence constantly in active exercise to be met and overcome. The devotion to amusements and the observance of so many holidays, give a large business to the courts, to officers and judges, and increase the poverty and squalor that need no increasing.

All this is a false education. We shall find it necessary to establish our schools out of, and away from, the cities, and yet not so far away that they cannot be in touch with them, to do them good, to let light shine amid the moral darkness. Students need to be placed under the most favorable circumstances to counteract very much of the education they have received.

Entire families are in need of thorough transformation in their habits and ideas before they can be true representatives of Jesus Christ. And to a great extent children who are to receive an education in our schools, will make far more advancement if separated from the family circle where they have received an erroneous education. It may be necessary for some families to locate where they can board their children and save expense, but in many cases it would prove a hindrance rather than a blessing to their children. The people of this country have so little appreciation of the importance of industrious habits that the children are not educated to do real, earnest work. This must be a part of the education given to the youth.

God gave Adam and Eve employment. Eden was the school for our first parents, and God was their instructor. They learned how to till the soil and to care for the things which the Lord had planted. They did not regard labor as degrading, but as a great blessing. Industry was a pleasure to Adam and Eve. The fall of Adam changed the order of things; the earth was cursed: but the decree that man should earn his bread by the sweat of his brow, was not given as a curse. Through faith and hope, labor was to be a blessing to the descendants of Adam and Eve. God never meant that man should have nothing to do. But the more and deeper the curse of sin, the more the order of God is changed. The burden of toil rests heavily upon a certain class, but the curse of idleness is upon many who are in possession of God's money, and all because of the false idea that money increases the moral worth of men. Labor is to human beings what they make it. To delve in constant toil, seeking momentary relief in liquor-drinking and exciting amusements, will make men little better than the brutes.

We need schools in this country to educate children and youth that they may be masters of labor, and not slaves of labor. Ignorance and idleness will not elevate one member of the human family. Ignorance will not lighten the lot of the hard toiler. Let the worker see what advantage he may gain in the humblest occupation, by using the ability God has given him as an endowment. Thus he can become an educator, teaching others the art of doing work intelligently. He may understand what it means to love God with the heart, the soul, the mind, and the strength. The physical powers are to be brought into service from love to God. The Lord wants the physical strength, and you can reveal your love for Him by the right use of your physical powers, doing the very work which needs to be done. There is no respect of persons with God.

When the tabernacle was built in the wilderness for the service of God, the work was done under divine direction. God was the designer, the workmen were educated by Him, and they put heart and soul and strength into the work. There was hard labor to be done, and the sturdy mechanic taxed muscle and sinew, manifesting his love to God in the toil for His honor.

There is in the world a great deal of hard, taxing work to be done, and he who labors without exercising the God-given powers of mind and heart and soul, he who employs the physical strength alone, makes the work a wearisome tax and burden. There are men with mind, heart, and soul who regard work as a drudgery, and settle down to it with self-complacent ignorance, delving without thought, without taxing the mental capabilities in order to do the work better.

There is science in the humblest kind of work, and if all would thus regard it, they would see nobility in labor. Heart and soul are to be put into work of any kind; then there is cheerfulness and efficiency. In agricultural or mechanical occupations men may give evidence to God that they appreciate His gift in the physical powers, and the mental faculties as well. Let the educated ability be employed in devising improved methods of work. This is what the Lord wants. There is honor in any class of work that is essential to be done. Let the law of God be made the standard of action, and it ennobles and sanctifies all labor. Faithfulness in the discharge of every duty makes the work noble, and reveals a character that God can approve.

"Thou shalt love the Lord thy God with all thy heart, and with all thy soul, and with all thy mind, and with all thy strength." God desires the love that is expressed in heart-service, in soul-service, in the service of the physical powers. We are not to be dwarfed in any kind of service for God. Whatever He has lent us is to be used intelligently for Him. The man who exercises his faculties will surely strengthen them, but he must seek to do his best. There is need of intelligence and educated ability to devise the best methods in farming, in building, and in every other department, that the worker may not labor in vain.

It is not a virtue for men or women to excuse slow bungling at work of any character. The slow habits must be overcome. The man who is slow, and does his work at a disadvantage, is an unprofitable workman. His slowness is a defect that needs to be seen and corrected. He needs to exercise his intellect in planning how to use his time so as to secure the best results.

When one is forever at work, and the work is never done, it is because mind and heart are not put into the work. It takes some persons ten hours to do that which another accomplishes readily in five. Such workmen do not bring tact and method into their labor. There is something to be learned every day as to how to improve in the manner of labor so as to get through the work, and have time for something else. It is the duty of every worker not merely to give his strength but his mind and intellect to that which he undertakes to do. Some who are engaged in domestic labor are always at work; it is not because they have so much to do, but they do not plan in such a way as to have time. They should give themselves a certain time to accomplish their task, and make every move tell. Dullness and ignorance are no virtue. You can choose to become stereotyped in a wrong course of action because you have not the determination to take yourselves in hand and to reform, or you may cultivate your powers to do the very best kind of service, and then you will find yourselves in demand anywhere and everywhere. You will be appreciated for all that you are worth. "Whatsoever thy hand findeth to do, do it with thy might." "Not slothful in business; fervent in spirit; serving the Lord."

317 Australia needs the leaven of sound, solid, common sense to be freely introduced into all her cities and towns. There is need of proper education. Schools should be established for the purpose of obtaining not only knowledge from books, but knowledge of practical industry. Men are needed in different communities to show the people how riches are to be obtained from the soil. The cultivation of land will bring its return.

Through the observance of holidays the people both of the world and of the churches have been educated to believe that these lazy days are essential to health and happiness; but the results reveal that they are full of evil, which is ruining the country. The youth generally are not educated to diligent habits. Cities and even country towns are becoming like Sodom and Gomorrah, and like the world in the days of Noah. The training of the youth in those days was after the same order as children are being educated and trained in this age, to love excitement, to glorify themselves, to follow the imagination of their own evil hearts. Now as then, depravity, cruelty, violence, and crime are the result.

All these things are lessons for us. Few now are really industrious and economical. Poverty and distress are on every hand. There are men who work hard, and obtain very little for their labor. There is need of much more extensive knowledge in regard to the preparation of the soil. There is not sufficient breadth of view as to what can be realized from the earth. A narrow and unvarying routine is followed with discouraging results. The land boom has cursed this country, extravagant prices have been paid for lands bought on credit; then the land must be cleared, and more money is hired; a house to be built calls for more money, and then interest with open mouth swallows up all the profits. Debts accumulate, and then come the closing and failure of banks, and then the foreclosure of mortgages.

Thousands have been turned out of employment; families lose their little all, they borrow and borrow, and then have to give up their property and come out penniless. Much money and hard labor have been put into farms bought on credit, or inherited with an incumbrance. The occupants lived in hope of becoming real owners, and it might have been so, but for the failure of banks throughout the country.

Now the case where a man owns his place clear is a happy exception to the rule. Merchants are failing, families are suffering for food and clothing. No work presents itself. But the holidays are just as numerous. Their amusements are entered into as eagerly. All who can do so will spend their hard-earned pence and shillings and pounds for a taste of pleasure, for strong drink, or some other indulgence. The papers that report the poverty of the people, have regular standing notices of the horse races, and of the prizes presented for different kinds of exciting sports. The shows, the theaters, and all such demoralizing amusements, are taking the money from the country, and poverty is continually increasing. Poor men will invest their last shilling in a lottery, hoping to secure a prize, and then they have to beg for food to sustain life, or go hungry. Many die of hunger, and many put an end to their existence. The end is not yet. Men take you to their orchards of oranges and lemons, and other fruits, and tell you that the produce does not pay for the work done in them. It is next to impossible to make ends meet, and parents decide that the children shall not be farmers; they have not the courage and hope to educate them to till the soil.

What is needed is schools to educate and train the youth so that they will know how to overcome this condition of things. There must be education in the sciences, and education in plans and methods of working the soil. There is hope in the soil, but brain and heart and strength must be brought into the work of tilling it. The money devoted to horse racing, theater going, gambling and lotteries; the money spent in the public houses for beer and strong drink,--let it be expended in making the land productive, and we shall see a different state of things.

This country needs educated farmers. The Lord gives the showers of rain and the blessed sunshine. He gives to men all their powers; let them devote heart and mind and strength to doing His will in obedience to His commandments. Let them cut off every pernicious habit, never expending a penny for beer or liquor of any kind, nor for tobacco, having nothing to do with horse racing or similar sports, and then commit themselves to God, working with their endowment of physical strength, and their labor will not be in vain. That God who has made the world for the benefit of man, will provide means from the earth to sustain the diligent worker. The seed placed in thoroughly prepared soil, will produce its harvest. God can spread a table for His people in the wilderness.

The various trades and occupations have to be learned, and they call into exercise a great variety of mental and physical capabilities; the occupations requiring sedentary habits are the most dangerous, for they take men away from the open air and sunshine, and train one set of faculties, while other organs are becoming weak from inaction. Men carry on their work, perfect their business, and soon lie down in the grave. Much more favorable is the condition of one whose occupation keeps him in the open air, exercising his muscles, while the brain is equally taxed, and all the organs have the privilege of doing their work. To those who can live outside of the cities, and labor in the open air, beholding the works of the great Master Artist, new scenes are continually unfolding. As they make the book of nature their study, a softening, subduing influence comes over them; for they realize that God's care is over all, from the glorious sun in the heavens to the little brown sparrow or the tiniest insect that has life. The Majesty of heaven has pointed us to these things of God's creation as an evidence of His love. He who fashioned the flowers has said: "Consider the lilies of the field, how they grow; they toil not, neither do they spin: and yet I say unto you, That even Solomon in all his glory was not arrayed like one of these. Wherefore, if God so clothe the grass of the field, which today is, and tomorrow is cast into the oven, shall He not much more clothe you, O ye of little faith?" The Lord is our teacher, and under His instruction we may learn the most precious lessons from nature.

The world is under the curse of sin, and yet even in its decay it is very beautiful. If it were not defiled by the wicked, corrupt deeds of the men who tread the soil, we could, with the blessing of God, enjoy our world as it is. But ignorance, pleasure loving, and sinful habits, corrupting soul, body, and spirit, make the world full of moral leprosy; a deadly moral malaria is destroying thousands and tens of thousands. What shall be done to save our youth? We can do little, but God lives and reigns, and He can do much. The youth are our hope for missionary labor.

Schools should be established where there is as much as possible to be found in nature to delight the senses and give variety to the scenery. While we shun the false and artificial, discarding horse racing, card playing, lotteries, prize fights, liquor drinking, and tobacco using, we must supply sources of pleasure that are pure and noble and elevating. We should choose a location for our school apart from the cities, where the eye will not rest continually upon the dwellings of men, but upon the works of God; where there shall be places of interest for them to visit, other than what the city affords. Let our students be placed where nature can speak to the senses, and in her voice they may hear the voice of God. Let them be where they can look upon His wondrous works, and through nature behold her Creator.

The youth in this country require more earnest spiritual labor than in any other country we have yet visited. Temptations are strong and numerous; the many holidays and the habits of idleness are most unfavorable for the young. Satan makes the idle man a partaker and co-worker in his schemes, and the Lord Jesus does not abide in the heart by faith. The children and youth are not educated to realize that their influence is a power for good or for evil. It should ever be kept before them how much they can accomplish; they should be encouraged to reach the highest standard of rectitude. But from their youth up they have been educated to the popular idea that the appointed holidays must be treated with respect and be observed. From the light that the Lord has given me, these days have no more influence for good than would the worship of heathen deities; for this is really nothing less. These days are Satan's special harvest seasons. The money drawn from men and women is expended for that which is not bread. The youth are educated to love those things which are demoralizing, things which the word of God condemns. The influence is evil and only evil continually.

Manual occupation for the youth is essential. The mind is not to be constantly taxed to the neglect of the physical powers. The ignorance of physiology, and a neglect to observe the laws of health, have brought many to the grave who might have lived to labor and study intelligently. The proper exercise of mind and body will develop and strengthen all the powers. Both mind and body will be preserved, and will be capable of doing a variety of work. Ministers and teachers need to learn in regard to these things, and they need to practice as well. The proper use of their physical strength, as well as of the mental powers, will equalize the circulation of the blood, and keep every organ of the living machinery in running order. Minds are often abused; they are goaded on to madness by pursuing one line of thought; the excessive employment of the brain power and the neglect of the physical organs create a diseased condition of things in the system. Every faculty of the mind may be exercised with comparative safety if the physical powers are equally taxed, and the subject of thought varied. We need a change of employment, and nature is a living, healthful teacher.

When students enter the school to obtain an education, the instructors should endeavor to surround them with objects of the most pleasing, interesting character, that the mind may not be confined to the dead study of books. The school should not be in or near a city, where its extravagance, its wicked pleasures, its wicked customs and practices, will require constant work to counteract the prevailing iniquity, that it may not poison the very atmosphere which the students breathe. All schools should be located, as far as possible, where the eye will rest upon the things of nature instead of clusters of houses. The ever-shifting scenery will gratify the taste, and control the imagination. Here is a living teacher, instructing constantly.

I have been troubled over many things in regard to our school. In their work the young men are associated with the young women, and are doing the work which belongs to women. This is nearly all that can be found for them to do as they are now situated; but from the light given me, this is not the kind of education that the young men need. It does not give them the knowledge they need to take with them to their homes. There should be a different kind of labor opened before them, that would give opportunity to keep the physical powers taxed equally with the mental. There should be land for cultivation. The time is not far distant when the laws against Sunday labor will be more stringent, and an effort should be made to secure grounds away from the cities, where fruits and vegetables can be raised. Agriculture will open resources for self-support, and various other trades also could be learned. This real, earnest work calls for strength of intellect as well as of muscle. Method and tact are required even to raise fruits and vegetables successfully. And habits of industry will be found an important aid to the youth in resisting temptation.

Here is opened a field to give vent to their pent-up energies, that, if not expended in useful employment, will be a continual source of trial to themselves and to their teachers. Many kinds of labor adapted to different persons may be devised. But the working of the land will be a special blessing to the worker. There is a great want of intelligent men to till the soil, who will be thorough. This knowledge will not be a hindrance to the education essential for business or for usefulness in any line. To develop the capacity of the soil requires thought and intelligence. Not only will it develop muscle, but capability for study, because the action of brain and muscle is equalized. We should so train the youth that they will love to work upon the land, and delight in improving it. The hope of advancing the cause of God in this country is in creating a new moral taste in love of work, which will transform mind and character.

False witness has been borne in condemning land which, if properly worked, would yield rich returns. The narrow plans, the little strength put forth, the little study as to the best methods, call loudly for reform. The people need to learn that patient labor will do wonders. There is much mourning over unproductive soil, when if men would read the Old Testament Scriptures they would see that the Lord knew much better than they in regard to the proper treatment of land. After being cultivated for several years, and giving her treasure to the possession of man, portions of the land should be allowed to rest, and then the crops should be changed. We might learn much also from the Old Testament in regard to the labor problem. If men would follow the directions of Christ in regard to remembering the poor and supplying their necessities, what a different place this world would be!

Let God's glory be kept ever in view; and if the crop is a failure, be not discouraged; try again; but remember that you can have no harvest unless the ground is properly prepared for the seed; failure may be wholly due to neglect on this point.

The school to be established in Australia should bring the question of industry to the front, and reveal the fact that physical labor has its place in God's plan for every man, and that His blessing will attend it. The schools established by those who teach and practice the truth for this time, should be so conducted as to bring fresh and new incentives into all kinds of practical labor. There will be much to try the educators, but a great and noble object has been gained when students shall feel that love for God is to be revealed, not only in the devotion of heart and mind and soul, but in the apt, wise appropriation of their strength. Their temptations will be far less;

from them by precept and example a light will radiate amid the erroneous theories and fashionable customs of the world. Their influence will tend to correct the false idea that ignorance is the mark of a gentleman.

God would be glorified if men from other countries who have acquired an intelligent knowledge of agriculture, would come to this land, and by precept and example teach the people how to cultivate the soil, that it may yield rich treasures. Men are wanted to educate others how to plow, and how to use the implements of agriculture. Who will be missionaries to do this work, to teach proper methods to the youth, and to all who feel willing and humble enough to learn? If any do not want you to give them improved ideas, let the lessons be given silently, showing what can be done in setting out orchards and planting corn; let the harvest be eloquent in favor of right methods of labor. Drop a word to your neighbors when you can, keep up the culture of your own land, and that will educate.

It may be urged by some that our school must be in the city in order to give influence to our work, and that if it is in the country, the influence is lost to the cities; but this is not necessarily the case.

The youth who attend our school for the first time, are not prepared to exert a correct influence in any city as lights shining amid the darkness. They will not be prepared to reflect light until the darkness of their own erroneous education is dispelled. In the future our school will not be the same as it has been in the past. Among the students there have been reliable, experienced men who have taken advantage of the opportunity to gain more knowledge in order to do intelligent work in the cause of God. These have been a help in the school, for they have been as a balance wheel; but in the future the school will consist mostly of those who need to be transformed in character, and who will need to have much patient labor bestowed upon them; they have to unlearn, and learn again. It will take time to develop the true missionary spirit, and the farther they are removed from the cities and the temptations that are flooding them, the more favorable will it be for them to obtain the true knowledge and develop well-balanced characters.

Farmers need far more intelligence in their work. In most cases it is their own fault if they do not see the land yielding its harvest. They should be constantly learning how to secure a variety of treasures from the earth. The people should learn as far as possible to depend upon the products that they can obtain from the soil. In every phase of this kind of labor they can be educating the mind to work for the saving of souls for whom Christ has died. "Ye are God's husbandry; ye are God's building." Let the teachers in our schools take their students with them into the gardens and fields, and teach them how to work the soil in the very best manner. It would be well if ministers who labor in word or doctrine could enter the fields and spend some portion of the day in physical exercise with the students. They could do as Christ did in giving lessons from nature to illustrate Bible truth. Both teachers and students would have much more healthful experience in spiritual things, and much stronger minds and purer hearts to interpret eternal mysteries, than they can have while studying books so constantly, and working the brain without taxing the muscles. God has given men and women reasoning powers, and He would have men employ their reason in regard to the use of their physical machinery. The question may be asked, How can he get wisdom that holdeth the plow, and driveth oxen?--by seeking her as silver, and searching for her as for hid treasures. "For his God doth instruct him to discretion, and doth teach him." "This also cometh forth from the Lord of hosts, which is wonderful in counsel, and excellent in working."

He who taught Adam and Eve in Eden how to tend the garden, would instruct men today. There is wisdom for him who holds the plow, and plants and sows the seed. The earth has its concealed treasures, and the Lord would have thousands and tens of thousands working upon the soil who are crowded into the cities to watch for a chance to earn a trifle; in many cases that trifle is not turned into bread, but is put into the till of the publican, to obtain that which destroys the reason of man formed in the image of God. Those who will take their families into the country, place them where they have fewer temptations. The children who are with parents that love and fear God, are in every way much better situated to learn of the Great Teacher, who is the source and fountain of wisdom. They have a much more favorable opportunity to gain a fitness for the kingdom of heaven. Send the children to schools located in the city, where every phase of temptation is waiting to attract and demoralize them, and the work of character building is tenfold harder for both parents and children.

The earth is to be made to give forth its strength; but without the blessing of God it could do nothing. In the beginning, God looked upon all that He had made, and pronounced it very good. The curse was brought upon the earth in consequence of sin. But shall this curse be multiplied by increasing sin? Ignorance is doing its baleful work. Slothful servants are increasing the evil by their lazy habits. Many are unwilling to earn their bread by the sweat of their brow, and they refuse to till the soil. But the earth has blessings hidden in her depths for those who have courage and will and perseverance to gather her treasures. Fathers and mothers who possess a piece of land and a comfortable home are kings and queens.

Many farmers have failed to secure adequate returns from their land because they have undertaken the work as though it was a degrading employment; they do not see that there is a blessing in it for themselves and their families. All they can discern is the brand of servitude. Their orchards are neglected, the crops are not put in at the right season, and a mere surface work is done in cultivating the soil. Many neglect their farms in order to keep holidays and to attend horse races and betting clubs; their money is expended in shows and lotteries and idleness, and then they plead that they cannot obtain money to cultivate the soil and improve their farms; but had they more money, the result would still be the same.--"Special Testimonies on Education," February, 1894.

The Basis of True Education

True education is a grand science; for it is founded on the fear of the Lord, which is the beginning of wisdom. Christ is the greatest Teacher this world ever knew, and it is not the pleasure of the Lord Jesus that the subjects of His kingdom, for whom He died, shall be educated in such a way that they will be led to place the wisdom of men in the forefront, and delegate to the wisdom of God, as revealed in His holy word, a place in the rear. True education is that which will train children and youth for the life that now is, and in reference to that which is to come; for an inheritance in that better country, even in an heavenly. They are to be trained for the country for which patriarchs and prophets looked. "These all died in faith, not having received the promises, but having seen them afar off, and were persuaded of them, and embraced them, and confessed that they were strangers and pilgrims on the earth. For they that say such things declare plainly that they seek a country. And truly, if they had been mindful of that country from whence they came out, they might have had opportunity to have returned. But now they desire a better country, that is, an heavenly: wherefore God is not ashamed to be called their God, for He hath prepared for them a city."

The general method of educating the youth does not meet the standard of true education. Infidel sentiments are interwoven in the matter placed in schoolbooks, and the oracles of God are placed in a questionable or even an objectionable light. Thus the minds of the youth become familiar with Satan's suggestions, and the doubts once entertained become to those who entertain them, assured facts, and scientific research is made misleading on account of the way its discoveries are interpreted and perverted. Men take it upon themselves to rein up the word of God before a finite tribunal, and sentence is pronounced upon the inspiration of God according to finite measurement, and the truth of God is made to appear as a thing uncertain before the records of science. These false educators exalt nature above nature's God, and above the Author of all true science. At the very time when teachers should have been firm and unwavering in their testimony, at the very time when it should have been made manifest that their souls were riveted to the eternal Rock, when they should have been able to inspire faith in those who were doubting, they made admission of their own uncertainty as to whether the word of God or the discoveries of science, falsely so called, were true. Those who were truly conscientious have been made to waver in their faith because of the hesitation of those who were professed expositors of the Bible when they dealt with the living oracles. Satan has taken advantage of the uncertainty of the mind, and through unseen agencies, he has crowded in his sophistries, and has caused men to become befogged in the mists of skepticism.

Learned men have given lectures in which have been mingled truth and error; but they have unbalanced the minds of those who leaned toward error instead of toward truth. The nicely woven sophistries of the so-called wise men have a charm for a certain class of students; but the impression that these lectures leave upon the mind is that the God of nature is restricted by His own laws. The immutability of nature has been largely dwelt upon, and skeptical theories have been readily adopted by those whose minds chose the atmosphere of doubt, because they were not in harmony with God's holy law, the foundation of His government in heaven and earth. Their natural tendency to evil made it easy for them to choose false paths, and to doubt the reliability of both the Old and the New Testament's records and history. Poisoned with error themselves, they have watched every opportunity to sow the seeds of doubt in other minds. Nature is exalted above the God of nature, and the simplicity of faith is destroyed; for the foundation of faith is made to appear uncertain. Befogged in skepticism, the minds of those who doubt are left to beat on the rocks of infidelity.--The Youth's Instructor, January 31, 1895.

Beware of Imitations

Association with learned men is esteemed by some more highly that communion with the God of heaven. The statements of learned men are thought of more value than the highest wisdom revealed in the word of God. But while infidelity is proudly lifting up its head, Heaven looks down upon the vanity and nothingness of human reasoning; for man in and of himself is vanity. All the merit, all the moral dignity, of men has been theirs simply in and through the merits of Jesus Christ. What, then, are the speculations of the greatest minds of the greatest men that have ever lived? Yet men place their human reasonings before the revealed will of God, and present to the world that which they claim is higher wisdom than the wisdom of the Eternal. In their vain imaginations, they would bring down the economy of heaven to suit their own inclinations and desires.

The great God has a law by which to govern His kingdom, and those who trample upon that law will one day find that they are amenable to its statutes. The remedy for transgression is not to be found in declaring that the law is abolished. To abolish the law would be to dishonor it, and to cast contempt upon the Lawgiver. The only escape for the transgressor of law is found in the Lord Jesus Christ; for through the grace and atonement of the only-begotten Son of God, the sinner may be saved and the law vindicated. The men who parade before the world as wonderful specimens of greatness, and at the same time trample down the revealed will of God, robe man with honor and talk of the perfection of nature. They paint a very fine picture, but it is an illusion, a flattering deception; for they walk in the sparks of their own kindling.

Those who present a doctrine contrary to that of the Bible, are led by the great apostate who was cast out of the courts of God. Of him before his fall, it was written, "Thou sealest up the sum, full of wisdom, and perfect in beauty. Thou hast been in Eden the garden of God; every precious stone was thy covering. . . . Thou art the anointed cherub that covereth; and I have set thee so: thou wast upon the holy mountain of God; thou hast walked up and down in the midst of the stones of fire. Thou wast perfect in thy ways from the day that thou wast created, till iniquity was found in thee. . . . Thine heart was lifted up because of thy beauty, thou has corrupted thy wisdom by reason of thy brightness; I will cast thee to the ground, I will lay thee before kings, that they may behold thee. . . . I will bring thee to ashes upon the earth in the sight of all them that behold thee. All they that know thee among the people shall be astonished at thee: thou shalt be a terror, and never shalt thou be any more."

With such a leader--an angel expelled from heaven--these supposedly wise men of earth may fabricate bewitching theories with which to infatuate the minds of men. Paul said to the Galatians, "Who hath bewitched you, that ye should not obey the truth?" Satan has a masterly mind, and he has his chosen agents by which he works to exalt men, and clothe them with honor above God. But God is clothed with power; He is able to take those who are dead in trespasses and sins, and by the operation of the Spirit which raised Jesus from the dead, transform the human character, bringing back to the soul the lost image of God. Those who believe in Jesus Christ are changed from being rebels against the law of God into obedient servants and subjects of His kingdom. They are born again, regenerated, sanctified through the truth. This power of God the skeptic will not admit, and he refuses all evidence until it is brought under the domain of his finite faculties. He even dares to set aside the law of God, and prescribe the limit of Jehovah's power. But God has said, "I will destroy the wisdom of the wise, and will bring to nothing the understanding of the prudent. Where is the wise? where is the scribe? where is the disputer of this world? hath not God made foolish the wisdom of this world? For after that in the wisdom of God the world by wisdom knew not God, it pleased God by the foolishness of preaching to save them that believe. For the Jews require a sign, and the Greeks seek after wisdom: but we preach Christ crucified, unto the Jews a stumbling block, and unto the Greeks foolishness: but unto them which are called, both Jews and Greeks, Christ the power of God, and the wisdom of God."--The Youth's Instructor, February 7, 1895.

Speedy Preparation For the Work

I have been much perplexed for several nights. I am troubled so that I am unable to sleep well. Things are being urged upon my attention which I must present before you.

The teachers in our schools at the Sanitarium and College at Battle Creek must be on guard constantly, lest their plans and management shall depress and quench the faith of students who have had their hearts deeply impressed by the Holy Spirit. They have heard the voice of Jesus saying, "Son, go work today in My vineyard." They feel the need of a proper course of study, that they may be prepared to labor for the Master, and every effort should be made to hasten their advancement; but the object of their education should be kept constantly in view. Unnecessary delay should not be advised or allowed. Those persons who have engaged to help sustain the students during their course of study suffer great loss both in time and money spent unwisely. These people have manifested their earnestness and willingness to help; but they become discouraged as they see the time originally estimated as being necessary for the students to receive a fitting-up for the work, prolonged, and still the students are encouraged to take up another course of study at their expense. Years pass; and still there is urged upon the students the necessity of more education. This long-drawn-out process, adding and adding more time, more branches, is one of Satan's snares to keep laborers back.

The students themselves would not think of such a delay in entering the work, if it were not urged upon them by those who are supposed to be shepherds and guardians, and who are their teachers and physicians. If we had a thousand years before us, such a depth of knowledge would be uncalled for, although it might be much more appropriate; but now our time is limited. It is said, "Today if ye will hear His voice, harden not your hearts."

We are not of that class who define the exact period of time that shall elapse before the coming of Jesus the second time with power and great glory. Some have set a time, and when that has passed, their presumptuous spirits have not accepted rebuke, but they have set another and another time; but many successive failures have stamped them as false prophets. "The secret things belong unto the Lord our God; but those things which are revealed belong unto us and to our children forever." Notwithstanding the fact that there are false prophets, there are also those who are preaching the truth as pointed out in the Scriptures. With deep earnestness, with honest faith, prompted by the Holy Spirit, they are stirring minds and hearts by showing them that we are living near the second coming of Christ, but the day and hour of His appearing are beyond the ken of man; for "of that day and hour knoweth no man, no, not the angels of heaven, but My Father only."

But there is a day that God hath appointed for the close of this world's history. This gospel of the kingdom shall be preached in all the world for a witness unto all nations; and then shall the end come." Prophecy is fast fulfilling. More, much more, should be said about these tremendously important subjects. The day is at hand when the destiny of every soul will be fixed forever. This day of the Lord hastens on apace. The false watchmen are raising the cry, "All is well"; but the day of God is rapidly approaching. Its footsteps are so muffled that it does not arouse the world from the death-like slumber into which it has fallen. While the watchmen cry, "Peace and safety," "sudden destruction cometh upon them," "and they shall not escape"; "for as a snare shall it come on all them that dwell on the face of the whole earth." It overtakes the pleasure-lover and the sinful man as a thief in the night. When all is apparently secure, and men retire to contented rest, then the prowling, stealthy, midnight thief steals upon his prey. When it is too late to prevent the evil, it is discovered that some door or window was not secured. "Be ye also ready: for in an such hour as ye think not the Son of man cometh." People are now settling to rest, imagining themselves secure under the popular churches; but let all beware, lest there is a place left open for the enemy to gain an entrance. Great pains should be taken to keep this subject before the people. The solemn fact is to be kept not only before the people of the world, but before our own churches also, that the day of the Lord will come suddenly, unexpectedly. The fearful warning of the prophecy is addressed to every soul. Let no one feel that he is secure from the danger of being surprised. Let no one's interpretation of prophecy rob you of the conviction of the knowledge of events which show that this great event is near at hand.

The money which has been expended in additional buildings and in extensions on existing buildings in Battle Creek, should have been used for creating facilities for carrying on the work in places where there is nothing done at all. God is not pleased at the manner in which His goods have been disposed of. There is no respect of places or of persons, with Him.

The practice of furnishing a few persons with every advantage of perfecting their education in so many lines that it would be impossible for them to make use of all of them, is an injury rather than a benefit to the one who has so many advantages, besides depriving others of the privileges they need so much. If there were far less of this long continued preparation, far less exclusive devotion to study only, there would be much more opportunity for an increase of the student's faith in God. He who long devotes all his energies to his studies alone, becomes fascinated,--is actually absorbed in his books, and loses sight of the goal for which he started when he came to school. It has been shown to me that some of the students are losing their spirituality, that their faith is becoming weak, and that they do not hold constant communion with God. They spend nearly all their time in the perusal of books; they seem to know but little else. But what advantage will all this preparation be to them? What benefit will they derive for

Speedy Preparation For the Work

all the time and money spent? I tell you, it will be worse than lost. There must be less of this kind of work, and more faith in God's power. God's commandment-loving people are to testify to the world of their faith by their works.

When students come to Battle Creek from long distances at great expense, expecting to receive instruction as to how to become successful missionaries, that idea is not to be sunk out of sight in a variety of studies. Consider Moses; the one great burden of his soul was that the presence of God might be with him, and that he might behold His glory. But if the students are given more studies than are absolutely necessary, it is calculated to cause them to forget the real object of their coming to Battle Creek. Now is the time when it is essential that only such work as is necessary should be done. Long years of preparation are not a positive necessity. The preparation of the students has been managed on the same principle as have the building operations. Building has been added to building, simply to make things a little more convenient and thorough. God is calling, and has been calling for years, for a reform on these lines. He desires that there shall be no unnecessary outlay of means. The Lord is not in favor of having so much time and money expended upon a few persons who come to Battle Creek to get a better preparation for the work. In all cases there should be a most careful consideration as to the best manner of expending money in the education of the students. While so much is spent to put a few through an exhaustive course of study, there are many who are thirsting for the knowledge they could get in a few months; one or two years would be considered a great blessing. If all the means are used in putting a few through several years of study, many just as worthy young men and young women cannot be assisted at all.

I hope the managers of the Battle Creek school and Sanitarium will consider this matter prayerfully, intelligently, and without partiality. Instead of over-educating a few, enlarge the sphere of your charities. Resolve that the means which you mean to use in educating workers for the cause shall not be expended simply upon one, enabling him to get more than he really needs, while others are left without anything at all. Give students a start, but do not feel that it is your duty to carry them year after year. It is their duty to get out into the field to work, and it is your place to extend your charities to others who are in need of assistance.

Christ's work was not done in such a way as to dazzle men with His superior abilities. He came forth from the bosom of the All-wise, and could have astonished the world with the great and glorious knowledge which He possessed; yet He was reticent and uncommunicative. It was not His mission to overwhelm them with the immensity of His talents, but to walk in meekness and lowliness, that He might instruct the ignorant in the ways of salvation. Too great devotion to study, even of true science, creates an abnormal appetite, which increases as it is fed. This creates a desire to secure more knowledge than is essential to do the work of the Lord. The pursuit of knowledge merely for its own sake diverts the mind from devotion to God, checks advance along the path of practical holiness, and hinders souls from traveling in the way which leads to a holier, happier life. The Lord Jesus imparted only such a measure of instruction as could be utilized. My brethren, your way of representing the necessity for years of study is not pleasing to God.

The Lord Jesus would have men trade upon their talents, and Jesus has promised that He will give grace for grace. As we impart to others, we shall receive more richly. And as we thus labor, the mind will not become clogged with a mass of matter which has been crowded into it with no opportunity to impart what has been received. The student becomes a mental dyspeptic by being crammed with much that he cannot use. Much time has been wasted, and the progressive usefulness of students hindered, by the teaching of that which cannot be utilized by the Spirit of God.

Those who come to the Battle Creek school should be speedily and thoroughly pushed through such a course of study as would be of practical value in the healthy development of the body and holy activity of the soul. In His gospel, God speaks not merely to benefit the growth of the mental capacity of man, but to instruct how the moral senses may be quickened. This is illustrated in the case of Daniel and the three Hebrews. They kept the fear and love of God ever before them, and the result is recorded as follows: "As for these four children, God gave them knowledge and skill in all learning and wisdom: and Daniel had understanding in all visions and dreams."

Christ said, "Blessed are they that hear the word of God, and keep it." The bread of life alone can satisfy the hungering soul. The water of life alone will quench the thirst of the thirsty soul. The minds of the disciples were often excited by curiosity, but instead of gratifying their desire to know things which were not necessary for the proper conduct of their work, he opened new channels of thought to their minds. He gave them much needed instruction upon practical godliness.

The many branches which students are induced to take up in their studies, holding them from the work for years, are not in the order of God. Christ came to seek and to save that which was lost. When He said, "Follow Me," He assumed the position of instructor. All the light He brought to men from heaven is to be used in revealing to men the pit of destruction into which they have been plunged by their sins, and to point out to them the only path which can be traveled with hope of reaching a place of safety. The bright beams of the Sun of Righteousness are shining upon this path, and the wayfaring man, though a fool, need not err therein. Those who come to Battle Creek are not to be encouraged to absorb several years in study.

Intemperance in study is a species of intoxication, and those who indulge in it, like the drunkard, wander from safe paths, and stumble and fall in the darkness. The Lord would have every student bear in mind that the eye must be kept single to the glory of God. They are not to exhaust and waste their physical and mental powers in seeking to acquire all possible knowledge of the sciences; but every individual is to preserve the freshness and vigor of all his powers to engage in the work which the Lord has appointed him in helping souls to find the path of righteousness. All must preserve the vigor of their lives, their soul-energy and ambitions, and prepare to leave their studies in school, and take up the more practical studies in the sphere of activity, where angels cooperate with them. The intelligences of heaven will work through the human agents. The command of heaven is to do, work,--do something which will reflect glory to God by being a benefit to our fellow men who are ready to perish.

There is great danger that students in the schools will fail of learning the all-important lesson which our Master would have them taught. This lesson is conveyed to us in the following scripture: "Take My yoke upon you, and learn of Me; for I am meek and lowly in heart: and ye shall find rest unto your souls. For My yoke is easy, and My burden is light." Some have not only failed to learn to bear the yoke of the meek and lowly Jesus, but have been unable to stand against the temptations which have surrounded them. Inexperienced youth who have journeyed long distances to obtain the advantages of an education at our school, have lost their hold upon Jesus. These things ought not so to be.

The Lord does not choose or accept laborers according to the numerous advantages which they have enjoyed, or according to the superior education which they have received. The value of the human agent is estimated according to the capacity of the heart to know and understand God. "Thou therefore, my son, be strong in the grace that is in Christ Jesus. And the things that thou hast heard of me among many witnesses, the same commit thou to faithful men, who shall be able to teach others also. Thou therefore endure hardness, as a good soldier of Jesus Christ." The highest possible good is obtained through a knowledge of God. "This is life eternal, that they might know Thee the only true God, and Jesus Christ, whom Thou has sent."

This knowledge is the secret spring from which flows all power. It is through the exercise of the faculty of faith that we are enabled to receive and practice the word of God. No excuse can be accepted, no plea of justification received for the failure to know and understand the will of the Lord. The Lord will enlighten the heart that is loyal to Him. He can read the thoughts and intents of the heart. It is useless to plead that if it had been so and so, we would have done so and so. There is no if about God's requirements; His word is yea and amen. There can be no question in the heart of faith as to the power of God to perform His promises. Pure faith works by love, and purifies the soul.

To the distressed father, seeking for the tender love and pity of Christ to be exercised in behalf of his afflicted son, Jesus said: "If thou canst believe, all things are possible to him that believeth." All things are possible with God, and by faith we may lay hold on His power. But faith is not sight; faith is not feeling; faith is not reality. "Faith is the substance of things hoped for, the evidence of things not seen." To abide in faith is to put aside feeling and selfish desires, to walk humbly with the Lord, to appropriate His promises, and apply them to all occasions, believing that God will work out His own plans and purposes in your heart and life by the sanctification of your character; it is to rely entirely, to trust implicitly, upon the faithfulness of God. If this course is followed, others will see the special fruits of the Spirit manifested in the life and character.

The education received by Moses, as the king's grandson, was very thorough. Nothing was neglected that was calculated to make him a wise man, as the Egyptians understood wisdom. This education was a help to him in many respects; but the most valuable part of his fitting for his life work was that received while employed as a shepherd. As he led his flocks through the wilds of the mountains and into the green pastures of the valleys, the God of nature taught him the highest and grandest wisdom. In the school of nature, with Christ himself for teacher, he contemplated and learned lessons of humility, meekness, faith, and trust, and of a humble manner of living, all of which bound his soul closer to God. In the solitude of the mountains he learned that which all his instruction in the king's palace was unable to impart to him,--simple, unwavering faith, and constant trust in the Lord.

Moses supposed that his education in the wisdom of Egypt had fully qualified him to lead Israel from bondage. Was he not learned in all the things necessary for a general of armies? Had he not had the greatest advantages of the best schools in the land?--Yes; he felt that he was able to deliver them. He first set about his work by trying to gain the favor of his own people by redressing their wrongs. He killed an Egyptian who was imposing upon one of his brethren. In this he manifested the spirit of him who was a murderer from the beginning, and proved himself unfit to represent the God of mercy, love, and tenderness. He made a miserable failure of his first attempt. Like many another, he then immediately lost his confidence in God, and turned his back upon his appointed work; he fled from the wrath of Pharaoh. He concluded that because of his mistake, his great sin in taking the life of the cruel Egyptian, God would not permit him to have any part in the work of delivering His people from their cruel bondage. But the Lord permitted these things that He might be able to teach him the gentleness, goodness, long-suffering, which it is necessary for every laborer for the Master to possess; for it is these characteristics that constitute the successful workman in the Lord's cause.

A knowledge of the attributes of the character of Christ Jesus cannot be obtained by means of the highest education in the most scientific schools. This wisdom is learned from the great Teacher alone. The lessons of Christlike meekness, lowliness of heart, reverence for sacred things, are taught nowhere effectively except in the school of Christ. Moses had been taught to expect flattery and praise because of his superior abilities;

Speedy Preparation For the Work

but now he was to learn a different lesson. As a shepherd of sheep, Moses was taught to care for the afflicted, to nurse the sick, to seek patiently after the straying, to bear long with the unruly, to supply with loving solicitude the wants of the young lambs and the necessities of the old and feeble. As these phases of his character were developed, he was drawn nearer to his Chief Shepherd. He became united to, submerged in, the Holy One of Israel. He believed in the great God. He held communion with the Father through humble prayer. He looked to the Highest for an education in spiritual things, and for a knowledge of his duty as a faithful shepherd. His life became so closely linked with heaven that God talked with him face to face.

Thus prepared, he was ready to heed the call of God to exchange his shepherd's crook for the rod of authority; to leave his flock of sheep to take the leadership of more than a million idolatrous, rebellious people. But he was to depend upon the invisible Leader. Even as the rod was simply an instrument in his hand, so was he to be a willing instrument to be worked by the hand of Jesus Christ. Moses was selected to be the shepherd of God's own people, and it was through his firm faith and abiding trust in the Lord that so many blessings reached the children of Israel. The Lord Jesus seeks the co-operation of such men as will become unobstructed channels through which the riches of heaven may be poured out upon the people of His love. He works through man for the uplifting and salvation of His chosen.

Moses was called to labor in co-partnership with the Lord, and it was the simplicity of his character, combined with a practical education, that constituted him such a representative man. In the very height of his human glory the Lord permitted Moses to reveal the foolishness of man's wisdom, the weakness of human strength, that he might be led to understand his utter helplessness, and his inefficiency without being upheld by the Lord Jesus.

The rashness of Moses in slaying the Egyptian was prompted by a presumptuous spirit. Faith moves in the strength and wisdom of God, and not in the ways of men. By simple faith Moses was enabled to press through difficulties, and overcome obstacles which seemed almost insurmountable. When they relied upon Him, not trusting to their own power, the mighty General of armies was faithful to Israel. He delivered them from many difficulties from which they could never have escaped, if left to themselves. God was able to manifest His great power through Moses because of his constant faith in the power and in the loving intentions of their Deliverer. It was this implicit faith in God that made Moses what he was. According to all that the Lord commanded him, so did he. All the learning of the wise men could not make him a channel through which the Lord could labor, however, until he lost his self-confidence, realized his own helplessness, and put his trust in God; until he was willing to obey God's commands whether they seemed to his human reason to be proper or not.

Those persons who refuse to move forward until they see every step plainly marked out before them, will never accomplish much; but every man who shows his faith and trust in God by willingly submitting himself to Him, enduring the divine discipline imposed, will become a successful workman for the Master of the vineyard. In their efforts to qualify themselves to be colaborers with God, men frequently place themselves in such positions as will completely disqualify them for the molding and fashioning which the Lord desires to give them. Thus they are not found bearing, as did Moses, the divine similitude. By submitting to God's discipline, Moses became a sanctified channel through which the Lord could work. He did not hesitate to change his way for the Lord's way, even though it did lead in strange paths, in untried ways. He did not permit himself to make use of his education by showing the unreasonableness of God's commands, and the impossibility of obeying them. No; he placed a very low estimate upon his own qualifications to complete successfully the great work which the Lord had given him. When he started on his commission to deliver the people of God from their bondage, to all human appearances it was a most hopeless undertaking; but he confided in Him with whom all things are possible.

Many in our day have had far better opportunities, enjoyed far greater privileges, for obtaining a knowledge of God, than did Moses; but his faith puts to shame their manifest unbelief. At the command of God, Moses advanced, although there was nothing ahead for his feet to tread upon. More than a million people were depending upon him, but he led them forward step by step, day by day. God permitted these lonely travels through the wilderness so that they might obtain an experience in enduring hardships, and so that when they were in peril, they might know that there was relief and deliverance in God alone, and that thus they might learn to know and to trust God, and to serve Him with a living faith. It was not the teachings of the schools of Egypt that enabled Moses to triumph over all his enemies, but an ever-abiding faith, an unflinching faith, a faith that did not fail under the most trying circumstances.

When God commanded Moses to do anything, he did it without stopping to consider what the consequences might be. He gave God credit for wisdom to know what He meant and firmness of purpose to mean what He said; and therefore Moses acted as seeing the Invisible. God is not seeking for men of perfect education. His work is not to wait while His servants go through such wonderfully elaborate preparations as our schools are planning to give; but the Lord wants men to appreciate the privilege of being laborers together with God,--men who will honor Him by rendering implicit obedience to His requirements regardless of previously inculcated theories. There is no limit to the usefulness of those who put self to one side, make room for the working of the Holy Spirit upon their hearts, and live lives wholly sanctified to the service of God, enduring the necessary discipline imposed by the Lord without complaining or fainting by the way. If they will not faint at the rebuke of the Lord, and become hard-hearted and stubborn, the Lord will teach both young and old, hour by hour, day by day. He longs to reveal His salvation to the children of men; and if His chosen people will remove the obstructions, He will pour forth the waters of salvation in abundant streams through the human channels.

Many who are seeking efficiency for the exalted work of God by perfecting their education in the schools of men, will find that they have failed of learning the more important lessons which the Lord would teach them. By neglecting to submit themselves to the impressions of the Holy Spirit, by not living in obedience to all God's requirements, their spiritual efficiency has become weakened; they have lost what ability they had to do successful work for the Lord. By absenting themselves from the school of Christ, they have forgotten the sound of the voice of the Teacher, and He cannot direct their course. Men may acquire all the knowledge possible to be imparted by the human teacher; but there is still greater wisdom required of them by God. Like Moses, they must learn meekness, lowliness of heart, and distrust of self. Our Saviour himself, bearing the test for humanity, acknowledged that of himself He could do nothing. We must also learn that there is no strength in humanity alone. Man becomes efficient only by becoming a partaker of the divine nature.

From the first opening of a book, the candidate for an education should recognize God as the one who imparts true wisdom. He should seek His counsel at every step along the way. No arrangement should be made to which God cannot be made a party, no union formed of which He is not the approver. The Author of wisdom should be recognized as the Guide from first to last. In this manner the knowledge obtained from books will be bound off by a living faith in the infinite God. The student should not permit himself to be bound down to any particular course of studies involving long periods of time, but should be guided in such matters by the Spirit of God.

A course of study at Ann Arbor may be thought essential for some; but evil influences are there ever at work upon susceptible minds, so that the farther they advance in their studies, the less they deem it necessary to seek a knowledge of the will and ways of God. None should be allowed to pursue a course of study that may in any way weaken their faith in the truth and in the Lord's power, or diminish their respect for a life of holiness. I would warn the students not to advance one step in these lines,--not even upon the advice of their instructors or men in positions of authority,--unless they have first sought God individually, with their hearts thrown open to the influence of the Holy Spirit, and obtained His counsel concerning the contemplated course of study. Let every selfish desire to distinguish yourselves be set aside; take every suggestion from humanity, to God, trusting in the guidance of the Holy Spirit; every unholy ambition should be blotted out, lest the Lord shall say: "I have seen the foolish taking root: but suddenly I cursed his habitation." Everyone should move so that he can say: "Thou, O Lord, knowest me: Thou hast seen me, and tried mine heart toward Thee." "Thou God seest me." The Lord weighs every motive. He is a discerner of the thoughts and intents and purposes of the heart. Without God we are without hope; therefore let us fix our faith upon Him. "Thou art my hope, O Lord God: Thou art my trust from my youth."

Every ship sailing the sea of life needs to have the divine Pilot on board; but when storms arise, when tempests threaten, many persons push their Pilot overboard, and commit their bark into the hand of finite man, or try to steer it themselves. Then disaster and wreckage generally follow, and the Pilot is blamed for running them into such dangerous waters. Do not commit yourselves into the keeping of men, but say, "The Lord is my helper"; I will seek His counsel; I will be a doer of His will. All the advantages you may have cannot be a blessing to you, neither can the highest class education qualify you to become a channel of light, unless you have the co-operation of the divine Spirit. It is as impossible for us to receive qualification from man, without the divine enlightenment, as it was for the gods of Egypt to deliver those who trusted in them. Students must not suppose that every suggestion for them to prolong their studies is in harmony with God's plan. Let every such suggestion be taken to the Lord in prayer, and seek earnestly for His guidance,--not only once, but again and again. Plead with Him, until you are convinced whether the counsel is of God or man. Do not trust yourself to men. Act under the divine Guide.

You have been chosen by Christ. You have been redeemed by the precious blood of the Lamb. Plead before God the efficacy of that blood. Say unto Him: "I am Thine by creation; I am Thine by redemption. I respect human authority, and the advice of my brethren; but I cannot depend wholly upon these. I want Thee, O God, to teach me. I have covenanted with Thee to adopt the divine standard of character, and make Thee my counselor and guide,--a party to every plan of my life; therefore teach me." Let the glory of the Lord be your first consideration. Repress every desire for worldly distinction, every ambition to secure the first place. Encourage heart purity and holiness, that you may represent the true principles of the gospel. Let every act of your life be sanctified by a holy endeavor to do the Lord's will, that your influence may not lead others into forbidden paths. When God is the leader, His righteousness shall go before thee, and the glory of the Lord shall be thy reward.

The Lord says, "Watch and pray, that ye enter not into temptation." The advice of your own brethren may cause you to swerve from the path which the Lord has marked out for you to walk in; for the minds of men are not always under the control of the Holy Spirit. "Watch" lest your studies shall accumulate to such proportions, and become of such absorbing interest to you, that your mind shall become overburdened, and the desire for godliness be crushed out of your soul. With many students the motive and aim which caused them to enter school have gradually been lost sight of, and an unholy ambition to secure a high class education has led them to sacrifice the truth. Their intense interest to secure a high place among men has caused them to leave the will of their Heavenly Father out of their calculations; but true knowledge leads to holiness of life through the sanctification of the truth.

Too often, as the studies accumulate, the wisdom from above has been given a secondary place, and the further advanced the student becomes, the less confidence he has in God; he considers that much learning is the very essence of success in life; but if all would give due consideration to the statement of Christ, they would make different plans: "Without Me ye can do nothing." Without the vital principles of true religion, without knowledge of how to serve and glorify the Redeemer, education is more harmful than beneficial. When education in human lines is pushed to such an extent that the love of God wanes in the heart, that prayer is neglected, and that there is a failure to cultivate spiritual attributes, it is wholly disastrous. It would be far better to cease seeking to obtain an education, and to recover your soul from its languishing condition, than to gain the best of educations, and lose sight of eternal advantages. There are many who are crowding too many studies into a limited period of time. They are overworking their mental powers; and as a consequence they see many things in a perverted light. They are not content in following the prescribed course of study, but feel that injustice is done them when, in their selfish ambition, they are not permitted to carry all the studies that they desire to carry. They become unbalanced in mind. They do not consider the fact that they would obtain a better qualification for the work of the Master if they would pursue a course that would not work injury to their physical, mental, and moral powers; but in overburdening the mind, they bring upon themselves life-long physical infirmities that cripple their powers, and unfit them for future usefulness.

I would not in any case counsel restriction of the education to which God has set no limit. Our education does not end with the advantages that this world can give. Through all eternity the chosen of God will be learners. But I would advise restriction in following those methods of education which imperil the soul and defeat the purpose for which time and money are spent. Education is a grand life work; but to obtain true education, it is necessary to possess that wisdom that cometh alone from God. The Lord God should be represented in every phase of education; but it is a mistake to devote a period of years to the study of one line of book-knowledge. After a period of time has been devoted to study, let no one advise students to enter again upon a line of study but, rather, advise them to enter upon the work for which they have been studying. Let them be advised to put into practice the theories they have gained. Daniel pursued this course in Babylon. He put into practical use that which he had learned under tutors. Let students seek heavenly direction much more than they have done hitherto, and let them make no move, even though it be advised by their teachers, unless they have most humbly sought wisdom from God, and have received His guidance and counsel.

Students are authorized to go to school for a certain length of time in order to acquire scientific knowledge; but in doing this they should ever consider their physical necessities, and seek their education in such a way as not to injure in the least the temple of the body. Let them be sure not to indulge in any sinful practice, not to burden themselves with too many studies, not to become so absorbed in devotion to their studies that the truth will be supplanted, the knowledge of God expelled from the soul, by the inventions of men. Let every moment that is devoted to study be a moment in which the soul is conscious of its God-given responsibilities. There will be no need then of enjoining the students to be true and just, and to preserve their soul's integrity. They will breathe a heavenly atmosphere, and every transaction will be inspired by the Holy Spirit, and equity and righteousness will be revealed.

But if the body is neglected, if unsuitable hours are consumed in study, if the mind is overtaxed, if the physical powers are left unemployed and become enfeebled, then the human machinery is trammeled, and matters that are essential for our future welfare and eternal peace are neglected. Book-knowledge is made all-important, and God is dishonored. The student forgets the words of inspiration, and does not follow the instruction of the Lord when He says: "I beseech you therefore, brethren, by the mercies of God, that ye present your bodies a living sacrifice, holy, acceptable unto God, which is your reasonable service. And be not conformed to this world: but be ye transformed by the renewing of your mind, that ye may prove what is that good, and acceptable, and perfect will of God." The minds of many need to be renewed, transformed, and molded after God's plan. Many are ruining themselves physically, mentally, and morally, by over-devotion to study. They are defrauding themselves for time and eternity through practicing habits of intemperance in seeking to gain an education. They are losing their desire to learn, in the school of Christ, lessons of meekness and lowliness of heart. Every moment that passes is fraught with eternal results. Integrity will be the sure result of following in the way of righteousness.

Is it necessary that in order to solve the problem of education one must commit robbery toward God, and refuse to give God the willing service of the powers of the spirit, soul, and body? God calls upon you to be doers of His word, in order that you may be thoroughly educated in the principles that will give you a fitness for heaven. No method of education should be followed that will crowd out the word of God. Let the word of God be the man of your counsel. The purpose of education should be to take in light in order that you may impart light by letting it shine forth to others in good works. The highest of all education is the knowledge of God. "Thus saith the Lord, Let not the wise man glory in his wisdom, neither let the mighty man glory in his might, let not the rich man glory in his riches: but let him that glorieth glory in this, that he understandeth and knoweth Me, that I am the Lord which exercise lovingkindness, judgment, and righteousness, in the earth: for in these things I delight, saith the Lord." Read the first and second chapters of 1 Corinthians with deep interest, and pray that God will give you understanding so that you may comprehend and put into practice the truths there revealed. "For ye see your calling, brethren, how that not many wise men after the flesh, not many mighty, not many noble, are called: but God hath chosen the foolish things of the world to confound the wise; and God hath chosen the weak things of the world to confound the things that are mighty; and base things of the world, and things which are despised, hath God chosen, yea, and things which are not, to bring to naught things that are: that no flesh should glory in His presence. But of Him are ye in Christ Jesus, who of God is made unto us wisdom, and righteousness, and sanctification, and redemption: that, according as it is written, He that glorieth, let him glory in the Lord." "The Lord is exalted; for He dwelleth on high: He hath filled Zion with judgment and righteousness. And wisdom and knowledge shall be the stability of thy times, and strength of salvation: the fear of the Lord is his treasure."

Time is short, and there are but few workers in the vineyard of the Lord. Several have been sent from this part of the world to be educated at Battle Creek, in order that they may become laborers together with God. It was hoped that the Holy Spirit would work with them for the salvation of those who are in the shadow of death. These students have been supported by the sacrifices of men and women who, to my certain knowledge, have hired money to pay the tuition and to cover the expenses. The world is to be warned; and yet you have thought it necessary to consume time and money in making an unnecessarily large preparation for the work that these students may be called upon to do. The same God lives today that Isaiah saw in his vision, and can give enlightenment to those who are acting a part in the work of fitting men for a solemn, sacred work. He says: "I the Lord love judgment, I hate robbery for burnt offering; and I will direct their work in truth, and I will make an everlasting covenant with them."

Those who are directing in the work of education are placing too large an amount of study before those who have come to Battle Creek to fit up for the work of the Master. They have supposed that it was necessary for them to go deeper and deeper into educational lines; and while they are pursuing various courses of study, year after year of precious time is passing away, and golden opportunities are flitting by never to return. There is procrastination in setting these men to work; and students are losing their burden for souls, and are depending more and more upon an education in book-knowledge, rather than upon the efficiency of the Holy Spirit, and upon that which the Lord has promised to do for them.

This burden has been upon me for years. A course is pursued at Battle Creek such as the Lord does not approve. The end of all things is at hand. The day of distress, of anguish, of plague, of retribution, of judgment for sin, is coming on the world as a thief in the night. The time is near when sudden destruction will come upon the world, and they will not escape. I have a word of warning for you. You are viewing things in altogether too feeble a light, and far too much from a merely human standpoint. A very small portion of God's great moral vineyard has yet been worked. Only a few, comparatively, have received the last message of mercy that is to be given to the world. Students are led to suppose that their efficiency depends upon their education and training; but the success of the work does not depend upon the amount of knowledge men have in scientific studies. The thought to be kept before students is that time is short, and that they must make speedy preparation for doing the work that is essential for this time. Every man, in and through the grace given him of God, is to do the work, not depending on his human earnestness or ability; for God can remove human ability in a moment. Let each one in the strength of the living Saviour, who today is our Advocate in the courts of heaven, strive to do the will of God.

I am bidden to say to you that you know not how soon the crisis may come. It is stealing gradually upon us, as a thief. The sun shines in the heavens, passing over its usual round, and the heavens still declare the glory of God; men are still pursuing their usual course of eating and drinking, planting and building, marrying and giving in marriage; merchants are still engaged in buying and selling; publications are still issuing one upon another: men are jostling one against another, seeking to get the highest place; pleasure-lovers are still attending theaters, horse races, gambling hells, and the highest excitement prevails; yet probation's hour is fast closing, and every case is about to be eternally decided. There are few who believe with heart and soul that we have a heaven to win and a hell to shun; but these few show their faith by their works. The signs of Christ's coming are fast fulfilling. Satan sees that he has but a short time in which to work, and he has set his satanic agencies at work to stir the elements of the world, in order that men may be deceived, deluded, and kept occupied and entranced until the day of probation shall be ended, and the door be forever shut.

The kingdoms of this world have not yet become the kingdoms of our Lord and of His Christ. Do not deceive yourselves; be wide awake, and move rapidly, for the night cometh, in which no man can work. Do not encourage students, who come to you burdened for the work of saving their fellow men, to enter upon course after course of study. Do not lengthen out the time for obtaining an education to many years. By this course they suppose that there is time enough, and this very plan proves a snare to their souls. Many are better prepared, have more spiritual discrimination and knowledge of God, and know more of His requirements, when they enter upon a course of study than when they graduate. They become inspired with an ambition to become learned men, and are encouraged to add to their studies until they become infatuated. They make their books their idol, and are willing to sacrifice health and spirituality in order to obtain an education. They limit the time which they should devote to prayer, and fail to improve the opportunities which they have had to do good, and do not communicate light and knowledge. They fail to put to use the knowledge

Speedy Preparation For the Work

which they have already obtained, and do not advance in the science of winning souls. Missionary work becomes less and less desirable, while the passion to excel in book-knowledge increases abnormally. In pursuing their studies, they separate from the God of wisdom. Some congratulate them on their advance, and encourage them to take degree after degree, even though they are less qualified to do the work of God after Christ's manner of instruction than they were before they entered the school at Battle Creek.

The question was asked those assembled: "Do you believe the truth? do you believe the third angel's message? If you do believe, then act your faith, and do not encourage men to continue in Battle Creek when they should be away from that place doing their Master's business." The Lord is not glorified in this procrastination. Men go to Battle Creek, and receive a far higher idea of their capabilities than they should. They are encouraged to take a long, protracted course of study; but God's way is not in it. It does not have a heavenly endorsement. Precious probationary time will not permit of long protracted years of drill. God calls: hear His voice as He says, "Go work today in My vineyard." Now, just now, is the time to work. Do you believe that the Lord is coming, and that the last great crisis is about to break upon the world?

There will soon be a sudden change in God's dealings. The world in its perversity is being visited by casualties,--by floods, storms, fires, earthquakes, famines, wars, and bloodshed. The Lord is slow to anger, and great in power; yet He will not at all acquit the wicked. "The Lord hath His way in the whirlwind and in the storm, and the clouds are the dust of His feet." O that men might understand the patience and longsuffering of God! He is putting under restraint His own attributes. His omnipotent power is under the control of Omnipotence. O that men would understand that God refuses to be wearied out with the world's perversity, and still holds out the hope of forgiveness even to the most undeserving! But His forbearance will not always continue. Who is prepared for the sudden change that will take place in God's dealing with sinful men? Who will be prepared to escape the punishment that will certainly fall upon transgressors?

We have not a temporal millennium in which to do the work of warning the world. There is need of transformation of soul. The most effective intelligence that can be obtained will be obtained in the school of Christ. Understand that I say nothing in these words to depreciate education, but to warn those who are in danger of carrying that which is lawful to unlawful extremes, and of making altogether too much of human education. Rather insist upon the development of precious, Christian experience; for without this, the education of the student will be of no avail.

If you see that students are in danger of becoming engrossed in their studies to such an extent as to neglect the study of that Book which gives them information as to how to secure the future welfare of their souls, then do not present the temptation of going deeper, of protracting the time for educational discipline. In this way all that will make the student's education of value to the world will be sunk out of sight. Christ Jesus is to be loved more and more; but some have gone to Battle Creek in the pursuit of education, when, had they remained away, they would have been far better prepared for the work of God. They would have carried it forward in simplicity, in the manner in which Christ labored. They would have depended more upon God and upon the power of the Holy Spirit, and far less upon their education. Long periods of continual study are injurious to physical, mental, and moral well-being.

Read the Old and New Testaments with a contrite heart. Read them prayerfully and faithfully, pleading that the Holy Spirit will give you understanding. Daniel searched the portion of the Old Testament which he had at his command, and made the word of God his highest instructor. At the same time he improved the opportunities that were given him to become intelligent in all lines of learning. His companions did the same, and we read: "In all matters of wisdom and understanding, that the king inquired of them, he found them ten times better than all the magicians and astrologers that were in all his realm." "As for these four children [for they were mere youths], God gave them knowledge and skill in all learning and wisdom: and Daniel had understanding in all visions and dreams."

Students that exalt the sciences above the God of science, will be ignorant when they think themselves very wise. If you cannot afford time to pray, cannot give time for communion with God, for self-examination, and do not appreciate that wisdom which comes alone from God all your learning will be deficient, and your schools and colleges will be found wanting. "The fear of the Lord is the beginning of wisdom." What faith are we cherishing? Have we a faith that works by love and purifies the soul? Have we faith according to the light we have received? Satan would be exultant if he could work himself in at Battle Creek to deter the work of God by pressing in human inventions in advice and counsel. He would be delighted to have the workers absorbed in years of preparation, so that education would become a hindrance instead of an advancement.

The Holy Spirit of God has been striving with many youth, and has been urging them to give themselves to the cause and work of God. When they offer themselves to the Conference, they are advised to take a course of study at Battle Creek before they shall enter the work. This is all very well if the student is evenly balanced with principle; but it is not consistent that the worker should be long delayed in preparation. Most earnest work should be given to advance those who are to be missionaries. Every effort should tell to their advantage, so that they shall be sent forth as speedily as possible. They cannot afford to wait until their education is considered complete. This can never be attained; for there will be a constant course of education carried on throughout the ceaseless ages of eternity.

There is a large work to be done, and the vineyard of the Lord needs laborers. Missionaries should enter the field before they shall be compelled

Speedy Preparation For the Work

to cease labor. There are now open doors on every side; they cannot afford to wait to complete years of training; for the years before us are not many, and we need to work while the day lasts. It is not best to advise men and women to take a course of study at Ann Arbor. Many who have been there have not been benefited in the past, and will not be in the future.

Mark the features of Christ's work. He moved in the greatest simplicity. Although His followers were fishermen, He did not advise them to go first into the school of the rabbis before entering upon the work. He called His disciples from their fishers' nets, and said: "Follow Me, and I will make you fishers of men." He called Matthew from the receipt of customs, and said, "Follow Me." All that they were required to do was to follow Jesus, to do as He commanded them, and thus enter into His school, where God could be their teacher. As long as time shall last, we shall have need of schools. There will always be need for education; but we must be careful lest education shall absorb every spiritual interest.

There is positive peril in advising students to pursue one line of education after another, and to leave them to think that by so doing they will attain perfection. The education that will be obtained will only be deficient in every way. The Lord says: "I will destroy the wisdom of the wise, and will bring to nothing the understanding of the prudent. Where is the wise? where is the scribe? where is the disputer of this world? hath not God made foolish the wisdom of this world? For after that in the wisdom of God the world by wisdom knew not God, it pleased God by the foolishness of preaching to save them that believe." This is God's devised plan; and through successive generations, through centuries of heathenism, this plan has been carried forward, not as an experiment, but as an approved way for the spreading of the gospel. Through this method from the beginning, conviction came upon man, and the world was enlightened concerning the gospel of God. The highest grade of schooling that any human being can attain to is the schooling given by the Divine Teacher. This is the knowledge that in a special sense we shall greatly need as we draw near the close of this world's history, and everyone will do well to obtain this kind of education. The Lord requires that men shall be under His training. There is a great work to be done in bringing human minds out of darkness into the marvelous light of God. As His human instrumentalities, we are by living faith to carry out His plans. Are we in a condition in which our faith will not work to the glory of God, or are we vessels meet for the Master's use, prepared for every good work?

Moses was learned in all the wisdom of the Egyptians. He received an education in the providence of God; but a large part of that education had to be unlearned, and accounted as foolishness. Its impression had to be blotted out by forty years of experience in caring for the sheep and the tender lambs. If many who are connected with the work of the Lord could be isolated as was Moses, and could be compelled by circumstances to follow some humble vocation until their hearts became tender, they would make much more faithful shepherds than they now do in dealing with God's heritage. They would not be so prone to magnify their own abilities, or seek to demonstrate that the wisdom of an advanced education could take the place of a sound knowledge of God. When Christ came to the world, the testimony was that "the world by wisdom knew not God," yet that "it pleased God by the foolishness of preaching to save them that believe."

The experiment of the world's wisdom had been fully tested at the advent of Christ, and the boasted human wisdom had proved wanting. Men knew not the true wisdom that comes from the Source of all good. The world's wisdom was weighed in the balances, and found wanting. You are giving the students under your guardianship ideas that are not correct. If they had received far less of them, they would have been better fitted for the prosecution of their work. You do not properly consider the instruction and the method of our Lord Jesus Christ, yet He was the only perfect Educator in our world. "Now we have received, not the spirit of the world, but the Spirit which is of God; that we might know the things that are freely given to us of God. Which things also we speak, not in the words which man's wisdom teacheth, but which the Holy Ghost teacheth; comparing spiritual things with spiritual. But the natural man receiveth not the things of the Spirit of God: for they are foolishness unto him: neither can he know them, because they are spiritually discerned. But he that is spiritual judgeth all things, yet he himself is judged of no man. For who hath known the mind of the Lord, that he may instruct Him? But we have the mind of Christ."

You need to be learning in the school of Christ today. The Lord has power to work with His own agents. You are loading down poor finite men with weighty advantages to do a large work, when they will have no opportunity or call to use a large share of the burden of studies that they have undertaken to master. Golden opportunities are passing into eternity, and counsel has been given that should have been withheld; and much more and better work might have been done, than has been done, if the period spent in Battle Creek by many of the workers had been materially shortened. They should have been set at work communicating the light and knowledge they have received to those who are in darkness. The God of all grace will give grace for grace. Those who go to work in the Lord's vineyard will learn how to work, and will call to remembrance the instruction they have received during their student life. The Lord is not pleased with encouraging these workers to spend years in accumulating knowledge which they will have no opportunity to impart. Precious youth, who ought to be laboring for God, have come to Battle Creek to receive an education, and to gain a better knowledge as to how to work. They ought to have been taught that which is essential in a very short period. They ought not to require years for their education before they can respond to the call, "Go work today in my vineyard." Instead of sending them forth as laborers after they have put in months and years at the College, they are advised to take other studies, and to make progress along additional lines. They are counseled to spend months and years in institutions where the truth is denied and controverted, and where error of a most specious, unscriptural character is insidiously introduced. These doctrines become mingled with their studies. They become engrossed in advancing in educational lines, and they lose their love for Jesus; and before they know what is the matter with them, they are far from God, and are all unprepared to respond to the command, "Go work today in my vineyard." The desire for missionary effort is gone. They pursue their studies with an infatuation that closes the door to the entrance of Christ. When they graduate, and have full commission to go out as properly educated students, some have lost all burden for the work, and are far less prepared to engage in the service of God than when they came to Battle Creek at first.

The messenger turned to the congregation and said, "Do you believe the prophecies? Do you who know the truth, understand that the last message of warning is now being given to the world,--the last call of mercy is now being heard? Do you believe that Satan has come down with great power, working with all deceivableness of unrighteousness in every place? Do you believe that great Babylon has come up in remembrance before God, and that soon she will receive from God's hand double for all her sins and iniquities?" Satan is pleased to have you hold men and women in Battle Creek who should be laborers together with God in His great moral vineyard. If the enemy can keep workers out of the field on any pretext, he will do so. This advanced preparation which keeps talent out of the field gives no chance for the Lord to work with His workers. Many are led to occupy time, talent, and means selfishly in obtaining an advanced education, and at the same time the world is perishing for the knowledge which they could impart. Christ called the unlearned fishermen, and gave these men knowledge and wisdom to such a degree that their adversaries could not gainsay or resist their words. Their testimony has gone to the uttermost parts of the earth.

The disciples of Christ are not called upon to magnify men, but to magnify God, the source of all wisdom. Let educators give the Holy Spirit room to do its work upon human hearts. The greatest Teacher is represented in our midst by His Holy Spirit. However you may study, however you may reach higher and still higher, although you occupy every moment of your probationary time in the pursuit of knowledge, you will not become complete. When time is over, you would have to ask yourself the question, "What good have I done to those who are in midnight darkness? To whom have I communicated the knowledge of God, or even the knowledge of those things for which I have spent so much time and money?" It will soon be said in heaven, "It is done." "He that is unjust, let him be unjust still: and he which is filthy, let him be filthy still: and he that is righteous, let him be righteous still: and he that is holy, let him be holy still. And, behold, I come quickly; and My reward is with Me, to give every man according as his work shall be." When this fiat is spoken, every case will have been decided. Far better would it be for workers to take smaller work, and to go about it slowly and humbly, wearing the yoke of Christ and bearing His burdens, than to devote years in preparation for a large work, and then fail to bring sons and daughters to God, fail to have any trophies to lay at the feet of Jesus. Men and women are hovering altogether too long in Battle Creek. God calls them, but they do not hear His voice. Fields are neglected, and that means that minds are unenlightened. Corrupt seed is being rapidly sown in the hearts of our youth, and great practical truths must be brought in contact with the children and youth; for truth is powerful.

Christian teachers are called to work for God. The leaven of truth must be introduced before it can work transformation of character. It would be far better for our youth to be less accomplished in branches of study than to be lacking in humility and meekness, and to be devoid of contrite hearts. The work of some of our educators has been to unfit students to be laborers together with God. You should study to become acquainted with the manner in which Jesus worked and preached. He was self-denying and self-sacrificing. He did not shun toil; He suffered reproach, scorn, insult, mockery, and abuse; but are our students educated in such a way as will prepare them to walk in His footsteps? God is not in your procrastination. Your temptation to follow on year upon year in lines of study, is taking hold of minds, and they are gradually losing the spirit with which the Lord inspired them to go to work in His vineyard. Why cannot responsible men discern what will be the sure results of thus detaining the students, and of teaching them to put off the work of the Lord? Time is passing into eternity, and yet those who were sent to Battle Creek to be fitted up to work in the vineyard of the Lord are not encouraged to do what they could do to advance the cause of God. Many privileges are supplied to those who already know the truth, and yet are not practicing the truth. Money and strength that should be expended in the highways and hedges of the world, are expended on those who do not improve the light that they already have by communicating that light to those who are in darkness. When Philip received the light, he went and called Nathanael; but many youths who might do a special work for the Master, will not make a move until they have had multiplied opportunities.

Ministers of Jesus Christ should apportion some part of God's vineyard to men who are standing idle in the market place. If they blunder, then correct their mistakes, and set them at work again. Many more have been hindered from going forth into the work than have been encouraged to trade upon their talents, and yet it is by using their ability that they learn how to employ their talents. Many have gone to Battle Creek to obtain an education who could have been better instructed in their own country. Time has been lost, money has been needlessly expended, a work has been left undone, and souls have been lost, because of the miscalculations of those who thought they were serving God. The Lord lives, and His Holy Spirit presides everywhere. The impression must not prevail that Battle Creek is the Jerusalem of the world, and that all must go up there to worship. Those who desire to learn, and who make every possible effort to acquire knowledge, walking conscientiously in the light of the truth, need not journey to Battle Creek. God is our teacher; and those who would improve their talents where they are, will be blessed with teachers sent of God to instruct them,--teachers who have been preparing to do a work for the Master. To spend more time, to expend more money, is to do worse than to lose it; for those who seek to obtain an education at the expense of practical godliness are on the losing side. That which they acquire in educational lines during the time when they should have entered upon the work, is mere waste and loss. The heavenly intelligences are waiting for human agents with whom they can co-operate as missionaries in the dark parts of the earth. God is waiting for men to engage in home missionary work in our large cities, and men and women are retained in Battle Creek when they should be distributed in the cities and towns, along the highways and hedges. They should be calling and bidding men to come to the marriage supper, for all things are now ready. There will be missionaries who will do good work in the Master's vineyard who do not go to Battle Creek.

Those who go to Battle Creek meet with temptations that they did not suppose could exist in that place. They meet with discouragements which they need not have had, and they are not helped in their religious experience by going to that place. They lose much time because they know not what they are to do, and no one is prepared to tell them. They lose much time in following occupations which have no bearing upon the work for which they desire to fit themselves. The common and the sacred work are co-mingled, and stand on a level. But this is not a wise policy. God looks on and does not approve. Many things might have been done that would have had lasting influence, had they worked moderately and in humility in the place where they were. Time is passing; souls are deciding either for evil or good, and the warfare is constantly increasing. How many who know the truth for this time are working in harmony with its principles? It is true that something is being done; but more, far more, should have been done. The work is accumulating, and the time for doing the work is diminishing. It is now time for all to be burning and shining lights; and yet many are failing to keep their lamps supplied with the oil of grace, and trimmed and burning so that light may gleam out today.

Too many are counting on a long stretch of a tomorrow; but that is a mistake. Let everyone be educated in such a way as to show the importance for the special work for today. Let everyone work for God and work for souls; let each one show wisdom, and never be found in idleness, waiting for someone to come around and set him to work. The "someone" who could set you to work is overcrowded with responsibilities and time is lost in waiting for his directions. God will give you wisdom in reforming at once; for the call is still made, "Son, go work today in My vineyard."

Some may still be undecided, yet the call is still heard, "Go work today in My vineyard." "Today if ye will hear His voice, harden not your hearts." The Lord prefaces the requirement by the use of the word "son." How tender, how compassionate, yet withal, how urgent! His invitation to work in His vineyard is also a command. "What? know ye not that your body is the temple of the Holy Ghost which is in you, which ye have of God, and ye are not your own? For ye are bought with a price; therefore glorify God in your body, and in your spirit, which are God's."--"Special Testimonies on Education," March 21, 1895.

The Essential Education

I have written largely in reference to students spending an unreasonably long time in gaining an education; but I hope I shall not be misunderstood in regard to what is essential education. I do not mean that a superficial work should be done as is illustrated by the way in which some portions of the land are worked in Australia. The plow was only put in the depth of a few inches, the ground was not prepared for the seed, and the harvest was meager, corresponding to the superficial preparation that was given to the land.

God has given inquiring minds to youth and children. Their reasoning powers are entrusted to them as precious talents. It is the duty of parents to keep the matter of their education before them in its true meaning; for it comprehends many lines. They should be taught to improve every talent and organ, expecting that they will be used in the service of Christ for the uplifting of fallen humanity. Our schools are the Lord's special instrumentality to fit up the children and youth for missionary work. Parents should understand their responsibility, and help their children to appreciate the great privileges and blessings that God has provided for them in educational advantages.

But their domestic education should keep pace with their education in literary lines. In childhood and youth practical and literary training should be combined, and the mind stored with knowledge. Parents should feel that they have a solemn work to do, and should take hold of it earnestly. They are to train and mold the characters of their children. They should not be satisfied with doing surface work. Before every child is opened up a life involved with highest interests; for they are to be made complete in Christ through the instrumentalities which God has furnished. The soil of the heart should be preoccupied; the seeds of truth should be sown therein in the earliest years. If parents are careless in this matter, they will be called to account for their unfaithful stewardship. Children should be dealt with tenderly and lovingly, and taught that Christ is their personal Saviour, and that by the simple process of giving their hearts and minds to Him they become His disciples.

Children should be taught to have a part in domestic duties. They should be instructed how to help father and mother in the little things that they can do. Their minds should be trained to think, their memories taxed to remember their appointed work; and in the training to habits of usefulness in the home, they are being educated in doing practical duties appropriate to their age. If children have proper home training, they will not be found upon the streets receiving the haphazard education that so many receive. Parents who love their children in a sensible way will not permit them to grow up with lazy habits, and ignorant of how to do home duties.

Ignorance is not acceptable to God, and is unfavorable for the doing of His work. To be ignorant is not to be considered a mark of humility, or something for which men should be praised. But God works for people in spite of their ignorance. Those who have had no opportunity for acquiring knowledge, or who have had opportunity and have failed to improve it, and become converted to God, can be useful in the service of the Lord through the operation of His Holy Spirit. But those who have education, and who consecrate themselves to the service of God, can do service in a greater variety of ways, and can accomplish a much more extensive work in bringing souls to the knowledge of the truth than can those who are uneducated. They are on vantage ground, because of the discipline of mind which they have had. We would not depreciate education in the least, but would counsel that it be carried forward with a full sense of the shortness of time, and the great work that is to be accomplished before the coming of Christ. We would not have the students receive the idea that they can spend many years in acquiring an education. Let them use the education that they can acquire in a reasonable length of time, in carrying forward the work of God. Our Saviour is in the sanctuary pleading in our behalf. He is our interceding High Priest, making an atoning sacrifice for us, pleading in our behalf the efficacy of His blood. Parents should seek to represent this Saviour to their children to establish in their minds the plan of salvation, how that because of transgression of the law of God, Christ became our sin-bearer. The fact that the only-begotten Son of God gave His life because of man's transgression, to satisfy justice and to vindicate the honor of God's law, should be constantly kept before the minds of children and youth. The object of this great sacrifice should also be kept before them; for it was to uplift fallen man degraded by sin that this great sacrifice was made. Christ suffered in order that through faith in Him our sins might be pardoned. He became man's substitute and surety, Himself taking the punishment, though all undeserving, that we who deserved it might be free, and return to our allegiance to God through the merits of a crucified and risen Saviour. He is our only hope of salvation. Through His sacrifice we who are now on probation are prisoners of hope. We are to reveal to the universe, to the world fallen and to worlds unfallen, that there is forgiveness with God, that through the love of God we may be reconciled to God. Man repents, becomes contrite in heart, believes in Christ as His atoning sacrifice, and realizes that God is reconciled to him.

We should cherish gratitude of heart all the days of our life because the Lord has put on record these words: "For thus saith the high and lofty One that inhabiteth eternity, whose name is Holy; I dwell in the high and holy place, with him also that is of a contrite and humble spirit, to revive the spirit of the humble, and to revive the heart of the contrite ones." The reconciliation of God to man, and man to God, is sure when certain conditions are met. The Lord says, "The sacrifices of God are a broken spirit: a broken and a contrite heart, O God, Thou wilt not despise." Again He says,

The Essential Education

"The Lord is nigh unto them that are of a broken heart; and saveth such as be of a contrite spirit." "Though the Lord be high, yet hath He respect unto the lowly: but the proud He knoweth afar off." "Thus saith the Lord, The heaven is My throne, and the earth is My footstool: where is the house that ye build unto Me? and where is the place of My rest? For all those things hath Mine hand made, and all those things have been, saith the Lord: but to this man will I look, even to him that is poor and of a contrite spirit, and trembleth at My word." "The Spirit of the Lord God is upon Me; because the Lord hath anointed Me to preach good tidings unto the meek; He hath sent Me to bind up the broken-hearted, to proclaim liberty to the captives, and the opening of the prison to them that are bound; to proclaim the acceptable year of the Lord, and the day of vengeance of our God; to comfort all that mourn; to appoint unto them that mourn in Zion, to give unto them beauty for ashes, the oil of joy for mourning, the garment of praise for the spirit of heaviness; that they might be called trees of righteousness, the planting of the Lord, that He might be glorified." The psalmist writes, "He healeth the broken in heart, and bindeth up their wounds." Though He is the restorer of fallen humanity, yet "He telleth the number of the stars; He calleth them all by their names. Great is our Lord, and of great power: His understanding is infinite. The Lord lifteth up the meek: He casteth the wicked down to the ground. Sing unto the Lord with thanksgiving; sing praise upon the harp unto our God. . . . The Lord taketh pleasure in them that fear Him, in those that hope in His mercy. Praise the Lord, O Jerusalem; praise thy God, O Zion."

How precious are the lessons of this psalm. We might well devote study to the last four psalms of David. The words also of the prophet are very precious: "Will a man leave the snow of Lebanon which cometh from the rock of the field? or shall the cold flowing waters that come from another place be forsaken? Because my people hath forgotten Me, they have burned incense to vanity, and they have caused them to stumble in their ways from the ancient paths, to walk in paths, in a way not cast up." "Thus saith the Lord; Cursed be the man that trusteth in man, and maketh flesh his arm, and whose heart departeth from the Lord. For he shall be like the heath in the desert, and shall not see when good cometh; but shall inhabit the parched places in the wilderness, in a salt land and not inhabited. Blessed is the man that trusteth in the Lord, and whose hope the Lord is. For he shall be as a tree planted by the waters, and that spreadeth out her roots by the river, and shall not see when heat cometh, but her leaf shall be green; and shall not be careful in the year of drought, neither shall cease from yielding fruit."--"Special Testimonies on Education," April 22, 1895.

Diligent and Thorough Education

No movement should be made to lower the standard of education in our school at Battle Creek. The students should tax the mental powers; every faculty should reach the highest possible development. Many students come to the college with intellectual habits partially formed that are a hindrance to them. The most difficult to manage is the habit of performing their work as a matter of routine, instead of bringing to their studies thoughtful, determined effort to master difficulties, and to grasp the principles at the foundation of every subject under consideration. Through the grace of Christ it is in their power to change this habit of routine, and it is for their best interest and future usefulness rightly to direct the mental faculties, training them to do service for the wisest Teacher, whose power they may claim by faith. This will give them success in their intellectual efforts, in accordance with the laws of God. Each student should feel that, under God, he is to have special training, individual culture; and he should realize that the Lord requires of him to make all of himself that he possibly can, that he may teach others also. Indolence, apathy, irregularity, are to be dreaded, and the binding of one's self to routine is just as much to be dreaded.

I hope that no one will receive the impression from any words I have written, that the standard of the school is to be in any way lowered. There should be most diligent and thorough education in our school, and in order to secure this, the wisdom that comes from God must be made first and most important. The religion of Christ never sanctions physical or mental laziness.

We have before us the case of Daniel and his fellows, who made the most of their opportunities to obtain an education in the courts of Babylon. When tested by those who questioned both their faith and their knowledge, they were able to give a reason of the hope that was in them, and, as well, to stand the examination as to their knowledge in all learning and wisdom; and it was found that Daniel had understanding also in all visions and dreams, showing that he had a living connection with the God of all wisdom. "In all matters of wisdom and understanding, that the king inquired of them, he found them ten times better than all the magicians and astrologers that were in all his realm." Daniel's history is given us for our admonition upon whom the ends of the world are come. "The secret of the Lord is with them that fear Him." Daniel was in close connection with God. When the decree went forth from an angry, furious king, commanding that all the wise men of Babylon should be destroyed, Daniel and his fellows were sought for to be slain. Then Daniel answered, not with retaliation, but "with counsel and wisdom," the captain of the king's guard, who was gone forth to slay the wise men of Babylon. Daniel asked, "Why is the decree so hasty from the king?" He presented himself before the king, requesting that time be given him, and his faith in the God he served prompted him to say that he would show the king the interpretation. "Then Daniel went to his house, and made the thing known to Hananiah, Mishael, and Azariah, his companions: that they would desire mercies of the God of heaven concerning this secret; that Daniel and his fellows should not perish with the rest of the wise men of Babylon. Then was the secret revealed unto Daniel in a night vision. Then Daniel blessed the God of heaven." (Read Daniel 2:20-28.) Here the interpretation was made known to Daniel.

The close application of those Hebrew students under the training of God was richly rewarded. While they made diligent effort to secure knowledge, the Lord gave them heavenly wisdom. The knowledge they gained was of great service to them when brought into strait places. The Lord God of heaven will not supply the deficiencies that result from mental and spiritual indolence. When the human agents shall exercise their faculties to acquire knowledge, to become deep-thinking men; when they, as the greatest witnesses for God and the truth, shall have won in the field of investigation of vital doctrines concerning the salvation of the soul, that glory may be given to the God of heaven as supreme, then even judges and kings will be brought to acknowledge, in the courts of justice, in parliaments and councils, that the God who made the heavens and the earth is the only true and living God, the author of Christianity, the author of all truth, who instituted the seventh-day Sabbath when the foundations of the world were laid, when the morning stars sang together, and all the sons of God shouted together for joy. All nature will bear testimony, as designed, for the illustration of the word of God.

The natural and the spiritual are to be combined in the studies of our schools. The operations of agriculture illustrate the Bible lessons. The laws obeyed by the earth reveal the fact that it is under the masterly power of an infinite God. The same principles run through the spiritual and the natural world. Divorce God and His wisdom from the acquisition of knowledge, and you have a lame, one-sided education, dead to all the saving qualities which give power to man, so that he is incapable of acquiring immortality through faith in Christ. The author of nature is the author of the Bible. Creation and Christianity have one God. All who engage in the acquisition of knowledge should aim to reach the highest round of progress. Let them advance as fast and as far as they can; let their field of study be as broad as their powers can compass, making God their wisdom, clinging to Him who is infinite in knowledge, who can reveal the secrets hidden for ages, who can solve the most difficult problems for minds that believe in Him who only hath immortality, dwelling in the light that no man can approach unto. The living witness for Christ, following on to know the Lord, shall know that his goings forth are prepared as the morning. "Whatsoever a man soweth, that shall he also reap." By honesty and industry, with a proper care of the body, applying every power of the mind to the acquisition of knowledge and wisdom in spiritual things, every soul may be complete in Christ, who is the perfect pattern of a complete man.

He who chooses a course of disobedience to God's law is deciding his future destiny; he is sowing to the flesh, earning the wages of sin, even eternal destruction, the opposite of life eternal. Submission to God and obedience to His holy law bring the sure result. "This is life eternal, that they might know Thee the only true God, and Jesus Christ, whom Thou hast sent." This is a knowledge of such value that no language can describe it; it is of highest worth in this world, and is far-reaching as eternity. "Thus saith the Lord, Let not the wise man glory in his wisdom, neither let the mighty man glory in his might, let not the rich man glory in his riches: but let him that glorieth glory in this, that he understandeth and knoweth Me, that I am the Lord which exercise loving-kindness, judgment, and righteousness, in the earth: for in these things I delight, saith the Lord."

When we aim at a low standard, we shall reach only a low standard. We commend to every student the Book of books as the grandest study for the human intelligence, as the education essential for this life, and for eternal life. But I did not contemplate a letting down of the educational standard in the study of the sciences. The light that has been given on these subjects is clear, and should in no case be disregarded. But if the word of God which giveth light, and giveth understanding to the simple, had been welcomed into the mind and the soul-temple, as a counselor, as a guide and instructor, the human agent living by every word that proceedeth out of the mouth of God, there would have been no need of reproof because of the backslidings of the students after the blessing of God had come to them in rich rays of divine light, to glow in heaven's holy fire upon the altar of their hearts. Many allowed amusements to have the supremacy. This was not the course that Daniel pursued in obtaining the education which revealed through him the supremacy of heavenly wisdom above all the wisdom and knowledge of the highest schools in the courts of proud Babylon. God opens the understanding of men in a marked manner if His words are brought into the practical life of the student, and the Bible is recognized as the precious, wonderful book that it is. Nothing is to come between this book and the student as more essential; for it is that wisdom which, brought into the practical life, makes men wise through time and through eternity. God is revealed in nature; God is revealed in His word. The Bible is the most wonderful of all histories, for it is the production of God, not of the finite mind. It carries us back through the centuries to the beginning of all things, presenting the history of times and scenes which would otherwise never have been known. It reveals the glory of God in the working of His providence to save a fallen world. It presents in the simplest language the mighty power of the gospel, which, received, would cut the chains that bind men to Satan's chariot.

The light shines from the sacred pages, in clear, glorious beams, showing us God, the living God, as represented in the laws of His government, in the creation of the world, in the heavens which He hath garnished. His power is to be recognized as the only means of redeeming a world from degrading superstitions which are so dishonoring to God and man. Every student of the Bible who not only becomes familiar with revealed truth through the education of the intellect, but also through its transforming power upon heart and character, will represent the character of God to our world in a well-ordered life and a godly conversation. The entrance of the word giveth light. The mind is expanded, elevated, purified. But many have pursued a course of action inconsistent with the knowledge of truth and the wonderful light through the descent of the Holy Spirit of God in so marked a manner upon hearts in Battle Creek. Great sin and loss resulted from the neglect to walk in the light from heaven. In plunging into amusements, match games, pugilistic performances, they declared to the world that Christ was not their leader in any of these things. All this called forth the warning from God. Now that which burdens me is the danger of going into extremes on the other side; there is no necessity for this; if the Bible is made the guide, the counselor, it is calculated to have an influence on the mind and heart of the unconverted. Its study, more than any other, will leave a divine impress. It will enlarge the mind of the candid student, it will endow it with new impulses and fresh vigor. It will give greater efficiency to the faculties by bringing them in contact with grand and far-reaching truths. It is ever working, drawing; it is an effective instrument in the converting of the soul. If the human mind becomes dwarfed and feeble and inefficient, it is because it is left to deal with commonplace subjects only.

God can and will do a great work for every human being who will open the heart to the word of God, and let it enter the soul-temple and expel every idol. Summoned to the effort, mind and heart take in the wonderful disclosures of the revealed will of God. The soul that is converted will be made stronger to resist evil. In the study of the Bible the converted soul eats the flesh and drinks the blood of the Son of God, which He himself interprets as the receiving and doing of His words, that are spirit and life. The Word is made flesh, and dwells among us, in those who receive the holy precepts of the word of God. The Saviour of the world has left a holy, pure example for all men. It illuminates, uplifts, and brings immortality to all who obey the divine requirements. This is my reason for writing to you as I did. God forbid that through lack of discernment errors should be committed through misunderstanding of my words addressed to you I have had no other feeling than that of pleasure in knowing that students could come forth from the study of the words of life with minds expanded, elevated, ennobled, and with their slumbering powers aroused to engage in the study of the sciences with a keener appreciation; they may become learned as did Daniel, with a purpose to develop and employ every power to glorify God. But it becomes every student to learn of God, who giveth wisdom, how to learn to the best advantage; for all are candidates for immortality.

The Lord God came down to our world clothed with the habiliments of humanity, that He might work out in His own life the mysterious controversy between Christ and Satan. He discomfited the powers of darkness. All this history is saying to man, I, your substitute and surety, have taken your nature upon Me, showing you that every son and daughter of Adam is privileged to become a partaker of the divine nature, and through Christ Jesus lay hold upon immortality. Those who are candidates for this great blessing should in everything act in a manner to represent the advantages of their association with the Lord through His revealed truth and through the sanctification of his Holy Spirit. This will enlarge the mind of the human agent, fasten it upon sacred things, set it to receive truth, to comprehend truth, which will lead to the working out of truth through the sanctification of heart, soul, and character.

Those who have this experience will not condescend to engage in the amusements that have been so absorbing and so misleading in their influence, revealing that the soul has not been eating and drinking the words of eternal life. The departure from the simplicity of true godliness on the part of the students was having an influence to weaken character and lessen mental vigor. Their advancement in the sciences was retarded, while if they were like Daniel, hearers and doers of the word of God, they would advance as he did in all branches of learning they entered upon. Being pure minded, they would become strong minded. Every intellectual faculty would be sharpened. Let the Bible be received as the only food for the soul, as it is the very best and most effectual for the purifying and strengthening of the intellect.--"Special Testimonies on Education," April 22, 1895.

FOR ADDITIONAL READING

Avoid Trifling Speech, Youth's Instructor, May 30, 1895

Books and Authors in Our Schools

I have some matters which I wish to present before you in regard to education. The teachers in our schools have great respect for authors and books that are current in most of our educational institutions. All heaven has been looking upon our institutions of learning, and asking you, What is the chaff to the wheat? The Lord has given us the most precious instructions in His word, teaching us what characters we must form in this life to prepare us for the future, immortal life. It has been the custom to exalt books and authors that do not present the proper foundation for true education. From what source did these authors obtain their wisdom, a large share of which does not deserve our respect, even if the authors are regarded as being wise men? Have they taken their lessons from the greatest Teacher that the world ever knew? If not, they are decidedly in the fault. Those who are preparing for the heavenly abodes should be recommended to make the Bible their chief book of study.

These popular authors have not pointed out to the students the way that leads to eternal life. "And this is life eternal, that they might know Thee the only true God, and Jesus Christ, whom Thou hast sent." John 17:3. The authors of the books current in our schools are recommended and exalted as learned men; their education is in every way deficient, unless they themselves have been educated in the school of Christ, and by practical knowledge bear witness to the word of God as the most essential study for children and youth. "The fear of the Lord is the beginning of wisdom." Books should have been prepared to place in the hands of students that would educate them to have a sincere, reverent love for truth and steadfast integrity. The class of studies which are positively essential in the formation of character to give them a preparation for the future life should be kept ever before them. Christ should be uplifted as the first great teacher, the only-begotten Son of God, who was with the Father from eternal ages. The Son of God was the great teacher sent into the world as the light of the world. "The Word was made flesh, and dwelt among us." The Father was represented in Christ, and the attention in education must be of that character that they will look to Him and believe in Him as the likeness of God. He had a most wonderful mission to this world, and His work was not in a line to give a full relation of His personal claims to deity, but His humiliation was a concealment of His claims. This is why the Jewish nation did not acknowledge Christ as the Prince of life; because He did not come with display and outward appearance, for He hid under the garb of humanity His glorious character.

The human family was to consider Him in the light of the holy Scriptures, which were to testify of the manner of His coming. Had He come, displaying His glory that He had with His Father, then His pathway toward the cross would have been thwarted by the purpose of men, who would have taken Him by force, and made Him king. He was to close His life by making a solemn oblation of Himself. Type was to reach antitype in Jesus Christ. His whole life was a preface to His death on the cross. His character was a life of obedience to all God's commandments, and was to be a sample for all men upon the earth. His life was the living of the law in humanity. That law Adam transgressed. But Christ, by His perfect obedience to the law redeemed Adam's disgraceful failure and fall.

The prophecies are to be studied, and the life of Christ compared with the writings of the prophets. He identifies Himself with the prophecies, stating over and over again, They wrote of Me; they testify of Me. The Bible is the only book giving a positive description of Christ Jesus; and if every human being would study it as his lesson book, and obey it, not a soul would be lost.

383 All the rays of light shining in the Scriptures point to Jesus Christ, and testify of Him, linking together the Old and New Testament Scriptures. Christ is presented as the author and finisher of their faith, Himself the one in whom their hopes of eternal life are centered. "For God so loved the world, that He gave His only-begotten Son, that whosoever believeth in Him should not perish, but have everlasting life."

What book can begin to compare with the Bible? It is essential for every child, for youth, and for those of mature age to understand; for it is the word of God, the word to guide all the human family to heaven. Then why does not the word from God contain the chief elements which constitute education? Uninspired authors are placed in the hands of children and youth in our schools as lesson books--books from which they are to be educated. They are kept before the youth, taking up their precious time in studying those things which they can never use. Many books have been introduced into the schools which should never have been placed there. These books do not in any sense voice the words of John, "Behold the Lamb of God, which taketh away the sin of the world." The whole line of study in our schools should be to prepare a people for the future, immortal life.

Jesus Christ is the knowledge of the Father, and Christ is our great teacher sent from God. Christ has declared in the sixth chapter of John that He is that bread sent down from heaven. "Verily, verily, I say unto you, He that believeth on Me hath everlasting life. I am that bread of life. Your fathers did eat manna in the wilderness, and are dead. This is the bread which cometh down from heaven, that a man may eat thereof, and not die. I am the living bread which came down from heaven: if any man eat of this bread, he shall live forever: and the bread that I will give is My flesh, which I will give for the life of the world." The disciples did not comprehend His words. Says Christ, "It is the Spirit that quickeneth; the
384 flesh profiteth nothing: the words that I speak unto you, they are spirit, and they are life."

It is of immense importance, in the light of the lessons of Christ, that every human being should study the Scriptures, that he may be convinced in whom his hopes of eternal life are centered. The Bible should ever have been made the great, grand book of study, which has come down to us from heaven, and is the word of life. Should that book which tells us what we must do in order to be saved, be set aside in a corner, and human productions be exalted as the great wisdom in education? The very knowledge children and youth need to obtain for usefulness in this life, and that they may carry with them in the future life, is found in the word of God. But this is not encouraged and presented before them as the most essential knowledge, and as that which will give the most correct information of the true God, and Jesus Christ whom He hath sent. There are gods many and doctrines many. There are maxims and commandments placed before our youth as the commandments of God. It is impossible for them to understand what is truth, what is the sacred, and what is the common, only as they understand the Scriptures, both Old and New Testaments.

The word of God is to stand as the highest educating book in our world, and is to be treated with reverential awe. It is our guidebook; we shall receive from it the truth. We need to present the Bible as the great lesson book to place in the hands of our children and youth, that they may know Christ, whom to know aright is life eternal. It is the book to be studied by those of middle age, and those who are aged. The word contains promises, warnings, encouragement, and assurances of the love of God to all who accept Him as their Saviour. Then place the holy word in their hands. Encourage them to search the word, and they will in so doing find hidden treasures of inestimable value to them in this present life, and in receiving Christ as the bread of life they have the promise of eternal life.

The lesson book, the Bible, contains the instruction of the character they must have, the moral excellence of character which must be cultivated, which God and heaven require. "Blessed are the pure in heart: for they shall see God." "Follow peace with all men, and holiness, without which no man shall see the Lord." "Beloved, now are we the sons of God, and it doth not yet appear what we shall be: but we know that, when He shall appear, we shall be like Him; for we shall see Him as he is. And every man that hath this hope in him purifieth himself, even as He is pure. Whosoever committeth sin transgresseth also the law: for sin is the transgression of the law. And ye know that He was manifested to take away our sins; and in Him is no sin."

This all-important knowledge is to be kept before children and youth, not in an arbitrary, dictatorial manner, but as divine disclosures, which are of the highest value to secure their present peace, quietude, and rest of mind in this present world of turmoil and strife, and as a preparation for the future, eternal life in the kingdom of God, where they shall see God, and know God and Jesus Christ, who gave His precious life to redeem them.

Christ came in the form of humanity to live the law of God. He was the word of life. He came to be the gospel of salvation to the world, and to fulfill every specification of the law. Jesus is the word, the guidebook, which must be received and obeyed in every particular. How necessary that this mine of truth be explored, and the precious treasures of truth be discovered and secured as rich jewels. The incarnation of Christ, His divinity, His atonement, His wonderful life in heaven as our advocate, the office of the Holy Spirit,--all these living, vital themes of Christianity are revealed from Genesis to Revelation. The golden links of truth form a chain of evangelical truth, and the first, and staple, is found in the great teachings of Christ Jesus. Why, then, should not the Scriptures be ennobled and exalted in every school in our land? How little children are educated to study the Bible as the word of God, and feed upon its truths, which are the flesh and blood of the Son of God! "Except ye eat the flesh of the Son of man, and drink His blood, ye have no life in you. Whoso eateth My flesh, and drinketh My blood [that is, continues to receive the words of Christ, and practice them], hath eternal life; and I will raise him up at the last day. For My flesh is meat indeed, and My blood is drink indeed. He that eateth My flesh, and drinketh My blood, dwelleth in Me, and I in him." "And he that keepeth His commandments dwelleth in Him, and He in him. And hereby we know that He abideth in us, by the Spirit which He hath given us."

There is necessity for every family to make the Bible the book of their study. Christ's sayings are pure gold, without one particle of dross, unless men, with their human understanding, shall try to put it there, and make falsehood appear as a portion of truth. To those who have received the false interpretation of the word, when they search the Scriptures with the determined effort to obtain the very marrow of truth contained in them, the Holy Spirit opens the eyes of their understanding, and the truths of the word are to them as a new revelation. Their hearts are quickened to a new and living faith, and they behold wondrous things out of His law. The teachings of Christ have a breadth and depth to many which they have never understood before.

The doctrines of grace and truth are not really understood by the larger number of our students and church members. Blindness of mind has happened to Israel. For human agents to misconstrue and put a forced, half truthful, and mystical construction upon the oracles of God, is an act which endangers their own souls, and the souls of others. "For I testify unto every man that heareth the words of the prophecy of this book. If any man shall add unto these things, God shall add unto him the plagues that are written in this book: and if any man shall take away from the words of the book of this prophecy, God shall take away his part out of the book of life, and out of the holy city, and from the things which are written in this book." Revelation 22:18, 19. Those who, by their human construction, shall make the Scripture to utter that which Christ has never placed upon it, weaken its force, making the voice of God in instruction and warnings to testify falsehood, to avoid the inconvenience incurred by obedience to God's requirements, have become signboards, pointing in the wrong direction, into false paths, which lead to transgression and death.

The testimony of the Alpha and Omega in regard to the punishment for making nonessential one word spoken by the mouth of God, is the fearful denunciation that they shall receive of the plagues that are written in the book; their names shall be taken out of the book of life, and from the holy city.

How many can truthfully answer this question, What is the essential education for this time? Education means much more than many suppose. True education embraces physical, mental, and moral training, in order that all the powers shall be fitted for the best development, to do service for God, and to work for the uplifting of humanity. To seek for self-recognition, for self-glorification, will leave the human agent destitute of the Spirit of God, destitute of that grace which will make him a useful, efficient worker for Christ. Those who desire only to glorify God will not be striving to bring their supposed merits into notice, or striving for recognition, or for the highest place. They that hear the call of the world's Redeemer, and obey that call, will be recognized as a distinct, self-sacrificing, holy people.

If the students in our schools will listen for the purpose of hearing and obeying the invitation, "Come unto Me, all ye that labor and are heavy laden, and I will give you rest. Take My yoke upon you, and learn of Me; for I am meek and lowly in heart: and ye shall find rest unto your souls. For My yoke is easy, and My burden is light," they will be living epistles, known and read of all men. "Verily I say unto you, Except ye be converted, and become as little children, ye shall not enter into the kingdom of heaven. Whosoever therefore shall humble himself as this little child, the same is greatest in the kingdom of heaven." The youth are in need of educators who shall keep the word of God ever before them in living principles. If they will keep Bible precepts ever as their textbook, they will have greater influence over the youth; for the teachers will be learners, having a living touch with God. All the time they are inculcating ideas and principles that will lead to a greater knowledge of God, and earnest, growing faith in their behalf in the blood of Jesus, and the power and efficiency of the grace of our Lord Jesus Christ to keep them from falling; because they are constantly seeking the strongholds of a healthful and well-balanced Christian experience, carrying with them qualifications for future usefulness, and intelligence, and piety. The teachers see and feel that they must labor not to dwarf and taint the minds of their associates, with a sickly half-religious service. There is need of separating from our educational institutions an erroneous, polluted literature, so that ideas will not be received as seeds of sin. Let none suppose that education means a study of books that will lead to the reception of ideas of authors that will sow seed and spring up to bear fruit that must be bound up in bundles with the world, separating them from the Source of all wisdom, all efficiency, and all power, leaving them the sport of Satan's arch-deceiving power. A pure education for youth in our schools, undiluted with heathen philosophy, is a positive necessity in literary lines.

The well-being, the happiness, of the religious life in the families with which they are connected, the prosperity and piety of the church of which they are members, are largely dependent upon the religious education that the youth have received in our schools.--"Special Testimonies on Education," June 12, 1895.

FOR ADDITIONAL READING

Let your Speech Be with Grace Always Seasoned with Salt, The Youth's Instructor, June 27, 1895

Our Words, The Youth's Instructor, July 11, 1895

The Child Life of Jesus, The Youth's Instructor, November 21, 1895

The Great Lesson Book

The Sanitarium is a broad missionary field. Your medical students, in studying the word of God diligently, are far better prepared for all other studies; for enlightenment comes always with an earnest study of the word. Let it be understood by medical missionaries that the better acquainted they become with God and Jesus Christ whom He hath sent, the better acquainted they become with Bible history, the better qualified they will be to do their work. The students in the College at Battle Creek need to aspire to higher knowledge, and nothing can give them a knowledge of all lessons, and a retentive memory, like the searching of the Scriptures. Let there be genuine discipline in study. There should be a most humble, prayerful longing of soul to know the truth.

There should be most faithful teachers, who strive to make the students understand their lessons, not by explaining everything themselves but by letting the students explain thoroughly every passage which they read. Let the inquiring minds of the students be respected. Treat their inquiries with respect. To skim over the surface will do little good. Thoughtful investigation and earnest, taxing study are required to comprehend it. There are truths in the word which are like veins of precious ore concealed beneath the surface. By digging for them, as the man digs for gold and silver, the hidden treasures are discovered. Be sure that the evidence of truth is in the Scripture itself. One scripture is the key to unlock other scriptures. The rich and hidden meaning is unfolded by the Holy Spirit of God, making plain the word to our understanding: "The entrance of Thy words giveth light; it giveth understanding unto the simple."

The word is the great lesson book for the students in our schools. The Bible teaches the whole will of God concerning the sons and daughters of Adam. The Bible is the rule of life, teaching us of the character we must form for the future, immortal life. Our faith, our practice, may make us living epistles, known and read of all men. Men need not the dim light of tradition and custom to make the Scriptures comprehensible. It is just as sensible to suppose that the sun, shining in the heavens at noon-day, needs the glimmerings of the torchlight of earth to increase its glory. The fables or the utterances of priests or of ministers, are not needed to save the student from error. Consult the divine Oracle, and you have light. In the Bible every duty is made plain, every lesson is comprehensible, able to fit men with a preparation for eternal life. The gift of Christ and the illumination of the Holy Spirit reveal to us the Father and the Son. The word is exactly adapted to make men and women and youth wise unto salvation. In the word is the science of salvation plainly revealed. "All Scripture is given by inspiration of God, and is profitable for doctrine, for reproof, for correction, for instruction in righteousness: that the man of God may be perfect, throughly furnished unto all good works." "Search the Scriptures," for therein is the counsel of God, the voice of God speaking to the soul.--"Special Testimonies on Education," December 1, 1895.

Higher Education

The term "higher education" is to be considered in a different light from what it has been viewed by the students of the sciences. The prayer of Christ to His Father is full of eternal truth. "These words spake Jesus, and lifted up His eyes to heaven, and said, Father, the hour is come; glorify Thy Son, that Thy Son may also glorify Thee: as thou hast given Him power over all flesh, that He should give eternal life to as many as Thou hast given Him. And this is life eternal, that they might know Thee the only true God, and Jesus Christ, whom Thou hast sent." "For He whom God hath sent speaketh the words of God; for God giveth not the Spirit by measure unto Him. The Father loveth the Son, and hath given all things into His hands. He that believeth on the Son hath everlasting life; and he that believeth not the Son shall not see life; but the wrath of God abideth on him." The power and soul of true education is a knowledge of God, and of Jesus Christ whom He hath sent. "The fear of the Lord is the beginning of wisdom."

Of Jesus it is written: "And the child grew, and waxed strong in spirit, filled with wisdom: and the grace of God was upon Him. . . . And Jesus increased in wisdom and stature, and in favor with God and man." A knowledge of God will constitute a kind of knowledge that will be as enduring as eternity. To learn and to do the works of Christ, is to obtain a true education. Although the Holy Spirit worked the mind of Christ, so that He could say to His parents, "How is it that ye sought Me? wist ye not that I must be about My Father's business?" yet He worked at the carpenter's trade as an obedient sin. He revealed that He had a knowledge of His work as the Son of God, and yet He did not exalt His divine character. He did not offer as a reason why He should not bear the burden of temporal care, that He was of divine origin; but He was subject to His parents. He was the Lord of the commandments, yet He was obedient to all their requirements, thus leaving an example of obedience to childhood, youth, and manhood.

If the mind is set to the task of studying the Bible for information, the reasoning faculties will be improved. Under study of the Scriptures the mind expands, and becomes more evenly balanced than if occupied in obtaining general information from the books that are used which have no connection with the Bible. No knowledge is so firm, so consistent and far-reaching, as that obtained from a study of the word of God. It is the foundation of all true knowledge. The Bible is like a fountain. The more you look into it, the deeper it appears. The grand truths of sacred history possess amazing strength and beauty, and are as far-reaching as eternity. No science is equal to the science that reveals the character of God. Moses was educated in all the wisdom of the Egyptians, yet he said, "Behold, I have taught you statutes and judgments, even as the Lord my God commanded me, that ye should do so in the land whither ye go to possess it. Keep therefore and do them; for this is your wisdom and your understanding in the sight of the nations, which shall hear all these statutes, and say, Surely this great nation is a wise and understanding people. For what nation is there so great, who hath God so nigh unto them, as the Lord our God is in all things that we call upon Him for? And what nation is there so great, that hath statutes and judgments so righteous, as all this law, which I set before you this day? Only take heed to thyself, and keep thy soul diligently, lest thou forget the things which thine eyes have seen, and lest they depart from thy heart all the days of thy life: but teach them thy sons and thy sons' sons."

Where shall we find laws more noble, pure, and just, than are exhibited on the statute books wherein is recorded the instruction given to Moses for the children of Israel? Through all time these laws are to be perpetuated, that the character of God's people may be formed after the divine similitude. The law is a wall of protection to those who are obedient to God's precepts. From what other source can we gather such strength, or learn such noble science? What other book will teach men to love, fear, and obey God as does the Bible? What other book presents to students more ennobling science, more wonderful history? It clearly portrays righteousness, and foretells the consequence of disloyalty to the law of Jehovah. No one is left in darkness as to that which God approves or disapproves. In studying the Scriptures we become acquainted with God, and are led to understand our relation to Christ, who is the sin-bearer, the surety, the substitute, for our fallen race. These truths concern our present and eternal interests. The Bible stands the highest among books, and its study is valuable above the study of other literature in giving strength and expansion to the mind. Paul says: "Study to show thyself approved unto God, a workman that needeth not to be ashamed, rightly dividing the word of truth." "But continue thou in the things which thou hast learned and hast been assured of, knowing of whom thou hast learned them; and that from a child thou hast known the holy Scriptures, which are able to make thee wise unto salvation through faith which is in Christ Jesus. All Scripture is given by inspiration of God, and is profitable for doctrine, for reproof, for correction, for instruction in righteousness: that the man of God may be perfect, thoroughly furnished unto all good works." "For whatsoever things were written aforetime were written for our learning, that we through patience and comfort of the Scriptures might have hope."

The word of God is the most perfect educational book in our world. Yet in our colleges and schools, books produced by human intellect have been presented for the study of our students, and the Book of books, which God has given to men to be an infallible guide, has been made a secondary matter. Human productions have been used as most essential and the word of God has been studied simply to give flavor to other studies. Isaiah

Higher Education

describes the scenes of heaven's glory that were presented to him, in most vivid language. All through this book he pictures glorious things that are to be revealed to others. Ezekiel writes: "The word of the Lord came expressly unto Ezekiel the priest, the son of Buzi, in the land of the Chaldeans by the river Chebar; and the hand of the Lord was there upon him. And I looked, and behold, a whirlwind came out of the north, a great cloud, and a fire infolding itself, and a brightness was about it, and out of the midst thereof as the color of amber, out of the midst of the fire. Also out of the midst thereof came the likeness of four living creatures. And this was their appearance; they had the likeness of a man. And everyone had four faces, and everyone had four wings. And their feet were straight feet; and the sole of their feet was like the sole of a calf's foot; and they sparkled like the color of burnished brass. And they had the hands of a man under their wings on their four sides; and they four had their faces and their wings. Their wings were joined one to another; they turned not when they went; they went everyone straight forward. As for the likeness of their faces, they four had the face of a man, and the face of a lion, on the right side: and they four had the face of an ox on the left side; they four also had the face of an eagle." The book of Ezekiel is deeply instructive.

The Bible is designed of God to be the book by which the understanding may be disciplined, the soul guided and directed. To live in the world and yet to be not of the world, is a problem that many professed Christians have never worked out in their practical life. Enlargement of mind will come to a nation only as men return to their allegiance to God. The world is flooded with books on general information, and men apply their minds in searching uninspired histories; but they neglect the most wonderful book that can give them the most correct ideas and ample understanding.--Review and Herald, Feb. 25, 1896.

395

The Divine Teacher

Those who are daily learning of Jesus Christ are fitted to take their position as laborers together with God, and whatever their trade or business may be, they may exert their God-given powers after the similitude of Christ's character while He tabernacled in the flesh. The young will carry with them just the influence they received in their home life and school education. God holds teachers responsible for their work as educators. They must learn daily in the school of Christ, in order to uplift the youth who have had a lax training at home, who have not formed studious habits, who have little knowledge of the future immortal life, for which the highest price was paid by the God of heaven in giving His only-begotten Son to live a life of humiliation and die a most shameful death, "that whosoever believeth in Him should not perish, but have everlasting life."

God has given us a probation in which we may prepare for the higher school. For this school the youth are to be educated, disciplined, and trained by forming such characters, moral and intellectual, as God will approve. They are to receive a training, not in the customs and amusements and games of this worldly polluted society, but in Christ's lines, a training which will fit them to be colaborers with the heavenly intelligences. But what a farce is that education obtained in literary lines, if it must be stripped from the learner if he is accounted worthy to enter upon that life which measures with the life of God, he himself saved as by fire.

In the past, education has consisted in laboriously loading the minds of the students with material which cannot be of the least value to them, and which will not be recognized in the higher school. The teachers of the Jewish nation professed to educate the youth to understand the purity and excellence of the laws of that kingdom which is to stand forever and ever, but they perverted truth and purity. Though they said of themselves, "The temple of the Lord, the temple of the Lord are we," yet they crucified the Originator of all the Jewish economy, Him to whom all their ordinances pointed. They failed to discern the veiled mystery of godliness; Christ Jesus remained veiled to them. The truth, the life, the heart of all their service, was discarded. They held, and still hold, the mere husks, the shadows, the figures symbolizing the true. A figure for the time appointed, that they might discern the true, became so perverted by their own inventions, that their eyes were blinded. They did not realize that type met antitype in the death of Jesus Christ. The greater their perversion of figures and symbols, the more confused their minds became, so that they could not see the perfect fulfillment of the Jewish economy, instituted and established by Christ, and pointing to Him as the substance. Meats and drinks and divers ordinances were multiplied until ceremonial religion constituted their only worship.

In His teaching, Christ sought to educate and train the Jews to see the object of that which was to be abolished by the true offering of Himself, the living Sacrifice. "Go ye," said He, "and learn what that meaneth, I will have mercy and not sacrifice." He presented a pure character as of supreme importance. He dispensed with all pomp, demanding that faith that works by love and purifies the soul, as the only qualification required for the kingdom of heaven. He taught that true religion does not consist in forms or ceremonies, outward attractions or outward display. Christ would have taken these to Himself if they had been essential in the formation of a character after the divine similitude. But His citizenship, His divine authority, rested upon His own intrinsic merits. He, the Majesty of heaven, walked the earth, shrouded in the robe of humanity. All His attractions and triumphs were to be revealed in behalf of man, and were to testify to His living connection with God.

Christ's prediction regarding the destruction of the temple was a lesson on the purification of religion, by making of none effect forms and ceremonies. He announced Himself greater than the temple, and stood forth proclaiming, "I am the way, the truth, and the life." He was the one in whom all the Jewish ceremony and typical service was to find its fulfillment. He stood forth in the place of the temple; all the offices of the church centered in Himself alone.

In the past, Christ had been approached through forms and ceremonies, but now He was upon the earth, calling attention directly to Himself, presenting a spiritual priesthood, and placing the sinful human agent at the footstool of mercy. "Ask, and it shall be given you," He promised; "seek, and ye shall find; knock, and it shall be opened unto you." "If ye shall ask anything in My name, I will do it. If ye love Me, keep My commandments." "He that hath My commandments, and keepeth them, he it is that loveth Me: . . . and I will love him, and will manifest Myself to him." "As the Father hath loved Me, so have I loved you: continue ye in My love. If ye keep My commandments, ye shall abide in My love; even as I have kept My Father's commandments, and abide in His love."

These lessons Christ gave in His teaching, showing that the ritual service was passing away, and possessed no virtue. "The hour cometh," He said, "and now is, when the true worshipers shall worship the Father in spirit and in truth: for the Father seeketh such to worship Him. God is a Spirit; and they that worship Him must worship Him in spirit and in truth." True circumcision is the worship of Christ in spirit and truth, not in forms and ceremonies, with hypocritical pretense.

The deep necessity of man for a divine teacher was known in heaven. The pity and sympathy of God were exercised in behalf of man, fallen and bound to Satan's chariot-car; and when the fullness of time was come, He sent forth His Son. The One appointed in the counsels of heaven came to the earth as an instructor. He was no less a being than the Creator of the world, the Son of the Infinite God. The rich benevolence of God gave Him to our world; and to meet the necessities of humanity, He took on Him human nature. To the astonishment of the heavenly host, He walked this earth as the Eternal Word. Fully prepared, He left the royal courts to come to a world marred and polluted with sin. Mysteriously He allied Himself to human nature. "The Word was made flesh, and dwelt among us." God's excess of goodness, benevolence, and love was a surprise to the world, of grace which could be realized, but not told.

That Christ, during His childhood, should grow in wisdom, and in favor with God and man, was not a matter of astonishment; for it was according to the laws of His divine appointment that His talents should develop, and His faculties strengthen by exercise. He sought neither the schools of the prophets nor the learning received from the rabbinical teachers; He needed not the education gained in these schools; for God was His instructor. When in the presence of the teachers and rulers, His questions were instructive lessons, and He astonished the great men with His wisdom and deep penetration. His answers to their queries opened up fields of thought on subjects in reference to the mission of Christ, which had never before entered their minds.

The stores of wisdom and the scientific knowledge Christ displayed in the presence of the wise men, were a subject of surprise to His parents and brothers; for they knew He had never received from the great teachers instruction in human science. His brothers were annoyed at His questions and answers; for they could discern that He was an instructor to the learned teachers. They could not comprehend Him; for they knew not that He had access to the tree of life, a source of knowledge of which they knew nothing. He ever possessed a peculiar dignity and individuality distinct from earthly pride or assumption; for He did not strive after greatness. 401

After Christ had condescended to leave His high command, step down from an infinite height and assume humanity, He could have taken upon Him any condition of humanity He might choose. But greatness and rank were nothing to Him, and He selected the lowest and most humble walk of life. The place of His birth was Bethlehem, and on one side His parentage was poor, but God, the Owner of the world, was His Father. No trace of luxury, ease, selfish gratification, or indulgence was brought into his life, which was a continual round of self-denial and self-sacrifice. In accordance with His humble birth, he had apparently no greatness or riches, in order that the humblest believer need not say that Christ never knew the stress of pinching poverty. Had he possessed the semblance of outward show, of riches, of grandeur, the poorest class of humanity would have shunned His society; therefore He chose the lowly condition of the far greater number of the people. The truth of heavenly origin was to be His theme: He was to sow the earth with truth; and He came in such a way as to be accessible to all, that the truth alone might make an impression upon human hearts.

Christ's contentment in any position provoked His brethren. They could not explain the reason of His peace and serenity; and no persuasion of theirs could lead Him to enter into any plans or arrangements which bore the impression of commonness or of guilt. On every occasion He would turn from them, plainly stating that they would mislead others, and were unworthy of the sons of Abraham. He must set such an example that little children, the younger members of the Lord's family, would see nothing in His life or character to justify any evil deed. You are altogether too particular and peculiar, said the members of his own family. Why not be as other children? But this could not be; for Christ was to be a sign and a wonder from His youth, as far as strict obedience and integrity were concerned.

Always kind, courteous, ever taking the part of the oppressed, whether Jew or Gentile, Christ was beloved by all. By His perfect life and character, He answered the question asked in the fifteenth Psalm: "Lord, who shall abide in Thy tabernacle? who shall dwell in Thy holy hill? He that walketh uprightly, and worketh righteousness, and speaketh the truth in his heart." In childhood and youth His course was such that when engaged in work as a teacher, He could say to His disciples, "If ye keep My commandments, ye shall abide in My love: even as I have kept My Father's commandments, and abide in His love."

As Christ grew older, the work begun in His childhood went on, and He continued to increase in wisdom, and in favor with God and man. He did not take the part of His own family merely because they were related to Him by natural ties; He would not vindicate their case in a single instance where they had been guilty of injustice or wrong; but He ever vindicated that which He knew to be truth.

Christ applied Himself diligently to a study of the Scriptures; for He knew them to be full of precious instruction to all who will make it the man of their counsel. He was faithful in the discharge of His home duties, and the early morning hours, instead of being wasted in bed, often found Him in a retired place, meditating and searching the Scriptures and in prayer. Every prophecy concerning His work and mediation was familiar to Him, especially those having reference to His humiliation, atonement, and intercession. In childhood and youth the object of His life was ever before Him, an inducement for His undertaking the work of mediating in behalf of fallen man. He would see seed which should prolong their days, and the gracious purpose of the Lord should prosper in His hands.

"Wherefore seeing we also are compassed about with so great a cloud of witnesses, let us lay aside every weight, and the sin which doth so easily beset us, and let us run with patience the race that is set before us, looking unto Jesus the author and finisher of our faith; who for the joy that was set before Him endured the cross, despising the shame, and is set down at the right hand of the throne of God." These subjects, Christ studied in His youth, and the universe of heaven looked with interest upon the One who for the joy that was set before Him endured the cross, despising the shame. By offering Himself to make intercession for the transgression of the human race, Christ executed the office of priest. As a reward, He was to see of the travail of His soul, and be satisfied. His seed should prolong their days on the earth forever. "Honor thy father and thy mother: that thy days may be long upon the land which the Lord thy God giveth thee." By His obedience to His father and mother, Christ was an example to all children and youth; but today children are not following the example He has given and the sure result will be the shortening of their days.

"Blessed be the God and Father of our Lord Jesus Christ, who hath blessed us with all spiritual blessings in heavenly places in Christ: according as He hath chosen us in Him before the foundation of the world, that we should be holy and without blame before Him in love: having predestinated us unto the adoption of children by Jesus Christ to Himself, according to the good pleasure of His will." Before the foundations of the earth were laid, the covenant was made that all who were obedient, all who should through the abundant grace provided, become holy in character, and without blame before God, by appropriating that grace, should be children of God. This covenant, made from eternity, was given to Abraham hundreds of years before Christ came. With what interest and what intensity did Christ in humanity study the human race to see if they would avail themselves of the provision offered.

"This is life eternal, that they might know Thee the only true God, and Jesus Christ, whom Thou hast sent." These words are an eye opener to all who will see. The knowledge of God is a knowledge which will not need to be left behind when our probation closes, a knowledge which is of the most lasting benefit to the world and to us individually. Why, then, should we put the word of God in the background when it is wisdom unto salvation. "Therefore we ought to give the more earnest heed to the things which we have heard, lest at any time we should let them slip. For if the word spoken by angels was steadfast, and every transgression and disobedience received a just recompense of reward; how shall we escape, if we neglect so great salvation." We are neglecting our salvation if we give authors who have but a confused idea of what religion means, the most conspicuous place and devoted respect, and make the Bible secondary. Those who have been enlightened in reference to the truth for these last days will not find instruction in the books generally studied today, in regard to the things which are coming upon our world; but the Bible is full of the knowledge of God, and is competent to educate the student for usefulness in this life and for the eternal life.

Study carefully the first chapter of Hebrews. Become interested in the Scriptures. Read and study them diligently. "In them ye think ye have eternal life," Christ said, "and they are they which testify of Me." It means everything to us to have an experimental and individual knowledge of God and of Jesus Christ, "whom He hath sent." "For this is life eternal, that they might know Thee the only true God, and Jesus Christ, whom Thou hast sent."--"Special Testimonies on Education," March 23, 1896.

True Education

"The entrance of Thy words giveth light; it giveth understanding unto the simple,"--to those who are not self-sufficient, but who are willing to learn. What was the work of the God-given messenger to our world? The only-begotten Son of God clothed His divinity with humanity, and came to our world as a teacher, an instructor, to reveal truth in contrast with error. Truth, saving truth, never languished on His tongue, never suffered in His hands, but was made to stand out plainly and clearly defined amid the moral darkness prevailing in our world. For this work He left the heavenly courts. He said of Himself, "For this cause came I into the world, that I should bear witness unto the truth." The truth came from His lips with freshness and power, as a new revelation. He was the way, the truth, and the life. His life, given for this sinful world, was full of earnestness and momentous results; for His work was to save perishing souls. He came forth to be the True Light, shining amid the moral darkness of superstition and error, and was announced by a voice from heaven, proclaiming, "This is My beloved Son, in whom I am well pleased." And at His transfiguration this voice from heaven was again heard, "This is My beloved Son, in whom I am well pleased; hear ye Him."

"Moses truly said unto the fathers, A Prophet shall the Lord your God raise up unto you of your brethren, like unto me; Him shall ye hear in all things whatsoever He shall say unto you. And it shall come to pass, that every soul, which will not hear that Prophet, shall be destroyed from among the people." Christ brought to our world a certain knowledge of God, and to all who received and obeyed His word, gave He power to become the sons of God. He who came forth from God to our world gave instruction on every subject about which it is essential that man should know in order to find the pathway to heaven. To Him, truth was an ever-present, self-evident reality; He uttered no suggestions, advanced no sentiments, notions, or opinions, but presented only solid, saving truth.

Everything not comprehended in truth is the guesswork of man. Professedly high and learned men may be fools in the sight of God, and if so, the high and learned statements of their doctrines, however they may please and humor the senses, and though they may have been handed down from age to age, and rocked in the cradle of popular faith, are a delusion and a falsehood if not found in the inspired lessons of Christ. He is the source of all wisdom; for He placed Himself directly on a level with the eternal God. In His humanity the glory of heavenly illumination fell directly upon Him, and from Him to the world, to be reflected back by all who receive and believe on Him, mingled with His perfection of character and the luster of His own character. While Christ stood forth distinctly in His human personality, and appealed in striking but simple language to humanity, He was in such perfect oneness with God that His voice came with authority, as the voice of God from the center of glory.

In the record John was charged by the Holy Spirit to present, he says of Christ, "In the beginning was the Word, and the Word was with God, and the Word was God. The same was in the beginning with God. All things were made by Him; and without Him was not anything made that was made." This is the most precious unfolding of definite truth, flashing its divine light and glory upon all who will receive it. What more important knowledge can be received than that given in the Book which teaches of the fall of man and the consequences of that sin which opened the floodgates of woe upon our world; which teaches also of the first advent of Christ, a helpless babe, born in a stable and cradled in a manger. The history of Christ is to be searched, comparing scripture with scripture, that we may learn the all-important lesson. What are the terms of salvation? As intelligent agents, invested with personal attributes and responsibilities, we can know in regard to our future, eternal destiny; for the Scripture record given by John, at the dictation of the Holy Spirit, contains no terms that cannot be easily comprehended, and that will not bear the most searching and critical investigation.

Christ was a teacher sent from God, and His words did not contain a particle of chaff or a semblance of that which is nonessential. But the force of much human instruction is comprised in assertion, not in truth. The teachers of the present day can only use the educated ability of previous teachers; and yet with all the weighty importance which may be attached to the words of the greatest authors, there is a conscious inability to trace them back to the first great principle, the Source of unerring wisdom, from which teachers derive their authority. There is a painful uncertainty, a constant searching and reaching for assurances that can only be found in God. The trumpet of human greatness may be sounded, but it is with an uncertain sound; it is not reliable, and the salvation of human souls cannot be ventured upon it.

A mass of tradition, with merely a semblance of truth, is being brought into education, which will never fit the learner to live in this life so that he may obtain the higher immortal life. The literature placed in our schools, written by infidels and so-called wise men, does not contain the education that students should have. It is not essential that they shall be educated in these lines in order to graduate from these schools to the school which is in heaven. The mass of tradition taught will bear no comparison with the teachings of Him who came to show the way to heaven. Christ taught with authority. The sermon on the mount is a wonderful production, yet so simple that a child can study it without being misled. The mount of beatitudes is an emblem of the high elevation on which Christ ever stood. He spoke with an authority which was exclusively His own. Every sentence He uttered came from God. He was the Word and the Wisdom of God, and He ever presented truth with the authority of God. "The words that I speak unto you," He said, "they are spirit and they are life."

That which in the councils of heaven the Father and the Son deemed essential for the salvation of man, was defined from eternity by infinite truths which finite beings cannot fail to comprehend. Revelations have been made for their instruction in righteousness, that the man of God may glorify his own life and the lives of his fellow men, not only by the possession of truth, but by communicating it. "All Scripture is given by inspiration of God, and is profitable for doctrine, for reproof, for correction, for instruction in righteousness: that the man of God may be perfect, thoroughly furnished unto all good works. I charge thee therefore before God, and the Lord Jesus Christ, who shall judge the quick and the dead at His appearing and His kingdom; preach the word; be instant in season, out of season; reprove, rebuke, exhort with all longsuffering and doctrine. For the time will come when they will not endure sound doctrine; but after their own lusts shall they heap to themselves teachers, having itching ears."

Jesus brought into His teaching none of the science of men. His teaching is full of grand, ennobling, saving truth, to which man's highest ambitions and proudest inventions can bear no comparison; and yet things of minor consequence engross the minds of men. The great plan of the redemption of a fallen race was wrought out in the life of Christ in human flesh. This scheme of restoring the moral image of God in debased humanity entered into every purpose of the life and character of Christ. His majesty could not mingle with human science, which will disconnect from the great source of all wisdom in a day. The topic of human science never escaped His hallowed lips. By believing in and doing the words of God, He was severing the human family from Satan's chariot-car. He was alive to the terrible ruin hanging over the human race, and He came to save souls by His own righteousness, bringing to the world definite assurance of hope and complete relief. The knowledge current in the world may be acquired; for all men are God's property, and are worked by God to fulfill His will in certain lines, even when they refuse the man Christ Jesus as their Saviour. The way in which God uses men is not always discerned, but He does use them. God entrusts men with talents and inventive genius, in order that His great work in our world may be accomplished. The inventions of human minds are supposed to spring from humanity, but God is behind all. He has caused that the means of rapid traveling shall have been invented, for the great day of His preparation.

The use which men have made of their capabilities, by misusing and abusing their God-given talents, has brought confusion into the world. They have left the guardianship of Christ for the guardianship of the great rebel, the prince of darkness. Man alone is accountable for the strange fire which has been mingled with the sacred. The accumulation of many things which minister to lust and ambition has brought upon the world the judgment of God. When in difficulty, philosophers and the great men of earth desire to satisfy their minds without appealing to God. They ventilate their philosophy in regard to the heavens and the earth, accounting for plagues, pestilences, epidemics, earthquakes, and famines, by their supposed science. Hundreds of questions relating to creation and providence, they will attempt to solve by saying. This is a law of nature.

There are laws of nature, but they are harmonious, and conform with all God's working; but when the lords many and gods many set themselves to explain God's own principles and providences, presenting to the world strange fire in the place of divine, there is confusion. The machinery of earth and heaven needs many faces to every wheel in order to see the Hand beneath the wheels, bringing perfect order from confusion. The living and true God is a necessity everywhere.

A most interesting and important history is given in Daniel 2. Nebuchadnezzar, king of Babylon, dreamed a dream which he could not bring to his remembrance when he awoke. "Then the king commanded to call the magicians, and the astrologers, and the sorcerers, and the Chaldeans," those whom he had exalted and upon whom he depended, and, relating the circumstances, demanded that they should tell him the dream. The wise men stood before the king in terror; for they had no ray of light in regard to his dream. They could only say, "O king, live forever: tell thy servants the dream, and we will show the interpretation." "The king answered and said to the Chaldeans, The thing is gone from me: if ye will not make known unto me the dream with the interpretation thereof, ye shall be cut in pieces, and your houses made a dunghill. But if ye show the dream, and the interpretation thereof, ye shall receive of me gifts and rewards and great honor: therefore show me the dream, and the interpretation thereof." Still the wise men returned the same answer, "Let the king tell his servants the dream, and we will show the interpretation of it."

Nebuchadnezzar began to see that the men whom he trusted to reveal mysteries through their boasted wisdom, failed him in his great perplexity, and he said, "I know of certainty that ye would gain the time, because ye see the thing is gone from me. But if ye will not make known unto me the dream, there is but one decree for you: for ye have prepared lying and corrupt words to speak before me, till the time be changed: therefore tell me the dream, and I shall know that ye can show me the interpretation thereof. The Chaldeans answered before the king, and said, There is not a man upon the earth that can show the king's matter. . . . It is a rare thing that the king requireth, and there in none other that can show it before the king, except the gods, whose dwelling is not with flesh." Then was the king "angry and very furious, and commanded to destroy all the wise men of Babylon."

Hearing of this decree, "Daniel went in, and desired of the king that he would give him time, and that he would show the king the interpretation. Then Daniel went to his house, and made the thing known to Hananiah, Mishael, and Azariah, his companions: that they would desire mercies of the God of heaven concerning this secret." The Spirit of the Lord rested upon Daniel and his fellows, and the secret was revealed to Daniel in a night vision. As he related the facts, the dream came fresh to the king's mind, and the interpretation was given, showing the remarkable events that were to transpire in prophetic history.

The Lord was working in the Babylonian kingdom, communicating light to the four Hebrew captives, that He might represent His work before the people. He would reveal that He had power over the kingdoms of the world, to set up kings and to throw down kings. The King over all kings was communicating great truth to the king of Babylon, awakening in his mind a sense of his responsibility to God. He saw the contrast between the wisdom of God and the wisdom of the most learned men in his kingdom.

The Lord gave His faithful representatives lessons from heaven, and Daniel declared before the great men of the king of Babylon, "Blessed be the name of God forever and ever: for wisdom and might are His: and He changeth the times and the seasons: He removeth kings, and setteth up kings: He giveth wisdom unto the wise, and knowledge to them that know understanding: He revealeth the deep and secret things: He knoweth what is in the darkness, and the light dwelleth with Him." "There is a God in heaven that revealeth secrets, and maketh known to the king Nebuchadnezzar what shall be in the latter days." Glory was not given to the men who stood as oracles in the kingdom; but the men who put their entire trust in God, seeking for grace and strength and divine enlightenment, were chosen as representatives of the kingdom of God in wicked, idolatrous Babylon.

The historic events related in the king's dream were of consequence to him; but the dream was taken from him, that the wise men by their claimed understanding of mysteries, should not place upon it a false interpretation. The lessons taught in it were given by God for those who live in our day. The inability of the wise men to tell the dream, is a representation of the wise men of the present day, who have not discernment and learning and knowledge from the Most High, and therefore are unable to understand the prophecies. The most learned in the world's lore, who are not watching to hear what God says in His word, and opening their hearts to receive that word and give it to others, are not representatives of His. It is not the great and learned men of the earth, kings and nobles, who will receive the truth unto eternal life, though it will be brought to them.

Daniel's exposition of the dream given by God to the king, resulted in his receiving honor and dignity. "The king Nebuchadnezzar fell upon his face, and worshiped Daniel, and commanded that they should offer an oblation and sweet odors unto him. The king answered unto Daniel, and said, Of a truth it is, that your God is a God of gods, and a Lord of kings, and a revealer of secrets, seeing thou couldest reveal this secret. Then the king made Daniel a great man, and gave him many great gifts, and made him ruler over the whole province of Babylon, and chief of the governors over all the wise men of Babylon. Then Daniel requested of the king, and he set Shadrach, Meshach, and Abed-nego, over the affairs of the province of Babylon: but Daniel sat in the gate of the king,"--a place where judgment was dispensed, and his three companions were made counselors, judges, and rulers in the midst of the land. These men were not puffed up with vanity, but they saw and rejoiced that God was recognized above all earthly potentates, and that His kingdom was extolled above all earthly kingdoms.

So we see that the highest line of earthly education may be obtained, and yet the men possessing it may be ignorant of the first principles which would make them subjects of the kingdom of God. Human learning cannot qualify for that kingdom. The subjects of Christ's kingdom are not made thus by forms and ceremonies, by a large study of books. "This is life eternal, that they might know Thee the only true God, and Jesus Christ, whom Thou has sent." The members of Christ's kingdom are members of His body, of which He himself is the head. They are the elect sons of God, "a royal priesthood, an holy nation, a peculiar people," that they should show forth the praises of Him who has called them out of darkness into His marvelous light.

"For thou art an holy people unto the Lord thy God: the Lord thy God hath chosen thee to be a special people unto Himself, above all people that are upon the face of the earth. The Lord did not set His love upon you, nor choose you, because ye were more in number than any people; for ye were the fewest of all people: but because the Lord loved you, and because He would keep the oath which He had sworn unto your fathers, hath the Lord brought you out with a mighty hand, and redeemed you out of the house of bondmen, from the hand of Pharaoh king of Egypt. Know therefore that the Lord thy God, He is God, the faithful God, which keepeth covenant and mercy with them that love Him and keep His commandments to a thousand generations; and repayeth them that hate Him to their face, to destroy them: He will not be slack to him that hateth Him, He will repay him to his face. Thou shalt therefore keep the commandments, and the statutes, and the judgments, which I command thee this day, to do them." If God's commandments are to be binding for a thousand generations, it will take them into the kingdom of God, into the presence of God and His holy angels. This is an argument that cannot be controverted. The commandments of God will endure through all time and eternity. Are they, then, given us as a burden?--No. "And the Lord commanded us to do all these statutes, to fear the Lord our God, for our good always, that He might preserve us alive, as it is at this day." The Lord gave His people commandments, in order that by obeying them they might preserve their physical, mental, and moral health. They were to live by obedience; but death is the sure result of the disobedience of the law of God.

The Old and the New Testament Scriptures need to be studied daily. The knowledge of God and the wisdom of God come to the student who is a constant learner of His ways and works. The Bible is to be our light, our educator. When we will acknowledge God in all our ways; when the youth are educated to believe that God sends the rain and the sunshine from heaven, causing vegetation to flourish; when they are taught that all blessings come from Him, and that thanksgiving and praise are due to Him; when with fidelity they acknowledge God, and discharge their duties day by day, God will be in all their thoughts; they can trust Him for tomorrow, and that anxious care that brings unhappiness to so many lives, will be avoided. "Seek ye first the kingdom of God, and His righteousness; and all these things shall be added unto you."

The first great lesson in all education is to know and understand the will of God. Take the knowledge of God with you through every day of life. Let it absorb the mind and the whole being. God gave Solomon wisdom, but this God-given wisdom was perverted when he turned from God to obtain wisdom from other sources. We need the wisdom of Solomon after we have learned the wisdom of One greater than Solomon. We are not to go through human wisdom, which is termed foolishness, to seek true wisdom. For men to learn science through man's interpretation, is to obtain a false education, but to learn of God and Jesus Christ is to learn the science of the Bible. The confusion in education has come because of wisdom and knowledge of God have not been honored and exalted by the religious world. The pure in heart see God in every providence, in every phase of true education. They vibrate to the first approach of light which radiates from the throne of God. Communications from heaven are made to those who will catch the first gleams of spiritual knowledge.

The students in our schools are to consider the knowledge of God as above everything else. Searching the Scriptures alone will bring the knowledge of the true God and Jesus Christ whom He hath sent. "The preaching of the cross is to them that perish foolishness; but unto us which are saved it is the power of God. For it is written, I will destroy the wisdom of the wise, and will bring to nothing the understanding of the prudent." "Because the foolishness of God is wiser than men; and the weakness of God is stronger than men." "But of Him are ye in Christ Jesus, who of God is made unto us wisdom, and righteousness, and sanctification, and redemption: that, according as it is written, He that glorieth, let him glory in the Lord."--"Special Testimonies on Education," March 26, 1896.

FOR ADDITIONAL READING

Our Children Demand Our Care and Attention, The Review and Herald, April 28, 1896

The Childhood of Jesus, The Bible Echo, May 11, 1896

Manual Training

Life is not given to us to be spent in idleness or self-pleasing; but great possibilities have been placed before everyone who will develop his God-given capabilities. For this reason the training of the young is a matter of the highest importance. Every child born into the home is a sacred trust. God says to the parents, Take this child, and bring it up for Me, that it may be an honor to My name, and a channel through which My blessings shall flow to the world. To fit the child for such a life, something more is called for than a partial, one-sided education, which shall develop the mental at the expense of the physical powers. All the faculties of mind and body need to be developed; and this is the work which parents, aided by the teacher, are to do for the children and youth placed under their care.

The first lessons are of great importance. It is customary to send very young children to school. They are required to study from books things that tax their young minds, and often they are taught music. Frequently the parents have but limited means, and an expense is incurred which they can ill afford; but everything must be made to bend to this artificial line of education. This course is not wise. A nervous child should not be overtaxed in any direction, and should not learn music until he is physically well developed.

The mother should be the teacher, and home the school where every child receives his first lessons; and these lessons should include habits of industry. Mothers, let the little ones play in the open air; let them listen to the songs of the birds, and learn the love of God as expressed in His beautiful works. Teach them simple lessons from the book of nature and the things about them; and as their minds expand, lessons from books may be added, and firmly fixed in the memory. But let them also learn, even in their earliest years, to be useful. Train them to think that, as members of the household, they are to act an interested, helpful part in sharing the domestic burdens, and to seek healthful exercise in the performance of necessary home duties.

It is essential for parents to find useful employment for their children, which will involve the bearing of responsibilities as their age and strength will permit. The children should be given something to do that will not only keep them busy, but interest them. The active hands and brains must be employed from the earliest years. If parents neglect to turn their children's energies into useful channels, they do them great injury; for Satan is ready to find them something to do. Shall not the doing be chosen for them, the parents being the instructors?

When the child is old enough to be sent to school, the teacher should co-operate with the parents, and manual training should be continued as a part of his school duties. There are many students who object to this kind of work in the schools. They think useful employments, like learning a trade, degrading; but such persons have an incorrect idea of what constitutes true dignity. Our Lord and Saviour Jesus Christ, who is one with the Father, the Commander in the heavenly courts, was the personal instructor and guide of the children of Israel; and among them it was required that every youth should learn how to work. All were to be educated in some business line, that they might possess a knowledge of practical life, and be not only self-sustaining, but useful. This was the instruction which God gave to His people.

In His earth-life, Christ was an example to all the human family, and He was obedient and helpful in the home. He learned the carpenter's trade, and worked with His own hands in the little shop at Nazareth. He had lived amid the glories of heaven; but He clothed His divinity with humanity, that He might associate with humanity, and reach hearts through the common avenue of sympathy. When found in fashion as a man, He humbled Himself, and worked for the recovery of the human soul by adapting Himself to the situation in which He found humanity.

The Bible says of Jesus, "And the child grew, and waxed strong in spirit, filled with wisdom: and the grace of God was upon Him." As He worked in childhood and youth, mind and body were developed. He did not use his physical powers recklessly, but gave them such exercise as would keep them in health, that He might do the best work in every line. He was not willing to be defective, even in the handling of tools. He was perfect as a workman, as He was perfect in character. By precept and example, Christ has dignified useful labor.

The time spent in physical exercise is not lost. The student who is continually poring over his books, while he takes but little exercise in the open air, does himself an injury. A proportionate exercise of all the organs and faculties of the body is essential to the best work of each. When the brain is constantly taxed while the other organs of the living machinery are inactive, there is a loss of strength, physical and mental. The physical system is robbed of its healthful tone, the mind loses its freshness and vigor, and a morbid excitability is the result.

The greatest benefit is not gained from exercise that is taken as play or exercise merely. There is some benefit derived from being in the fresh air, and also from the exercise of the muscles; but let the same amount of energy be given to the performance of helpful duties, and the benefit will be greater, and a feeling of satisfaction will be realized; for such exercise carries with it the sense of helpfulness and the approval of conscience for duty well done.

In the children and youth an ambition should be awakened to take their exercise in doing something that will be beneficial to themselves and helpful to others. The exercise that develops mind and character, that teaches the hands to be useful, and trains the young to bear their share of life's burdens, is that which gives physical strength, and quickens every faculty.

And there is a reward in virtuous industry, in the cultivation of the habit of living to do good.

The children of the wealthy should not be deprived of the great blessing of having something to do to increase the strength of brain and muscle. Work is not a curse, but a blessing. God gave sinless Adam and Eve a beautiful garden to tend. This was pleasant work, and none but pleasant work would have entered our world, had not the first pair transgressed God's commandments. Delicate idleness and selfish gratification make invalids; they can make the life empty and barren in every way. God has not given human beings reason, and crowned their lives with His goodness, that they may be cursed with the sure results of idleness. The wealthy are not to be deprived of the privilege and blessing of a place among the world's workers. They should realize that they are responsible for the use they make of their entrusted possessions; that their strength, their time, and their money, are to be used wisely, and not for selfish purposes.

The Christian religion is practical. It does not incapacitate one for the faithful discharge of any of life's essential duties. When the lawyer asked Jesus, "What shall I do to inherit eternal life?" Jesus turned the question back upon himself, saying, "What is written in the law? how readest thou? And he answering said, Thou shalt love the Lord thy God with all thy heart, and with all thy soul, and with all thy strength, and with all thy mind; and thy neighbor as thyself." Jesus said to him, "Thou hast answered right: this do, and thou shalt live." Luke 10:25-28. It is not a religion of inaction that is here sketched, but one that requires the energetic use of all the mental and physical powers.

Mere indolent musing, idle contemplation, is not religion. God requires us to appreciate our varied endowments, and to multiply them by constant, practical use. His people are to be models of correctness in all the relations of life. To every one of us He has given a work to do, according to our ability; and it is our privilege to enjoy His blessing while devoting strength of body and mind to its faithful performance, with His name's glory in view.

The approval of God rests with loving assurance upon the children who cheerfully take their part in the duties of domestic life, sharing the burdens of father and mother. They will be rewarded with health of body and peace of mind; and they will enjoy the pleasure of seeing their parents take their share of social enjoyment and healthful recreation, thus prolonging their lives. Children trained to the practical duties of life, will go out from the home to be useful members of society. Their education is far superior to that gained by close confinement in the schoolroom at an early age, when neither the mind nor the body is strong enough to endure the strain.

The children and youth should have the lesson continually before them, at home and in the school, by precept and example, to be truthful, unselfish, and industrious. They should not be allowed to spend their time in idleness; their hands should not be folded in inaction. Parents and teachers should work for the accomplishment of this object,--the development of all the powers, and a formation of a right character; but when parents realize their responsibilities, there will be far less left for teachers to do in the training of their children.

Heaven is interested in this work in behalf of the young. The parents and teachers who by wise instruction, in a calm, decided manner, accustom them to think of and care for others, will help them to overcome their selfishness, and will close the door against many temptations. Angels of God will co-operate with these faithful instructors. Angels are not commissioned to do this work themselves; but they will give strength and efficiency to those who, in the fear of God, seek to train the young to a life of usefulness.--"Special Testimonies on Education," May 11, 1896.

Educational Influence of Surroundings

In the selection of a home, parents should not be governed by temporal considerations merely. It is not altogether a question of the place where they can make the most money, or where they will have the most pleasant surroundings, or the greatest social advantages. The influences that will surround their children, and sway them for good or evil, are of more consequence than any of these considerations. A most solemn responsibility rests upon parents in choosing a place of residence. As far as possible they are to place their families in the channel of light, where their affections will be kept pure, and their love to God and to one another active. The same principle applies to the location of our schools, where the youth will be gathered, and families will be attracted for the sake of the educational advantages.

No pains should be spared to select places for our schools where the moral atmosphere will be as healthful as possible; for the influences that prevail will leave a deep impress on young and forming characters. For this reason a retired locality is best. The great cities, the centers of business and learning, may seem to present some advantages; but these advantages are outweighed by other considerations.

Society at the present time is corrupt, as it was in the days of Noah. To the long-lived, antediluvian race, only a step from paradise, God gave rich gifts, and they possessed a strength of body and mind of which men now have but a faint idea; but they used His bounties, and the strength and skill He gave them, for selfish purposes, to minister to unlawful appetites, and to gratify pride. They expelled God from their thoughts; they despised His law; trampled His standard of character in the dust. They reveled in sinful pleasure, corrupting their ways before God, and corrupting one another. Violence and crime filled the earth. Neither the marriage relation nor the rights of property were respected; and the cries of the oppressed entered into the ears of the Lord of Sabaoth. By beholding evil, men became changed into its image, until God could bear with their wickedness no longer, and they were swept away by the flood.

The youth educated in large cities are surrounded by influences similar to those that prevailed before the flood. The same principles of disregard for God and His law; the same love of pleasure, of selfish gratification, and of pride and vanity are at work at the present time. The world is given up to pleasure; immorality prevails; the rights of the weak and helpless are disregarded; and, the world over, the large cities are fast becoming hotbeds of iniquity.

The love of pleasure is one of the most dangerous, because it is one of the most subtle, of the many temptations that assail the children and youth in the cities. Holidays are numerous; games and horse-racing draw thousands, and the whirl of excitement and pleasure attracts them away from the sober duties of life. Money that should have been saved for better uses--in many cases the scanty earnings of the poor--is frittered away for amusements.

The continual craving for pleasurable amusements reveals the deep longings of the soul. But those who drink at this fountain of worldly pleasure, will find their soul-thirst still unsatisfied. They are deceived; they mistake mirth for happiness; and when the excitement ceases, many sink down into the depths of despondency and despair. O what madness, what folly to forsake the "Fountain of living waters" for the "broken cisterns" of worldly pleasure! We feel to the depth of the soul the peril that surrounds the youth in these last days; and shall not those who come to us for an education, and the families that are attracted to our schools, be withdrawn, as far as possible, from these seductive and demoralizing influences?

423 In choosing retired localities for our schools, we do not for a moment suppose that we are placing the youth beyond the reach of temptation. Satan is a very diligent worker, and is untiring in devising ways to corrupt every mind that is open to his suggestions. He meets families and individuals on their own ground, adapting his temptations to their inclinations and weaknesses. But in the large cities his power over minds is greater, and his nets for the entanglement of unwary feet are more numerous. In connection with our schools, ample grounds should be provided. There are some students who have never learned to economize, and have always spent every shilling they could get. These should not be cut off from the means of gaining an education. Employment should be furnished them, and with their study of books should be mingled a training in industrious, frugal habits. Let them learn to appreciate the necessity of helping themselves.

There should be work for all students, whether they are able to pay their way or not; the physical and mental powers should receive proportionate attention. Students should learn to cultivate the land; for this will bring them into close contact with nature.

There is a refining, subduing influence in nature that should be taken into account in selecting the locality for a school. God has regarded this principle in training men for His work. Moses spent forty years in the wilds of Midian. John the Baptist was not fitted for his high calling as the forerunner of Christ by association with the great men of the nation in the schools at Jerusalem. He went out into the wilderness, where the customs and doctrines of men could not mold his mind, and where he could hold unobstructed communion with God.

When the persecutors of John, the beloved disciple, sought to still his voice and destroy his influence among the people, they exiled him to the Isle of Patmos. But they could not separate him from the Divine Teacher.

On lonely Patmos, John could study the things that God had created. In the rugged rocks, in the waters that surrounded the island, he could see the greatness and majesty of God. And while he was communing with God, and studying the book of nature, he heard a voice speaking to him, the voice of the Son of God. Jesus was John's teacher upon the Isle of Patmos, and He there unfolded to His servant wonderful things that were to take place in time to come.

God would have us appreciate His blessings in His created works. How many children there are in the crowded cities that have not even a spot of green grass to set their feet upon. If they could be educated in the country, amid the beauty, peace, and purity of nature, it would seem to them the spot nearest heaven. In retired places, where we are farthest from the corrupting maxims, customs, and excitements of the world, and nearest to the heart of nature, Christ makes His presence real to us, and speaks to our souls of His peace and Love.--"Special Testimonies on Education," May 11, 1896.

Importance of Physical Culture

Physical culture is an essential part of all right methods of education. The young need to be taught how to develop their physical powers, how to preserve these powers in the best condition, and how to make them useful in the practical duties of life. Many think that these things are no part of school work; but this is a mistake. The lessons necessary to fit one for practical usefulness should be taught to every child in the home and to every student in the schools.

The place for physical training to begin is in the home, with the little child. Parents should lay the foundation for a healthy, happy life. One of the first questions to be decided is that of the food on their tables; for this is a matter upon which the development of the little ones and the health of the family very largely depend. Skill in the preparation of food is very important, and it is not less important that the food be of the proper quantity and quality.

We all need to exercise wisdom in eating. If more food is eaten than can be digested and appropriated, a decaying mass accumulates in the stomach, causing an offensive breath and a bad taste in the mouth. The vital powers are exhausted in an effort to throw off the excess, and the brain is robbed of nerve force. Less food would have nourished the system, and not wasted its powers in overwork. Yet wholesome food should be supplied, sufficient in quantity and quality to nourish the system. If we follow the Bible rule, "Whether therefore ye eat, or drink, or whatsoever ye do, do all to the glory of God," we shall not indulge appetite at the expense of the physical health, which it is our duty to preserve.

Every mother should see that her children understand their own bodies, and how to care for them. She should explain the construction and use of the muscles given us by our kind Heavenly Father. We are God's workmanship, and His word declares that we are "fearfully and wonderfully made." He has prepared this living habitation for the mind; it is "curiously wrought," a temple which the Lord himself has fitted up for the indwelling of His Holy Spirit. The mind controls the whole man. All our actions, good or bad, have their source in the mind. It is the mind that worships God, and allies us to heavenly beings. Yet many spend all their lives without becoming intelligent in regard to the casket that contains this treasure.

All the physical organs are the servants of the mind, and the nerves are the messengers that transmit its orders to every part of the body, guiding the motions of the living machinery. Exercise is an important aid to physical development. It quickens the circulation of the blood, and gives tone to the system. If the muscles are allowed to remain unused, it will soon be apparent that the blood does not sufficiently nourish them. Instead of increasing in size and strength, they will lose their firmness and elasticity, and become soft and weak. Inactivity is not the law the Lord has established in the human body. The harmonious action of all the parts,--brain, bone, and muscle,--is necessary to the full and healthful development of the entire human organism.

The work of physical training, begun in the home, should be carried on in the schools. It is the design of the Creator that man shall know himself; but too often in the pursuit of knowledge this design is lost sight of. Students devote years to different educational lines; they become engrossed in the study of the sciences and of things in the natural world; they are intelligent on most subjects, but they do not become acquainted with themselves. They look upon the delicate human organism as something that will take care of itself; and that which is in the highest degree essential--a knowledge of their own bodies--is neglected.

Every student should understand how to take such care of himself as to preserve the best possible condition of health, resisting feebleness and disease; and if from any cause disease does come, or accidents occur, he should know how to meet ordinary emergencies without calling upon a physician, and taking his poisonous drugs.

The Lord himself has spoken upon this subject of the care of the body. He says in His word, "If any man destroyeth the temple of God, him shall God destroy; for the temple of God is holy, which temple ye are." 1 Corinthians 3:17, R. V. This scripture enjoins a conscientious care of the body, and condemns all ignorant or careless neglect. And again: "Know ye not that your body is the temple of the Holy Ghost which is in you, which ye have of God, and ye are not your own? For ye are bought with a price: therefore glorify God in your body, and in your spirit, which are God's." "Whether therefore ye eat, or drink, or whatsoever ye do, do all to the glory of God." 1 Corinthians 6:19,20; 10:31.

The intelligent, conscientious care of our bodies is due to our Heavenly Father, who "so loved the world, that He gave His only-begotten Son, that whosoever believeth in Him should not perish, but have everlasting life." We are individually the property of Christ, His purchased possession. It is required of each one of us to preserve our health and strength by the practice of temperance in all things. The appetites and passions must be controlled, that through them we shall not weaken or defile God's human temple.

Anything that lessens the physical power enfeebles the mind, and makes it less clear to discriminate between good and evil, between right and wrong. This principle is illustrated in the case of Nadab and Abihu. God gave them a most sacred work to perform, permitting them to come near to Himself in their appointed service; but they had a habit of drinking wine, and they entered upon the holy service in the sanctuary with confused minds. There was the sacred fire, which was kindled by God himself; but they used the common fire upon their censers, when they offered incense to ascend as a sweet fragrance with the prayers of God's people.

Because their minds were clouded by an unholy indulgence, they disregarded the divine requirement; "and there went out fire from the Lord, and devoured them, and they died before the Lord."

God prohibited the use of wine to the priests ministering in His sanctuary, and the same injunction would have been made against tobacco, had its use been known; for it, too, has a benumbing influence upon the brain. And besides clouding the mind, it is unclean and defiling. Let everyone resist the temptation to use wine, tobacco, flesh-meats, tea, or coffee. Experience has demonstrated that far better work can be accomplished without these harmful things.

Let it be deeply impressed on the minds of the young by both parents and teachers, that Christ has paid an infinite price for our redemption. He has left nothing undone that He might win us back to allegiance to God. He wants us to remember our royal birth and high destiny as sons and daughters of God, and have genuine respect for ourselves. He would have all our powers developed, and kept in the best possible condition, that He may fill us with His grace and use us in His service, making us co-workers with Himself for the salvation of souls.

It is the duty of each student, of each individual, to do all in his power to present his body to Christ, a cleansed temple, physically perfect as well as morally free from defilement,--a fit abode for God's indwelling presence.--"Special Testimonies on Education," May 11, 1896.

The True Higher Education

God is love. The evil that is in the world comes not from His hands, but from our great adversary, whose work it has ever been to deprave man, and enfeeble and pervert his faculties. But God has not left us in the ruin wrought by the fall. Every faculty has been placed in reach by our Heavenly Father, that men may, through well-directed efforts, regain their first perfection, and stand complete in Christ. In this work God expects us to do our part. We are His--His purchased possession. The human family cost God and His Son Jesus Christ an infinite price.

The world's Redeemer, the only-begotten Son of God, by His perfect obedience to the law, by His life and character, redeemed that which was lost in the fall, and made it possible for man to obey that holy law of righteousness which Adam transgressed. Christ did not exchange His divinity for humanity, but combined humanity with divinity; and in humanity He lived the law in behalf of the human family. The sins of everyone who will receive Christ were set to His account, and He has fully satisfied the justice of God.

All the plan of redemption is expressed in these precious words: "For God so loved the world, that He gave his only-begotten Son, that whosoever believeth in Him should not perish, but have everlasting life." Christ actually bore the punishment of the sins of the world, that His righteousness might be imputed to sinners, and through repentance and faith they might become like Him in holiness of character. He says, "I bear the guilt of that man's sins. Let Me take the punishment and the repenting sinner stand before Thee innocent." The moment the sinner believes in Christ, he stands in the sight of God uncondemned; for the righteousness of Christ is his: Christ's perfect obedience is imputed to him. But he must co-operate with divine power, and put forth his human effort to subdue sin, and stand complete in Christ.

The ransom paid by Christ is sufficient for the salvation of all men; but it will avail for only those who become new creatures in Christ Jesus, loyal subjects of God's everlasting kingdom. His suffering will not shield from punishment the unrepenting, disloyal sinner.

Christ's work was to restore man to his original state, to heal him, through divine power, from the wounds and bruises made by sin. Man's part is to lay hold by faith of the merits of Christ, and co-operate with the divine agencies in forming a righteous character; so that God may save the sinner, and yet be just and His righteous law vindicated.

The price paid for our redemption lays a great obligation upon everyone of us. It is our duty to understand what God requires of us, and what He would have us to be. The educators of youth should realize the obligation resting upon them, and do their best to obliterate defects, whether physical, mental, or moral. They should aim at perfection in their own case, that the students may have a correct model.

Teachers should work circumspectly. Those who are often with God in prayer, have holy angels by their side. The atmosphere that surrounds their souls is pure and holy; for their whole soul is imbued with the sanctifying influence of the Spirit of God. They should be learners every day in the school of Christ, that they may be teachers under the great Teacher. They must learn of Christ, and become one with Him in the work of training minds, before they can be efficient teachers in the higher education--the knowledge of God.

God is revealed in His word. "For whatsoever things were written aforetime were written for our learning, that we through patience and comfort of the Scriptures might have hope." "And again, Praise the Lord, all ye Gentiles; and laud him, all ye people. And again, Esaias saith, There shall be a root of Jesse, and He that shall rise to reign over the Gentiles; in Him shall the Gentiles trust."

431   The true higher education is what makes students acquainted with God and His word, and fits them for eternal life. It was to place this life within their reach that Christ gave Himself an offering for sin. His purpose of love and mercy is expressed in his prayer for His disciples. "These words spake Jesus, and lifted up His eyes to heaven and said, Father, the hour is come; glorify Thy Son, that Thy Son also may glorify Thee: as Thou hast given Him power over all flesh that He should give eternal life to as many as Thou hast given Him. And this is life eternal, that they might know Thee the only true God, and Jesus Christ, whom Thou hast sent." Every instructor of youth is to work in harmony with this prayer, leading the students to Christ.

Jesus continues, expressing His care for His own: "And now I am no more in the world, but these are in the world, and I come to Thee. Holy Father, keep through Thine own name those whom Thou hast given Me, that they may be one, as we are. While I was with them in the world, I kept them in Thy name: those that Thou gavest Me I have kept, and none of them is lost, but the son of perdition; that the scripture might be fulfilled. And now I come to Thee; and these things I speak in the world, that they might have My joy fulfilled in themselves. I have given them Thy word; and the world hath hated them, because they are not of the world."

Suppose we catch the spirit that breathed in this prayer that ascended to heaven. Christ here shows what methods and force He used to keep His disciples from worldly practices, maxims, and dispositions: "I have given them Thy word; and the world hath hated them, because they are not of the world." Their actions, their words, their spirit, are not in harmony with the world, "even as I am not of the world." And the Saviour adds, "I pray not that Thou shouldest take them out of the world, but that Thou shouldest 432 keep them from the evil." The children and youth should receive an education in the line that Christ has here indicated, that they may be separate from the world.

"Sanctify them through Thy truth: Thy word is truth." The word of God should be made the great educating power. How shall students know the truth, except by a close, earnest, persevering study of the word? Here is the grand stimulus, the hidden force which quickens the mental and physical powers, and directs the life into right channels. Here in the word is wisdom, poetry, history, biography, and the most profound philosophy. Here is a study that quickens the mind into a vigorous and healthy life, and awakens it to the highest exercise. It is impossible to study the Bible with a humble, teachable spirit, without developing and strengthening the intellect. Those who become best acquainted with the wisdom and purpose of God as revealed in His word, become men and women of mental strength; and they may become efficient workers with the great Educator, Jesus Christ.

"As Thou hast sent Me into the world, even so have I also sent them into the world." There is a work to be done for the world, and Christ sends His messengers, who are to be workers together with Himself. Christ has given His people the words of truth, and all are called to act a part in making them known to the world.

"And for their sakes I sanctify Myself, that they also might be sanctified through the truth." Teachers may suppose that they can teach in their own wisdom, retaining their human imperfections; but Christ, the divine Teacher, whose work is to restore to man that which was lost through the fall, sanctified Himself for His work. He offered Himself unto God as a sacrifice for sin, giving His life for the life of the world. He would have those for whom He paid such a ransom, sanctified "through the truth," and He has set them an example. The Teacher is what He would have His disciples become. There is no sanctification aside from the truth--the word. Then how essential that it should be understood by everyone!

The prayer of Christ embraces more than those who were then His disciples; it takes in all who should receive Him in faith. He says, "Neither pray I for these alone, but for them also which shall believe on Me through their word; that they all may be one; as Thou, Father, art in Me, and I in Thee, that they also may be one in us: that the world may believe that Thou hast sent me. And the glory which Thou gavest Me I have given them; that they may be one, even as we are one: I in them, and Thou in Me, that they may be made perfect in one; and that the world may know that Thou hast sent Me, and hast loved them, as Thou hast loved Me."

Wonderful, wonderful words, almost beyond comprehension! Will the teachers in our schools understand this? Will they take the word of God as the lesson book able to make them wise unto salvation? This book is the voice of God speaking to us. The Bible opens to us the words of life; for it makes us acquainted with Christ who is our life. In order to have true, abiding faith in Christ, we must know Him as He is represented in the word. Faith is trustful. It is not a matter of fits and starts, according to the impulse and emotion of the hour; but it is a principle that has its foundation in Jesus

Christ. And faith must be kept in constant exercise through the diligent, persevering study of the word. The word thus becomes a living agency; and we are sanctified through the truth.

The Holy Spirit has been given to us as an aid in the study of the word. Jesus promises, "The Comforter, which is the Holy Ghost, whom the Father will send in My name, He shall teach you all things, and bring all things to your remembrance, whatsoever I have said unto you." Those who are under the training of the Holy Spirit will be able to teach the word intelligently. And when it is made the study book, with earnest supplication for the Spirit's guidance, and a full surrender of the heart to be sanctified through the truth, it will accomplish all that Christ has promised. The result of such Bible study will be well-balanced minds; for the physical, mental, and moral powers will be harmoniously developed. There will be no paralysis in spiritual knowledge. The understanding will be quickened; the sensibilities will be aroused; the conscience will become sensitive; the sympathies and sentiments will be purified; a better moral atmosphere will be created; and a new power to resist temptation will be imparted. And all, both teachers and students, will become active and earnest in the work of God.

But there is a disposition on the part of many teachers not to be thorough in religious education. They are satisfied with a half-hearted service themselves, serving the Lord only to escape the punishment of sin. Their half-heartedness affects their teaching. The experience that they do not desire for themselves, they are not anxious to see their pupils gain. That which has been given them in blessing has been cast aside as a dangerous element. The offered visits of the Holy Spirit are met with the words of Felix to Paul, "Go thy way for this time; when I have a convenient season, I will call for thee." Other blessings they desire; but that which God is more willing to give than a father to give good gifts to his children; that Holy Spirit, which is offered abundantly according to the infinite fullness of God, and which, if received, would bring all other blessings in its train,—what words shall I use sufficiently to express what has been with reference to it? The heavenly messenger has been repulsed by the determined will. "Thus far shalt Thou go with my students, but no farther. We need no enthusiasm in our school, no excitement. We are much better satisfied to work with the students ourselves." It is thus that despite has been done to God's gracious messenger, the Holy Spirit.

Are not the teachers in our schools in danger of blasphemy, of charging the Holy Spirit of God with being a deceiving power, and leading into fanaticism. Where are the educators that choose the snow of Lebanon which cometh from the rock of the field, or the cold, flowing waters that come from another place, instead of the murky waters of the valley? A succession of showers from the living waters has come to you at Battle Creek. Each shower was a consecrated inflowing of divine influence; but you did not recognize it as such. Instead of drinking copiously of the streams of salvation, so freely offered through the influence of the Holy Spirit, you turned to common sewers, and tried to satisfy your soul-thirst with the polluted waters of human science. The result has been parched hearts in the school and in the church. Those who are satisfied with little spirituality have gone far in unfitting themselves to appreciate the deep movings of the Spirit of God. But I hope the teachers have not yet passed the line where they are given over to hardness of heart and blindness of mind. If they are again visited by the Holy Spirit, I hope they will not call righteousness sin, and sin righteousness.

There is need of heart conversions among the teachers. A genuine change of thoughts and methods of teaching is required to place them where they will have a personal relation to a living Saviour. It is one thing to assent to the Spirit's work in conversion, and another thing to accept that Spirit's agency as a reprover, calling to repentance. It is necessary that both teachers and students not only assent to truth, but have a deep, practical knowledge of the operations of the Spirit. Its cautions are given because of the unbelief of those who profess to be Christians. God will come near to the students because they are misled by the educators in whom they put confidence; but both teachers and students need to be able to recognize the voice of the Shepherd.

You who have long lost the spirit of prayer, pray, pray, earnestly, "Pity Thy suffering cause; pity the church; pity the individual believers, Thou Father of mercies. Take from us everything that defiles, deny us what Thou wilt; but take not from us Thy Holy Spirit."

There are and ever will be persons who do not move wisely, who will, if words of doubt or unbelief are spoken, throw off conviction and choose to follow their own will; and because of their deficiencies Christ has been reproached. Poor finite mortals have judged the rich and precious outpouring of the Spirit, and passed sentence upon it, as the Jews passed sentence upon the work of Christ. Let it be understood in every institution in America that it is not commissioned to you to direct the work of the Holy Spirit, and tell how it shall represent itself. You have been guilty of doing this. May the Lord forgive you, is my prayer. Instead of being repressed and driven back, as it has been, the Holy Spirit should be welcomed and its presence encouraged. When you sanctify yourself through obedience to the word, the Holy Spirit will give you glimpses of heavenly things. When you seek God with humiliation and earnestness, the words which you have spoken in freezing accents will burn in your hearts; the truth will not then languish upon your tongues.

Eternal interest should be the great theme of teachers and students. Conformity to the world should be strictly guarded against. The teachers need to be sanctified through the truth, and the all-important thing should be the conversion of their students, that they may have a new heart and life. The object of the Great Teacher is the restoration of the image of God in the soul, and every teacher in our schools should work in harmony with this purpose.

Teachers, trust in God, and go forward, "My grace is sufficient for you" is the assurance of the Great Teacher. Catch the inspiration of the words, and never, never talk doubt and unbelief. Be energetic. There is no half-and-half service in pure and undefiled religion. "Thou shalt love the Lord thy God with all thy heart, and with all thy soul, and with all thy strength, and with all thy mind." The very highest sanctified ambition is demanded of those who believe the word of God.

437 Teachers, tell your students that the Lord Jesus Christ has made every provision that they should go onward, conquering and to conquer. Lead them to trust in the divine promise: "If any of you lack wisdom, let him ask of God, that giveth to all men liberally, and upbraideth not; and it shall be given him. But let him ask in faith, nothing wavering. For he that wavereth [talks faith one moment, and acts unbelief the next] is like a wave of the sea driven with the wind and tossed. For let not that man think that he shall receive anything of the Lord. A double-minded man is unstable in all his ways."

From God, the fountain of wisdom, proceeds all the knowledge that is of value to man, all that the intellect can grasp or retain. The fruit of the tree representing good and evil is not to be eagerly plucked, because it is recommended by one who was once a bright angel in glory. He has said that if men eat thereof, they shall know good and evil. But let it alone. The true knowledge comes not from infidels or wicked men. The word of God is light and truth. The true light shines from Jesus Christ, who "lighteth every man that cometh into the world." From the Holy Spirit proceeds divine knowledge. He knows what humanity needs to promote peace, happiness, and restfulness here in this world, and secure eternal rest in the kingdom of God.

"I Jesus have sent Mine angel to testify unto you these things in the churches. I am the root and the offspring of David, and the bright and morning star. And the Spirit and the bride say, Come. And let him that heareth say, Come. And let him that is athirst come. And whosoever will, let him take the water of life freely."--"Special Testimonies on Education," June 12, 1896.

Christ's Example in Contrast with Formalism

Of the Lord Jesus Christ in His youth, the divine testimony is given, "And the child grew, and waxed strong in spirit, filled with wisdom; and the grace of God was upon Him." After the visit to Jerusalem in His boyhood, He returned with His parents, "and came to Nazareth, and was subject unto them. . . . And Jesus increased in wisdom and stature, and in favor with God and man."

In the days of Christ, the educators of the youth were formalists. During His ministry, Jesus declared to the rabbis, "Ye do err, not knowing the Scriptures, nor the power of God." And He charged them with "teaching for doctrines the commandments of men." Tradition was dwelt upon, amplified, and reverenced far above the Scriptures. The sayings of men, and an endless round of ceremonies, occupied so large a share of the student's life, that the education which imparts a knowledge of God was neglected. The great teachers were continually enlarging upon little things, specifying every detail to be observed in the ceremonies of religion, and making its observance a matter of highest obligation. They paid "tithe of mint and anise and cummin," while they "omitted the weightier matters of the law, judgment, mercy, and faith." Thus there was brought in a mass of rubbish that hid from the view of the youth the great essentials of the service of God.

In the educational system there was no place for that personal experience in which the soul learns for itself the power of a "Thus saith the Lord," and gains that reliance upon the divine word which alone can bring peace, and power with God. Busied with the round of forms, the students in these schools found no quiet hours in which to commune with God and hear His voice speaking to their hearts. That which the rabbis regarded as superior education was in reality the greatest hindrance to true education. It was opposed to all real development. Under their training, the powers of the youth were repressed, and their minds were cramped and narrowed.

The brothers and sisters of Jesus were taught the multitudinous traditions and ceremonies of the rabbis, but Christ himself could not be induced to interest Himself in these matters. While hearing on every hand the reiterated "Thou shalt," and "Thou shalt not," He moved independently of these restrictions. The requirements of society and the requirements of God were ever in collision; and while in His youth he made no direct attack upon the customs or precepts of the learned teachers, He did not become a student in their schools.

Jesus would not follow any custom that would require Him to depart from the will of God, nor would He place Himself under the instruction of those who exalted the words of men above the word of God. He shut out of His mind all the sentiments and formalities that had not God for their foundation. He would give no place for these things to influence Him. Thus He taught that it is better to prevent evil than to attempt to correct it after it has gained a foothold in the mind. And Jesus would not by His example lead others to place themselves where they would be corrupted. Nor would He needlessly place Himself in a position where He would be brought into conflict with the rabbis, which might in after years result in weakening His influence with the people. For the same reasons He could not be induced to observe the meaningless forms or rehearse the maxims that afterward in His ministry He so decidedly condemned.

Though Jesus was subject to His parents, He began at a very early age to act for Himself in the formation of His character. While His mother was His first human teacher, He was constantly receiving an education from His Father in heaven. Instead of poring over the learned lore handed down by the rabbis from century to century, Jesus, under the Divine Teacher, studied the words of God, pure and uncorrupted, and studied also the great lesson-book of nature. The words, "Thus saith the Lord," were ever upon His lips, and "It is written," was His reason for every act that varied from the family customs. He brought a purer atmosphere into the home life. Though He did not place Himself under the instruction of the rabbis by becoming a student in their schools, yet He was often brought in contact with them, and the questions He asked, as if He were a learner, puzzled the wise men; for their practices did not harmonize with the Scriptures, and they had not the wisdom that comes from God. Even to those who were displeased at His noncompliance with popular customs, His education seemed of a higher type than their own.

The life of Jesus gave evidence that He expected much, and therefore He attempted much. From His very childhood He was the true light shining amid the moral darkness of the world. He revealed Himself as the truth, and the guide of men. His conceptions of truth and His power to resist temptation were proportionate to His conformity to that word which He himself had inspired holy men to write. Communion with God, a complete surrender of the soul to Him, in fulfilling His word irrespective of false education or the customs or traditions of His time, marked the life of Jesus.

To be ever in a bustle of activity, seeking by some outward performance to show their superior piety, was, in the estimation of the rabbis, the sum of religion; while at the same time, by their constant disobedience to God's word, they were perverting the way of the Lord. But the education that has God back of it, will lead men to seek after God, "if haply they might feel after Him, and find Him." The infinite is not, and never will be, bound about by human organizations or human plans. Every soul must have a personal experience in obtaining a knowledge of the will and ways of God. In all who are under the training of God is to be revealed a life that is not in harmony with the world, its customs, its practice, or its experiences. Through study of the Scriptures, through earnest prayer, they may hear His message to them, "Be still and know that I am God." When every other voice is hushed, when every earthly interest is turned aside, the silence of the soul makes more distinct the voice of God. Here rest is found in Him. The peace, the joy, the life of the soul, is God.

When the child seeks to get nearest to his father, above every other person, he shows his love, his faith, his perfect trust. And in the father's wisdom and strength the child rests in safety. So with the children of God. The Lord bids us, "Look unto Me, and be ye saved!" "Come unto Me, . . . and I will give you rest." "If any of you lack wisdom, let him ask of God, that giveth to all men liberally, and upbraideth not; and it shall be given him."

"Thus saith the Lord; cursed be the man that trusteth in man, and maketh flesh his arm, and whose heart departeth from the Lord. For he shall be like the heath in the desert, and shall not see when good cometh; but shall inhabit the parched places in the wilderness, in a salt land and not inhabited. Blessed is the man that trusteth in the Lord, and whose hope the Lord is. For he shall be as a tree planted by the waters, and that spreadeth out her roots by the river, and shall not see when heat cometh, but her leaf shall be green; and shall not be careful in the year of drought, neither shall cease from yielding fruit."--"Special Testimonies on Education," August 27, 1896.

A Divine Example

From the earliest times the faithful in Israel had given much attention to the matter of education. The Lord had directed that the children, even from babyhood, should be taught of His goodness and His greatness, especially as revealed in His law, and shown in the history of Israel. Through song and prayer, and lessons from the Scriptures, adapted to the opening mind, fathers and mothers were to instruct their children that the law of God is an expression of His character, and that as they received the principles of the law into the heart, the image of God was traced on mind and soul. In both the school and the home, much of the teaching was oral, but the youth also learned to read the Hebrew writings; and the parchment rolls of the Old Testament Scriptures were open to their study.

In the days of Christ, the religious instruction of the young was thought to be so important that the town or city which did not provide schools for this purpose, was regarded as under the curse of God. Yet in both the school and the home, the teaching had become mechanical and formal. Since "in all things it behooved Him to be made like unto His brethren" (Hebrews 2:17), and Jesus gained knowledge as we may do, the intimate acquaintance with the Scriptures, which He evinced in His ministry, testifies to the diligence with which, in those early years, He gave Himself to the study of the sacred word.

And day by day He gained knowledge from the great library of animate and inanimate nature. He who had created all things, was now a child of humanity, and He studied the lessons which His own hand had written in earth and sea and sky. The parables by which, during His ministry, He loved to teach His lessons of truth, show how open His spirit was to the influences of nature, and how, in His youth, He had delighted to gather the spiritual teaching from the surroundings of His daily life. To Jesus the significance of the word and the works of God unfolded gradually, as He was seeking to understand the reason of things, as any youth may seek to understand. The culture of holy thoughts and communings was His. All the windows of His soul were open toward the sun; and in the light of heaven His spiritual nature waxed strong, and His life made manifest the wisdom and grace of God.

Every child may gain knowledge as Jesus did, from the works of nature and the pages of God's holy word. As we try to become acquainted with our Heavenly Father through His word, angels will come near, our minds will be strengthened, our character will be elevated and refined, and we shall become more like our Saviour. And as we behold the beautiful and grand in nature, our affections go out after God; while the spirit is awed, the soul is invigorated by coming in contact with the Infinite through His works. Communion with God through prayer develops the mental and moral faculties, and the spiritual powers strengthen as we cultivate thoughts upon spiritual things.

The life of Jesus was a life in harmony with God. While He was a child, He thought and spoke as a child, but no trace of sin marred the image of God within Him. From the first dawning of intelligence He was continually growing in heavenly grace, and knowledge of truth.--"Special Testimonies on Education," 1896.

The Bible the Most Important Book for Education in Our Schools

The Bible is the revelation of God to our world, telling us of the character we must have in order to reach the paradise of God. We are to esteem it as God's disclosure to us of eternal things,--the things of most consequence for us to know. By the world it is thrown aside, as if the perusal of it were finished, but a thousand years of research would not exhaust the hidden treasure it contains. Eternity alone will disclose the wisdom of this book. The jewels buried in it are inexhaustible; for it is the wisdom of an infinite mind.

At no period of time has man learned all that can be learned of the word of God. There are yet new views of truth to be seen, and much to be understood of the character and attributes of God,--His benevolence, His mercy, His long forbearance, His example of perfect obedience. "And the Word was made flesh, and dwelt among us, (and we beheld His glory, the glory as of the only-begotten of the Father,) full of grace and truth." This is a most valuable study, taxing the intellect, and giving strength to the mental ability. After diligently searching the word, hidden treasures are discovered, and the lover of truth breaks out in triumph, "Without controversy great is the mystery of godliness: God was manifest in the flesh, justified in the Spirit, seen of angels, preached unto the Gentiles, believed on in the world, received up into glory." "Let this mind be in you, which was also in Christ Jesus: who, being in the form of God, thought it not robbery to be equal with God: but made Himself of no reputation, and took upon Him the form of a servant, and was made in the likeness of men."

The Bible, fully received and studied as the voice of God, tells the human family how to reach the abodes of eternal happiness, and secure the treasures of heaven. "All Scripture is given by inspiration of God, and is profitable for doctrine, for reproof, for correction, for instruction in righteousness: that the man of God may be perfect, throughly furnished unto all good works." Are we then so dull that we cannot comprehend it? Shall we cultivate a deep hunger for the productions of learned authors, and disregard the word of God? It is this great longing for something they never ought to crave, that makes men substitute for knowledge, that which cannot make them wise unto salvation.

"For we have not followed cunningly devised fables, when we make known unto you the power and coming of our Lord Jesus Christ, but were eyewitnesses of His majesty. For He received from God the Father honor and glory, when there came such a voice to Him from the excellent glory, This is my beloved Son, in whom I am well pleased. And this voice which came from heaven we heard, when we were with Him in the holy mount. We have also a more sure word of prophecy; whereunto ye do well that ye take heed, as unto a light that shineth in a dark place, until the day dawn, and the day star arise in your hearts: knowing this first, that no prophecy of the Scripture is of any private interpretation. For the prophecy came not in old time by the will of man: but holy men of God spake as they were moved by the Holy Ghost." "For whatsoever things were written aforetime were written for our learning, that we through patience and comfort of the Scriptures might have hope." "Meditate upon these things; give thyself wholly to them; that thy profiting may appear to all." "For all flesh is as grass, and all the glory of man as the flower of grass. The grass withereth, and the flower thereof falleth away: but the word of the Lord endureth forever."

It is by the perusal of the Bible that the mind is strengthened, refined, and elevated. If there were not another book in the wide world, the word of God, lived out through the grace of Christ, would make man perfect in this world, with a character fitted for the future, immortal life. Those who study the word, taking it in faith as the truth, and receiving it into the character, will be complete in Him who is all and in all. Thank God for the possibilities set before humanity. But a study of the many different authors confuses and wearies the mind, and has a detrimental influence upon the religious life. In the Bible are specified distinctly man's duties to God and to his fellow men; but without a study of the word, how can these requirements be met? We must have a knowledge of God; for "this is life eternal," said Christ, "that they might know Thee the only true God, and Jesus Christ, whom Thou hast sent."

Let not man's assertions be considered as truth when they are contrary to the word of God. The Lord God, the Creator of the heavens and the earth, the source of all wisdom, is second to none. But those supposed great authors, who give to our schools their textbooks for study, are received and glorified, even though they have no vital connection with God. By such study man has been led away from God into forbidden paths; minds have been wearied to death through unnecessary work in trying to obtain that which is to them as the knowledge which Adam and Eve disobeyed God in obtaining. If Adam and Eve had never touched the tree of knowledge, they would have been where the Lord could impart to them knowledge from His word, knowledge which would not have had to be left behind with the things of this world, but which they could carry with them to the paradise of God. But today young men and women spend years and years in acquiring an education which is but wood and stubble, to be consumed in the last great conflagration. Many spend years of their life in the study of books, obtaining an education that will die with them. Upon such an education God places no value. This supposed wisdom gained from the study of different authors, has excluded and lessened the brightness and value of the word of God. Many students have left school unable to receive the word of God with the reverence and respect that they gave it before they entered, their faith eclipsed in the effort to excel in the various studies. The Bible has not been made a standard matter in their education, but books mixed with infidelity and propagating unsound theories have been placed before them.

There is nothing so ennobling and invigorating as a study of the great themes which concern our eternal life. Let students seek to grasp these God-given truths; let them seek to measure these precious things, and their minds will expand and grow strong in the effort. But a mind crowded with a mass of matter it will never be able to use, is a mind dwarfed and enfeebled, because only put to the task of dealing with commonplace material. It has not been put to the task of considering the high, elevated disclosures coming from God.

"For God so loved the world, that He gave His only-begotten Son, that whosoever believeth in Him should not perish, but have everlasting life." As the mind is summoned to the consideration of these great themes, it will rise higher and higher in the comprehension of these subjects of eternal importance, leaving the cheaper and insignificant matters to drop as a dead weight.

All unnecessary matters need to be weeded from the course of study, and only such studies placed before the student as will be of real value to him. With these alone he needs to become familiarized, that he may secure for himself that life which measures with the life of God. And as he learns of these, his mind will strengthen and expand as did the mind of Christ and of John the Baptist. What was it that made John great?--He closed his mind to the mass of tradition taught by the teachers of the Jewish nation, opening it to the wisdom "which cometh down from above." Before his birth, the Holy Spirit testified of John: "For he shall be great in the sight of the Lord, and shall drink neither wine nor strong drink; and he shall be filled with the Holy Ghost, even from his mother's womb. And many of the children of Israel shall he turn to the Lord their God. And he shall go before Him in the spirit and power of Elias, to turn the hearts of the fathers to the children, and the disobedient to the wisdom of the just; to make ready a people prepared for the Lord." And in his prophecy, Zacharias said of John, "And thou, child, shalt be called the prophet of the Highest: for thou shalt go before the face of the Lord to prepare His ways; to give knowledge of salvation unto His people by the remission of their sins, through the tender mercy of our God; whereby the dayspring from on high hath visited us, to give light to them that sit in darkness and in the shadow of death, to guide our feet into the way of peace. And the child grew, and waxed strong in spirit, and was in the deserts till the day of his showing unto Israel."

Simeon said of Christ, "Lord, now lettest Thou Thy servant depart in peace, according to Thy word: for mine eyes have seen Thy salvation, which Thou hast prepared before the face of all people; a light to lighten the Gentiles, and the glory of Thy people Israel." "And Jesus increased in wisdom and stature, and in favor with God and man." Jesus and John were represented by the educators of that day as ignorant, because they had not learned under them. But the God of heaven was their teacher, and all who heard were astonished at their knowledge of the Scripture, having never learned. Of them, they had not, truly; but from God they had learned the highest kind of wisdom.

The judgment of men, even of teachers, may be very wide of the mark as to what constitutes true education. The teachers in the days of Christ did not educate the youth in the correct knowledge of the Scriptures, which lie at the foundation of all education worthy of the name. Christ declared to the Pharisees, "Ye do err, not knowing the Scriptures, nor the power of God," "teaching for doctrines the commandments of men." And He prayed for His disciples, "Sanctify them through Thy truth: Thy word is truth. As Thou hast sent Me into the world, even so have I also sent them into the world. And for their sakes I sanctify Myself, that they also might be sanctified through the truth."

"And the Lord spake unto Moses, saying, Speak thou also unto the children of Israel, saying, Verily My Sabbaths ye shall keep: for it is a sign between Me and you throughout your generations; that ye may know that I am the Lord that doth sanctify you." "Six days may work be done; but in the seventh is the Sabbath of rest, holy to the Lord: whosoever doeth any work in the Sabbath day, he shall surely be put to death." Has Satan succeeded in removing the sanctity from the day thus distinguished above all others? He has succeeded in putting another day in its stead, but never can he take from it the blessing of the Lord. "Wherefore the children of Israel shall keep the Sabbath, to observe the Sabbath throughout their generations, for a perpetual covenant." What can be more positive and clear than these words? And has God changed? He will remain the same through all eternity, but man "has sought out many inventions."

The Bible is full of knowledge, and all who come to its study with a heart to understand, will find the mind enlarged and the faculties strengthened to comprehend these precious, far-reaching truths. The Holy Spirit will impress them upon the mind and soul. But those who give instruction to the young, need first to become fools that they may be wise. If they ignore a plain "Thus saith the Lord," and pluck from the tree of knowledge that which God has forbidden them to have, which is a knowledge of disobedience, their transgression brings them into condemnation and sin. Shall we extol such men for their great knowledge? Shall we sit at the feet of those who ignore the truths which sanctify the soul? "As I live, saith the Lord God, surely with a mighty hand, and with a stretched out arm, and with fury poured out, will I rule you." Why do not the educators of today heed these warnings? Why are they stumbling, not knowing at what they stumble? It is because Satan has blinded their eyes, and the stumbling block of their iniquity is presented before others by their precept and example. Thus other eyes are blinded, and those who ought to walk in the light, are walking in darkness; for they do not steadfastly behold Jesus, the Light of the world.

Great light was given to the Reformers, but many of them received the sophistry of error through misinterpretation of the Scriptures. These errors have come down through the centuries, but although they be hoary with age, yet they have not behind them a "Thus saith the Lord." For the Lord has said, I will not "alter the thing that is gone out of My lips." In His great mercy the Lord has permitted still greater light to shine in these last days. To us He has sent His message, revealing His law and showing us what is truth.

In Christ is the fountain of all knowledge. In Him our hopes of eternal life are centered. He is the greatest teacher the world has ever known, and if we desire to enlarge the minds of the children and youth, and win them, if possible, to a love of the Bible, we should fasten their minds upon the plain and simple truth, digging out that which has been buried beneath the rubbish of tradition, and letting the jewels shine forth. Encourage them to search into these subjects, and the effort put forth will be an invaluable discipline. The unfolding of God, as represented in Jesus Christ, furnishes a theme that is grand to contemplate, and that will, if studied, sharpen the mind, and elevate and ennoble the faculties. As the human agent learns these lessons in the school of Christ, trying to become as Christ was, meek, and lowly of heart, he will learn the most useful of all lessons,--that intellect is supreme only as it is sanctified by a living connection with God.

The warning and instruction given in the word of God with regard to false shepherds, should have some weight with the teachers and students in our schools. Advice should be given to the students not to take such shepherds as their highest authority. What need is there for students to bind off their education by attending at Ann Arbor to receive the finishing touch? It has proved to be the finishing touch to very many as far as spirituality and belief in the truth are concerned. It is unnecessary discipline, opening the mind to the sowing of tares among the wheat; and it is not pleasing to our Great Teacher thus to glorify teachers who have not ears to hear or minds to comprehend a plain "Thus saith the Lord." In thus honoring those who are educating directly away from the truth, we do not meet the approval of God. Let the words of the Lord, spoken to the world through the prophet Isaiah, have weight with us. "For thus saith the high and lofty One that inhabiteth eternity, whose name is Holy; I dwell in the high and holy place, with him also that is of a contrite and humble spirit, to revive the spirit of the humble, and to revive the heart of the contrite ones." "The Lord is nigh unto them that are of a broken heart; and saveth such as be of a contrite spirit." "To this man will I look," saith the Lord, "even to him that is poor and of a contrite spirit, and trembleth at My word." The humble, who seek the Lord, have wisdom unto eternal life.

The greatest wisdom, and most essential, is the knowledge of God. Self sinks into insignificance as it contemplates God and Jesus Christ whom He hath sent. The Bible must be made the foundation for all study. Individually we must learn from this lesson-book which God has given us, the condition of the salvation of our souls; for it is the only book that tells us what we must do in order to be saved. Not only this, but from it strength may be received for the intellect. The many books which education is thought to embrace, are misleading, a deception and a delusion. "What is the chaff to the wheat?" Satan is now stirring up the minds of men to furnish to the world literature which is of a cheap, superficial order, but which fascinates the mind, and fastens it in a network of Satan's contrivance. After reading these books, the mind lives in an unreal world, and the life, so far as usefulness is concerned, is as barren as a fruitless tree. The brain is intoxicated, making it impossible for the eternal realities, which are essential for the present and the future, to be pressed home. A mind educated to feed upon trash is unable to see in the word of God the beauty that is there. Love for Jesus and inclination to righteousness are lost; for the mind is built up from that upon which it feeds. By feeding the mind upon exciting stories of fiction, man is bringing to the foundation "wood, hay, stubble." He loses all taste for the divine Guidebook, and cares not to study the character he must form in order to dwell with the redeemed host, and inhabit the mansions which Christ has gone to prepare.

God has most graciously granted us a probation in which to prepare for the test which will be brought upon us. Every advantage is given us through the mediation of Christ. If the human agent will study the word, he will see that every facility has been freely provided for those who are seeking to be overcomers. The Holy Spirit is present to give strength for victory, and Christ has promised, "Lo, I am with you alway, even unto the end of the world."--"Special Testimonies on Education," 1896.

FOR ADDITIONAL READING

1896 Publication of " Special Testimonies on Education"

A Lesson from One of the Prophets of God, The Youth's Instructor, January 7, 1897

Worldly Amusements, The Youth'Instructor, February 4, 1897

Words to Parents, The Review and Herald, April 6, 1897,

The Review and Herald, April 13, 1896

Benefits of Nature, The Youth's Instructor, May 6, 1897

Don't Send the Children too Early to School, The Bible Echo, June 28, 1897

Correct School Discipline

We had in the school in-----unruly students, who were disposed to disregard the instructions given from the word of God, and by their course of action betray sacred trusts. The Lord looked down from heaven upon them, and beheld their deceptive practices, and their false denial of their actions. They were labored for faithfully; but they were altogether too near the city, and temptations were constantly arising. They forgot to be true and loyal to God's holy law. They transgressed His commandments. They were infatuated, and revealed that as students they had not moral integrity to be true. There seemed to be a Satanic agency at work to discourage the teachers and demoralize the school. Some acting as teachers did not exert a correct influence. When every jot of influence should have been placed on the side of discipline and order, these teachers, though knowing all the trials that disorderly students were bringing upon the principal and his co-workers, who were burdened and oppressed, and who were seeking the Lord most earnestly, showed sympathy for the ones who were serving the enemy most earnestly. The students--the wrongdoers--knew this. A few took courage to brave out their wrong course of action, until it was brought home so strongly to them that they acknowledged that they had disobeyed the rules of the school, and had then tried to hide behind falsehood.

The school faculty held private consultations to consider what was best to be done. There was a voice in these counsels that tried to counterwork the plans introduced to keep discipline and order. By this sympathizing voice indiscreet words were dropped to the students in reference to the matters under consideration in the council. These things were caught up by the students. They thought that such a teacher was all right; that she was a clever teacher. She would have sympathy for the wrongdoer. Thus the hands of those carrying a heavy load were not strengthened, but weakened. The efforts made to repress evil were looked upon as harsh and uncharitable. "Young folks must have their jolly times," was repeated, with other insipid speeches. A word dropped here and a word there left its baneful impression; and the wrong-doers knew that there were those in the school who did not think that their course of deception and falsehood was a great sin. But to continually take up the cause of the wrongdoer, making of no account his departure from righteousness and truth and steadfast integrity, is a grievous sin against God.

There were those in the school who were carried through the terms of study because they had no means themselves. These should have made every effort to obtain all the advantages possible, and thus show their gratitude to God, and for the kindness of the friends who had helped them.

When young men and young women are in deed and in truth converted, a decided change will be seen by all who have any connection with them. Their frivolity will leave them; the continual desire for amusement and selfish pleasure, the longing for some kind of change, to be in parties and excursions, will no longer be seen.

Hear the words of the great Teacher: "For the bread of God is He that cometh down from heaven, and giveth life unto the world." There is no need to be dull and indolent, to live only for common, earthly excitement. Life is given to every believer, as well as comfort and sobriety. All may have joy, because of the satisfaction of having Christ as an abiding guest in the soul.

When Jesus said to the multitude, "The bread of God is He which cometh down from heaven, and giveth life unto the world," some in the multitude said, "Lord, evermore give us this bread." The bread of heaven was in their midst, but they did not recognize Him as the bread of life. Jesus then stated plainly, "I am the bread of life he that cometh to Me shall never hunger, and he that believeth on Me shall never thirst."

This sixth chapter of John contains the most precious and important lessons for all who are being educated in our schools. If they want that education that will endure through time and through eternity, let them bring the wonderful truths of this chapter into their practical life. The whole chapter is very instructive, but is only faintly understood. We urge students to take in these words of Christ, that they may understand their privileges. The Lord Jesus teaches us what He is to us, and what advantage it will be to us individually to eat His words, realizing that He himself is the great center of our life, "The words that I speak unto you," He said, "they are spirit, and they are life."

Having Christ in the heart, we have an eye single to the glory of God. We should strive to comprehend what it means to be in complete union with Christ, who is the propitiation for our sins, and for the sins of the whole word, our substitute and surety before the Lord God of heaven. Our life should be bound up in the life of Christ, we should draw constantly from Him, partaking of Him, the living bread that came down from heaven, drawing from a fountain ever fresh, ever giving forth its abundant treasures. When this is in truth the experience of the Christian, there is seen in his life a freshness, a simplicity, a humility, meekness, and lowliness of heart, that show all with whom he associates that he has been with Jesus, and learned of Him.

This experience gives every teacher the very qualifications that will make him a representative of Christ Jesus. The methods of Christ's teaching will, if followed, give a force and directness to his communications and to his prayers. His witness for Christ will not be a narrow, tame, lifeless testimony, but will be like plowing up the field, quickening the conscience, opening the heart, and preparing it for the seeds of truth.

None who deal with the youth should be iron-hearted, but affectionate, tender, pitiful, courteous, winning, and companionable; yet they should know that reproofs must be given, and that even rebuke may have to be spoken to cut off some evildoing. Encourage the youth to glorify God by giving expression to their gratitude to the Lord for all His mercies. Let their thanks be spoken often in the heart and with the voice, and let self-denial and self-sacrifice be shown. If those who claim to be Christ's disciples will eat His flesh and drink His blood, which is His word, they will have eternal life. "And I will raise him up at the last day," Christ says. "For My flesh is meat indeed, and My blood is drink indeed. He that eateth My flesh and drinketh My blood, dwelleth in Me, and I in him."

"As the living Father hath sent Me, and I live by the Father: so he that eateth Me, even he shall live by Me." How many have experienced this? How many realize the true meaning of these words? Will we individually seek to understand the word of God, and practice it? This word, believed, is to every truly converted soul, the free gift of grace. It cannot be bought with money. We should continually realize that we do not deserve grace because of our merit, for all that we have is God's gift. He says to us, "Freely ye have received, freely give."

The atmosphere of unbelief is heavy and oppressive. The giddy laugh, the jesting, the joking, sickens the soul that is feeding on Christ. Cheap, foolish talk is painful to Him. With a humble heart read carefully 1 Peter 1:13-18. Those who enjoy talking should see that their words are select and well chosen. Be careful how you speak. Be careful how you represent the religion you have accepted. You may feel it no sin to gossip and talk nonsense, but this grieves your Saviour, and saddens the heavenly angels.

What testimony does Peter bear? "Wherefore laying aside all malice, and all guile, and hypocrisies, and envies, and all evil speakings, as newborn babes, desire the sincere milk of the word, that ye may grow thereby: if so be that ye have tasted that the Lord is gracious." Here again the same principle is brought out distinctly. No one need make a mistake. If as newborn babes you desire the sincere milk of the word, that you may grow thereby, you will have no appetite to partake of a dish of evil speaking, but all such food will be at once rejected, because those who have tasted that the Lord is gracious cannot partake of the dish of nonsense, and folly, and backbiting. They will say decidedly, "Take this dish away. I do not want to eat such food. It is not the bread from heaven. It is eating and drinking the very spirit of the devil; for it is his business to be an accuser of the brethren."

It is best for every soul to closely investigate what mental food is served up for him to eat. When those come to you who live to talk, and who are all armed and equipped to say, "Report, and we will report it," stop and think if the conversation will give spiritual help, spiritual efficiency, that in spiritual communication you may eat of the flesh and drink the blood of the Son of God. "To whom coming, as unto a living stone, disallowed indeed of men, but chosen of God, and precious." These words express much. We are not to be tattlers, or gossipers, or talebearers; we are not to bear false witness. We are forbidden by God to engage in trifling, foolish conversation, in jesting, joking, or speaking any idle words. We must give an account of what we say to God. We will be brought into judgment for our hasty words, that do no good to the speaker or to the hearer. Then let us all speak words that will tend to edification. Remember that you are of value with God. Allow no cheap, foolish talk or wrong principles to compose your Christian experience.

"Chosen of God and precious." Consider, everyone who names the name of Christ, have you tasted that the Lord is gracious? Has this become a part of your actual experience, represented in John six as eating the flesh and drinking the blood of the Son of God? As newborn babes, are you learning to desire the sincere milk of the word, that you may grow thereby? Have you at any time in your life been truly converted? Have you been born again? If you have not, then it is time for you to obtain the experience that Christ told one of the chief rulers that he must have. "Ye must be born again," He said. "Except a man be born again, he cannot see the kingdom of God." That is, he cannot discern the requirements essential to having a part in that spiritual kingdom. "Marvel not that I said unto thee, Ye must be born again." If you open your mind to the entrance of God's word, with a determination to practice that word, light will come; for the word gives understanding to the simple.

This is the very education that every student needs. When this is obtained, if they are converted, the frivolous life they have heretofore lived will change. The universe of heaven will look upon characters that have been transformed. The frivolous, common level will be forsaken, and their feet will be placed upon the first round of the ladder, which is Christ Jesus. They will mount step by step, one round after another, heavenward. Christ will be revealed in their spirit, in their words, in their actions.

"Ye also, as lively stones, are built up a spiritual house, an holy priesthood, to offer up spiritual sacrifices acceptable to God by Jesus Christ." Will teachers and students study this representation, and see if they are in that class who, through the abundant grace given, are obtaining an experience which is in harmony with the real, genuine experience which every child of God must have if he enters the higher grade.

When Nicodemus came to Jesus, Christ laid before him the conditions of divine life, teaching him the very alphabet of conversion. Nicodemus asked, "How can these things be?" "Art thou a master of Israel," Christ answered, "and knowest not these things?" This question might be addressed to many who are holding positions of responsibility as teachers, but who have neglected the work essential for them to do before they were qualified to be teachers. If Christ's words were received into the soul, there would be a much higher intelligence, and a much deeper spiritual knowledge of what constitutes one a disciple and a sincere follower of Christ. When the test and trial comes to every soul, there will be apostasies. Traitors, heady, highminded and self-sufficient men will turn away from the truth, making shipwreck of their faith. Why?--Because they did not dig deep, and make their foundation sure. They were not riveted to the eternal Rock. When the words of the Lord, through His chosen messengers, are brought to them, they murmur and think the way is made too strait. Like those who were thought to be the disciples of Christ, but who were displeased by His words, and walked no more with Him, they will turn away from Christ.

"No man can come to Me, except the Father which hath sent Me, draw him: and I will raise him up at the last day." What is the drawing?--"It is written in the prophets, And they shall be all taught of God. Every man therefore that hath heard and hath learned of the Father, cometh unto Me." There are men who hear, but who do not learn the lesson as diligent students. They have a form of godliness, but are not believers. They know not the truth by practice. They receive not the engrafted word. "Wherefore lay apart all filthiness and superfluity of naughtiness, and receive with meekness the engrafted word, which is able to save your souls. But be ye doers of the word, and not hearers only, deceiving your own selves. For if any man be a hearer of the word, and not a doer, he is like unto a man beholding his natural face in a glass: for he beholdeth himself, and goeth his way, and straightway forgetteth what manner of man he was." He did not receive the impression made upon his mind when comparing his course of action with the great moral looking-glass. He did not see his defects of character. He did not reform, and forgetting all about the impression made, he went not God's way, but his way, continuing to be unreformed.

Hear the only correct way for each human being to do if he would have a safe, all-round experience. "But whoso looketh into the perfect law of liberty, and continueth therein, he being not a forgetful hearer, but a doer of the work, [for there is a work to be done, that is neglected at the peril of the soul], this man shall be blessed in his deed. If any man among you seem to be religious, and bridleth not his tongue, but deceiveth his own heart, this man's religion is vain. Pure religion and undefiled before God and the Father is this, To visit the fatherless and the widows in their affliction, and to keep himself unspotted from the world." Carry this out, as a test of pure and undefiled religion, and the blessing of God will surely follow.

"Wherefore also it is contained in the Scripture, Behold, I lay in Zion a chief corner stone, elect, precious: and he that believeth on Him shall not be confounded." Mark the figure presented in verse five: "Ye also, as lively stones, are built up a spiritual house, an holy priesthood, to offer up spiritual sacrifices, acceptable to God by Jesus Christ." Then these lively stones are exerting a tangible, practical influence in the Lord's spiritual house. They are a holy priesthood, performing pure, sacred service. They offer up spiritual sacrifices, acceptable to God.

The Lord will not accept a heartless service, a round of ceremonies that are really Christless. His children must be lively stones in God's building. If all would give themselves unreservedly to God, if they would cease to study and plan for their amusement, for excursions, and pleasure-loving associations, and would study the words, "Ye are not your own; for ye are bought with a price: therefore glorify God in your body, and in your spirit, which are God's," they would never hunger or thirst for excitement or change. If it is for our true interest to be spiritual and if the salvation of our people depends on our being riveted on the Eternal Rock, would we not better be engaged in seeking for that which will hold the whole building to the chief corner stone, that we may not be confused and confounded in our faith.

"Unto you therefore which believe He is precious: but unto them which be disobedient, the stone which the builders disallowed, the same is made the head of the corner, and a stone of stumbling, and a rock of offense, even unto them which stumble at the word, being disobedient: whereunto also they were appointed." All men, women, and youth are appointed to do a certain work. But some stumble at the word of truth. It does not harmonize with their inclinations, and therefore they refuse to be doers of the word. They will not wear Christ's yoke of perfect obedience to the law of God. They look upon this yoke as a burden, and Satan tells them that if they will break away from it, they will become as gods. No one shall rule them or dictate to them; they will be able to do as they please, and have all the liberty they desire. True, they have been oppressed and cramped in every way in their religious life, but that religious life was a farce. They were appointed to be co-laborers with Jesus Christ, and yoking up with Christ was their only chance for perfect rest and freedom. Had they done this, they would never have been confounded.

"But ye are a chosen generation, a royal priesthood, an holy nation, a peculiar people; that ye should show forth [your own sufficiency, and attract attention to yourself, and seek your own glory?--No; no] that ye should show forth the praises of Him who hath called you [to a distasteful, hard life of bondage?] out of darkness into His marvelous light."

Will you think of the high position to which we were appointed? Will those who name the name of Christ depart from all evil? Will you or I fret under Christ's yoke? When you cherish unrest and love for amusement, and to have a high stirring time of exhibition of self, enjoying and pleasing the natural will in the place of doing the will of God, is there any rest? Is the temple of God upbuilt in your life by the frivolous view you take of Christianity? "Having your conversation honest among the Gentiles: that whereas they speak against you as evildoers, they may by your good works, which they shall behold, glorify God in the day of visitation." Is not the word of God to be our guide and our director? Shall any be slow to study that word? Shall any profess to be Christians, and yet by their course of action become a reproach to the faith, just because they desire to live to please their own natural inclinations? Will they, though professing faith in the truth, pursue a course to abuse that faith and dishonor the truth of heavenly origin? Who have appreciated the precious opportunities granted them in probationary time to form characters that God can approve, because they wear the yoke of obedience that Christ wore? What does He say in regard to this? "Take My yoke upon you, and learn of Me; for I am meek and lowly in heart, and ye shall find rest unto your souls. For My yoke is easy, and My burden is light."

Many who profess to believe in Christ do not wear His yoke. They think that they do, but if they were not deluded and deceived by Satan, they would have thoughts corresponding with their faith, and with the great truths which they profess to believe. They would realize that the words of Christ mean something to them. "If any man will come after Me, let him deny himself, and take up his cross, and follow Me." If you follow Jesus, you are His disciple; if you follow your own impulses, your own unsanctified heart, you say plainly, I want not Thy way, O Lord, but mine.

We are to take in the situation, and decide what is our purpose. I have a deep interest in the young men and young women who have enlisted in the army of the Lord. My love for Jesus Christ imbues me with a love for the souls of all for whom Christ has died. The words, "Ye are laborers together with God," mean much. No one can make conditions with God. We are servants of the living God, and all who shall be educated in our school, are to be trained to be workers. They labor to acquire correct principles. They are to connect with Christ by faith. Thus they can give great satisfaction to the heavenly universe. If each volunteer in the army of the Lord will do his best, God will do the rest. They are to call nothing their own. When striving for the victory, they are to strive lawfully. The Word is to be their teacher. Unholy ambition will not advance them, for God only can give them true wisdom and understanding; but He will not work with Satan. If envy and unholy ambition are cherished, if they wrestle for the victory to obtain human glory, the mind will be filled with confusion. Do your best. Advance as fast as possible to reach a high standard in spiritual things. Sink self in Jesus Christ, and aim ever to glorify His name. Bear in mind that talent, learning, position, wealth, and influence are gifts from God; therefore they should be consecrated to Him. Seek to obtain an education that will qualify you to be wise stewards of the manifold grace of Christ Jesus, servants under Christ, to do His bidding.

Let all students seek to take as broad a view as possible of their obligations to God. They are not to look forward to a time after the school term closes, when they will do some large, noted work. But they are to study earnestly how they can commence practical working in their student life by yoking up with Christ. Let every impulse be on the Lord's side. Do not pull down and discourage those who are your teachers. Do not burden their souls by manifesting a spirit of levity and a careless disregard of rules.

Students, you can make this school first class in success by being laborers together with your teachers to help other students, and by zealously uplifting yourselves from a cheap, common, low standard. Let each see what improvement he can make in conforming his conduct to Bible rules. Those who will seek to be themselves elevated and ennobled are cooperating with Jesus Christ by becoming refined in speech, in temper, under the control of the Holy Spirit. They are yoked up with Jesus Christ. They will not flounce about, and become unruly and self-caring, studying their own selfish pleasures and gratification. They bend all their efforts with Jesus Christ as the messengers of His mercy and love, ministering to others of His grace. Their hearts throb in unison with Christ's heart. They are one with Christ in spirit, one with Christ in action. They seek to store the mind with the precious treasures of the word of God, that each may do the work appointed him by God, to gather in the bright rays of the Sun of Righteousness, that they may shine unto others.

If you will watch and pray, and make earnest efforts in the right direction, you will be thoroughly imbued with the spirit of Jesus Christ. "Put ye on the Lord Jesus Christ and make not provision for the flesh, to fulfil the lusts thereof." Be determined that you will make this school a success, and if you will heed the instruction given in the word of God, you may go forth with a development of intellectual and moral power that will cause even angels to rejoice, and God will rejoice over you with singing. If you are under God's discipline, you will secure the harmony and co-operation of the physical, mental, and moral powers, and the fullest development of your God-given faculties. Let not the buoyancy and the lust of youth through manifold temptations make your opportunities and privileges a failure. Day by day put on Christ, and in the brief season of your test and trial here below, maintain your dignity in the strength of God, as co-workers with the highest agencies during your scholastic life.

All should say, I will not fail. I will not through my influence betray myself or my companions into the hands of the enemy. I will heed the words of the Lord. "Let him take hold of My strength, that he may make peace with Me, and he shall make peace with Me." Ever remember that you have One by your side who says to you, "Be not afraid." "I have overcome the world." Bear in mind that Christ came as the Prince of heaven, and has engaged in an eternal warfare against the principles of sin. All who will unite with Christ will be workers together with God in this warfare.

"For their sakes I sanctify Myself," Christ said, "that they also might be sanctified through the truth." The Lord Jesus is the way, the truth, and the life; and those who unite with Him, putting Him on, will work as colaborers with Him, by conforming to the principles of truth. By beholding, they become imbued with truth, and unite with Christ to transform the living temple given to idols, that human beings may become cleansed, refined, sanctified, temples for the indwelling of the Holy Spirit.

"I have declared unto them Thy name," Christ said, "and will declare it: that the love wherewith Thou hast loved Me may be in them, and I in them." The Lord has made abundant provision that His love may be given to us as His free, abundant grace, as our inheritance in this life, to enable us to diffuse the same by being yoked up with Christ. Jesus conveys the circulating vitality of a pure and sanctified Christlike love through every part of our human nature. When this love is expressed in the character, it reveals to all those with whom we associate that it is possible for God to be formed within, the hope of glory. It shows that God loved the obedient ones as He loves Jesus Christ; and nothing less than this satisfies His desires in our behalf. As soon as the human agent becomes united with Christ in heart, soul, and spirit, the Father loves that soul as a part of Christ, as a member of the body of Christ, He himself being the glorious head.--MSS., June 21, 1897.

The Bible in Our Schools

It is not wise to send our youth to universities where they devote their time to gaining a knowledge of Greek and Latin, while their heads and hearts are being filled with the sentiments of the infidel authors whom they study in order to master these languages. They gain a knowledge that is not at all necessary, or in harmony with the lessons of the great Teacher. Generally those educated in this way have much self-esteem. They think they have reached the height of higher education, and carry themselves proudly, as though they were no longer learners. They are spoiled for the service of God. The time, means, and study that many have expended in gaining a comparatively useless education should have been used in gaining an education that would make them all-round men and women, fitted for practical life. Such an education would be of the highest value to them.

What do students carry with them when they leave our schools? Where are they going? What are they going to do? Have they the knowledge that will enable them to teach others? Have they been educated to be wise fathers and mothers? Can they stand at the head of a family as wise instructors? In their home life can they so instruct their children that theirs will be a family that God can behold with pleasure, because it is a symbol of the family in heaven? Have they received the only education that can truly be called "higher education"?

What is higher education? No education can be called higher education unless it bears the similitude of heaven, unless it leads young men and young women to be Christlike, and fits them to stand at the head of their families in the place of God. If, during his school life, a young man has failed to gain a knowledge of Greek and Latin and the sentiments contained in the works of infidel authors, he has not sustained much loss. If Jesus Christ had deemed this kind of education essential, would He not have given it to His disciples, whom He was educating to do the greatest work ever committed to mortals, to represent Him in the world? But, instead, He placed sacred truth in their hands, to be given to the world in its simplicity.

There are times when Greek and Latin scholars are needed. Some must study these languages. This is well. But not all, and not many should study them. Those who think that a knowledge of Greek and Latin is essential to a higher education, cannot see afar off. Neither is a knowledge of the mysteries of that which the men of the world call science necessary for entrance into the kingdom of God. It is Satan who fills the mind with sophistry and tradition, which exclude the true higher education, and which will perish with the learner.

Those who have received a false education do not look heavenward. They cannot see the One who is the true Light, "which lighteth every man that cometh into the world." They look upon eternal realities as phantoms, calling an atom a world, and a world an atom. Of many who have received the so-called higher education, God declares, "Thou art weighed in the balances, and art found wanting,"--wanting in a knowledge of practical business, wanting in a knowledge of how to make the best use of time, wanting in a knowledge of how to labor for Jesus.

The practical nature of the teaching of Him who gave His life to save men is an evidence of the value He places upon men. He gave the education which alone can be called the higher education. He did not turn His disciples away because they had not received their instruction from pagan and infidel teachers. These disciples were to proclaim truth that was to shake the world, but before they could do this, before they could be the salt of the earth, they must form new habits, they must unlearn many things learned from priest and rabbi. And today those who would represent Christ must form new habits. Theories which originate with the world must be given up. Their words and their works must be after the divine similitude. They must not place themselves in connection with the debasing principles and sentiments that belong to the worship of other gods. They cannot with safety receive their education from those who know not God, and acknowledge Him not as the life and light of men. These men belong to another kingdom. They are ruled by a disloyal prince, and they mistake phantoms for realities.

Our schools are not what they should be. The time which should be devoted to laboring for Christ is exhausted on unworthy themes and self-pleasing. Controversy arises in a moment if once-stated opinions are crossed. So it was with the Jews. To vindicate personal opinion and petty interests, to gratify worldly ambition, they rejected the Son of God. Time is passing. We are nearing the great crisis of this earth's history. If teachers continue to close their eyes to the necessities of the time in which we are living, they should be disconnected from the work.

Many of the instructors in the schools of the present day are practicing deception by leading their students over a field of study that is comparatively useless, that takes time, study, and means that should be used to gain that higher education that Christ came to give. He took upon Him the form of humanity, that He might lift the mind from the lessons men deemed essential to lessons which involve eternal results. He saw the world wrapped in satanic deception. He saw men earnestly following their own imagination, thinking they had gained everything if they had found how they might be called great in the world. But they gained nothing but death. Christ took His stand in the highways and byways of this earth, and looked upon the crowd eagerly seeking for happiness, thinking that in every new scheme they had discovered how they might be gods in this world. Christ pointed men upward, telling them that the only true knowledge is a knowledge of God and of Christ. This knowledge will bring peace and happiness in this present life, and will secure God's free gift, eternal life. He urged His hearers, as men possessing reasoning powers, not to lose eternity out of their reckoning. "Seek ye first the kingdom of God, and His righteousness," He said, "and all these things shall be added unto you." You are then co-workers with God. For this I have bought you with My suffering, humiliation, and death.

The great lesson to be given to the youth is that, as worshipers of God, they are to cherish Bible principles, and hold the world as subordinate. God would have all instructed as to how they can work the works of Christ, and enter in through the gates into the heavenly city. We are not to let the world convert us; we are to strive most earnestly to convert the world. Christ has made it our privilege and duty to stand up for Him under all circumstances. I beg of parents to place their children where they will not be bewitched by a false education. Their only safety is in learning of Christ. He is the great central Light of the world. All other lights, all other wisdom, are foolishness.

Men and women are the purchase of the blood of God's only-begotten Son. They are Christ's property, and their education and training are to be given, not with reference to this short, uncertain life, but to the immortal life, which measures with the life of God. It is not His design that those whose services He has purchased, shall be trained to serve mammon, trained to receive human praise, human glorification, or to be subservient to the world.

"Then said Jesus unto them, Verily, verily, I say unto you, Except ye eat the flesh of the Son of man, and drink His blood, ye have no life in you. Whoso eateth My flesh, and drinketh My blood, hath eternal life; and I will raise him up at the last day. For My flesh is meat indeed, and My blood is drink indeed. He that eateth My flesh, and drinketh My blood, dwelleth in Me, and I in Him." These are the terms of life made by the world's Redeemer, before the foundations of the earth were laid. Are the teachers in our schools giving the students to eat of the bread of life? Many of them are leading their students over the same track that they themselves have trod. They think this the only right way. They give students food which will not sustain spiritual life, but which will cause those who partake of it to die. They are fascinated by that which God does not require them to know.

Those teachers who are as determined as were the priests and rulers to carry their students over the same old path in which the world continues to travel will go into still greater darkness. Those who might have been co-laborers with Christ, but who have spurned the messengers and their message, will lose their bearings. They will walk in darkness, knowing not at what they stumble. Such are ready to be deceived by the delusions of the last day. Their minds are preoccupied with minor interests, and they lose the blessed opportunity of yoking up with Christ, and being laborers together with God.

The tree of knowledge, so-called, has become an instrument of death. Satan has artfully woven himself, his dogmas, his false theories into the instruction given. From the tree of knowledge he speaks the most pleasing flattery in regard to the higher education. Thousands partake of the fruit of this tree, but to them it means death. Christ says to them: "Ye spend money for that which is not bread. You are using your God-entrusted talents to secure an education which God pronounces foolishness."

Satan is striving to gain every advantage. He desires to secure, not only students, but teachers. He has his plans laid. Disguised as an angel of light, he will walk the earth as a wonder-worker. In beautiful language he will present lofty sentiments. Good words will be spoken by him, and good deeds performed. Christ will be personified, but on one point there will be a marked distinction. Satan will turn the people from the law of God. Notwithstanding this, so well will he counterfeit righteousness, that if it were possible, he would deceive the very elect. Crowned heads, presidents, rulers in high places, will bow to his false theories. Instead of giving place to criticism, division, jealousy, and rivalry, those in our schools should be one in Christ. Only thus can they resist the temptations of the arch-deceiver.

Time is passing, and God calls for every watchman to be in his place. He has been pleased to lead us to a crisis greater than any since our Saviour's first advent. What shall we do? God's Holy Spirit has told us what to do; but, as the Jews in Christ's day rejected light and chose darkness, so will the religious world reject the message for today. Men professing godliness have despised Christ in the person of His messengers. Like the Jews, they reject God's message. The Jews asked regarding Christ, "Who is this? Is not this Joseph's son?" He was not the Christ that the Jews looked for. So today the agencies that God sends are not what men have looked for. But the Lord will not ask any man by whom to send. He will send by whom he will. Men may not be able to understand why God sends this one or that one. His work may be a matter of curiosity. God will not satisfy this curiosity; and His word will not return unto Him void.

Let the work of preparing a people to stand in the day of God's preparation be entered upon by all who believe the word. During the last few years serious work has been done. Serious questions have agitated the minds of those who believe present truth. The light of the Son of Righteousness has been shining in every place, and by some it has been received, and perseveringly held. The work has been carried forward in Christ's lines.

Every soul that names the name of Christ should be under service. All should say, "Here I am; send me." The lips that are willing to speak, though unclean, will be touched with the living coal, and purified. They will be enabled to speak words that will burn their way to the soul. The time will come when men will be called to give an account for the souls to whom they should have communicated light, but who have not received it. Those who have thus failed in their duty, who have been given light, but who have not cherished it, so that they have none to impart, are classed in the books of heaven with those that are at enmity with God, not subject to His will or under His guidance.

The Bible in Our Schools

A Christian influence should pervade our schools, our sanitariums, our publishing houses. Under the direction of Satan, confederacies are being formed, and will be formed to eclipse the truth by human influence. Those who join these confederacies can never hear the welcome, "Well done, thou good and faithful servant; . . . enter thou into the joy of thy Lord." The instrumentalities established by God are to press forward, making no compromise with the power of darkness. Much more must be done in Christ's lines than has yet been done.

Strict integrity should be cherished by every student. Every mind should turn with reverent attention to the revealed word of God. Light and grace will be given to those who thus obey God. They will behold wondrous things out of His law. Great truths that have lain unheeded and unseen since the day of Pentecost, are to shine from God's word in their native purity. To those who truly love God the Holy Spirit will reveal truths that have faded from the mind, and will also reveal truths that are entirely new. Those who eat the flesh and drink the blood of the Son of God will bring from the books of Daniel and Revelation truth that is inspired by the Holy Spirit. They will start into action forces that cannot be repressed. The lips of children will be opened to proclaim the mysteries that have been hidden from the minds of men. The Lord has chosen the foolish things of this world to confound the wise, and the weak things of the world to confound the mighty.

The Bible should not be brought into our schools to be sandwiched in between infidelity. The Bible must be made the groundwork and subject matter of education. It is true that we know much more of the word of the living God than we knew in the past, but there is still much more to be learned. It should be used as the word of the living God, and esteemed as first, and last, and best in everything. Then will be seen true spiritual growth. The students will develop healthy religious characters, because they eat the flesh and drink the blood of the Son of God. But unless watched and nurtured, the health of the soul decays. Keep in the channel of light. Study the Bible. Those who serve God faithfully will be blessed. He who permits no faithful work to go unrewarded will crown every act of loyalty and integrity with special tokens of His love and approbation.--Review and Herald, August 17, 1897.

FOR ADDITIONAL READING

A Lesson from the Three Hebrew Children, Signs of the Times, September 2, 1897

What Think Ye of Christ? The Youth's Instructor, September 16, 1897

The True Object of Education, The Youth's Instructor, March 31, April 7, 1898

Timothy, The Youth's Instructor, May 5, 1898

Parental Responsibility, The Review and Herald, May 10, 17, 1898

The Unseen Watcher, The Youth's Instructor, May 19, 26, 1898

God's Word Our Study Book, The Youth's Instructor, June 30, July 7, 1898

Prayer Our Stronghold, The Youth's Instructor, August 18, 1898

And the Grace of God was upon Him, The Youth's Instructor, September 8, 1898

The Higher Education, The Youth's Instructor, December 8, 1898

As a Child, The Desire of Ages, 68-74 (1898)

The Passover Visit, The Desire of Ages, 75-83 (1898)

Special Testimony Relating to Politics

To the Teachers and Managers of our Schools:--

Those who have charge of our institutions and our schools should guard themselves diligently, lest by their words and sentiments they lead the students into false paths. Those who teach the Bible in our churches and in our schools are not at liberty to unite in making apparent their prejudices for or against political men or measures, because by so doing they stir up the minds of others, leading each to advocate his favorite theory. There are among those professing to believe present truth some who will thus be stirred up to express their sentiments and political preferences, so that division will be brought into the church.

The Lord would have His people bury political questions. On these themes silence is eloquence. Christ calls upon His followers to come into unity on the pure gospel principles which are plainly revealed in the word of God. We cannot with safety vote for political parties; for we do not know whom we are voting for. We cannot with safety take part in any political schemes. We cannot labor to please men who will use their influence to repress religious liberty, and to set in operation oppressive measures to lead or compel their fellow men to keep Sunday as the Sabbath. The first day of the week is not a day to be reverenced. It is a spurious sabbath, and the members of the Lord's family cannot participate with the men who exalt this day, and violate the law of God by trampling upon His Sabbath. The people of God are not to vote to place such men in office; for when they do this, they are partakers with them of the sins which they commit while in office.

We are not compromise principle by yielding to the opinions and prejudices which we may have encouraged before we united with God's commandment-keeping people. We have enlisted in the army of the Lord, and we are not to fight on the enemy's side, but on the side of Christ, where we can be a united whole, in sentiment, in action, in spirit, in fellowship. Those who are Christians indeed will be branches of the true vine, and will bear the same fruit as the vine. They will act in harmony, in Christian fellowship. They will not wear political badges, but the badge of Christ.

What are we to do, then?--Let political questions alone. "Be ye not unequally yoked together with unbelievers: for what fellowship hath righteousness with unrighteousness? and what communion hath light with darkness? and what concord hath Christ with Belial? or what part hath he that believeth with an infidel?" What can there be in common between these parties? There can be no fellowship, no communion. The word fellowship means participation, partnership. God employs the strongest figures to show that there should be no union between worldly parties and those who are seeking the righteousness of Christ. What communion can there be between light and darkness, truth and unrighteousness?--None whatever. Light represents righteousness; darkness, error, sin, unrighteousness. Christians have come out of darkness into the light. They have put on Christ, and they wear the badge of truth and obedience. They are governed by the elevated and holy principles which Christ expressed in His life. But the world is governed by principles of dishonesty and injustice.

"Therefore seeing we have this ministry, as we have received mercy, we faint not; but have renounced the hidden things of dishonesty, not walking in craftiness, nor handling the word of God deceitfully; but by manifestation of the truth commending ourselves to every man's conscience in the sight of God. But if our gospel be hid, it is hid to them that are lost: in whom the god of this world hath blinded the minds of them which believe not, lest the light of the glorious gospel of Christ, who is the image of God, should shine upon them. For we preach not ourselves, but Christ Jesus the Lord; and ourselves your servants for Jesus' sake. For God, who commanded the light to shine out of darkness, hath shined in our hearts, to give the light of the knowledge of the glory of God in the face of Jesus Christ." Two parties are here brought to view, and it is shown that there can be no union between them.

Those teachers in the church or in the school who distinguish themselves by their zeal in politics, should be relieved of their work and responsibilities without delay; for the Lord will not co-operate with them. The tithe should not be used to pay anyone for speechifying on political questions. Every teacher, minister, or leader in our ranks who is stirred with a desire to ventilate his opinions on political questions, should be converted by a belief in the truth, or give up his work. His influence must tell as a laborer together with God in winning souls to Christ, or his credentials must be taken from him. If he does not change, he will do harm, and only harm.

In the name of the Lord I would say to the teachers in our schools, Attend to your appointed work. You are not called upon by God to engage in politics. "All ye are brethren," Christ declares, "and as one you are to stand under the banner of Prince Emmanuel." "What doth the Lord thy God require of thee, but to fear the Lord thy God, to walk in all His ways, and to love Him, and to serve the Lord thy God with all thy heart and with all thy soul, to keep the commandments of the Lord, and His statutes, which I command thee this day for thy good? . . . For the Lord your God is God of gods, and Lord of lords, a great God, a mighty, and a terrible, which regardeth not persons, nor taketh reward: He doth execute the judgment of the fatherless and widow, and loveth the stranger, in giving him food and raiment. Love ye therefore the stranger: for ye were strangers in the land of Egypt. Thou shalt fear the Lord thy God; Him shalt thou serve, and to Him shalt thou cleave, and swear by His name. He is thy praise, and He is thy God."

The Lord has given great light and privileges to His people. "Behold, I have taught you statutes and judgments," He says; "keep therefore and do them; for this is your wisdom and your understanding in the sight of the nations, which shall hear all these statutes, and say, Surely this great nation is a wise and understanding people. For what nation is there so great, who hath God so nigh unto them, as the Lord our God is in all things that we call upon Him for? And what nation is there so great, that hath statutes and judgments so righteous as all this law, which I have set before you this day? Only take heed to thyself, and keep thy soul diligently, lest thou forget the things which thine eyes have seen, and lest they depart from thy heart all the days of thy life: but teach them thy sons, and thy sons' sons."

As a people we are to stand under the banner of Jesus Christ. We are to consecrate ourselves to God as a distinct, separate, and peculiar people. He speaks to us, saying, "Incline your ear, and come unto Me: hear, and your soul shall live; and I will make an everlasting covenant with you, even the sure mercies of David." "In righteousness shalt thou be established: thou shalt be far from oppression; for thou shalt not fear: and from terror; for it shall not come near thee. Behold, they shall surely gather together, but not by Me: whosoever shall gather together against thee shall fall for thy sake. . . . No weapon that is formed against thee shall prosper; and every tongue that shall rise against thee in judgment thou shalt condemn. This is the heritage of the servants of the Lord, and their righteousness is of Me, saith the Lord."

I call upon my brethren who are appointed to educate, to change their course of action. It is a mistake for you to link your interests with any political party, to cast your vote with them or for them. Those who stand as educators, as ministers, as laborers together with God in any line, have no battles to fight in the political world. Their citizenship is in heaven. The Lord calls upon them to stand as separate and peculiar people. He would have no schisms in the body of believers. His people are to possess the elements of reconciliation. Is it their work to make enemies in the political world?--No, no. They are to stand as subjects of Christ's kingdom, bearing the banner on which is inscribed, "The commandments of God, and the faith of Jesus." They are to carry the burden of a special work, a special message. We have a personal responsibility, and this is to be revealed before the heavenly universe, before angels, and before men. God does not call upon us to enlarge our influence by mingling with society, by linking up with men on political questions, but by standing as individual parts of His great whole, with Christ as our head. Christ is our Prince, and as His subjects we are to do the work appointed us by God.

It is of the highest importance that the youth understand that Christ's people are to be united in one; for this unity binds men to God by the golden cords of love, and lays each one under obligation to work for his fellow men. The Captain of our salvation died for the human race that men might be made one with Him and with each other. As members of the human family we are individual parts of one mighty whole. No soul can be made independent of the rest. There is to be no party strife in the family of God; for the well-being of each is the happiness of the whole. No partition walls are to be built up between man and man. Christ as the great center must unite all in one.

Christ is our teacher, our ruler, our strength, our righteousness; and in Him we are pledged to shun any course of action that will cause schism. The questions at issue in the world are not to be the theme of our conversation. We are to call upon the world to behold an uplifted Saviour, through whom we are made necessary to one another and to God. Christ trains His subjects to imitate His virtues, His meekness and lowliness, His goodness, patience, and love. Thus He consecrates heart and hand to His service, making man a channel through which the love of God can flow in rich currents to bless others. Then let there be no shade of strife among Seventh-day Adventists. The Saviour invites every soul, "Come unto Me, all ye that labor and are heavy laden, and I will give you rest. Take My yoke upon you, and learn of Me; for I am meek and lowly in heart: and ye shall find rest unto your souls. For My yoke is easy, and My burden is light." He who approaches nearest to the perfection of Christ's divine benevolence causes joy among the heavenly angels. The Father rejoices over him with singing; for is he not working in the spirit of the Master, one with Christ as He is one with the Father?

In our periodicals we are not to exalt the work and characters of men in positions of influence, constantly keeping human beings before the people. But as much as you please you may uplift Christ our Saviour. "We all, with open face beholding as in a glass the glory of the Lord, are changed into the same image from glory to glory [from character to character], even as by the Spirit of the Lord." Those who love and serve God are to be the light of the world, shining amid moral darkness. But in the places which have been given the greatest light, where the gospel has been preached the most, the people--fathers, mothers, and children--have been moved by a power from beneath to unite their interests with worldly projects and enterprises.

Great blindness is upon the churches, and the Lord says to His people, "What agreement hath the temple of God with idols? for ye are the temple of the living God; as God hath said, I will dwell in them, and walk in them; and I will be their God, and they shall be My people. Wherefore come out from among them, and be ye separate, saith the Lord, and touch not the unclean thing; and I will receive you, and will be a father unto you, and ye shall be My sons and daughters, saith the Lord Almighty."

The condition of being received into the Lord's family is coming out from the world, separating from all its contaminating influences. The people of God are to have no connection with idolatry in any of its forms. They are to reach a higher standard. We are to be distinguished from the world, and then God says, "I will receive you as members of My royal family, children of the heavenly King." As believers in the truth we are to be distinct in practice from sin and sinners. Our citizenship is in heaven.

We should realize more clearly the value of the promises God has made to us, and appreciate more deeply the honor He has given us. God can bestow no higher honor upon mortals than to adopt them into His family, giving them the privilege of calling Him Father. There is no degradation in becoming children of God. "My people shall know My name," the Lord declares; "therefore they shall know in that day that I am He that doth speak: behold, it is I." The Lord God omnipotent reigneth. "How beautiful upon the mountains are the feet of him that bringeth good tidings, that publisheth peace; that bringeth good tidings of good, that publisheth salvation; that saith unto Zion, Thy God reigneth! Thy watchmen shall lift up the voice; with the voice together shall they sing: for they shall see eye to eye, when the Lord shall bring again Zion."

Why is so much attention given to human agencies, while there is so little reaching up of the mind to the eternal God? Why are those who claim to be children of the heavenly King so absorbed in the things of this world? Let the Lord be exalted. Let the word of the Lord be magnified. Let human beings be placed low, and let the Lord be exalted. Remember that earthly kingdoms, nations, monarchs, statesmen, counselors, great armies, and all worldly magnificence and glory are as the dust of the balance. God has a reckoning to make with all nations. Every kingdom is to be brought low. Human authority is to be made as naught. Christ is the King of the world, and His Kingdom is to be exalted.

The Lord desires all who bear the message for these last days to understand that there is a great difference between professors of religion who are not doers of the word, and the children of God, who are sanctified through the truth, who have that faith that works by love and purifies the soul. The Lord speaks of those who claim to believe the truth for this time, yet see nothing inconsistent in their taking part in politics, mingling with the contending elements of these last days, as the circumcised who mingle with the uncircumcised, and He declares that He will destroy both classes together without distinction. They are doing a work that God has not set them to do. They dishonor God by their party spirit and contention, and He will condemn both alike.

The question may be asked, Are we to have no union whatever with the world? The word of the Lord is to be our guide. Any connection with infidels and unbelievers which would identify us with them is forbidden by the word. We are to come out from them and be separate. In no case are we to link ourselves with them in their plans or work. But we are not to live reclusive lives. We are to do worldlings all the good we possibly can. Christ has given us an example of this. When invited to eat with publicans and sinners, He did not refuse; for in no other way than by mingling with them could He reach this class. But on every occasion He gave them talents of words and influence. He opened up themes of conversation which brought things of eternal interest to their minds. And this Teacher enjoins us, "Let your light so shine before men, that they may see your good works, and glorify your Father which is in heaven." On the temperance question take your position without wavering. Be as firm as a rock. Be not partakers of other men's sins. Acts of dishonesty in business deal, with believers or unbelievers, should be reproved; and if they give no evidence of reformation, come out from among them and be separate.

There is a large vineyard to be cultivated; but while Christians are to work among unbelievers, they are not to appear like worldlings. They are not to spend their time talking politics or acting as politicians; for by so doing, they give the enemy opportunity to come in and cause variance and discord. Those in the ministry who desire to stand as politicians should have their credentials taken from them; for this work God has not given to high or low among His people. God calls upon all who minister in doctrine to give the trumpet a certain sound. All who have received Christ, ministers and lay members, are to arise and shine; for great peril is right upon us. Satan is stirring the powers of earth. Everything in the world is in confusion. God calls upon His people to hold aloft the banner bearing the message of the third angel. We are not to go to Christ through any human being, but through Christ we are to understand the work He has given us to do for others.

God calls to His people, saying, "Come out from among them, and be ye separate." He asks that the love which He has shown for them may be reciprocated and revealed by willing obedience to His commandments. His children are to separate themselves from politics, from any alliance with unbelievers. They are not to link their interests with the interests of the world. "Give proof of your allegiance to Me" He says, "by standing as My chosen heritage, as a people zealous of good works." Do not take part in political strife. Separate from the world, and refrain from bringing into the church or school ideas that will lead to contention or disorder. Dissension is the moral poison taken into the system by human beings who are selfish. God wants His servants to have clear perceptions, true and noble dignity, that their influence may demonstrate the power of truth. The Christian life is not to be a haphazard, emotional life. True Christian influence, exerted for the accomplishment of the work God has appointed, is a precious agency, and it must not be united with politics, or bound up in a confederacy with unbelievers. God is to be the center of attraction. Every mind that is worked by the Holy Spirit will be satisfied with Him.

God calls upon the teachers in our schools not to become interested in the study of political questions. Take the knowledge of God into our schools. Your attention may be called to worldly wise men, who are not wise enough to understand what the Scriptures say in regard to the laws of God's kingdom; but turn from these to Him who is the source of all wisdom. Seek first the kingdom of God and His righteousness. Make this first and last. Seek most earnestly to know Him whom to know aright is life eternal. Christ and His righteousness is the salvation of the soul. Teach the little children what obedience and submission means. In our schools science, literature, painting, and music, and all that the world's learning can teach are not to be made first. Let the knowledge of Him in whom our eternal life is centered come first. Plant in the hearts of the students that which will adorn the character and fit the soul, through sanctification of the Spirit, to learn lessons from the greatest Teacher the world has ever known. Thus students will be fitted to be heirs of the kingdom of God.--June 16, 1899.

FOR ADDITIONAL READING

God's Purpose Concerning Our Youth Today, The Youth's Instructor, June 22, 29, 1899

Marriages, Wise and Unwise, The Youth's Instructor, August 10, 1899

Self-culture, The Youth's Instructor, August 17, 1899

True Education, The Youth's Instructor, August 31, 1899

The Need of Reform in Our Educational Work, General Conference Daily Bulletin, March 6, 1899

The Tree of Life and the Tree of Knowledge, General Conference Daily Bulletin, March 6, 1899

The Need of Church Schools, General Conference Daily Bulletin, March 6, 1899

The Apostle Paul and Manual Labor, The Review and Herald, March 6, 13, 1900

The Student's s Privileges and Responsibilities, The Youth's Instructor, May 3, 10, 1900

The Example of Solomon, The Bible Echo, May, 1900

Our Words, The Youth's Instructor, July 26, 1900

Our Influence, The Youth's Instructor, August 2, 1900

A Lesson from Daniel's Experience, The Youth's Instructor, September 6, 1900

Words to the Youth, The Youth's Instructor, October 25, 1900

The Burning Bush, The Youth's Instructor, December 13, 1900

From the Natural to the Spiritual, Christ's Object Lessons, 17-27

The Talents, Christ's Object Lessons, 325-369

Children's Meetings and Church Schools, Testimonies for the Church, 6:105-109

Need of Educational Reform, Testimonies for the Church, 6:126-140

Hindrances to Educational Reform, Testimonies for the Church, 6:141-151

Character and Work of Teachers, Testimonies for the Church, 6:152-161

Words from a Divine Instructor, Testimonies for the Church, 6:162-167

School Homes, Testimonies for the Church, 6:168-170

Industrial Reform, Testimonies for the Church, 6:176-180

The Avondale School Farm, Testimonies for the Church, 6:181-198

Church Schools, Testimonies for the Church, 6:193-205

486 School Management and Finance, Testimonies for the Church, 6:206-218

The Importance of Voice Training, Testimonies for the Church, 6:380-383

The Relief of Our Schools, Testimonies for the Church, 6:468-478

Idleness is Sin, The Youth's Instructor, January 31, February 7, 1901

Our Duty as Parents, Signs of the Times, April 3, 1901

How to Meet Criticism, The Youth's Instructor, April 4, 1901

No Other Gods Before Me, The Review and Herald, September 10, 1901

The Mother's Work, Signs of the Times, January 1, 1902

God's Purpose for the Youth, The Youth's Instructor, February 13, 1902

Lesson for Mothers Signs of the Times, Signs of the Times, February 26, 1902

The Blessing of Labor, The Youth's Instructor, February 27, 1902

What Shall the Youth Read? The Youth's Instructor, October 9, 1902

Centers of Influence, Testimonies for the Church, 7: 231-234

To the Teachers in Our Schools, Testimonies for the Church, 7: 267-276

The Divine Teacher, The Youth's Instructor, March 19, 1903

Sowing Beside all Waters, The Review and Herald, July 14, 1903

Words to Parents Signs of the Times, Signs of the Times, September 16, 1903

Lessons from the Life of Daniel, The Youth's Instructor, April 23-February 2, 1904

1903 Publication of the book " Education (See table of contents for topics treated)

Lessons from the Life of Daniel, The Youth's Instructor, March 8, 1904

Cooperation between the Home and School, The Review and Herald, April 21, 1904

Sowing Beside All Waters

By invitation I attended the meeting held at Healdsburg in connection with the closing of the school year, May 29, 1903. I was glad to learn that teachers and students had united in dispensing with the wearisome and profitless exercises that usually attend the closing of a school, and that the energies of all, to the very close, were devoted to profitable study.

On Friday morning the certificates were quietly handed to those who were entitled to them, and then students and teachers united in an experience meeting, in which many recounted the blessings that they had freely received from God during the year.

On Sabbath morning I spoke to a large audience in the commodious meetinghouse of the Healdsburg church. The students and teachers were seated in front, and I was blessed in presenting to them their responsibility as laborers together with God. The Saviour calls upon our teachers and students to render efficient service as fishers of men.

In the evening a large audience assembled in the church to listen to a musical program rendered by Brother Beardslee and his pupils. Good singing is an important part of the worship of God. I am glad that Brother Beardslee is training the students, so that they can be singing evangelists.

I was much pleased with what I saw of the school. During the past year it has made marked progress. Both teachers and students are reaching higher and still higher in the spiritual life. During the past year there have been remarkable conversions. Lost sheep have been found and brought back to the fold.--Review and Herald, July 14, 1903.

The Work of Our Training Schools

The work of our colleges and training schools should be strengthened year by year.

No Time for Delay

Time is short. Workers for Christ are needed everywhere. There should be one hundred earnest, faithful laborers in home and foreign mission fields where now there is one. The highways and the byways are yet unworked. Urgent inducements should be held out to those who ought now to be engaged in missionary work for the Master.

The signs which show that Christ's coming is near are fast fulfilling. The Lord calls upon our youth to labor as canvassers and evangelists, to do house-to-house work in places that have not yet heard the truth. He speaks to our young men, saying, "Ye are not your own; for ye are bought with a price; therefore glorify God in your body, and in your spirit, which are God's." Those who will go forth to the work under God's direction will be wonderfully blessed. Those who in this life do their best will obtain a fitness for the future, immortal life.

The Lord calls for volunteers who will take their stand firmly on His side, and will pledge themselves to unite with Jesus of Nazareth in doing the very work that needs to be done now, just now.

There are among us many young men and women who, if inducements are held out, would naturally be inclined to take several years' course of study at Battle Creek. But will it pay? The talents of God's people are to be employed in giving the last message of mercy to the world. The Lord calls upon those connected with our sanitariums, publishing houses, and other institutions to teach the youth to do evangelistic work. Our time and money must not be so largely employed in establishing sanitariums, food factories, food stores, and restaurants, that other lines of work shall be neglected. Young men and young women who should be engaged in the ministry, in Bible work, and in the canvassing work, should not be bound down to mechanical employment.

The youth are to be encouraged to attend our schools, which should become more and more like the schools of the prophets. Our schools have been established by the Lord; and if they are conducted in harmony with His purpose, the youth sent to them will quickly be prepared to engage in various branches of missionary work. Some will be trained to enter the field as missionary nurses, some as canvassers, some as evangelists, some as teachers, and some as gospel ministers.

The Lord has plainly instructed me that our young people should not be encouraged to devote so much of their time and strength to medical missionary work as it has been carried forward of late. The instruction they receive regarding Bible doctrines is not such as to fit them to perform properly the work that God has entrusted to His people.

Satan is earnestly striving to lead souls away from right principles. Multitudes who profess to belong to God's true church are falling under the enemy's deceptions. They are being led to swerve from their allegiance to the blessed and only Potentate.

A Present Duty

All our denominational colleges and training schools should make provision to give their students the education essential for evangelists and for Christian business men. The youth and those more advanced in years who feel it their duty to fit themselves for work requiring the passing of certain legal tests should be able to secure at our Union Conference training-schools all that is essential, without having to go to Battle Creek for their preparatory education.

Prayer will accomplish wonders for those who give themselves to prayer, watching thereunto. God desires us all to be in a waiting, hopeful position. What He has promised He will do, and if there are legal requirements making it necessary that medical students shall take a certain preparatory course of study, let our colleges teach the required additional studies in a manner consistent with Christian education. The Lord has signified His displeasure that so many of our people are drifting into Battle Creek; and since He does not want so many to go there, we should understand that He wants our schools in other places to have efficient teachers, and to do well the work that must be done. They should arrange to carry their students to the point of literary and scientific training that is necessary. Many of these requirements have been made because so much of the preparatory work done in ordinary schools is superficial. Let all our work be thorough, faithful, and true.

In our training-schools the Bible is to be made the basis of all education. And in the required studies, it is not necessary for our teachers to bring in the objectionable books that the Lord has instructed us not to use in our schools. From the light that the Lord has given me, I know that our training-schools in various parts of the field should be placed in the most favorable position possible for qualifying our youth to meet the tests specified by state laws regarding medical students. To this end the very best teaching talent should be secured, that our schools may be brought up to the required standard.

But let not the young men and young women in our churches be advised to go to Battle Creek in order to obtain a preparatory education. There is a congested state of things at Battle Creek that makes it an unfavorable place for the proper education of Christian workers. Because the warnings in regard to the work in that congested center have not been heeded, the

Lord permitted two of our institutions to be consumed by fire. Even after this revealing of His signal displeasure His warnings were not heeded. The Sanitarium is still there. If it had been divided into several plants, and its work and influence given to several different places, how much more God would have been glorified! But now that the Sanitarium has been rebuilt, we must do our very best to help those who are there struggling with many difficulties.

Let me repeat: It is not necessary for so many of our youth to study medicine. But for those who should take medical studies our Union Conference training-schools should make ample provision in facilities for preparatory education. Thus the youth of each Union Conference can be trained nearer home, and be spared the special temptations that attend the work in Battle Creek.--Review and Herald, October 15, 1903.

Shall We Colonize Around Our Institutions

Special light has been given me in regard to moving our publishing houses and sanitariums and schools out of the cities into places more favorable for their work, where those connected with them will not be exposed to all the temptations of city life. Especially should our schools be away from the cities. It is not for the spiritual good of the workers in our institutions for them to be located in the cities, where the temptations of the enemy abound on every hand.

The instruction given regarding the removal of the publishing work from Battle Creek to some rural place near Washington, D.C., was clear and distinct, and I earnestly hope that this work may be hastened.

Instruction has also been given that the Pacific Press should be moved from Oakland. As the years have passed by, the city has grown and it is now necessary to establish the printing plant in some more rural place, where land can be secured for the homes of the employees. Those who are connected with our offices of publication should not be obliged to live in the crowded cities. They should have opportunity to obtain homes where they will be able to live without requiring high wages.

The apprentices in our publishing houses should receive more fatherly care than they have had. They are to be given a thorough training in the different lines of the printing business; and they are also to be given every opportunity to gain a knowledge of the Bible; for the time is at hand when believers will be scattered into many lands. The workers in our publishing houses are to be taught what it means to be sincere followers of our Lord and Saviour Jesus Christ. In the past, many souls have been left unguarded. They have not been taught what is comprehended in the science of godliness. Not all of those who have borne responsibilities have lived the Christian life.

Consecrated Workers Needed

I listened to words spoken by One who understands the past, the present, and the future. A most solemn representation was given, delineating the characters that should be possessed by those who are accepted as yokefellows in our institutions. These institutions need men who are temperate in the full acceptance of the term. God forbid that men who have not learned to control themselves, and who neglect their own character-building in order to make plans for someone else, should be brought into our institutions at Washington, D.C., and Mountain View, California.

The workers in our institutions are to heed the instruction given by Christ. When the truth abides in the hearts of those in charge, when they walk in the light shining from God's word, the younger workers will wish to understand better the words they hear in the assembly of God's people. They will ask for fuller explanations, and there will be special seasons of seeking the Lord and studying His word. It was in some quiet room or some retired spot in the country that Christ explained to the disciples the parables which He had spoken before the multitude. This is the work that will need to be done for the youth in our publishing houses.

The Tendency to Colonize

Those who are necessarily situated near our institutions should be careful how they send out glowing reports of the place. Everywhere there are people who are restless and dissatisfied, and who long to go to some place where they think they will do better than in their present surroundings. They think that if they could be given work in connection with someone of our institutions, they would have a better chance to earn a living.

Those who are tempted to gather about our institutions should understand that it is skilled workers that are needed, and that heavy burdens fall upon all who are properly related to the work. Those who are connected with our institutions must be producers as well as consumers. To those who desire to change their location, and settle near one of our institutions, I would say: Do you think that in settling near an institution you will be able to get a living without perplexity or hard work? Have you counseled with the Lord in regard to this matter? Have you evidence that your desire for a change of location is free from selfish motives, and would be for the honor of God?

From letters received by those connected with our institutions, and by movements already made, we see that many desire to obtain homes near these institutions. My mind is weighed down with perplexity regarding this, because I have received instruction from the Lord in regard to the influence that would be exerted upon individuals and upon our work for our people selfishly to gather around our institutions.

For years, in warnings often repeated, I have testified to our people that God was not pleased to see families leaving the smaller churches, and gathering into the places where our publishing houses, sanitariums, and schools are established, for their own convenience, ease, or worldly profit.

In Australia, we went into the forest and secured a large tract of land for our school. Plans were laid to sell to our brethren building lots near the school homes and near the meetinghouse. But I was instructed to protest against permitting families to settle near our school homes. The counsel given was that it would be much better for families not to live near the school, and not to live too close to one another.

Those who feel like settling close to our publishing house or our sanitarium and school at Takoma Park, should take counsel before they move.

To those who are looking toward Mountain View as a favorable place in which to live, because the Pacific Press is to be established there, I would say: Look to other parts of the world, which need the light that you have received in trust. Remember that God has given to every man his work. Choose some locality where you will have opportunity to let your light shine forth amid the moral darkness.

It is always the case that when an institution is established in a place, there are many families who desire to settle near it. Thus it has been in Battle Creek and in Oakland, and, to some extent, in almost every place where we have a school or a sanitarium.

There are restless ones who, were they to go to a new place to live, would still be dissatisfied, because the spirit of disaffection is in their hearts, and a change of place does not bring a change of heart. Their characters have not been refined and ennobled by the Spirit of Christ. They need to learn the lesson of contentment. They do not study from cause to effect. They do not seek to understand the Bible tests of character, which are essential to true success.

There are many who are desirous of changing their employment. They wish to obtain advantages which they suppose exist in some other place. Let them ask themselves of what benefit it would be to them to move if they have not learned to be kind and patient and helpful where they are. Let them look at themselves in the light of the word of God, and then work to the point where improvement is needed.

Let those who are thinking of settling at Mountain View remember that this is not wisdom unless they are called there to connect with the publishing work. The world is large; its needs are great. Go, make new centers in places where there is need of light. Do not crowd into one place, making the same mistake that has been made in Battle Creek. There are hundreds of places that need the light God has given you.

And wherever you live, whatever your circumstances may be, be sure to bring the teachings of the Word of God into your homes, into your daily life. Seek God as your light, your strength, your way to heaven. Remember that to every man God has entrusted talents, to be used for Him. Learn at the feet of Jesus the lessons of meekness and lowliness, and then work in the spirit of the Saviour for those around you. By willing obedience to the commandments, make your home a place where God's honor will love to dwell. "Thus saith the high and lofty One that inhabiteth eternity, whose name is Holy; I dwell in the high and holy place, with him also that is of a contrite and humble spirit, to revive the spirit of the humble, and to revive the heart of the contrite ones."

We each have an individual work to do. We are to consecrate ourselves, body and soul and spirit, to God. Each child of His has something to do for His name's honor and glory. Wherever you are, you may be a blessing.

If there seems to be but a slender chance of obtaining a livelihood where you are, make the most of every opportunity. Devise wise plans. Put to use every jot of ability that God has given you. Do your duty to yourself, improving in understanding and adaptability, daily becoming better able to turn to the best account the mental and physical powers that God has given you. He wants you to be a success. He wants you to be a blessing in your home and in the neighborhood in which you live.

Parents, help your children to help you and to help one another. Be kind and courteous to your neighbors. By good works let your light shine forth amid the moral darkness. If you are true Christians, you will become more and more able to understand what the will of the Lord is, and you will move forward step by step in the light of His word.

Study the life of Christ, and strive to follow the pattern He has given you. Ask yourselves if you have done your whole duty to the church in your own house, and your duty to your neighbors. Have you been faithful in teaching your children lessons of Christian politeness? Are there not many opportunities for improvement in the government of your home? Do not neglect your children. Learn how to discipline yourselves, that you may be worthy of the respect of your children and your neighbors. If Christ is not abiding in your hearts, how can you teach others the lessons of patience and kindness that must be manifest in the life of every Christian? Be sure that you are keeping the way of the Lord, and then teach the truth to those around you.--Review and Herald, June 2, 1904.

FOR ADDITIONAL READING

Training Children for God, The Review and Herald, September 8, September 15, 1904

How Shall Our Youth be Trained, Testimonies for the Church, 8:221-230

God in Nature, Idem, 8:239-243

A Personal God, Idem, 8:263-278

A False and True Knowledge of God, Idem, 8: 279-289

Danger in Speculative Knowledge, Idem, 8:290-308

The False and True in Education, Idem, 8:305-311

Importance of Seeking True Knowledge, Idem, 8:312-318

Knowledge Received Through God's Word, Idem, 8:319-328

Lessons from the Life of Daniel, The Youth's Instructor, April 4, 1905

Instruction for Helpers and Students at Tahoma, The Review and Herald, April 27, 1905

Lessons from the Life of Solomon

"Be Ye Separate"

Placed at the head of a nation that had been set as a light to the surrounding nations, Solomon might have brought great glory to the Lord of the universe by a life of obedience. He might have encouraged God's people to shun the evils that were practiced in the surrounding nations. He might have used his God-given wisdom and power of influence in organizing and directing a great missionary movement for the enlightenment of those who were ignorant of God and of His truth. Thus multitudes might have been won to an allegiance to the King of kings.

Satan well knew the results that would attend obedience, and during the earlier years of Solomon's reign,--years glorious because of the wisdom, the beneficence, and the uprightness of the king,--he sought to bring in influences that would insidiously undermine Solomon's loyalty to principle, and cause him to separate from God. And that the enemy was successful in this effort, we know from the record: "Solomon made affinity with Pharaoh king of Egypt, and took Pharaoh's daughter, and brought her into the city of David."

In forming an alliance with a heathen nation, and sealing the compact by marriage with an idolatrous princess, Solomon rashly disregarded the wise provisions that God had made for maintaining the purity of His people. The hope that this Egyptian wife might be converted, was but a feeble excuse for the sin. In violation of a direct command to remain separate from other nations, the king united his strength with the arm of flesh.

For a time, God in His compassionate mercy overruled this terrible mistake. Solomon's wife was converted; and the king, by a wise course, might have done much to check the evil forces that his imprudence had set in operation. But Solomon began to lose sight of the Source of his power and glory. Inclination gained the ascendency over reason. As his self-confidence increased, he sought to carry out the Lord's purpose in his own way. He reasoned that political and commercial alliances with the surrounding nations would bring them to a knowledge of the true God; and so he entered into unholy alliance with nation after nation. Often these alliances were sealed by marriage with heathen princesses. The commands of Jehovah were set aside for the customs of the surrounding nations.

During the years of Solomon's apostasy, the spiritual decline of Israel was rapid. How could it have been otherwise, when their king united with satanic agencies? Through these agencies the enemy worked to confuse the minds of the people in regard to true and false worship. They became an easy prey. It came to be a common practice to intermarry with the heathen. The Israelites rapidly lost their abhorrence of idolatry. Heathen customs were introduced. Idolatrous mothers brought their children up to observe heathen rites. The Hebrew faith was fast becoming a mixture of confused ideas. Commerce with other nations brought the Israelites into intimate contact with those who had no love for God, and their own love for Him was greatly lessened. Their keen sense of the high and holy character of God was deadened. Refusing to follow in the path of obedience, they transferred their allegiance to Satan. The enemy rejoiced in his success in effacing the divine image from the minds of the people that God has chosen as His representatives. Through inter-marriage with idolaters and constant association with them, Satan brought about that for which he had long been working,--a national apostasy.

Unscriptural Alliances

The Lord desires His servants to preserve their holy and peculiar character. "Be ye not unequally yoked together with unbelievers," is His command; "for what fellowship hath righteousness with unrighteousness? and what communion hath light with darkness? and what concord hath Christ with Belial? or what part hath he that believeth with an infidel? and what agreement hath the temple of God with idols? for ye are the temple of the living God; as God hath said, I will dwell in them, and walk in them; and I will be their God, and they shall be My people. Wherefore come out from among them, and be ye separate, saith the Lord, and touch not the unclean thing; and I will receive you, and will be a Father unto you, and ye shall be My sons and daughters, saith the Lord Almighty."

Never was there a time in earth's history when this warning was more appropriate than at the present time. Many professed Christians think, like Solomon, that they may unite with the ungodly, because their influence over those who are in the wrong will be beneficial; but too often they themselves, entrapped and overcome, yield their sacred faith, sacrifice principle, and separate themselves from God. One false step leads to another, till at last they place themselves where they cannot hope to break the chains that bind them.

Great care should be taken by Christian youth in the formation of friendships and in the choice of companions. Take heed, lest what you now think to be pure gold turns out to be base metal. Worldly associations tend to place obstructions in the way of your service to God, and many souls are ruined by unhappy unions, either business or matrimonial, with those who can never elevate or ennoble. Never should God's people venture upon forbidden ground. Marriage between believers and unbelievers is forbidden by God. But too often the unconverted heart follows its own desires, and marriages unsanctioned by God are formed. Because of this many men and women are without hope and without God in the world. Their noble aspirations are dead; by a chain of circumstances they are held in Satan's net. Those who are ruled by passion and impulse will have a bitter harvest to reap in this life, and their course may result in the loss of their souls.

Institutional Work

Those who are placed in charge of the Lord's institutions are in need of much of the strength and grace and keeping power of God, that they shall not walk contrary to the sacred principles of the truth. Many, many are very dull of comprehension in regard to their obligation to preserve the truth in its purity, uncontaminated by one vestige of error. Their danger is in holding the truth in light esteem, thus leaving upon minds the impression that it is of little consequence what we believe, if, by carrying out plans of human devising, we can exalt ourselves before the world as holding a superior position, as occupying the highest seat.

God calls for men whose hearts are as true as steel, and who will stand steadfast in integrity, undaunted by circumstances. He calls for men who will remain separate from the enemies of the truth. He calls for men who will not dare to resort to the arm of flesh by entering into partnership with worldlings in order to secure means for advancing His work--even for the building of institutions. Solomon, by his alliances with unbelievers, secured an abundance of gold and silver, but his prosperity proved his ruin. Men today are no wiser than he, and they are as prone to yield to the influences that caused his downfall. For thousands of years Satan has been gaining an experience in learning how to deceive; and to those who live in this age he comes with almost overwhelming power. Our only safety is found in obedience to God's word, which has been given us as a sure guide and counselor. God's people today are to keep themselves distinct and separate from the world, its spirit, and its influences.

"Come out from among them, and be ye separate." Shall we hear the voice of God and obey, or shall we make halfway work of the matter, and try to serve God and Mammon? There is earnest work before each one of us. Right thoughts, pure and holy purposes, do not come to us naturally. We shall have to strive for them. In all our institutions, our publishing houses and colleges and sanitariums, pure and holy principles must take root. If our institutions are what God designs they should be, those connected with them will not pattern after worldly institutions. They will stand as peculiar, governed and controlled by the Bible standard. They will not come into harmony with the principles of the world in order to gain patronage. No motives will have sufficient force to move them from the straight line of duty. Those who are under the control of the Spirit of God will not seek their own pleasure or amusement. If Christ presides in the hearts of the members of His church, they will answer to the call, "Come out from among them, and be ye separate." "Be not partakers of her sins."

God would have us learn the solemn lesson that we are working out our own destiny. The characters we form in this life decide whether or not we are fitted to live through the eternal ages. No man can with safety attempt to serve both God and Mammon. God is fully able to keep us in the world, but not of the world. His love is not uncertain and fluctuating. Ever He watches over His children with a care that is measureless and everlasting. But He requires us to give Him our undivided allegiance. "No man can serve two masters: for either he will hate the one, and love the other; or else he will hold to the one, and despise the other. Ye cannot serve God and Mammon."

Solomon was endowed with wonderful wisdom; but the world drew him away from God. We need to guard our souls with all diligence, lest the cares and the attractions of the world absorb the time that should be given to eternal things. God warned Solomon of his danger, and today He warns us not to imperil our souls by affinity with the world. "Come out from among them," He pleads, "and be ye separate, . . . and touch not the unclean thing; and I will receive you, and will be a Father unto you, and ye shall be My sons and daughters, saith the Lord God Almighty."--Review and Herald, February 1, 1906.

FOR ADDITIONAL READING

Lessons in Economy and Self-denila, The Youth's Instructor, September 10, 1907

Teachers as Examples of Christian Integrity

I have a message for those standing at the head of our educational institutions. I am instructed to call the attention of everyone occupying a position of responsibility, to the divine law as the basis of all right conduct. I am to begin by calling attention to the law given in Eden, and to the reward of obedience and the penalty of disobedience.

In consequence of Adam's transgression, sin was introduced into the fair world that God had created, and men and women became more and still more bold in disobeying His law. The Lord looked down upon the impenitent world, and decided that He must give transgressors an exhibition of His power. He caused Noah to know His purpose, and instructed him to warn the people while building an ark in which the obedient could find shelter until God's indignation was overpast. For one hundred and twenty years Noah proclaimed the message of warning to the antediluvian world; but only a few repented. Some of the carpenters he employed in building the ark, believed the message, but died before the flood; others of Noah's converts backslid. The righteous on the earth were but few, and only eight lived to enter the ark. These were Noah and his family.

The rebellious race was swept away by the flood. Death was their portion. By the fulfillment of the prophetic warning that all who would not keep the commandments of heaven should drink the waters of the flood, the truth of God's word was exemplified.

After the flood the people once more increased on the earth, and wickedness also increased. Idolatry became well-nigh universal, and the Lord finally left the hardened transgressors to follow their evil ways, while He chose Abraham, of the line of Shem, and made him the keeper of His law for future generations. To him the message came, "Get thee out of thy country, and from thy kindred, and from thy father's house, unto a land that I will show thee." And by faith Abraham obeyed. "He went out, not knowing whither he went."

Abraham's seed multiplied, and at length Jacob and his sons and their families went down into Egypt. Here they and their descendants sojourned for many years, till at last the Lord called them out, to lead them into the land of Canaan. It was His purpose to make of this nation of slaves a people who would reveal His character to the idolatrous nations of the world. Had they been obedient to His word, they would soon have entered the promised land. But they were disobedient and rebellious, and for forty years they journeyed in the wilderness. Only two of the adults who left Egypt entered Canaan.

It was during the wilderness wandering of the Israelites that God gave them His law. He led them to Sinai, and there, amid scenes of awful grandeur, proclaimed the ten commandments.

We may with profit study the record of the preparation made by the congregation of Israel for the hearing of the law. "In the third month, when the children of Israel were gone forth out of the land of Egypt, the same day came they into the wilderness of Sinai. For they were departed from Rephidim, and were come to the desert of Sinai, and had pitched in the wilderness: and there Israel camped before the mount. And Moses went up unto God, and the Lord called unto him out of the mountain, saying, Thus shalt thou say to the house of Jacob, and tell the children of Israel: Ye have seen what I did unto the Egyptians, and how I bare you on eagles' wings, and brought you unto Myself. Now therefore, if ye will obey My voice indeed, and keep My covenant, then ye shall be a peculiar treasure unto Me above all people: for all the earth is Mine."

Who, then, is to be regarded as the Ruler of the nations?--The Lord God Omnipotent. All kings, all rulers, all nations, are His under His rule and government.

"And Moses came and called for the elders of the people, and laid before their faces all these words which the Lord commanded him."

What was the response of the congregation, numbering more than a million people?

"And all the people answered together, and said, All that the Lord hath spoken we will do. And Moses returned the words of the people unto the Lord."

Thus the children of Israel were denominated as a special people. By a most solemn covenant they were pledged to be true to God.

Then the people were bidden to prepare themselves to hear the law. On the morning of the third day the voice of God was heard. Speaking out of the thick darkness that enshrouded Him, as He stood upon the mount, surrounded by a retinue of angels, the Lord made known His law.

God accompanied the proclamation of His law with manifestations of His power and glory, that His people might be impressed with a profound veneration for the Author of the law, the Creator of heaven and earth. He would also show to all men the sacredness, the importance, and the permanence of His law.

The people of Israel were overwhelmed with terror. They shrank away from the mountain in fear and awe. The multitude cried out to Moses, "Speak thou with us, but let not God speak with us, lest we die."

The minds of the people, blinded and debased by slavery, were not prepared to appreciate fully the far-reaching principles of God's ten precepts. That the obligations of the decalogue might be more fully understood and enforced, additional precepts were given, illustrating and applying the precepts of the ten commandments. Unlike the decalogue, these were delivered privately to Moses, who was to communicate them to the people.

Upon descending from the mountain, Moses "came and told the people all the words of the Lord, and all the judgments: and all the people answered with one voice, and said, All the words which the Lord hath said will we do. And Moses wrote all the words of the Lord, and rose up early in the morning, and builded an altar under the hill, and twelve pillars, according to the twelve tribes of Israel. And he sent young men of the children of Israel, which offered burnt offerings, and sacrificed peace offerings of oxen unto the Lord. And Moses took half of the blood, and put it in basins; and half of the blood he sprinkled on the altar. And he took the book of the covenant, and read in the audience of the people: and they said, All that the Lord hath said will we do, and be obedient. And Moses took the blood, and sprinkled it on the people, and said, Behold the blood of the covenant, which the Lord hath made with you concerning all these words."

Thus by a most solemn service the children of Israel were once more set apart as a peculiar people. The sprinkling of the blood represented the shedding of the blood of Jesus, by which human beings are cleansed from sin.

Once more the Lord has special words to speak to His people. In the thirty-first chapter of Exodus we read:

"The Lord spake unto Moses, saying, Speak thou also unto the children of Israel, saying, Verily My Sabbaths ye shall keep: for it is a sign between Me and you throughout your generations; that ye may know that I am the Lord that doth sanctify you. . . . Wherefore the children of Israel shall keep the Sabbath, to observe the Sabbath throughout their generations, for a perpetual covenant. It is a sign between Me and the children of Israel forever: for in six days the Lord made heaven and earth, and on the seventh day He rested, and was refreshed. And He gave unto Moses, when he had made an end of communing with him upon Mount Sinai, two tables of testimony, tables of stone, written with the finger of God."

Many other scriptures on the sacredness of God's law have been presented before me. Scene after scene, reaching down to the present time, passed before me. The word spoken by God to Israel was verified. The people disobeyed, and only two of the adults who left Egypt entered Canaan. The rest died in the wilderness. Will not the Lord today vindicate His word if the leaders of His people depart from His commandments?

I was referred to the fourth chapter of Deuteronomy. The whole of this chapter is to be studied. Notice particularly the statement: "Know therefore this day, and consider it in thine heart, that the Lord He is God in heaven above, and upon the earth beneath: there is none else. Thou shalt keep therefore His statutes, and His commandments, which I command thee this day, that it may go well with thee, and with thy children after thee, and that thou mayest prolong thy days upon the earth, which the Lord thy God giveth thee, forever."

The eighth and eleventh chapters of Deuteronomy also mean much to us. The lessons that they contain are of the greatest importance, and are given to us as verily as to the Israelites. In the eleventh chapter God says: "Behold I set before you this day a blessing and a curse; a blessing if ye obey the commandments of the Lord your God, which I command you this day: and a curse, if ye will not obey the commandments of the Lord your God, but turn aside out of the way which I command you this day, to go after other gods, which ye have not known."

I have been instructed, as God's messenger, to dwell particularly upon the record of Moses' sin and its sad result, as a solemn lesson to those in positions of responsibility in our schools, and especially to those acting as presidents of these institutions.

Of Moses God's word declares, "Now the man Moses was very meek, above all the men which were upon the face of the earth." Long had he borne with the rebellion and obstinacy of Israel. But at last his patience gave way. They were on the borders of the promised land. But before they entered Canaan, they must show that they believed God's promise. The supply of water ceased. Here was an opportunity for them to walk by faith instead of by sight. But they forgot the hand that for so many years had supplied their wants, and instead of turning to God for help, they murmured against Him.

Their cries were directed against Moses and Aaron: "Why have ye brought up the congregation of the Lord into this wilderness, that we and our cattle should die there? And wherefore have ye made us to come up out of Egypt, to bring us in unto this evil place? It is no place of seed, or of figs, or of vines, or of pomegranates; neither is there any water to drink."

The two brothers went before the multitude. But instead of speaking to the rock, as God had directed, Moses smote the rock angrily, crying, "Hear now, ye rebels; must we fetch you water out of this rock?"

Bitter and deeply humiliating was the judgment immediately pronounced. "The Lord spake unto Moses and Aaron, Because ye believed Me not, to sanctify Me in the eyes of the children of Israel, therefore ye shall not bring this congregation into the land which I have given them." With rebellious Israel they must die before crossing the Jordan.

From the experience of Moses the Lord would have His people learn that when they do that which gives prominence to self, His work is neglected, and He is dishonored. The Lord will work counter to those who work counter to Him. His name, and His alone, is to be magnified on the earth.

For more than twenty years strange things have at different times been coming in among us. Those who have become unfaithful, who have not exalted the principles of righteousness, need now to seek the Lord with deep humiliation of soul, and be converted, that God may heal their transgressions.

The one standing at the head of a school is to put his undivided interests into the work of making the school just what the Lord designed it to be. If he is ambitious to climb higher and still higher, if he gets above the real virtues of his work, and above its simplicity, and disregards the holy principles of heaven, let him learn from the experience of Moses that the Lord will surely manifest His displeasure because of his failure to reach the standard set before him.

Especially should the president of a school look carefully after the finances of the institution. He should understand the underlying principles of bookkeeping. He is faithfully to report the use of all moneys passing through his hand for the use of the school. The funds of the school are not to be overdrawn, but every effort is to be made to increase the usefulness of the school. Those entrusted with the financial management of our educational institutions, must allow no carelessness in the expenditure of means. Everything connected with the finances of our schools should be perfectly straight. The Lord's way must be strictly followed, though this may not be in harmony with the ways of man.

To those in charge of our schools I would say, Are you making God and His law your delight? Are the principles that you follow, sound and pure and unadulterated? Are you keeping yourselves, in the life practice, under the control of God? Do you see the necessity of obeying Him in every particular? If you are tempted to appropriate the money coming into the school, in ways that bring no special benefit to the school, your standard of principle needs to be carefully criticized, that the time may not come when you will have to be criticized and found wanting. Who is your bookkeeper? Who is your treasurer? Who is your business manager? Are they careful and competent? Look to this. It is possible for money to be misappropriated without anyone's understanding clearly how it came about; and it is possible for a school to be losing continually because of unwise expenditures. Those in charge may feel this loss keenly, and yet suppose they have done their best. But why do they permit debts to accumulate? Let those in charge of a school find out each month the true financial standing of the school.

My brethren in responsibility, exalt the law of Christ's kingdom by giving to it willing obedience. If you are not yourselves under the control of the Ruler of the universe, how can you obey His law, as required in His word? Those who are placed in positions of authority are the very ones who need most fully to realize their amenability to God's law and the importance of obeying all His requirements.

In some respects, many of those connected with our schools should be standing on a higher platform. We know that it is the determined purpose of some to be obedient to every word that proceedeth out of the mouth of God. Such men and women will be given power of intellect to discern the difference between righteousness and unrighteousness. They have the faith that works by love and purifies the soul, and they reveal God to the world.

We all need to gain a much deeper experience in the things of God than we have gained. Self is to die, and Christ is to take possession of the soul temple. Physicians, ministers, teachers, and all others in responsible positions, must learn the humility of Christ before He can be revealed in them. Too often self is so important an agency in the life of a man that the Lord is not able to mold and fashion him. Self rules on the right hand and on the left, and the man presses his way forward as he pleases. Christ says to self, "Stand out of My path. Whosoever will come after Me, let him deny himself, and take up his cross, and follow Me. Then I can accept him as My disciple. In order to serve Me acceptably, he must do the work I have given him in harmony with My instructions."--Review and Herald, August 16, 23, 1906.

The Essential in Education

The most essential education for our youth today to gain, and that which will fit them for the higher grades of the school above, is an education that will teach them how to reveal the will of God to the world. To neglect this phase of their training, and to bring into our schools a worldly method, is to bring loss to both teachers and students.

Just before Elijah was taken to heaven, he visited the schools of the prophets, and instructed the students on the most important points of their education. The lessons he had given them on former visits, he now repeated, impressing upon the minds of the youth the importance of letting simplicity mark every feature of their education. Only in this way could they receive the mold of heaven, and go forth to work in the ways of the Lord. If conducted as God designs they should be, our schools in these closing days of the message will do a work similar to that done by the schools of the prophets.

Those who go forth from our schools to engage in mission work will have need of an experience in the cultivation of the soil and in other lines of manual labor. They should receive a training that will fit them to take hold of any line of work in the fields to which they shall be called. No work will be more effectual than that done by those who, having obtained an education in practical life, go forth prepared to instruct as they have been instructed.

In His teachings the Saviour represented the world as a vineyard. We would do well to study the parables in which this figure is used. If in our schools the land were more faithfully cultivated, the buildings more disinterestedly cared for by the students, the love of sports and amusements, which causes so much perplexity in our school work, would pass away.

When the Lord placed our first parents in the garden of Eden, it was with the injunction that they "dress it" and "keep it." God had finished His work of creation, and had pronounced all things very good. Everything was adapted to the end for which it was made. While Adam and Eve obeyed God, their labors in the garden were a pleasure; the earth yielded of its abundance for their wants. But when man departed from his obedience to God, he was doomed to wrestle with the seeds of Satan's sowing, and to earn his bread by the sweat of his brow. Henceforth he must battle in toil and hardship against the power to which he had yielded his will.

It was God's purpose to remove by toil the evil which man brought into the world by disobedience. By toil the temptations of Satan might be made ineffectual, and the tide of evil be stayed. The Son of God was given to the world, by His death to make atonement for the sins of the world, by His life to teach men how the plans of the enemy were to be thwarted. Taking upon Himself the nature of man, Christ entered into the sympathies and interests of His brethren, and by a life of untiring labor taught how men might become laborers together with God in the building up of His kingdom in the world.

If those who have received instruction concerning God's plan for the education of the youth in these last days, will surrender their wills to God, He will teach them His will and His way. Christ is to be the teacher in all our schools. If teachers and students will give Him His rightful place, He will work through them to carry out the plan of redemption.

Students are to be taught to seek the counsel of God in prayer. They are to be taught to look to their Creator as their unerring guide. They are to be taught the lessons of forbearance and trust, of true goodness and kindness of heart. They are to learn the lesson of perseverance. Their characters are to answer to the words of David, "That our sons may be as plants grown up in their youth; that our daughters may be as corner stones, polished after the similitude of a palace." In all this they are qualifying for service in the missionary field.

The converted student has broken the chain which bound him to the service of sin, and has placed himself in the right relation to God. His name is enrolled in the Lamb's book of life. He is under solemn obligation to renounce evil, and come under the jurisdiction of God. Through earnest prayer he is to cleave to Christ. To neglect this, to refuse his service, is to forfeit the favor of the Great Teacher, and to become the sport of Satan's wiles. It was the design of heaven by the infinite sacrifice of Christ, to bring men and women into favor again with God. The education that brings the student into close relation with the Teacher sent from God, is true education.

God's people are His chosen instrumentalities for the enlargement of His church in the earth. They are to seek the counsel of God. Worldly amusements and entertainments are to have no place in the life of the Christian. In following the way of the Lord is to be the strength of His people. Their faith in the gift of God's only-begotten Son is to be manifest. This will make its impression on the mind of the worldling. He who takes his position as separate from the world, and strives to become one with Christ, will be successful in drawing souls to God. The grace of Christ will be so apparent in his life that the world will take knowledge of him that he has been with Jesus, and has learned of Him.

"Go work today in my vineyard," the Saviour commands. "Whether therefore ye eat, or drink, or whatsoever ye do, do all to the glory of God." Let everyone who claims to be a child of the heavenly King seek constantly to represent the principles of the kingdom of God. Let each remember that in spirit, in words, and in works, he is to be loyal and true to all the precepts and commandments of the Lord. We are to be faithful, trustworthy subjects of the kingdom of Christ, that those who are worldly wise may have a true representation of the riches, the goodness, the mercy, the tenderness, and the courtesy of the citizens of the kingdom of God.-- Review and Herald, October 24, 1907.

A Message to Teachers

A message has been given me for the teachers in all our schools. Those who accept the sacred responsibility resting upon teachers need to be constantly advancing in their experience. They should not be content to remain upon the lowlands, but should ever be climbing heavenward. With the word of God in their hands, and the love of souls pointing them to diligence, they should advance step by step in efficiency.

A deep Christian experience will be combined with the work of true education. Our schools are to advance steadily in Christian development; and in order to do this, the words and example of the teacher should be a constant help. "Ye also, as lively stones," the apostle declares, "are built up a spiritual house, an holy priesthood, to offer up spiritual sacrifices, acceptable to God by Jesus Christ." It would be well for every teacher and student to study carefully these words, asking himself the question, Am I, through the abundant grace given, obtaining the very experience that as a child of God I must have in order to advance constantly step by step to the higher grade?

In every line of instruction, teachers are to seek to impart light from the word of God, and to show the importance of obedience to a "Thus saith the Lord." The education should be such that the students will make right principles the guide of every action: This is the education that will abide through the eternal ages.

I am given words of caution to the teachers in all our established schools. The work of our schools must bear a different stamp from that borne by some of our most popular schools. The mere study of the ordinary textbook is not sufficient; and many of the books that are used are unnecessary for those schools that are established to prepare students for the school above. As a result, the students in these schools are not receiving the most perfect Christian education. The very points of study are neglected that are most needed to prepare the students to stand the last great examination, and to fit them for missionary work in home and foreign fields. The education that is needed now is one that will qualify the students for practical missionary work, by teaching them to bring every faculty under the control of the Spirit of God. The study book which is of the highest value is that which contains the instruction of Christ, the Teacher of teachers.

The Lord expects our teachers to expel from our schools those books that teach sentiments which are not in accordance with His word, and to give place to those books that are of the highest value. The Lord designs that the teachers in our schools shall excel in wisdom the wisdom of the world, because they study His wisdom. God will be honored when the teachers in our schools, from the highest grades to the lowest, show to the world that a more than human wisdom is theirs, because the Master Teacher is standing at their head.

Our teachers need to be constant learners. All reformers need to place themselves under discipline to God. Their own lives need to be reformed, their own hearts subdued by the grace of Christ. Every worldly habit and idea that is not in harmony with the mind of God should be renounced.

When Nicodemus, a learned teacher in Israel, came to Jesus to inquire of Him, Christ laid before him the first principles. Nicodemus, though holding an honorable position in Israel, had not a true conception of what a teacher in Israel should be. He needed instruction in the very first principles of the divine life, for he had not learned the alphabet of true Christian experience.

In response to Christ's instruction Nicodemus said, "How can these things be?" Christ answered, "Art thou a master of Israel, and knowest not these things?" The same question might be asked of many who are holding responsible positions as teachers, physicians, and ministers of the gospel, but who have neglected the most essential part of their education, that which would fit them to deal in a Christlike manner with human minds.

In the instruction that Christ gave to His disciples, and to the people of all classes who came to hear His words, there was that which lifted them to a high plane of thought and action. If the words of Christ, instead of the words of men, were given to the learner today, we would see evidences of higher intelligence, a clearer comprehension of heavenly things, a deeper knowledge of God, a purer and more vigorous Christian life. "Verily, verily, I say unto you," Christ said, "he that believeth on Me hath everlasting life. I am that bread of life. Your fathers did eat manna in the wilderness, and are dead. This is the bread which cometh down from heaven, that a man may eat thereof, and not die. I am the living bread which came down from heaven: if any man eat of this bread, he shall live forever."

"When Jesus knew in Himself that His disciples murmured at it, He said unto them, Doth this offend you? What and if ye shall see the Son of man ascend up where He was before? It is the spirit that quickeneth; the flesh profiteth nothing: the words that I speak unto you, they are spirit, and they are life."

We are slow to understand how much we need to study the words of Christ and His methods of labor. If His teachings were better understood, much of the instruction that is now given in our schools would be valued at its true worth. It would be seen that much that is now taught does not develop the simplicity of godliness in the life of the student. Then finite wisdom would receive less honor, and the word of God would have a more honored place.

When our teachers are truly converted, they will experience a soul hunger for the knowledge of God, and as humble learners in the school of Christ, they will study to know His righteousness. Righteous principles will rule the life, and will be taught as the principles that rule in the education of heaven. When teachers seek with all their heart to bring true principles into the work of education, angels of God will be present to make impressions upon the heart and mind.--Review and Herald, November 7, 1907.

FOR ADDITIONAL READING

With Full Purpose of Heart, The Youth's Instructor, November 12, 1907
From Prison Cell to Egypt's Throne, The Youth's Instructor, March 17, 1908
Knowing God, The Youth's Instructor, April 7, 1908
Wise Counsel to the Youth, The Youth's Instructor, April 28, 1908

Provision Made for Our Schools

AN APPEAL TO MINISTERS, PHYSICIANS, AND TEACHERS IN SOUTHERN CALIFORNIA:

The men who stand as leaders in any part of the solemn work of the last gospel message must cultivate and cherish broad views and ideas. It is the privilege of all who bear responsibilities in the work of the gospel to be apt learners in the school of Christ. The professed follower of Christ must not be led by the dictates of his own will; his mind must be trained to think Christ's thoughts, and enlightened to comprehend the will and way of God. Such a believer will be a follower of Christ's methods of work.

Our brethren should not forget that the wisdom of God has made provision for our schools in a way that will bring blessing to all who participate in the enterprise. The book, "Christ's Object Lessons," was donated to the educational work, that the students and other friends of the schools might handle these books, and by their sale raise much of the means needed to lift the school indebtedness. But this plan has not been presented to our schools as it should have been; the teachers and students have not been educated to take hold of this book and courageously push its sale for the benefit of the educational work.

Long ago the teachers and students in our schools should have learned to take advantage of the opportunity to raise means by the sale of "Christ's Object Lessons." In selling these books the students will serve the cause of God, and, while doing this, by the dissemination of precious light, they will learn invaluable lessons in Christian experience. All our schools should now come into line, and earnestly endeavor to carry out the plan presented to us for the education of the workers, for the relief of the schools, and for the winning of souls to the cause of Christ.

In the cities of Riverside, Redlands, and San Bernardino a mission field is open to us that we have as yet only touched with the tips of our fingers. A good work has been done there as far as our workers have had encouragement to do it; but there is need of means to carry the work forward successfully. It was God's purpose that by the sale of "Ministry of Healing" and "Christ's Object Lessons" much means should be raised for the work of our sanitariums and schools, and that our people would thereby be left more free to donate of their means for the opening of the work in new missionary fields. If our people will now engage in the sale of these books as they ought, we shall have much more means to carry the work in the way the Lord designed.

Wherever the work of selling "Christ's Object Lessons" has been taken hold of in earnest, the book has done good. And the lessons that have been learned by those who have engaged in this work, have well repaid their efforts. And now our people should all be encouraged to take part in this special missionary effort. Light has been given me that in every possible way instruction should be given to our people as to the best methods of presenting these books to the people.

I have been instructed that at our large gatherings, workers should be present who will teach our people how to sow the seeds of truth. This means more than instructing them how to sell the Signs of the Times and other periodicals. It includes thorough instruction in how to handle such books as "Christ's Object Lessons" and "Ministry of Healing." These are books which contain precious truths, and from which the reader can draw lessons of highest value.

Why was not someone appointed at your camp-meeting [in 1907] to present the interests of this line of work to our people? In your failure to do this, you lost a precious opportunity to place large blessings within the reach of the people, and you also lost an opportunity of raising means for the relief of our institutions. My brethren, let us encourage our people to take up this work without further delay.

There are some who have had experience in the sale of health foods who should now interest themselves in the sale of our precious books; for in them is food unto eternal life. Los Angeles has been presented to me as a very fruitful field for the sale of "Christ's Object Lessons" and "Ministry of Healing." The thousands of transient residents and visitors would be benefited by the lessons they contain, and those who bear responsibilities in our sanitariums should act wisely in this matter, encouraging all, nurses, helpers, and students, to gather by this means as much as possible of the money required to meet the expenses of the different institutions.

Why are our people so slow to understand what the Lord would have them do? Our leading workers should prepare beforehand to use their opportunities at our large and small gatherings to present these books to our people, and call for volunteers who will engage in their sale. When this work is entered into with the earnestness which our times demand, the indebtedness which now rests upon our schools will be greatly lessened. And then the people who are now being called upon to give largely of their means to support these institutions, will be free to turn a larger part of their offerings to missionary work in other needy places, where special efforts have not yet been made.

Great good will result from bringing these books to the attention of the leaders in the Woman's Christian Temperance Union. We should invite these workers to our meetings, and give them an opportunity to become acquainted with our people. Place these precious books in their hands, and tell them the story of their gift to the cause, and its results. Explain how, by the sale of "Ministry of Healing," patients may be brought to the sanitarium for healing who could never get there unaided; and how through this means assistance will be rendered in the establishment of sanitariums in

Provision Made for Our Schools

places where they are greatly needed. If our sanitariums are wisely managed by men and women who have the fear of God before them, they will be a means of bringing us in connection with workers in the Woman's Christian Temperance Union, and these workers will not be slow to see the advantage of the medical branch of our work. As a result of their contact with our medical work, some of them will learn truths that they need to know for the perfection of Christian character.

One point that should never be forgotten by our workers is that the Lord Jesus Christ is our chief director. He has outlined a plan by which the schools may be relieved of their indebtedness; and He will not vindicate the course of those who lay this plan aside for lack of confidence in its success. When His people will come up unitedly to the help of His cause in the earth, no good thing that God has promised will be withheld from them.

In places like Los Angeles, where the population is constantly changing, wonderful opportunities are presented for the sale of our books. A great loss has been sustained because our people have not more fully embraced this opportunity. Why should not the teachers and students from the San Fernando School make Los Angeles a special field for the sale of "Object Lessons"? If with earnestness and faith they will work out the plan that has been given us for the use of this book, angels of God will attend their steps, and the blessing of heaven will be upon their efforts.

It would have been an excellent thing if the teachers of the San Fernando School had, during the vacation, availed themselves of this opportunity to push the work with "Christ's Object Lessons." They would have found a blessing in going out with the students and teaching them how to meet the people, and how to introduce the book. The story of the gift of the book and its object would lead some to have a special interest in the book and in the school for which it is sold.

Why have not the teachers in our schools done more of this work? If our people would only realize it, there is no more acceptable work to be done in the home field than to engage in the sale of "Object Lessons"; for while they are thus helping to carry out the Lord's plan for the relief of our schools, they are also bringing the precious truths of the word of God to the attention of the people.

The indifference that has been manifested by some toward this enterprise is displeasing to God. He desires that it shall be recognized by all our people as His method of relieving our schools from debt. It is because this plan has been neglected that we now feel so keenly our lack of means for the advancing work. Had the schools availed themselves of the provision thus made for them, there would be more money in the school treasury, and more money in the hands of His people, to relieve the necessities of other needy departments of the cause, and, best of all, teachers and students would have received the very lessons that they needed to learn in the Master's service.

I send you these lines because I see that there is need of a deeper intuition, a wider perception, on the part of our medical and educational workers, if they would get all the benefit that God intends shall come to them through the use of "Object Lessons" and "Ministry of Healing." I ask you, my brethren, to read these words to our people, that they may learn to show the spirit of wisdom, and of power, and of a sound mind.--Review and Herald, September 3, 1908.

Teacher, Know Thyself

To know one's self is great knowledge. True self-knowledge will lead to a humility that will allow the Lord to train the mind, and mold and discipline the character. The grace of humility is greatly needed by the workers for Christ in this period of the world's history. No teacher can do acceptable work who does not bear in mind his own deficiencies and who does not drop out from his reckoning all plans that will weaken his spiritual life. When teachers are willing to drop out from their work everything that is unessential for the life eternal, then they can be said indeed to be working out their salvation with fear and trembling, and to be building wisely for eternity.

I am instructed to say that some of our teachers are far behind in an understanding of the kind of education needed for this period of earth's history. This is not a time for students to be gathering up a mass of knowledge that they cannot take with them to the school above. Let us carefully weed out from our course of study all that can be spared, that we may have room in the minds of the students in which to plant the seeds of righteousness. This instruction will bear fruit unto eternal life.

Every teacher should be a daily learner in the school of Christ, lest he lose the sense of what constitutes true physical, mental, and moral excellence. No one should place himself as a teacher of others who is not constantly working out his own salvation by receiving and imparting an all-round education. The true teacher will educate himself in moral excellence, that by precept and example he may lead souls to understand the lessons of the Great Teacher. No one should be encouraged to do the work of teaching who will be satisfied with a low standard. No one is fitted to teach the grand mysteries of godliness till Christ is formed within, the hope of glory.

Every teacher needs to receive the truth in the love of its sacred principles; then he cannot fail of exerting an influence that is purifying and uplifting. The teacher whose soul is stayed upon Christ will speak and act like a Christian. Such a one will not be satisfied until the truth cleanses his life from every unessential thing. He will not be satisfied unless his mind is day by day molded by the holy influences of the Spirit of God. Then Christ can speak to the heart, and His voice, saying, "This is the way; walk ye in it," will be heard and obeyed.

The teacher who has a right understanding of the work of true education, will not think it sufficient now and then to make casual reference to Christ. With his own heart warm with the love of God, he will constantly uplift the Man of Calvary. His own soul imbued with the Spirit of God, he will seek to fasten the attention of the students upon the pattern, Christ Jesus, the chiefest among ten thousand, the One altogether lovely.

The Holy Spirit is greatly needed in our schools. This divine agency comes to the world as Christ's representative. It is not only the faithful and true witness of the Word of God, but it is the searcher of the thoughts and purposes of the heart. It is the source to which we must look for efficiency in the restoration of the moral image of God in man. The Holy Spirit was eagerly sought for in the schools of the prophets; its transforming influence was to bring even the thoughts into harmony with the will of God, and establish a living connection between earth and heaven.

Teachers, if you will open your hearts to the indwelling of the Spirit of God, if you will welcome the heavenly Guest, God will make you laborers together with Him. In co-operation with the Master Teacher, the spirit of selfishness will be expelled, and wonderful transformations will take place.

In the night season these words were spoken to me: "Charge the teachers in our schools to prepare the students for what is coming upon the world." The Lord has been waiting long for our teachers to walk in the light He has sent them. There is need of a humbling of self, that Christ may restore the moral image of God in man. The character of the education given must be greatly changed before it can give the right mold to our institutions. It is only when intellectual and moral powers are combined for the attainment of education, that the standard of the word of God is reached.

These words were clearly and forcibly spoken: "Confess your faults one to another, and pray one for another, that ye may be healed. Press together; press together, and love as brethren. Pray together." The Lord has paid the price of His own blood for the salvation of the world. He suffered every indignity that men could devise and Satan could invent, in order to carry out the plan of salvation. Let not the teacher seek to exalt self, but let him see the necessity of learning of Christ daily, and making Him the pattern. For teachers and students our Lord and Saviour Jesus Christ should be the only example.

Bear in mind that the Lord will accept as teachers only those who will be gospel teachers. A great responsibility rests upon those who attempt to teach the last gospel message. They are to be laborers together with God in the training of human minds. The teacher who fails to keep the Bible standard always before him, misses an opportunity of being a laborer together with God in giving to the mind the mold that is essential for a place in the heavenly courts.--Review and Herald, September 3, 1908.

FOR ADDITIONAL READING

The Business Principles of the Christian, Signs of the Times, February 24, 1909

The Aim of Our Schools, The Review and Herald, March 4, 1909

Higher Education a Preparation for Service, The Review and Herald, March 25, 1909

God in Nature, The Signs of the Times, May 5, 12, 19, 1909

Home Schools, The Review and Herald, May 6, 1909.

Christ the Example of the Children and Youth, The Youth's Instructor, May 25, 1909

The Work Before Us

There is a very great and important work for our conferences in America to do. We are to carry the work in America in such a way that we shall be a strength and help to those who are proclaiming the message in distant countries. Every nation, tongue, and people is to be aroused and brought to a knowledge of the truth. Something is being done, but there is much yet to be done, much to be learned right here at this Conference, in order that the work may go forward in a way that will honor and glorify God.

My soul has been so burdened that I have not been able to rest. What line can we dwell upon that will make the deepest impression upon the human mind? There are our schools. They are to be conducted in such a way that they will develop missionaries who will go out to the highways and hedges to sow the seeds of truth. This was the commission of Christ to His followers. They were to go to the highways and the byways bearing the message of truth to souls that would be brought to the faith of the gospel. I felt deeply in earnest as I saw how much needs to be done in the places I have recently visited. We must stand in the strength of God if we are to accomplish this work.

In his labors each worker is to look to God. We are to labor as men and women who have a living connection with God. We are to learn how to meet the people where they are. Let not such conditions exist as we found in some places when we returned to America, in which individual church-members, instead of realizing their responsibility, looked to men for guidance, and men to whom had been committed sacred and holy trusts in the carrying forward of the work, failed of understanding the value of personal responsibility and took upon themselves the work of ordering and dictating what their brethren should do or should not do. These are things that God will not allow in His work. He will put His burdens upon His burden-bearers. Every individual soul has a responsibility before God, and is not to be arbitrarily instructed by men as to what he shall do, what he shall say, and where he shall go. We are not to put confidence in the counsel of men and assent to all they shall say unless we have evidence that they are under the influence of the Spirit of God.

Study the first and second chapters of Acts. Light has been given me that our work must be carried forward in a higher and broader way than it has ever yet been carried. The light of heaven is to be appreciated and cherished. This light is for the laborers. It is for those who feel that God has given them a message, and that they have a sacred responsibility to bear in its proclamation.

The message of present truth is to prepare a people for the coming of the Lord. Let us understand this, and let those placed in responsible positions come into such unity that the work shall go forward solidly. Do not allow any man to come in as an arbitrary ruler, and say, You must go here, and you must not go there; and you must do this, and you must not do that. We have a great and important work to do, and God would have us take hold of that work intelligently. The placing of men in positions of responsibility in the various conferences, does not make them gods. No one has sufficient wisdom to act without counsel. Men need to consult with their brethren, to counsel together, to pray together, and to plan together for the advancement of the work. Let laborers kneel down together and pray to God, asking Him to direct their course. There has been a great lack with us on this point. We have trusted too much to men's devisings. We cannot afford to do this. Perilous times are upon us, and we must come to the place where we know that the Lord lives and rules, and that He dwells in the hearts of the children of men. We must have confidence in God.

531 Wherever you may be sent, cherish in your hearts and minds the fear and love of God. Go daily to the Lord for instruction and guidance; depend upon God for light and knowledge. Pray for this instruction and this light, until you get it. It will not avail for you to ask, and then forget the thing for which you prayed. Keep your mind upon your prayer. You can do this while working with your hands. You can say, Lord, I believe; with all my heart I believe. Let the Holy Spirit's power come upon me.

If there were more praying among us, more exercise of a living faith, and less dependence upon someone else to have an experience for us, we would be far in advance of where we are today in spiritual intelligence. What we need is a deep, individual heart and soul experience. Then we shall be able to tell what God is doing and how He is working. We need to have a living experience in the things of God; and we are not safe unless we have this. There are some who have a good experience, and they tell you about it; but when you come to weigh it up, you see that it is not a correct experience, for it is not in accordance with a plain, Thus saith the Lord. If ever there was a time in our history when we needed to humble our individual souls before God, it is today. We need to come to God with faith in all that is promised in the word, and then walk in all the light and power that God gives.

I felt very deeply when our brethren who have come from foreign fields told me a little of their experiences and of what the Lord is doing in bringing souls to the truth. This is what we want at this time. God does not want us to go on in ignorance. He wants us to understand our individual responsibilities to Him. He will reveal Himself to every soul who will come to Him in all humility and seek Him with the whole heart.

There are schools to be established in foreign countries and in our own country. We must learn from God how to manage these schools. They are not to be conducted as many of them have been conducted. Our institutions
532 are to be regarded as God's instrumentalities for the furtherance of His work in the earth. We must look to God for guidance and wisdom; we must plead with Him to teach us how to carry the work solidly. Let us recognize

the Lord as our teacher and guide, and then we shall carry the work in correct lines. We need to stand as a united company who shall see eye to eye. Then we shall see the salvation of God revealed on the right hand and on the left. If we work in harmony, we give God a chance to work for us.

In all our school work we need to have a correct understanding of what the essential education is. Men talk much of higher education, but who can define what the higher education is? The highest education is found in the word of the living God. That education which teaches us to submit our souls to God in all humility, and which enables us to take the word of God and believe just what it says, is the education that is most needed. With this education we shall see of the salvation of God. With the Spirit of God upon us, we are to carry the light of truth into the highways and the byways, that the salvation of God may be revealed in a remarkable manner.

Will we carry forward the work in the Lord's way? Are we willing to be taught of God? Will we wrestle with God in prayer? Will we receive the baptism of the Holy Spirit? This is what we need and may have at this time. Then we shall go forth with a message from the Lord, and the light of truth will shine forth as a lamp that burneth, reaching to all parts of the world. If we will walk humbly with God, God will walk with us. Let us humble our souls before Him, and we shall see of His salvation.--Review and Herald, October 21, 1909.

Counsel to Teachers

[Mrs. E. G. White and her party on their way to the general conference, spent five days in Collegeview. Friday morning she spoke to five hundred students in the college chapel, and Sabbath and Sunday she spoke to large congregations in the church. Monday morning, by request, she met with the college faculty. The following is a portion of her address to the thirty teachers assembled. –W. C. White]

I will read 2 Corinthians, the sixth chapter:

"We then, as workers together with Him, beseech you also that ye receive not the grace of God in vain. (For He saith, I have heard thee in a time accepted, and in the day of salvation have I succored thee: behold, now is the accepted time; behold, now is the day of salvation.) Giving no offense in anything, that the ministry be not blamed; but in all things approving ourselves as the ministers of God, in much patience, in afflictions, in necessities, in distresses, in stripes, in imprisonments, in tumults, in labors, in watchings, in fastings; by pureness, by knowledge, by longsuffering, by kindness, by the Holy Ghost, by love unfeigned, by the word of truth, by the power of God, by the armor of righteousness on the right hand and on the left, by honor and dishonor, by evil report and good report: as deceivers, and yet true; as unknown, and yet well known; as dying, and, behold, we live; as chastened, and not killed; as sorrowful, yet always rejoicing; as poor, yet making many rich; as having nothing, and yet possessing all things. . . .

"Be ye not unequally yoked together with unbelievers: for what fellowship hath righteousness with unrighteousness? and what communion hath light with darkness? and what concord hath Christ with Belial? or what part hath he that believeth with an infidel? and what agreement hath the temple of God with idols? for ye are the temple of the living God; as God hath said, I will dwell in them, and walk in them; and I will be their God, and they shall be My people. Wherefore come out from among them, and be ye separate, saith the Lord, and touch not the unclean thing; and I will receive you, and will be a Father unto you, and ye shall be My sons and daughters, saith the Lord Almighty."

You should study also the seventh chapter, but I will not take time to read it now.

There is constant danger among our people that those who engage in labor in our schools and sanitariums will entertain the idea that they must get in line with the world, study the things which the world studies, and become familiar with the things that the world becomes familiar with. This is one of the greatest mistakes that could be made. We shall make grave mistakes unless we give special attention to the searching of the word.

The question is asked, What is the higher education? There is no education higher than that contained in the principles laid down in the words I have read to you from this sixth chapter of Second Corinthians. Let our students study diligently to comprehend this. There is no higher education to be gained than that which was given to the early disciples, and which is given to us through the word. May the Holy Spirit of God impress your minds with the conviction that there is nothing in all the world in the line of education that is so exalted as the instruction contained in the sixth and seventh chapters of Second Corinthians. Let us advance in our work just as far as the word of God will lead us. Let us work intelligently for this higher education. Let our righteousness be the sign of our understanding of the will of God committed to us through His messengers.

It is the privilege of every believer to take the life of Christ and the teachings of Christ as his daily study. Christian education means the acceptance, in sentiment and principle, of the teachings of the Saviour. It includes a daily conscientious walking in the footsteps of Christ, who consented to lay off His royal robe and crown and to come to our world in the form of humanity, that He might give to the human race a power that they could gain by no other means. What was that power? It was the power resulting from the human nature uniting with the divine, the power to take the teachings of Christ and follow them to the letter. In His resistance of evil and His labor for others Christ was giving to men an example of the highest education that it is possible for anyone to attain.

The Son of God was rejected by those whom He came to bless. He was taken by wicked hands and crucified. But after He had risen from the dead, He was with His disciples forty days, and in this time He gave them much precious instruction. He laid down to His followers the principles underlying the higher education. And when He was about to leave them and go to His Father, His last words to them were, "I am with you alway, even unto the end of the world."

To many who place their children in our schools, strong temptations will come, because they desire them to secure what the world regards as the most essential education. Who knows what constitutes the most essential education, unless it is the education to be obtained from that Book which is the foundation of all true knowledge? Those who regard as essential the knowledge to be gained along the line of worldly education are making a great mistake, one which will cause them to be swayed by individual opinions that are human and erring. To those who feel that their children must have what the world calls the essential education, I would say, Bring your children to the simplicity of the word of God, and they will be safe. We are going to be greatly scattered before long, and what we do must be done quickly.

The light has been given me that tremendous pressures will be brought upon every Seventh-day Adventist with whom the world can get into close connection. Those who seek the education that the world esteems so highly, are gradually led further and further from the principles of truth until they become educated worldlings. At what a price have they gained their education! They have parted with the Holy Spirit of God. They have chosen to accept what the world calls knowledge in the place of the truths which God has committed to men through His ministers and prophets and apostles. And there are some who, having secured this worldly education, think that they can introduce it into our schools. But let me tell you that you must not take what the world calls the higher education and bring it into our schools and sanitariums and churches. We need to understand these things. I speak to you definitely. This must not be done.

Upon the mind of every student should be impressed the thought that education is a failure unless the understanding has learned to grasp the truths of divine revelation, and unless the heart accepts the teachings of the gospel of Christ. The student who, in the place of the broad principles of the word of God, will accept common ideas, and will allow the time and attention to be absorbed in commonplace, trivial matters, will find his mind becoming dwarfed and enfeebled. He has lost the power of growth. The mind must be trained to comprehend the important truths that concern eternal life.

I am instructed that we are to carry the minds of our students higher than it is now thought to be possible. Heart and mind are to be trained to preserve their purity by receiving daily supplies from the fountain of eternal truth. The divine Mind and Hand has preserved through the ages the record of creation in its purity. It is the word of God alone that gives to us an authentic account of the creation of our world. This word is to be the chief study in our schools. In it we may hold converse with patriarchs and prophets. In it we may learn what our redemption has cost Him who was equal with the Father from the beginning, and who sacrificed His life that a people might stand before Him redeemed from everything earthly and commonplace, renewed in the image of God.

If we are to learn of Christ, we must pray as the apostles prayed when the Holy Spirit was poured upon them. We need a baptism of the Spirit of God. We are not safe for one hour while we are failing to render obedience to the word of God.

I do not say that there should be no study of the languages. The languages should be studied. Before long there will be a positive necessity for many to leave their homes and go to work among those of other languages; and those who have some knowledge of foreign languages will thereby be able to communicate with those who know not the truth. Some of our people will learn the languages in the countries to which they are sent. This is the better way. And there is One who will stand right by the side of the faithful worker to open the understanding and to give wisdom. The Lord can make their work fruitful where men do not know the foreign language. As they go among the people, and present the publications, the Lord will work upon minds, imparting an understanding of the truth. Some who take up the work in foreign fields can teach the word through an interpreter. As the result of faithful effort there will be a harvest gathered, the value of which we do not now understand.

There is another line of work to be carried forward, the work in the large cities. There should be companies of earnest laborers working in the cities. Men should study what needs to be done in the places that have been neglected. The Lord has been calling our attention to the neglected multitudes in the large cities, yet little regard has been given to the matter.

We are not willing enough to trouble the Lord with our petitions, and to ask Him for the gift of the Holy Spirit. The Lord wants us to trouble Him in this matter. He wants us to press our petitions to the throne. The converting power of God needs to be felt throughout our ranks. The most valuable education that can be obtained will be found in going out with the message of truth to the places that are now in darkness. We should go out just as the first disciples went out in obedience to the commission of Christ. The Saviour gave the disciples their directions. In a few words He told them what they might expect to meet. "I send you forth," He said, "as sheep in the midst of wolves: be ye therefore wise as serpents, and harmless as doves." These workers were to go forth as the representatives of Him who gave His life for the life of the world.

The Lord wants us to come into harmony with Him. If we will do this, His Spirit can rule our minds. If we have a true understanding of what constitutes the essential education, and endeavor to teach its principles, Christ will help us. He promised His followers that when they should stand before councils and judges, they were to take no thought what they should speak. I will instruct you, He said. I will guide you. Knowing what it is to be taught of God, when words of heavenly wisdom are brought to our mind, we shall distinguish them from our own thoughts. We shall understand them as the words of God, and we shall see in the words of God wisdom and life and power. . . .

We are to educate the youth to exercise equally the mental and the physical powers. The healthful exercise of the whole being will give an education that is broad and comprehensive. We had stern work to do in Australia in educating parents and youth along these lines; but we persevered in our efforts until the lesson was learned that in order to have an education that was complete, the time of study must be divided between the gaining of book-knowledge and the securing of a knowledge of practical work. Part of each day was spent in useful work, the students learning how to clear the land, how to cultivate the soil, and how to build houses, using time that would otherwise have been spent in playing games and seeking amusement. And the Lord blessed the students who thus devoted their time to acquiring habits of usefulness.

Instruct the students not to regard as most essential the theoretical part of their education. Let it be more and more deeply impressed upon every student that we should have an intelligent understanding of how to treat the physical system. And there are many who would have greater intelligence in these matters if they would not confine themselves to years of study without a practical experience. The more fully we put ourselves under the direction of God, the greater knowledge we shall receive from God. Let us say to our students: Keep yourselves in connection with the Source of all power. Ye are laborers together with God. He is to be our chief instructor.--Review and Herald, November 11, 1909.

FOR ADDITIONAL READING

Loma Linda College of Evangelists, Testimonies for the Church, 9:173-178 (1909)

The Physician an Educator, The Ministry of Healing, 125-136 (1909)

General Hygiene, The Ministry of Healing, 171-176 (1909)

Hygiene Among the Israelites, The Ministry of Healing, 276-186 (1909)

Dress, The Ministry of Healing, 287-294 (1909)

Diet and Health, The Ministry of Healing, 295-310 (1909)

True Education and Missionary Training, The Ministry of Healing, 395-406 (1909)

A True Knowledge of God, The Ministry of Healing, 409-426 (1909)

Danger in Speculative, The Ministry of Healing, 427-438 (1909)

Knowledge The False and True in Education, The Ministry of Healing, 439-450 (1909)

Importance of Seeking True Knowledge, The Ministry of Healing, 451-458 (1909)

The Knowledge Received through God's Word, The Ministry of Healing, 458-466 (1909)

Decision of Character, The Youth's Instructor, January 25, 1910

The Gift of Speech, The Review and Herald, May 12, 1910

Unholy Knowledge, The Review and Herald, August 4, 1910

Temperance in the Family, Signs of the Times, September 13, 1910

The Mother a Missionary, Signs of the Times, September 20, 1910

The Father's Duty, Signs of the Times, October 18, 1910

Christian Homes, The Review and Herald, November 22, 1910

The Home School, Signs of the Times, January 12, 1911

Walk in the Light, The Youth's Instructor, January 17, 1911

Woman in the Home, Signs of the Times, April 4, 1911
Woman in the Home, Signs of the Times, June 30, 1911
Parents as Character Builders, Signs of the Times, October 5, 1911
A Godly Example in the Home, Signs of the Times, October 12, 1911
A Message to Parents, The Review and Herald, February 1, 8, 1912
Words to the Young, The Youth's Instructor, April 23, 1912
Training the Youth to be Workers, The Review and Herald, May 16, 1912
Young Men as Missionaries, The Review and Herald, May 23, 1912

The True Ideal for Our Youth

By a misconception of the true nature and object of education many have been led into serious and even fatal errors. Such a mistake is made when the regulation of the heart or the establishment of right principles is neglected in an effort to secure intellectual culture, or when eternal interests are overlooked in the eager desire for temporal advantage.

It is right for the youth to feel that they must reach the highest development of their natural powers. We would not restrict the education to which God has set no limit. But our attainments will avail nothing if not put to use for the honor of God and the good of humanity. Unless our knowledge is a stepping-stone to the accomplishment of the highest purposes, it is worthless.

The necessity of establishing Christian schools is urged upon me very strongly. In the schools of today many things are taught that are a hindrance rather than a blessing. Schools are needed where the word of God is made the basis of education. Satan is the great enemy of God, and it is his constant aim to lead souls away from their allegiance to the King of heaven. He would have minds so trained that men and women will exert their influence on the side of error and moral corruption, instead of using their talents in the service of God. His object is effectually gained, when, by perverting their ideas of education, he succeeds in enlisting parents and teachers on his side; for a wrong education often starts the mind on the road to infidelity.

In many of the schools and colleges of today, the conclusions which learned men have reached as the result of their scientific investigations are carefully taught and fully explained; while the impression is distinctly made that if these learned men are correct, the Bible cannot be. The thorns of skepticism are disguised; they are concealed by the bloom and verdure of science and philosophy. Skepticism is attractive to the human mind. The young see in it an independence that captivates the imagination, and they are deceived. Satan triumphs; it is as he meant it should be. He nourishes every seed of doubt that is sown in young hearts, and soon a plentiful harvest of infidelity is reaped.

We cannot afford to allow the minds of our youth to be thus leavened; for it is on these youth we must depend to carry forward the work of the future. We desire for them something more than the opportunity for education in the sciences. The science of true education is the truth, which is to be so deeply impressed on the soul that it cannot be obliterated by the error that everywhere abounds.

The word of God should have a place--the first place--in every system of education. As an educating power, it is of more value than the writings of all the philosophers of all ages. In its wide range of style and subjects there is something to interest and instruct every mind, to ennoble every interest. The light of revelation shines undimmed into the distant past where human annals cast not a ray of light. There is poetry which has called forth the wonder and admiration of the world. In glowing beauty, in sublime and solemn majesty, in touching pathos, it is unequaled by the most brilliant productions of human genius. There is sound logic and impassioned eloquence. There are portrayed the noble deeds of noble men, examples of private virtue and public honor, lessons of piety and purity.

There is no position in life, no phase of human experience, for which the Bible does not contain valuable instruction. Ruler and subject, master and servant, buyer and seller, borrower and lender, parent and child, teacher and student--all may here find lessons of priceless worth.

But above all else, the word of God sets forth the plan of salvation: shows how sinful man may be reconciled to God, lays down the great principles of truth and duty which should govern our lives, and promises us divine aid in their observance. It reaches beyond this fleeting life, beyond the brief and troubled history of our race. It opens to our view the long vista of eternal ages,--ages undarkened by sin, undimmed by sorrow. It teaches us how we may share the habitations of the blessed, and bids us anchor our hopes and fix our affections there.

The true motives of service are to be kept before old and young. The students are to be taught in such a way that they will develop into useful men and women. Every means that will elevate and ennoble them is to be employed. They are to be taught to put their powers to the best use. Physical and mental powers are to be equally taxed. Habits of order and discipline are to be cultivated. The power that is exerted by a pure, true life is to be kept before the students. This will aid them in the preparation for useful service. Daily they will grow purer and stronger, better prepared through His grace and a study of His word, to put forth aggressive efforts against evil.

True education is the inculcation of those ideas that will impress the mind and heart with the knowledge of God the Creator and Jesus Christ the Redeemer. Such an education will renew the mind and transform the character. It will strengthen and fortify the mind against the deceptive whisperings of the adversary of souls, and enable us to understand the voice of God. It will fit the learned to become a co-worker with Christ.

If our youth gain this knowledge, they will be able to gain all the rest that is essential; but if not, all the knowledge they may acquire from the world will not place them in the ranks of the Lord. They may gather all the knowledge that books can give, and yet be ignorant of the first principles of that righteousness which could give them a character approved of God.

Those who are seeking to acquire knowledge in the schools of earth should remember that another school also claims them as students,--the school of Christ. From this school the students are never graduated. Among the pupils are both old and young. Those who give heed to the instructions of the divine Teacher are constantly gaining more wisdom and nobility of soul, and thus they are prepared to enter that higher school, where advancement will continue throughout eternity.

Infinite Wisdom sets before us the great lessons of life,--the lessons of duty and happiness. These are often hard to learn, but without them we can make no real progress. They may cost us effort, tears, and even agony; but we must not falter nor grow weary. It is in this world, amid its trials and temptations, that we are to gain a fitness for the society of the pure and holy angels. Those who become so absorbed in less important studies that they cease to learn in the school of Christ, are meeting with infinite loss.

Every faculty, every attribute, with which the Creator has endowed the children of men, is to be employed for His glory; and in this employment is found its purest, noblest, happiest exercise. The principles of heaven should be made paramount in the life, and every advance step taken in the acquirement of knowledge or in the culture of the intellect should be a step toward the assimilation of the human to the divine.

To many who place their children in our schools strong temptations will come because they desire them to secure what the world regards as the most essential education. But what constitutes the most essential education, unless it be the education to be obtained from that Book which is the foundation of all true knowledge? Those who regard as essential the knowledge to be gained along the line of worldly education are making a great mistake, one which will cause them to be swayed by opinions that are human and erring.

Those who seek the education that the world esteems so highly are gradually led farther and farther from the principles of truth until they become educated worldlings. At what a price have they gained their education! They have parted with the Holy Spirit of God. They have chosen to accept what the world calls knowledge in place of the truths that God has committed to men through His ministers and prophets and apostles.

Upon fathers and mothers devolves the responsibility of giving a Christian education to the children entrusted to them. In no case are they to let any line of business so absorb mind and time and talents that their children are allowed to drift until they are separated far from God. They are not to allow their children to slip out of their grasp into the hands of unbelievers. They are to do all in their power to keep them from imbibing the spirit of the world. They are to train them to become workers together with God. They are to be God's human hand, fitting themselves and their children for an endless life.

There is earnest work to be done for the children. Before the overflowing scourge shall come upon all the dwellers on the earth, the Lord calls on those who are Israelites indeed to serve Him. Gather your children into your own houses; gather them in from the classes who are voicing the words of Satan, who are disobeying the commandments of God. Let us in our educational work embrace far more of the children and youth, and there will be a whole army of missionaries raised up to work for God.

Our educational institutions are to do much toward meeting the demands for trained workers for the mission fields. Workers are needed all over the world. The truth of God is to be carried to foreign lands, that those who are in darkness may be enlightened. Cultivated talents are needed in every part of the work of God. God has designed that our schools shall be an instrumentality for developing workers for Him,--workers of whom He will not be ashamed. He calls upon our young people to enter our schools, and quickly fit themselves for service.--Review and Herald, August 22, 1912.

FOR ADDITIONAL READING

Dangerous Amusements for the Young, The Review and Herald, August 29, 1912

Dignity of Labor, The Review and Herald, October 3, 1912

What Shall Our Children Read? The Review and Herald, January 23, The Review and Herald, 30, 1913

1913 Publication of book "Counsels to Teachers" (for topics see table of contents)

Looking Unto Jesus, The Review and Herald, July 16, 1914

Simplicity and Economy, The Review and Herald, July 30, 1914

Effect of Mind on Health, Signs of the Times, October 6, 1914

Women as Missionaries, The Review and Herald, December 10, 1914

A Message for Our Young People

There are books that are of vital importance that are not looked at by our young people. They are neglected because they are not so interesting to them as some lighter reading.

We should advise the young to take hold of such reading matter as recommends itself for the upbuilding of Christian character. The most essential points of our faith should be stamped upon the memory of the young. They have had a glimpse of these truths, but not such an acquaintance as would lead them to look upon their study with favor. Our youth should read that which will have a healthful, sanctifying effect upon the mind. This they need in order to be able to discern what is true religion. There is much good reading that is not sanctifying.

Now is our time and opportunity to labor for the young people. Tell them that we are now in a perilous crisis, and we want to know how to discern true godliness. Our young people need to be helped, uplifted, and encouraged, but in the right manner; not, perhaps, as they would desire it, but in a way that will help them to have sanctified minds. They need good, sanctifying religion more than anything else.

I do not expect to live long. My work is nearly done. Tell our young people that I want my words to encourage them in that manner of life that will be most attractive to the heavenly intelligences, and that their influence upon others may be most ennobling.

In the night season I was selecting and laying aside books that are of no advantage to the young. We should select for them books that will encourage them to sincerity of life, and lead them to the opening of the word. This has been presented to me in the past, and I thought I would get it before you and make it secure. We cannot afford to give to young people valueless reading. Books that are a blessing to mind and soul are needed. These things are too lightly regarded; therefore our people should become acquainted with what I am saying.

I do not think I shall have more Testimonies for our people. Our men of solid minds know what is good for the uplifting and upbuilding of the work. But with the love of God in their hearts, they need to go deeper and deeper into the study of the things of God. I am very anxious that our young people shall have the proper class of reading; then the old people will get it also. We must keep our eyes on the religious attraction of the truth. We are to keep mind and brain open to the truths of God's word. Satan comes when men are unaware. We are not to be satisfied because the message of warning has been once presented. We must present it again and again.

We could begin a course of reading so intensely interesting that it would attract and influence many minds. If I am spared for further labor, I should gladly help to prepare books for the young.

There is a work to be done for the young by which their minds will be impressed and molded by the sanctifying truth of God. It is my sincere wish for our young people that they find the true meaning of justification by faith, and the perfection of character that will prepare them for eternal life. I do not expect to live long, and I leave this message for the young, that the aim which they make shall not miscarry.

I exhort my brethren to encourage the young ever to keep the preciousness and grace of God highly exalted. Work and pray constantly for a sense of the preciousness of true religion. Bring in the blessedness and the attractiveness of holiness and the grace of God. I have felt a burden regarding this because I know it is neglected.

I have no assurance that my life will last long, but I feel that I am accepted of the Lord. He knows how much I have suffered as I have witnessed the low standards of living adopted by so-called Christians. I have felt that it was imperative that the truth should be seen in my life, and that my testimony should go to the people. I want that you should do all you can to have my writings placed in the hands of the people in foreign lands.

Tell the young that they have had many spiritual advantages. God wants them to make earnest efforts to get the truth before the people. I am impressed that it is my special duty to say these things.--Review and Herald, April 15, 1915.

FOR ADDITIONAL READING

Solomon, Prophets and Kings, pp. 25-34 (1917)

In the Court of Babylon, Prophets and Kings, pp. 479-490

In the Days of Queen Esther, Prophets and Kings, pp. 598-606

Ezra the Priest and Scribe, Prophets and Kings, pp. 607-617

A Spiritual Revival, Prophets and Kings, pp. 618-627

A Man of Opportunity, Prophets and Kings, pp. 628-634

General Index

Please note that the original pagination is used here.

Ability, educated, dearth of 256
Acts, study first and second chapters 530
Adam, after fall, access to God through Christ only 237
   fell through appetite 23
   vital force of 23
Adam to Noah, long life of patriarchs 24
Adelaide 212
Africa 208
Agricultural occupations 315
Agriculture, illustrates Bible lessons 375
   in connection with schools 38, 40
   means of self-support 322
   provision for, in every institution 72
   to be encouraged in other countries 72
   See also Schools; Education.
Agriculturists, need education 204
Alliances, unscriptural 499
Amusements 63, 75, 139, 141, 397, 462
   becoming absorbed in 220
   Christ devoted no time to 229
   Christ not the leader of 378
   Christ's disciples indulged not in 229
   condescending to engage in 379
   counteract working of Holy Spirit 221
   crowd out work 228
   demoralizing 318
   desire for, converted students have not 455
   detrimental to study 303
   effect on other students 246
   idle 300
   love of, how taken away 512
   money frittered away for 422
   of the world 514
   question to be carefully studied 302
   regulation of, necessary 22, 26, 60
   result of devotion to 228
   simplicity of 288
   supremacy of interest directing to 376
   teachers to join with children in 116
   tend to poverty 312, 313
   time for, spent in missionary work 290
   unbalance minds 229
   watched by Satan 225
   work takes place of 538
   See also Recreation.
Angels, part in education and refinement 443
   presence of, an aid to teachers 519
Ann Arbor 347, 359, 451
Archery 75
Articulation, distinct and intelligent 215
Artist, master, works of, displayed in nature 319
Association, worldly, obstruction to service 500
   young men and young women 62
Astronomy 71
Atonement, antitypical day of, now 272
Australia, 203, 204, 208, 316, 323, 368, 494, 538
Australian Bible School, location 310
Authors 388
   irreligious to be discarded 404
   of textbooks, are glorified 446
   productions of compared with Bible 445
   study of many, confusing 446

Backbiting 458
Balanced minds, all faculties used 40
   amusements do not cultivate 229
   difficult to produce 53, 118
   excess of mental work does not obtain 350
   labor and study united 38
   learned lectures do not produce 329
   reaching highest point of intellectual greatness 48
   required of teachers 266, 267
   result of moral, intellectual, and physical culture 42
   result of threefold education 71
   teacher's duty to produce 54
   to be developed, 37
   See also Mind; Education.
Balances, world's wisdom weighed and found wanting 361
Balancing of mind, most important work 30
Battle Creek, 51-53, 56, 220-222, 224, 336, 337, 340, 353, 354, 356, 358, 361-366, 373, 377, 435, 488-492, 495
Battle Creek College, 50, 52, 55, 62, 64,

220, 224, 225, 227, 334, 338, 339, 390
Beer, 63, 318, 319
Bethel, location of school of prophets 97
Bible, alone, furnishes distinction between life and death 200
  Angels surround students of 195
  as a textbook 84, 131, 388
  basis of all education 490
  boundless field for imagination 165
  comparable with no book 181, 383
  defines whole duty of man 186
  disciplines the understanding 395
  discloses principles of truth 131
  duties made plain in 391
  enlarges mind and strengthens faculties 449
  excluded for a time 130
  foundation of all study 451
  great book of study and education 171, 256, 384
  ground work of education 474
  helps in resisting temptation 92
  high standards set up by 288
  highest among books 394
  highest and most important textbook 231
  history, most wonderful 377
  comprehensive, 84
  improves reasoning faculties 393
  in our schools 467-474
  instruction for every human experience 542
  intellect strengthened by 432
  Interpreted by fathers of Romish church 308
  its own expositor 187
  knowledge of God, full of 104
  lesson book 385
  loss of souls impossible while studying 382
  most important book in our schools 129, 384, 444, 451
  not made a standard in education 447
  only history of Jesus Christ 382
  only rule of doctrine 126
  our educator 414
  our study book 133
  pages must be searched 307
  perfect standard of character 100
  placed in background 182
  potent in elevating thoughts 126, in giving vigor to faculties 126

  produces enlightened people 165, strength of intellect 111, 129, 165, 379-380, 432, 445
  rules of conduct in 464
  sandwiched in between infidelity 474
  soul's only food 379
  study for yourself 307-309
  study of, produces balanced mind 433-434
  teaches whole will of God 390
  treasures not exhausted in thousand years 444
  without a rival 84
Bible and history 393
Bible and learned men disagree 541
Bible and nature have the same author 375
Bible readings 107
  essential part of missionary work 121
  given by inexperienced girls 113
Bible study, value of 123
  See also Bible
Bible teachers, manifesting prejudices for political measures 475
Biography, in the Word 432
Boarding department, healthful principles to be brought into 226
  religion to be manifest in 82
Bookkeeping, college presidents to understand 510
Book knowledge, desire for missionary work destroyed by 356
  God may be dishonored by 351
Book of books 129
  commended as grandest study 376
  See also Bible.
Book of nature, reveals working of God 85
Book of Revelation, reveals working of God 85
Books, Christ would expel many
  Christ's work not based on study of 413
  harmful, expulsion of 517
  in our schools 167
  mind in unreal world by reading 452
  misleading 451
  not to be made idols 355
  profitless, to be laid aside 547
  specious errors taught through 184
  time wasted in perusal of 337
  training in industries mingled with

study of 423
Books and authors, custom to exalt 381
    in our schools 381-389
Boos of biography and narrative sold by colporteurs 123
Brain, congestion of blood in 146
    equally taxed 319
    excessive use creates diseased condition 321
    harmonious action with muscles 426
    intoxicated by reading books 452
    invents, works, and wrestles, solves problems 226
    overtaxing lessens physical and mental strength 418
    overworked 34, 42
    put to the stretch 226
    relation to diet and healthful food 227
    using one's own 307
    vitalizes system by electrical force 43
Breathing to be taught 147
Building, need of intelligence in 316
Buildings, cared for by students 512
Business, all to be educated in 417
    not to neglect study of 38
    practical knowledge of 26, 468

Canvassers 106, 488, 489
Card playing 63, 320
Carpenters employed in building ark 504
Carpentry, trade learned by Jesus 142, 417
Chaldeans, Daniel's skill in the learning of the 77, 87
Chapel exercises, vitalized by Spirit of God 116
Children, all need education 204
    babes not to attend school 27
    confined to books 22
    domestic labor of, God's approval upon 420
    educate to deny appetites 25
    imitate examples of parents 28
    lips will proclaim mysteries 473
    music taught too early 416
    need proper education 27
    need words of encouragement 32
    nervous, not to be overtaxed 416
    of wealthy, to be taught to work 419
    perseverance to be taught to 32
    play instead of work 65
    rights of 67
    sacred trusts 416
    separated from family circle in education 313
    useful employment need for 417
    trained to practical duties 420
    thorough work done for 161
    to be as free as lambs 21, 146
    to play out of doors 60
    to learn responsibility 16
    to respect judgment 17
China 208
Christ, accused of being peculiar 401
    as teacher 236-241
    brothers and sisters of, taught traditions 439
    disciples of, not educated in games and amusements 229
    dignified useful labor 418
    diligent student of scriptures 402
    drew illustrations from nature 243
    educator for future life 48, 229
    example to poor and lowly 401
    familiar with every prophecy 402
    fed with pure truth 243
    fountain of all knowledge 450
    Great Teacher 184
    Greatest Educator 48, 224, 450
    history of, to be searched 406
    learning of rabbinical teachers not sought by 400
    lesson book of nature studied by 440
    life of, to be studied 382
    manner of teaching to be followed 243
    mother of, first teacher 439
    not under instruction of rabbis 439, 440
    pattern in all things 229
    perfect as a workman 418
    reticent and uncommunicative 338
    schools of prophets not sought by 400
    taught with authority 236, 407
    teacher sent from God 407, 479
    teaching of, not science of men 238, 408
    to be teacher in all our schools 513
    to sow the world with truth 177
    would cleanse institutions of leanring 174
Christian education, meaning of 534
Christian endeavor society, duty to form 292
Christ's Object Lessons 524
    devoted to educational work 520

sale of to provide means for our
schools 521
to be sold in Los Angeles 522
Christ's school, teachers and pupils in
280
Chow-chow 151
Circulation, unbalanced 60, 146
Cities, conditions in 312, 322
Cities, thousands to move out 326
Citizenship, in heaven 481
Classical literature questionably value 98
Coffee 428
College City 62
Colleges, Bible not to be in secondary
position 394
found wanting may be pronounced
upon 358
holy principles to take root in 502
missionary work to be encouraged in
113
premedical work in 490
provision to educate evangelists 489
to be different from schools of today
115, 290
to educate Christian businessmen 489
Colleges, modern, teach conclusions of
learned men 541
College View 533
Collegiate education, not absolutely
essential 242
Colonization, around our institutions
492-497
Colporteurs 107
Commencement exercises 487
Commentaries, to be used with caution
187, 188
Condiments, produce irritability 151
Confinement, in school 19, 59
to close study 146
Controversy, if opinions are crossed 469
Cook, importance of position 43, 44
Cooking 74, 425
Children to be taught 160
life long injury may result from 226
requires intelligence 43
students to be taught 41, 227
teaches to be provided 41
to be skillful 226
Corinthians II, educational message in
sixth chapter 533
Counsels to teachers 533-539
Course of study 490

Course after course 355
many should pursue by 337, 338
unnecessary matters to be weeded
from 447, 525
Courses of study, not to be forced upon
every student 347
not to be prolonged 334
Courtesy 515
in the home 154
lack of 157
Courtship, danger of premature 62
Courtship and marriage 100, 102, 103
Cramming, mental dyspepsia from 339
Creation, not solved by laws of nature
409
only authentic account 84, 536
Crocheting, in relation to domestic work
36
Croquet 75
Crisis, imminence of 354
"Cube root" in contrast with cooking and
sewing 74
Culture, for each individual 373
of jesus 443
of the mind 44, 47
to be measured by intellect 39
Curriculum, weeding non-essentials
from 447, 525
Custom, 20
no help in understanding Scriptures
391
Customs, 311, 397, 423, 499
in the cities 312
of the Battle Creek school 224
Customs and maxims, break away from
149, 313
of world, to be avoided 115, 324, to be
opposed 288
of worldly schools, not to be followed
98, 289

Daniel, choice of, result of education 86
course of, pleasing to God 87
diet of, simple, nutritious 227
faithful statesman 205
firm in his integrity 78
guided by Spirit of the Lord 411
history of given for our admonition
374
illustration of sanctified character 80
imitate faithfulness of 305
integrity under test 77

model for youth 192
not corrupted by temptation 248
opportunities improved to utmost by 373
powers of, how educated 230
striking example to world 79
students may become as learned as 379
thorough consecration of 205
thoroughness put into practice by 351
Dancing, 75, 111
Daughters, spending precious hours in sleep 36
David, study last four psalms of 371
Degrees, taking one after another 356
Delay, not to be advised 334
Deportment, correct habits in 267
 example of teachers in 191
Desserts, detrimental to health 226, 227
Diet 75, 140, 425
 affects physical and moral health 143
 every youth to study 72
 influence upon health 147
 of children 20, 143, 150, 153
 of Daniel 227
 simplicity of 288
 to be carefully studied 226
Diligence and thoroughness in education 373
Discipline 16, 58
 caution in enforcing strict 249
 for the young 63
 lax in many institutions 64
Disease, treatment of 75
Divine example 442, 443
Divine Teacher 397-404
Domestic duties, children to be taught 369, 417
Domestic education, to keep pace with literary 368
Domestic science 74
Domestic work, importance of 75, 316
 young men and women separate at 322
Dress 75, 139
 example of teachers 191
 love of not to be encouraged 286
 separate from the world 311
 simplicity of 288
Dyspepsia, mental 339

Early education 27
 shapes character 15, 19

Economy, to be practiced 152
Eden, school for our first parents 314
Educated laborers, dearth of 217
Educated worldlings, produced by education of the world 536, 544
Education, aim, shaped by inducements of better world 235
 all-round men and women to gain 467
 balanced by religious experience 119
 basis of 328
 best, purpose of 231-235
 brings into relation with Great Teacher 514
 confusion in 415
 diligent and thorough 373-380
 domestic, to keep pace with literary 368
 early 15, 19, 27
 affects mature life 33
 embraces physical, mental, moral 387
 essential, 368-372, true understanding of what constitutes 538
 false 171
 first lesson to know God 414
 fitness for work not gained merely by 196
 fits for variety of service 369
 general interest in 64
 grand life work 350
 grand science 328
 great change in the character of 527
 health may be affected by 19
 higher 392-396
 importance of 82-91
 in israel 442
 in school most lasting 397
 knowledge of God 392
 lasting, regarded as old-fashioned 111
 lengthened to many years 355, 368
 means much more than many suppose 387
 missionary in need of 202
 most essential for gospel workers 242-244
 most valuable, world's great men disregard 169
 need of, permanent 359
 neglect of, sinful 216
 not a necessary recommendation for God's service 341
 not for a few only 336
 not the result of chance 193-194

not to be depreciated 357, 369
object to prepare zealous missionaries 231
one-sided 41, 73, 416
perfect, not required for God's service 346
perfected in schools of men 346
popular, not a remedy for evils 64
prayer not to be neglected for 350
purpose of to receive light 352
qualifies for service only with divine spirit 348
relation to work of God 201-211
religion not divorced from science 135
religious, importance of 311, 388, 434
restricted 350, 541
spiritual 19
standard of, not met by general methods 328
standard of, not to be lowered 373
teaching of rabbis greatest hindrance to 438
theory less essential in 539
thoughts on 57-61
to be obtained 350
trains for life to come 328
true object of 45, 82
truth 542
used in work of God 370
weeding non-essentials from 447, 525
workers to feel need of 113
See also Higher education.
Education and health 145-148
Educational institutions 220-230
to meet demand for trained workers 545
Educational standard, not to be lowered 376
Educator, the only safe 174-180
Educators, as overseers of flock 220
students may be unfitted by 364
Electrical energy given at creation 23
may resist disease 43
Elijah, instructor in schools of prophets 512
Eloquence, 241
Employment, characteristic of true gentlemen and lady 75
for exercise of muscles 44
Engagements 105
Entertainments, of the world 514
See also Amusements.

Equalization of mental and physical powers 146
See also Labor; Manual labor; Mind; Mental labor.
Essential, in education 512-515
Evangelism, to be taught in various institutions 489
Evangelists 488, 489
Examination, preparation for last great 517
Example, divine 442-443
Excursions 455
Exercises, out of school hours 26
regular 74
Expelling students, only for depravity 277
Expenditures, unwise 510
Experience, Bible instruction for every 542
Expulsion of students, usually avoidable 277
Extremes, caution against 378
Extremists, considered so, because loyal to God's standards 289

Fables, may tempt carnal appetites 184
not needed by students 391
Faculties, to reach highest development 373
Faculty ethics, indiscreet words dropped to students 454
Families, located near schools 313
Family circle, first school 65
Fancy work, contrasted with cooking and sewing 74
Farmer, healthier than mechanic 73
in contrast with student 74
Farmers, inadequate returns of 327
Farming, need of more intelligence in 316, 325
Fascination, by long devotion to studies 336
Fashion, 20
not to absorb attention 149
Fashions, not to be followed 155
oppose, 288, 298, 311
schools not to follow 289
Father, duty not transferable to mother 69
pleads "no time" 65
Fathers and mothers, instruct children in the law of God 442

land important for family 327
make life-study of children 67
not seconding efforts of teachers 64
relation of, to teacher's work 70
responsibility of, to give Christian education to children 545
set example to children 161
study characters of children 66
Fathers, bring business troubles home 154
   smiling countenance in home 159
   with warm sympathy 115
Fatigue, healthful 151
Fiction, danger of reading 92-94
   destructive of true piety 162
   profitless 92
   wood, hay, and stubble 452
Figures of speech 236
Finances, uniting with world in securing 501
Financial management not to be conducted carelessly 510
Flattery, Christ gave no place to 304
   injurious to precious souls 304
   lifted by aid of 305
Flesh meats 140, 150, 151, 428
   becloud brain 226
Flirtation 62
Food factories, establishment of 489
Foods, solid better than liquid 227
Food stores, establishment of 489
Football, Christ's disciples knew not 229
   objectionable game 225
Foreign countries, schools to be established in 531
Foreign fields, work accomplished as in America 208
Foreign missions, call for thorough Christians 112
Formalism, Christ's example in contrast with 438-441
Formality, not organization 253-259
Frivolity, converted students will leave 455
Frolic, foolish 300
Funds, of school, not to be overdrawn 510

Gambling 63, 318
   species of idolatry 312
Games 397
   Christ not the leader of 378
   detract from duties 422
   football 229
   intensity in 228
   produce excitement of minds 225
   pugilistic 229
   relation of, to prayer 303
   teachers not to invent 220
   work takes place of 538
Genesis no record of imbeciles 22
Geology 71
Gilgal, location of school of prophets 97
God, revealed in His word 377
   revealed in nature 377
Gospel workers, education most essential for 242-244
Gossiping 457-458
Governments, earthly, under God's government 505
Grammar 242, 243
Greek 467
Greek and Latin, few scholars needed in 468
Greeks sought after wisdom 333
Gymnastic exercises, in relation to labor 73

Habits, correct, to be formed in youth 67, 268
   in accordance with physical law 22
   in youth, manifested in manhood 27
   strengthen with strength 28
   of usefulness, train children to 369
Healdsburg 487
Health, foundation of student's ambitions 72
   great treasure 35
   guard as sacredly as character 147
   in open air 21-22
   in relation to education 72
   in relation to mental powers 36
   instruction in preservation of 26
   most important for students 426
   not to be sacrificed for money 155
   of body and soul 76
   of children, to be preserved 20, 59
   relation of, to labor 35
   relation of, to study, labor, amusement 60
   result of physical and mental labor 42
Health reform, in last days 139
Heart, neglecting in securing intellectual culture 541

Heavenly school 512, 517, 525
Hebrew, cultivated as sacred tongue 97
Hebrews, faith of mixed with confused
  ideas 499
  schools of 95-99
  study carefully first chapter 404
  See also Israelites.
Hebrew writings, learned by children of
  Israelites 442
Heredity, 25 278
  noble aspirations not by 87
Higher education 392-396
  vaining, instead of useless facts 469
Height of 360, 467
  in word of God 532
  presented in flattering terms by Satan
    471
  so-called, not to be brought into our
    schools 536
  who can define 467, 532
  See also Education.
Higher school, our preparation for 397
  See also School; schools
Historical events, of consequence to
  Nebuchadnezzar 412
History, Bible most wonderful 377, 394,
  432
  important study 192
  sacred, extending into eternity 393
  uninspired, often searched 395
Holy Spirit, aid in the study of Scriptures
  433
  Divine knowledge proceeds from 437
  essential to our perfection 218
  give room to work of 346, 363
  gives strength for victory 452
  helps worker's infirmities 242
  influence of 167
  counteracted by amusements 221
  in schools of prophets 526
  leads men to Christ 210
  not to be directed 436
  opens eyes of understanding 386
  presides everywhere 365
  schools in great need of 526
  shines upon pages of sacred Book 189
  strives with many youth 358
  teachers do not appreciate 434
  teachers to be susceptible to 269
  thoughts to be purified by 227
  working for our perfection 215
  works for salvation 353

  See also Bible.
Home and school 64-70
  teaching became mechanical in Israel
    442
  to be one 95
Home education 149-161
Home, first school 416
  to be most attractive place 155
  See also Education.
Homesickness, free from 300
Home training, importance of 25
Honor, encourage a sense of 114
  students to place themselves upon
    249, 250
Honors, not to encourage strife for 286
Hours, of study and recreation 164
  of study, too long 33
  unsuitable time in study 351
Household duties, highly important for
  a lady 37
  See also Domestic work.
Human intellect, to gain expansion and
  vigor 226
  See also Intellect; Mind.
Human learning, cannot qualify for
  kingdom 413
  See also Education.
Human science 435
  not mingled with teaching of Christ
    408
Hygiene, principles of 75

Idleness, a sin 75
Ignorance, humility not increased by 45
  not acceptable to God 369
  not a virtue 316
  not a characteristic of devoted life 74
  not the mark of the gentleman 324
  produces moral leprosy 320
  result of folly 75
  Satan would keep men in 256
  toil not lightened by 314
Illustrations, drawn from nature 236
Image, divine, effaced from minds of
  people 499
In the soul 436
Imagery 243
Imagination, diseased 163
Imitations 331-333
Indebtedness, of schools to be relieved
  523
  by sale of Christ's Object Lessons 520

India 208
Individuality, Christ possessed peculiar 400
  not to be merged 16, 58
  of each student 373
Industries, to be taught in our school 317
Inebriates, mental 162-166
Infants, affected by sins of parents 24
  See also Children; Parents.
Infidel books, danger of reading 92-94
  placed before students 447
  true education not in 407
Infidelity 474
  doctrine of eternal punishment 176
In school books 99, 167
  mind befogged by 330
  not to be countenanced 231
  turn away from teaching of 172-173
Infidels, not to be identified with 482
  sentiments of not valuable 174, 467
  not to be interwoven with school books 328
  true knowledge comes not from 437
  works not to be studied 167, 168
  writings of may contain elevated thoughts 175
Infidel writers 467
  to be avoided 93
  See also Authors.
Institutional work 501
Institutions, danger in attending worldly 362
  educational, would be closed Christ 174
Instruction to those in charge of 501
  need skilled workers 494
  people not to settle near 494
  school most important of 226
  swinging into worldly conformity 290
  two, consumed by fire 490-491
  worldly, not our pattern 502
Institutions of learning, counteract influence of world 286
  See also Schools; Colleges.
Instruction, to be varied 15
  See also Education.
Instructor, Jesus came to earth as 400
Instructors, not to lead through useless studies 469
  See also Teachers
Intellect, effect of continual study upon 27
  not to be urged 21
  sound, in sound body 37
  taxing 444
Intellectual culture, not to replace spiritual 541
Intellectual greatness, right to aspire to 82
Intellectual powers, strengthen by every means 165
  See also Mind; Intellect.
Intemperance, in eating and drinking 153
In study 340
Investigation, to be encouraged 27
Islands of the sea 204, 209
Israelites, saw importance of education 442

Jericho, school of prophets at 97
Jesting, 457, 458
Jesus, see Christ.
Jews, lessons from offerings not understood by 398
  Old Testament mingled with human opinions 309
  required a sign 333
  Scriptures not known by 128
John, sixth chapter precious lessons in 456
Joking, 457, 458
Justification by faith, youth to find true meaning of 548

Kings, some will stand before 217
Kirjathejearam, school of prophets at 96
Knowledge, practical, essential, secular 136

Labor, a blessing 40, 75
  advantage to girls 37
  aid to purity 36
  cultivation of intellect not hindered by 37
  dignified by Christ 418
  educated to be masters of, not slaves 314
  education in different branches of 40
  in place of gymnastics 73
  in schools of prophets 97
  masters of 314
  on tabernacle in the wilderness 315
  portion of each day devoted to 38, 41, 44

powers exercised by 229
practical 41
prolonged into the night 154
regulated 60
slaves of 314
time to be given for 60
to be connected with schools 26, 44
youth to be educated to 35
Laborers, educated, dearth of 217
hundred to be where now one 488
See also Workers.
Ladies and gentlemen, development by meditation upon holy things 132
Land, families need piece of 327
schools to cultivate more faithfully 512
students to cultivate 423
working of, special blessing 323
yielding returns 317
Language, correct, study earnestly 256
separate from world 311
simplicity in 236
Languages 71, 467
familiarity with 187
Greek and Latin few need to study 468
study of, important 537
Latin 467-468
Leaders, cultivate broad views 520
Learned lore, Jesus did not study 439
Learned of the earth, some will stand before 217
Legal requirements, for medical students 490
Legal tests 489
Legislative councils, student may sit in 82
Legislative courts, many to stand in 217
Lesson book, great 390-391
of nature, studied by Jesus 440
Word of God 433
Libraries, containing works of skeptics 173
Library, of animate and inanimate nature 442
Life, long of patriarchs 24
Liquor drinking 320
species of idolatry 312
Literary attainments, not indispensable for usefulness 193
religion no handicap to 118
Literary lines 388
education obtained from 397
Literary qualifications, pressing need for future 192

Literary talent, to be appreciated 120-121
Literary training, combined with practical 368
minds of men need 255-256
Literature, alone, cannot enlighten mind 199
Bible study more valuable than 394
classical, questionable value of 98
infidel, dangers in reading 92-94, 99, 167, 173, 175, 330, 407, 474
not to be made first 484
pollution, eliminate from institutions 388
Literature of Satan, hellish fascination 93
Logical reasoning, scarce 27
Lore, learned, Jesus did not study 439
Los Angeles, fruitful field for Christ Object Lessons 522, 523
for Ministry of Healing 522
Lotteries 318. 320, 327

Machinery, to be avoided 253
Management of schools, to be learned 531
See also School; Schools.
Manual labor, by teachers in schools of prophets 97
conducive to rest 54
excess harmful 42
Missionaries to have knowledge of 512
stated hours for 146
See also Labor; Exercise.
Manual occupation, essential for youth 321
Manual training, 416-420
part of school duties 417
Manners 108, 214
God's people models of correct 419
improved by Bible study 129
Manufacturers, need education 204
Manufacturing establishments, connected with schools 38, 40
Marriage, with unbelievers, forbidden 500
unwise 62
Master artist, works displayed outside cities 319
Mathematics 71
Maxims and customs of world, of worldly schools, not to be followed 98
relation to 115, 298, 384, 424, 431, 439
to be opposed 288

Means, uniting with world in securing 501
Mechanical arts, provision for, in every institution 72
Mechanics, need education 204, 315
Medical course, not many to take 491
Medical missionaries, great demand for 231
　to become acquainted with God 390
Medical schools brought up to standard for 490
Medical students, importance of Bible study for 390
Melbourne 202, 203, 212
Memory, taxation of, profitable 369
Mental discipline, aim for 115
　Must be acquired 205
Mental dyspepsia, produced by cramming 339
Mental improvement, part of each day 73
Mental inebriates, 162-166
Mental labor, more efficient by union with physical 44
　See also Mind
Mental powers, equally taxed with physical 543
　girded for work 257
Men and women, bunging at work 316
　to gain all-round education 467
　trained for usefulness and influence 202
Message to teachers 516-519
Methods, in teaching 390
　of Christ's teaching 456
　of labor, need to study Christ's 518
Mind, abused by one line of thought 321
　action of, not preventable 38
　balanced, all faculties used 30, 40
　　difficult to find 118
　　labor and study united 38
　　mental work alone does not attain to 350
　　result of threefold education 71, 266, 267
　　teachers' duty to produce 53-54
　clogged with mass of matter 339
　controlled by another 18
　disadvantage of undisciplined 108
　dwarfed by mass of matter 447
　educated to enjoy physical taxation 229
　enlargement of 127
　law of 127
　of students, carry higher than thought possible 536
　rising higher and higher in comprehension 447
　stamped with idolatry 186
　susceptible to highest cultivation 47
　to receive culture 229
　treasures to be stored in 181
　worships God 426
　See also Balanced minds; Education.
Missionaries, dearth of 201
　importance of encouraging 113
　to be developed in our schools 529
Missionary nurses 489
Missionary work, taking place of amusements 290
Ministerial labor, entrusted to boys 113
Ministers, assign work to those idle 365
　Need knowledge of physiology 321
　not the only workers 212
　spending time in politics, to surrender credentials 483
　unite with teachers in saving youth 117
Ministry, importance of common branches for 45
　lack of cultivated 215
　young men to be encouraged 114
Ministry of Healing, sale to provide means for our sanitariums 521, 524
　to be sold in Los Angeles 522
Moses, educated in the school of nature 342
　education of, very thorough 342
　greatest laws recorded by 393
　lessons to be learned from experience of 509
　schools of Egypt not accountable for success of 345
Mother, first teacher 416
Mothers, condition of daughters attributable to 36
　cultivate love for beautiful 21
　importance of work 139, 149
Manifest cruel kindness 25, idolatrous love 25
　sacredness of duties 139
　seeking excitement of world 31
　sowing seed; will reap fruit 25-26
　work of, begins with babe in arms 150, rarely appreciated 185

Motherhood, story reading detrimental to 37
Motive of youth attending school 301
Mountain View 493, 494, 495
Muscles, becoming weak 34
   exercise of, each day 146
Music, cultivated in schools of prophets 97
   flippant song, 97
   in contrast with domestic science 74
   instruments of 111
Made to serve holy purpose 97
   not to be made first 484
   not to take the place of practical subjects 41
   Psalms sung in schools of prophets 97
   undeveloped children not to be taught 416
   waltz 97
Musical display, not to be introduced 253
Musical program, rendered in Healdsburg College 487
Mustard, 151
Mysteries, Christ could open 237

Names, of believers, graven on Christ's palms 273
Narcotics 144
Nationalities, connected with schools 111
Nature and Bible, have one Author 375
Nature, Christ used illustrations from 243
   exalted above God 329
   great library 442
   illustrates word of God 375
   knowledge from for every child 443
   laws of, cannot ignore 409
   lesson book studied by Jesus 440
   reveals God 377
   students brought into contact with 423
   study in book of 424
Nature study 21
Nebuchadnezzar, purpose of, for Daniel 77
   See also Daniel.
Nerve power, relation of, to healthful food 227
Nerves, messengers transmitting orders 426
Nervous system, taxed by passion for reading 163
   unbalanced 147
   well balanced 143

New Testament, study daily 414
   See also Bible
New Zealand 204, 208, 248
Nicodemus, needed instruction 517
Noah, backsliding converts of 504
   life tapering since time of 24
Non-essentials, infidel literature 407
Novels, effect on lives 36
   greatest evil 37
   in relation to active labor 35
   produce dislike for Bible 92
Unhappiness 163

Oakland 492, 495
Obituary notices in book of Genesis 22
   See also Life; Patriarchs.
Objectionable books, in required studies 490
   See also Books; Authors; Textbooks.
Old Testament 384
   studied by Israelites 442
   study daily 414
   See also Bible.
One-sided education, God divorced from knowledge 375
   See also Education.
Oral teaching, in schools of Israel 442
Organization, God wrought in 254

Pacific Press 492, 495
Pagan and infidel teachers 468
Pagans, sentiments of, not valuable 174
   works of, may contain elevated thoughts 175
   not to be studied 167, 168
   See also Authors; Infidel authors.
Painting, in contrast with practical duties 74
  not to be made first 484
Paralysis, effect of excessive reading 163
Parental responsibility 139-144
Parents, an example to children 67
   arouse to sense of responsibility 30
   build firm constitution in children 36
   co-operate with teacher 270
   disease bequeathed to children 24, 25
   educate children for usefulness 32, 139
   education and discipline fundamental 69
   encourage study of physiology 159
   evenings to be spent with children 154
   example and discipline of 28

guard children against false education 470
keeping children at school too steadily 26
lack of obligation 25
no time to improve mind 29
overrating good qualities children 33
Preserve simplicity 29
  seeds of disease sown by 21
  school discipline to be recognized by 53
  teachers, only, to ages eight and ten 21, 61, 157
  to meet children at final reckoning 140
Parents, too little anxiety for environment of children 50
  to respect claims of children 67
  to teach God in His works 21
  training in domestic duties neglected 65
  work of, cannot be done by another 69
  worldly education of children desired by 544
Parents and teachers, all powers to be developed by 420
  causing fear in children 68
  close door against temptation of children 420
  controlling wills of children 17
  danger in dictating too much 21, 58
  grieved by foolish children 300
  guides of children 17
  instruct, polish, refine, etc. 27
  intellects of children not to be forced 21
  remember that you were children 68
  responsibility of training children 145
  self-control to be manifest by 15
  smile 68
  to preserve life and health of children 145
  to understand physiology 20
Parchment rolls, of Old Testament were studied 442
Parties 141, 455
Patriarchs, long life of 24
Patronage, not to be gained by uniting with world 502
Pattern, not after worldly institutions 502
  See also Institutions; Schools.
Pedagogy 390
Periodicals, not to exalt men of influence 480

Philosophy, complete system in Bible 129, 432
  dangers in 541-542
  divine, foundation of education 194
  false, regarding heavens and earth 409
  heathen 388
  important study 192
  mixed with error 171
Physical and mental powers, proportionate attention to 27, 423
Physical culture 425-428
Physical exercise, combine with mental effort 146
  in harmony with lessons of Christ 220
  marked out by God 228
  may lead to excess 228
  result of neglect of 60
  to accompany study 22
  to recover normal condition 146
Physical labor, benefits for students 33
  combined with mental taxation 229
  discipline in practical life 229
  healthful weariness to muscles 151
  not to be shunned 42, 43
  part of each day 73
  time to be spent in 146
  See also Labor; Manual labor.
Physical law, consequences of violation 23-24
Physical powers, amusements not to claim 229
  brought into service 314
  equally taxed with mental 543
  mind enfeebled by weakening 427
  neglect to strengthen 21
Physical training, important factor 59, 71
Physical training, to begin in the home 425
  See also Manual labor; Trades.
Physiology 71
  apparatus for 147
  for the children 159
  importance of lessons in 160, 321
  study of, neglected 20
  teachers to understand 20, 26
Pickles 151
Play, Christ devoted no time to 229
  duties, helpful, more important than 418
  unessential 228
Playground, Satan's presence on 225
Pleasure, dangerous to develop love of 422

Poetry, 542
  in the Bible 432
Politeness, to be taught to children 496
Political parties, affiliation with 476
  mistake of linking interests with 478
Politics, Christian influence not to be united with 479, 484
  ministers spending time on, withdraw credentials from 477, 483
  special testimony relating to 475-484
  spending time talking 483
  teachers not to manifest zeal in 477, 484
  to be buried by God's people 475
  to be let alone 476, 477
Position of usefulness, no one drifts into 256
Practical duties, children to be educated in 35
  graduates to be prepared for 73
  of life 75
  students to be taught 228
  See also Duties.
Practical knowledge, essential 132
  See also Knowledge.
Practical training, essential for instructors 512
  See also Training.
Practices of the world, to be separate from 288, 311
Preparation, speedy 334-367
Presidents of schools, bookkeeping necessary knowledge for 510
  guard yourselves diligently 475
  message for 504, 510
  responsible for finances of institutions 510
  subject of students' prayers 293
Principals of schools 504, 510
  disorderly students bring trials upon 454
  effect of insubordination upon 248
  to make God's law their delight 510
  See also Management; School; Schools.
Prize fights, 320
Pronunciation, incorrect 242, 243
  not to criticize. 242
Prophecies, to be studied 382
Prophecy, fast fulfilling 335
  lectures on, given in school 46
Publications, silently working 212
Public speaking, to be taught 147

Publishing houses, Christian influence to prevail 473
Pugilistic games 220, 229
  Christ not leader of 378

Qualifications, of teacher 19
  See also Teachers.

Rabbis, brothers of Jesus taught ceremonies of 439
  Christ not connected with 310, schools of 438
  Christ not student in 439
  disciples not students in 359
  teaching of, greatest hindrance to true education 438-439, To be unlearned 468-469
  wearying round of exactions 237
Ramah, school of prophets at 96
Reading, excessive, effects of 163
  impressions remain through life 163
  intemperate habits of 164
  possible hindrance to reform 163-164
  taxes nervous system 163
  teaching correct 147
  wrong habits of 162
Reading course, should be interesting and instructive 548
Reasoning, logical, scarce 27
Reasoners, close, are few 27
Recreation, 75
  hours for, regulated 146
  proper kind 84
Reflection, to be encouraged 27
Refinement, of mind 132
Reformation, in our educational work, urgent call for 337, 367
Reformers, great light given to 450
  to be under discipline of God 517
  we are 44
Regulations, obedience to 302
  See also School; Schools.
Religious exercises, prolonged to weariness 115
Religious liberty, liable to repression 475
Religious principle, guide to any height 83
Requirements, legal 490
Restaurants, establishment of 489
Reverence, for sacred things 194
Rewards, encouraging strife for 286
Rhetoric, contrasted with domestic science 74

Romance, unfits for real life 37
Romish church, Bible interpreted by "fathers" of 308
Roommates 55
Routine, in habits of work 373
Rules 16
   breakers of, cannot be trusted 246-247
   deviation from, no sin 222
   of association 62
   of conduct, found in Bible 464
   of school, disobeyed 302, 454
   Regarding rooms 54
   Regulating hours for study 22
   Result of disobedience to 297
   slight violations of 222

Sabbath meetings, vitalized by the Spirit of God 116
Sabbath schools, 68, 256, 257, 271
   warning against superficiality 121
Sabbath school teachers, to unite with ministers in saving youth 117
Sabbath school work 253, 254
Samaria, school of prophets at 97
Sanitariums, Christian influence to prevail in 473
   danger of getting in line with the world 534
   establishment of 489
   See also Institutions.
Satan, in school room and on school ground 225
Scholar, Christian 230
See also Students.
Scholarship, high, to be attained to 204
   not sought for rewards 286
School, babes not to attend 27
   heavenly 512, 517, 525
   higher, our preparation for 397
   motive of youth attending 301
   most important institution in world 226
   seed sown will bear harvest 191
   time spent in, the most favorable 191
School age 21, 27, 61, 145, 156, 157, 416, 420
Schoolbooks, interwoven with infidel sentiments 328
School discipline, correct 454-466
School ground, visited by Satan 225
School homes, families not to settle near 494
formalists in 50
function of 89
rooms to be inspected 54
rules necessary 54
School management, to be learned 531
School of Christ, teaches Christlike meekness 343
   teachers and pupils in 280
Schoolroom, fields and hills for little children 61
Satan's presence in 225
   teachers not to enter when irritated 266
Schools, all students trained to be workers 463
   Bible to be chief study in 536
   books of wrong sentiments expelled from 517
   danger of getting in line with world 534
   different stamp to be borne by 516
   disparaged by students 293
   christian influence to prevail in 473
   diligent and thorough education in 373
   educate to be masters not slaves of labor 314
   establish for practical industry 317
   families located near 313
   God expects more of than seen 185
   ideas of contention separated from 483
   impart knowledge of truth 206
   improvements needed in 469
   incentives to practical labor given by 324
   instruction in, not all valuable 518
   instrumentalities for developing workers 368, 545
   land to be cultivated in 512
   location of 312, 313, 320, 322, 324, 326, 421-424, 492
   management of, to be learned 531
   manufacturing establishments at 38, 40
   may be found wanting 358
   mechanical arts in all 72, 315, 324
   missionaries to be developed in 273, 368, 529
   nationalities connected with 111
   needed as long as time lasts 359
   no place for criticism, division, jealousy, and rivalry 472
   object of establishment 289

of other denominations not our pattern 231, 290
true Christian education, needed 541
preparation for immortal life 383
preparation, giving too elaborate 346
provision made for 520-524
qualify to meet state laws 490
satanic agency may demoralize 454
spectacle unto men and angels 186
supplements for home training 288
support of 211
temptation to place children in worldly 535
to be established in fields 204
to be established in foreign countries 531
worldly methods bring loss to 290, 512
Schools of prophets, established by Samuel 96, 99
established to prepare workers for God 489
Holy Spirit was sought in 526
models for our schools 184, 223, 228, 512
ours to be more and more like 489
teachers noted for learning and piety 96
visited by Elijah 512
Schools of world, learners in know not the Teacher 346
ours, to be different from 290
teach conclusions of learned men 541
temptation to place children in 535
Science, advanced, to be taught in our schools 186
alone, cannot enlighten mind 199
become engrossed in the study of 426
dangers in 541-542
interpreted by man 414
not to be made first 484
of salvation 186-190
revelation of God superior to 393
steppingstone to higher purposes 192
Sciences, Christ could have made disclosures in 183
education in 318
not to be exalted above God 358
Scientists, falsely so called 181
Scripture, easily comprehended 407
See also Bible.
Secular knowledge 136
Self-improvement, each day 73
Self-reliance, to be taught 57

Sentimentalism, produces sick fancies 37, 99, 103
Seventh-day Adventists, called extremists for reaching God's standard
strife not to be known among 480
sewing 74
teachers of 41
Shepherd, good, represents work of Christian teacher 273
Signs of the Times 521
Simplicity, to mark every feature of education 512
Singing evangelists, trained in schools 487
Skepticism, attractive to human mind 542
in school books 99
mind befogged by 330
result of evil literature 93
thorns in disguise 541
Skeptics, works of not to appear in libraries 173
Sleep, spending precious hours in 36
Smoking, a species of idolatry 312
Social meetings, pleasant and attractive 116
Soil, methods of working 318
missionaries to understand cultivation of 512
riches may be obtained from 317
Solomon, apostasy of 499
defines whole duty of man 186
lessons from life of 498-503
mistake in procuring gold and silver from unbelievers 501
on child training 15
Son of God, great teacher sent into world 382
See also Christ; Teacher.
Song, flippant 97
Sowing beside all waters 487
Speaking, to be taught 147
Speech, correct habits of 267
figures of 236
See also Language.
Spices 151
Sports 63, 319
conditions creating distaste for 512
wicked, engage not in 297
Standard, educational, not to be lowered 376
higher, call for 306

Standards, elevate higher and higher 285, 288
State laws to qualify to meet 490
Statesman, Daniel a faithful 205
"Steps to Christ" 212
Stimulants 144
Stories, continued, impressions of 162
　exciting cripple mental strength 163
　sensational pervert mental tastes 163
Story books, danger of reading 92
　greatest evil 37
Story papers 163
Story reading, detrimental to motherhood 37
Students advised to prolong studies 348
　appeal for 50-56
　appeal to 137
　approved in heaven 247
　at Battle Creek College 285-290
　attend school for certain period 351
　becoming engrossed in studies 357
　bound down to particular course of study 347
　brought in contact with nature 423
　burdening teachers by disregarding rules 464
　careless, doing themselves great injury 247
　climb educational ladder 192
　complaining, have superficial education 65
　consider knowledge of god above everything 415
　co-operate with teachers 246
　deciding their eternal destiny 245-252
　degrading God-given powers 251
　devoting long periods to study 350
　discouraging teachers 464
　each to have special training 373
　earnest cast influence on right side 297
　education in practical duties needed 228
　elijah instructed in schools of prophets 512
　encourage teachers 250
　exposure of errors of, harmful to school 277
　expulsion of, usually avoidable 277, only for depravity 277
　faithful, help themselves 247
　forming divine characters 251
　free from homesickness 300
　from foreign fields, not to be sent to America 204
　games deeply excite minds of 225
　health most important for 428
　"i study, i work, for eternity" 229
　infatuated 454
　learn to cultivate land 423
　leaving college in better health 146
　life of interwoven with all others 191
　lighten work of teachers 246
　literary and scientific training necessary 490
　losing burden for soul winning 354, 362
　losing reverence while in school 446-447
　make school life success 297
　mental dyspeptics 339
　mental powers to be put to stretch 170
　to be taxed 373
　missionaries in school 464
　missionary motive lost while securing education 349
　mistake of humiliating before school 277
　never graduated from school of Christ 544
　physical powers neglected by some 34
　preparation, speedy 354
　preparation for what is coming 526
　present bodies to Christ 428
　pursuing one line after another 359
　raising standard of school 464
　reaching highest standard 246
　remember time is short 354
　required to be workers with God 291-296
　responsibility to make school orderly 292
　restraining power in school 297
　satan desires to secure 471
　satisfaction derived from obedience 251
　seasons of prayer among 293
　seek heavenly direction 351
　speedy preparation for service 354
　study for eternity 229
　supported by hired money 353
　surround with pleasing objects 321-322
　suspension of exercise care in 277, 282

taking many studies 146
teachers' advice not to be followed wholly 347
thorough training needed 148
training peculiar to each 373
urged to take long courses 334
warning against mass of knowledge 525
words to 297-306
work for all, to be provided 423
Studies, combine natural and spiritual 375
  few and well-chosen 115
  crowding out physical training 146
  required, 490
  restricted to proper hours 60
  results of too many 337, 349
  destroy desire for missionary work 337
  weeding, non-essentials from 447, 525
  wisdom from above crowded to secondary place 349
Study, diligent, essential 228
  for eternity 229
  long periods of injurious 357
  portion of each day 41
  pursuing year upon year 364
  result of great devotion to 338
  strenuous, not destructive to health 74
  superficial, degenerating effect of 257-258
  to be regulated 60
  unfits some for practical life 38
  useless, not to be stressed 469
Sunday 475
Sunday labor 322
Superficiality, age of 28
Surroundings, educational influence of 421-424
Suspension of students 277-284
  See also Students.

Takoma Park 494
Talent, to be appreciated 120-121
Tatting, in relation to domestic work 36
Tea 428
Teacher, Christian, Good Shepherd represents work of 273
  qualifications of 19
  relation to pupil 66
Teachers, 260-276, 489
  advancement in experience 516

  as examples of Christian integrity 504-511
  assisted by angels 268, 519
  hear in mind deficiencies 525
  books of wrong sentiments to be expelled by 517
  carrying students over old paths 471
  ceasing to be students 107, 120, 517, 525
  children catch spirit of 269
  christ in your school every day 262
  christian, great demand for 231
  co-operate with parents 417
  constrained by love of Christ 264
  counsels to 533-539
  dealing with children, not men 269
  discouraged by satanic agency 454
  discouragements not evadable 117
  disobedience of students not to burden 247
  efficient 119
  exacting in denunciation 222
  exercise necessary 221
  exerting wrong influence 454
  exhorted to set right example 191
  eyes of, closed to the times 469
  failing to comprehend true education 448
  for different branches of labor 40
  heart conversion needed 435
  holy spirit not appreciated by 434, 435
  humility of Christ to be learned by 511
  impatience held in subjection 260
  indiscreet words dropped by 454
  in Christ's day 183
  interested in political questions 484
  "know thyself" 525-527
  laws of health to be respected by 147
  message to 516-519
  not satisfied with low standard 525
  obligations of, weighty and sacred 116
  of cooking and sewing 41, 74
  of industrial pursuits 72
  of the gospel, God accepts 527
  of the world, not to be glorified 451
  opened field for labor for 271
  physiology, requisite of 321
  piety of 116
  practical work done by 221
  prepare students for what is coming 526-527
  pupils rise no higher than 58

religious education paramount to 434
respect of, for authors and books 381
responsibility of, heavy 90, 397
sanctified 263
satan desires to secure 471
study from cause to effect 266
sympathy with unruly students 454
trust in God 436
unbend from your dignity 116
unite with ministers in saving youth 117
useless studies not to be stressed 469
warning for, 220
  regarding fitness 223
weaker faculties to be cultivated 16
words of caution to 516
work circumspectly 430
  in the sight of heaven 261
  with students in gardens and fields 325
Teachers and Students 220-230, 451
  Christ works through 513
  eternal interest, theme of 436
  exemplifying Christian character 191-195
  fishers of men 487
  genuine experience for entering higher grade 459
  obligations of, mutual 246
  selling "Christ's Object Lessons" 520
Teaching, oral, in schools of Israel 442
Temperance question, taking position without wavering 482
Testimonies, in hands of foreign peoples 549
Textbook, Bible highest and most important 131, 231
Textbooks, by supposed great authors 446
  by uninspired authors 383
  errors in 167
  expressing pagan and infidel sentiments 168
  mere study not sufficient 516
  nature's treasures as 21, 61
  students to be considered in preparation of 381
Theater, demoralizing amusements 318
  See also Amusements.
Theatergoing, 318
  species of idolatry 312
Theatrical performances, not to be introduced 253

Theology, unfolded in Bible 129
Theories of the world, give up 469
Theory, less essential in education 539
Thinkers, logical, are few 27
"Thoughts on Daniel and Revelation" 212
Threefold education 57, 59, 71, 218, 387, 418, 430, 434, 465
  See also Education.
Time, "is passing" 472
  setting of 335
  shortness of, 488
  education to be gained in view of 389
Tithe, used for speechifying on political questions 477
  See also Politics.
Tobacco 144, 319, 320, 428
Tools, Jesus handled with skill 418
Trade, not degrading 417
Trades, to be learned 319
To be taught 41
  See also Manual labor; Labor.
Tradition, 468
  brought into education 407
Tradition, 468
  buries jewels of truth 188, 450
  Christ's brothers were taught 439
  Christ showed no regard for 238
  false estimates of 171
  no aid in understanding Scriptures 391
  silenced truth of God 238
Training, for usefulness, and influence 202
  in work of God 107-112
  of children, not like that of animals 57
  of youth, severity in 17
  peculiar to each student 373
Training schools 108
  Christian business men educated in 489
  in most favorable position 490
  strengthening of 488
  work of 488-491
"Twig is bent," quotation used 156

Union Conference training schools 489, 491
Universities, studying Greek and Latin in 467

Ventilation, danger from lack of 27
  effects of improper 59

of school rooms, 19, 145
Voice, correct habits in 267
   cultivation of, study earnestly 256
   precious talent 214, 215
Volunteers, called to work just now 488
   Christ's Object Lessons to be sold by 522
   in the army of the Lord 464

Washington D.C. 492, 493
Weariness, healthful 151
Will, to obey conscience 57
Wine 63, 427, 428
Wisdom, in the Word 432
World's, weighed and found wanting 361
Woman, her husband's equal 141
   her position more sacred than a king 141
Woman's Christian Temperance Union 522, 523
Word of God, first place in all education 542
   Only authentic account of creation 536
   Perfect educational book 394
   See also Bible.
Work, before us 529-532
   blessing, not a curse 419
   command of heaven 340
   for all students 423
   for children of wealthy 419
   for eternity 229
   in open air 73
   part of each day 228, 538
   preparation for large or small 364
   strenuous and diligent 228
   superficial 368
Work and education 310-327
Workers, for foreign fields, to be trained in fields 204
   need of consecration 493
   trained, need of 212
World, absorbing our time 502
   come out from 502
   conformity with, strictly guarding against 436
Worldlings, in education 536
   securing means in partnership with 501
Worldly associations, obstructions in God's service 500
Worldly education, gradually leads from principles 536

not to be introduced 536
See also Education.

Young ladies, neglecting essentials for practical life 34
Young men and women, acquiring education that is wood and stubble 466
   converted, decided change in 455
   employed with care 266, 269
   engaged in ministry 489
   find true meaning of justification by faith 548
   ignorant of future responsibility 217
   in bible work 489
   in canvassing work 489
   knowledge of bible truths needed by 45
   message for 547-549
   "must have their jolly time" 455
   not to associate in domestic work 322
   to become well disciplined 216
   to place themselves in our schools 216
   under direction of others, away from home 51
   urged to enter our schools 545
Youth, all appointed for certain work 462
   begin at lowest round of ladder 213
   choice of companions for 500
   exercise equally mental and physical powers 538
   future of work depends on 542
   habits of 27
   habits will grow with growth of 28
   higher standard set before 306
   labor as canvassers and evangelists 488
   learners for next world 49
   like impressible wax 51
   minds of, to be trained 213
   motive in going to school to be considered by 301
   precept and example in education of 231
   reaching highest development 541
   to be in earnest 191
   to be trusted 114
   true ideal for 541-545

Printed in Great Britain
by Amazon